Young Minds in Social Worlds

Young Minds in Social Worlds

EXPERIENCE, MEANING, AND MEMORY

Katherine Nelson

HARVARD UNIVERSITY PRESS

Cambridge, Massachusetts
London, England

First Harvard University Press paperback edition, 2009.

Library of Congress Cataloging-in-Publication Data

Nelson, Katherine.
Young minds in social worlds : experience, meaning, and memory /
Katherine Nelson.
    p.   cm.
  Includes bibliographical references and index.
  ISBN 978-0-674-02335-2 (cloth : alk. paper)
  ISBN 978-0-674-03486-0 (pbk.)
  1. Child psychology.   2. Child psychology—Social aspects.   3. Cognition in
children.   4. Human information processing in children.   I. Title.
BF721.N42   2007
155.4—dc22   2006046720

To my granddaughter, Noa

Contents

Preface   *ix*

1   Modern Metaphors of the Developing Child   *1*

2   Perspectives on Meaning   *29*

3   Being an Infant, Becoming a Child   *58*

4   Toddling toward Childhood   *87*

5   Experiential Semantics of First Words   *117*

6   Entering the Symbolic World   *149*

7   Finding Oneself in Time   *179*

8   Entering a Community of Minds   *209*

9   The Study of Developing Young Minds   *239*

Notes   *269*

References   *277*

Acknowledgments   *301*

Index   *305*

Preface

This book had its genesis in a seminar—New Models in Developmental Psychology—that I cotaught with Joe Glick at the Graduate Center of CUNY (City University of New York), first in 1999 and again in 2003 and 2005. The seminar was primarily organized around a group of provocative books, many published between 1996 and 1999 (around the same time as my last book, *Language in Cognitive Development: The Emergence of the Mediated Mind*), and included works by Elman et al. (1996), Hendriks-Jansen (1996), Hutchins (1996), Clark (1997), Deacon (1997), Gottlieb (1997), Damasio (1999), Hrdy (1999), and Tomasello (1999). Not all addressed developmental issues, but all challenged basic tenets of contemporary theory in cognitive science as well as cognitive and language development. They added to and enriched ideas that I had been accumulating around new views of the human evolution of language and cognition (especially as put forth in Merlin Donald's 1991 *Origins of the Modern Mind*), embodiment (Varela, Thompson, and Rosch, 1991), and dynamic and developmental systems theories (Oyama, 1985; Thelen and Smith, 1994).

The readings and discussions in our first seminar confirmed my growing conviction that two basic conceptions of mind compete in contemporary research: one a top-down, abstract, genes-first, neural-first nativism realized in terms of domain-specific modular theories; and the other a bottom-up, pragmatic, experience-dependent, biosocial-cultural developmental system of knowing. These different conceptions imply different views of evolution, representation, conceptual development, and the role of language in cognitive development, and different ideas about critical research questions in developmental and cognitive psychology. This book takes the second stance—pragmatic, experience-dependent—with the goal of delineating the developmental path toward the full, symbolic, cultural mind, what Donald (2001) calls the "mind-culture symbiosis."

It should be said at the outset that a pragmatic, experiential approach to developmental psychology is not an endorsement of the infant mind as a "blank slate" (as Pinker has charged against virtually all of psychology). Indeed, it takes the rich evolutionary heritage of *Homo sapiens*, much of it shared with the other primates, as critical to understanding development in children (Nelson, 1996; Tomasello, 1999), recognizing that significant aspects of this heritage—not all well understood at present—are either unique to humans or vastly more complex in humans than in other species. Our symbolic capacity, which must be a primary focus of any attempt to understand cognitive development from birth to school age, is a prime example. Other recent efforts to reorient the developmental enterprise, such as dynamic systems theory or connectionism, although they address many important and basic issues in cognition, have failed to engage these most important characteristics of the human mind: its symbolic, social, and cultural intelligence. It is no help to imagine that symbols are somehow written on the "slate" prior to birth and simply called into use when the occasion arises. The challenge is to discover how the mind-culture symbiosis comes about in the course of every normally developing child. This is a central part of the story that I lay out here.

Another component of the story involves the crucial fact that learning and knowing are products of each individual child's limited experience—limited by the biological constraints of the long period of postnatal neural and motor development, and by similarly constrained opportunities for varied ecological and social interactions. Developmental theorists typically envision the child as constructing an abstract, epistemic model of how the world works. This has led developmentalists to attribute excessive levels of abstraction to the infant mind. I argue that by sticking close to the level of the child's experience in the world, without importing our own scientific language into the child's conceptual system, we can make better progress in understanding the child's knowledge state at each period in development, and thus succeed in unveiling the developmental connections between states, an achievement that often eludes us at present. In place of the abstractions of the current cognitive jargon (in which infants are said to conceptualize people as "autonomous agents" and the like) I opt for plain English, assuming that infants are no more abstract thinkers than their parents are, or than the young of other closely related species, and that they come to see the people around them as valued persons, not as members of some universal class of possible agents.

This stance relates to my rejection of the characterization of infants and young children as theorists or scientists; instead, I interpret their behavior in terms of their pragmatic experience within a rather limited view of the world around them. I appreciate the contributions of researchers who, over the past forty years, have shown that infants and young children see, hear, and know more about the world they're engaged in than most professionals had imagined. But I believe that the implications of this knowledge are too easily overextended, and that a modest reinterpretation from the perspective of the infant and young child can help us to recapture a developmental-systems account that is true to all facets of experience—embodiment, ecology, social support, cultural givens, and symbolic and private meanings. Relevant studies by researchers who have explored how children develop in their real-world environments fill out and support this account.

Young Minds in Social Worlds

❧ 1

Modern Metaphors of the Developing Child

Above all, one must have "a feeling for the organism."
~ *Barbara McClintock, quoted by E. F. Keller, 1983*

*T*oo often something seems to be missing in our studies of children, as they are conducted in experimental laboratories—what Barbara McClintock called "a feeling for the organism."[1] The idea of the "experiential child" captures some of what is missing: the fact that development depends on experience and learning gained from the unique perspective of an infant or child in the midstream of becoming a person. This child actively seeks meaningful experiences relevant to her current needs and interests and makes pragmatic sense of her encounters in the world, in close relation with adults who care for, support, and guide her. I have adopted the experiential child here as a model to aid in rethinking theory and empirical research in developmental psychology, particularly in its cognitive branch. Over the past century theorists have generated a plethora of metaphors and models as they have struggled to understand how development of the human person can be best conceptualized and studied. The experiential child must compete with these others for the defining position in contemporary developmental studies of the child. In this chapter, I will consider some of these other metaphors before defining the experiential position in more detail.

Today the most striking conception of children in developmental psychology—and arguably the most widely accepted one—is that the very young are "little scientists" or "theorists," specialists in different domains of knowledge who are actively attempting to carve out coher-

1

ent theories about the real observed world (see, for example, *The Scientist in the Crib*, Gopnik, Meltzoff, and Kuhl, 1999). In my conception of the experiencing child, I take on many of the theoretical goals of this and other current models and metaphors, but I take issue with the cognitive premises on which the little scientist model is based. A broader perspective on the pros and cons of current models can be achieved by considering a number of the alternatives that have dotted the history of developmental psychology.

Old Metaphors

Piaget, the preeminent developmental psychologist of the twentieth century, introduced the concept of the "epistemic child": the child seeking knowledge of how the world is structured and, in the process, constructing the structure of his own mind. In Piaget's view, the child begins life endowed only with sensorimotor capacities and struggles, through the exercise of these capacities in action, to attain concepts such as the Permanent Object and Means-Ends relations. After a decade or so, the child might achieve Formal Operations that enable her to approach problems from the perspective of the formal theorist or scientist, the presumed telos of development.

In contrast to Piaget's view, the model of the "cultural-historical child" was advanced by Lev Vygotsky in Russia in the early days of the Soviet Union (1920s and 1930s). This child, unlike the epistemic child, is thoroughly social, situated in a specific historical context and within a culture that might or might not nurture the mind through facilitative processes of interpersonal scaffolding. This model has been revived in contemporary theory and constitutes the underpinning of modern social-cultural developmental psychology, including important aspects of the positions I take in this book.

Piaget and Vygotsky are now viewed as founding fathers of opposing conceptions of development. Of course other models were proposed during the twentieth century—ontogeny recapitulating phylogeny (Hall, 1904); behaviorism (Skinner, 1957); maturationism (Gesell and Amatruda, 1945); symbol-formation (Werner and Kaplan, 1963)—but they did not outlast their time to compete or influence theory today to a significant degree.

Revisionist Metaphors: The Competent Infant and Beyond

Throughout the early days of child development theory, infancy was presented as a period of helplessness in view of the primitive capacities of newborn and young infants, including their perceptual and motor capacities. As late as the 1960s, pediatricians were informing mothers that newborn infants could neither see nor hear. But a revolution in experimental investigation of infant perception and learning that began in the 1950s and came into full bloom in the 1970s and 1980s overrode the old views, and a new model was born: the "competent infant." Originally the competent infant model was proposed simply to combat older views of inert beginnings, and to account for the findings from experiments, with infants as young as two months, that indicated a considerable ability to perceive, categorize, and remember visually presented stimuli in brief laboratory sessions. As time went on, mere competence metamorphosed into an updated version of Piaget's epistemologist, the "scientist in the crib," who generated theories about the world as she viewed it with knowing eyes. The basic mechanics of information processing, the dominant theory in cognitive psychology, appeared to have an early start in infancy, and it was a short step to the idea that the mechanisms required for information processing were in place "from the beginning" (that is, from birth). Thus no change in basic structures, mechanisms, or processes needed to be contemplated in developmental theorizing, an important step in the move from the competent infant to the child as theorist.

The Child Theorist

No doubt the most important precedent for the view of the child as theorist was set by Noam Chomsky's (1965) conception of language acquisition, derived from his immensely influential generative theory of grammar. Chomsky claimed that the abstract structure of language was such that it could not be learned in an ordinary sense from exposure to examples in everyday speech. Therefore he proposed that a special language acquisition device (LAD) existed in the child's brain for the purpose of analyzing samples of sentences and producing a grammar based on the models available in the Universal Grammar residing in all human brains. Chomsky's theories have undergone quite radical changes over the decades since he first stated this claim, but his view of the necessity for an innate language theory has not, a view broadly accepted in the linguistic community as well as among many philosophers and psychologists. Much more has and could be said on the pros and cons of this position; for now the idea is mainly historical, as a primary source idea of the idea of child as theorist.

In the 1980s two cognitive developmental psychologists made related claims about the role of child theories in the acquisition of knowledge in well-specified domains. Carey (1985) proposed that children's knowledge of the biological world was first included within a psychology-based conceptual theory of which humans were the prototype members. Carey anchored her theory in the history and philosophy of science, where basic concepts may change over time as theories become reassembled, and in the process, the concepts of old and new theory may become incommensurable (Kuhn, 1970). Carey viewed changes in child theories as analogous to those in science. From a different position, Spelke (1988) conceptualized the perceptual knowledge that young infants displayed in the laboratory with regard to objects (such as continuity of movement through space, and no more than one object in a given space at a given time) as a "folk theory of physics." Spelke viewed this folk theory as unchanging in development, with adults as well as infants using it as a basis of perception and action.

Over the same period of time, interest grew in what Premack and Woodruff (1978) had called "theory of mind" (referring to the question of whether chimpanzees have one). Developmental psychologists soon picked up the term, referring to achievements that in earlier work were termed "perspective taking" (Astington, Harris, and Olson, 1988). In the years since these initial forays into theory analogies, the child as theorist has proliferated into many specialized domains: the physics theorist, the psychology theorist, the biology theorist, the linguistics theorist, the "mind" theorist, and more.

What is this "theory," anyway? Although it has crept into the field via metaphor, it is no longer held to metaphorical proportions. In many guises it appears to be a novel invention: an implicit, unconscious theory that acts precisely like an explicit, communally derived scientific theory (Gopnik, 1993). Children are said to be born with theories that guide their knowledge gathering but that are subject to revision in light of new data (Gopnik and Meltzoff, 1996). Assuming their innate origins takes some of the burden off the child as scientist. In this view, children seem to come into the world equipped with a set of "ghost children"[2]—a physicist, a linguist, a psychologist—who do the data gathering and theorizing for them. These ghosts, of which the actual child interacting in the world is unaware, are presumed to do the heavy cognitive work early in life, before the child is able to take on the task of managing her own cognitive affairs. The child need take no responsibility for whatever follows, as she has no access to the knowledge being organized on her behalf.

Scientists' theories of course are not out of reach of consciousness, nor is most of what we ordinarily call "knowledge." It is therefore legitimate to ask how helpful this kind of language and theorizing is in understanding children's developing knowledge. The theory construct is now widespread within the contemporary field of developmental psychology. Even those who feel a little uneasy about the idea of infant theorizing, or about the "theory theory" of mind ("So good they named it twice," Russell, 1992) seem to feel comfortable with the idea of children's theories as conceptual structures. However, I believe it to be a seriously misleading construct in confronting the problems of development. The real difference between being a child with limited resources operating pragmatically in a limited corner of the world and being a scientist in a social-historical community of science, symbols, and technologies, is obscured in this simile, to the detriment of both sides.

Problems with Theories

What are the problems with theory theories, and what should be the alternative? First, to clearly identify the problems we need to examine the major assumptions, insofar as they have been made apparent in basic writings. Consider the following set:[3]

1. The basic architecture of the cognitive system does not change from infancy to adulthood, despite changes in neural development, language acquisition, and the growth of knowledge.
2. Cognition is modular: there are some inborn modules, such as

vision, and some that develop over time, such as language and conceptual domains of knowledge. Most conceptual domains are characterized by "core concepts" that are inborn and appear in early infancy. These may be elaborated later as knowledge accumulates, or transformed as concepts change with additional knowledge. Such domains include objects, space, number, mind, emotion, biology, and physics. There may be others not yet identified.

3. Domain-specific cognition is organized in terms of intuitive or folk theories that are not accessible to consciousness, but that organize data within a field of knowledge. Concepts within a domain of "natural kinds" are "essentialist," based on the idea of essential properties of things. Development takes place when theories change over time; conceptual domains develop through a process of constrained construction. The state of a theory determines a person's understanding of the domain. Learning within the domain is organized by the theory.

4. Thinking takes place within domains. To "cross classify" or to combine two domains in problem solving, some domain-independent means is required. Language has been proposed as serving this purpose.

Each of these assumptions is antithetical to development from an experientialist perspective. Among the major weaknesses of the theory theory from this perspective is its solipsistic stance—that is, its imperviousness to influences on basic cognitive processes or cognitive growth from outside the mind, including major changes in neurological development, physical growth, motor skills, and particularly language and social interactions. What the child "brings" to any conceptual domain is assumed to be built-in structure, not experiential knowledge, and is seen as the necessary beginning point for any developmental investigation in that domain. Outside influence on development comes in the form of "data" that may support or challenge the theory.

This stance seriously obscures the complexity of cognition and its development. In the basic cognitive structure of theory theory, change occurs only in terms of content, not basic structure. But every theory of development must account for the dimension of change as well as for the dimension of continuity across change. Change must be given its due; it is unrealistic to assume that inside the rapidly changing physical form of the growing infant and child there is a mind that remains ever the same.

Neither biology nor culture are accounted for in the singular focus of theory theory on what's in the head, a focus that obscures the significance of sources of knowledge in the social and cultural world inhabited by the child, and the problems of how the child's own conceptual structures and experience become coordinated with the social world. Such coordination is simply assumed. Yet despite its reliance on innate theories, there is also no accounting for the biology of how such theories arise or for their phylogenetic history.

Finally, theory theorists appear to be consciously committing the "psychologists' fallacy" of assuming that those they study have the same perspective on the world that they themselves do (Dewey, 1973). In this case the theorist takes an adultomorphic stance and attributes the structure and content of adult minds to those of newly born infants and young children. This critique largely applies as well to other contemporary cognitive development theories derived from information processing and computational models. We need to recognize not only that the child is not a machine, but also that *the child is not us*.

I suggest that instead we turn to the project of acquiring a "feeling for the organism" in its natural surroundings in the real world, where the organism is the experiencing child. The quotation from McClintock that opens this chapter continues as follows:

> One must understand "how it grows, understand its parts, understand when something is going wrong with it. [An organism] isn't just a piece of plastic, it's something that is constantly being affected by the environment, constantly showing attributes or disabilities in its growth. You have to be aware of all of that . . . You need to know those plants well enough so that if anything changes, . . . you [can] look at the plant and right away you know what this damage you see is from . . . You need to have a feeling for every individual plant." (Excerpted in Keller, 1983, p. 198)

McClintock, who won the Nobel Prize for the discovery of gene transposition, was referring to the corn plants that she studied. But the advice seems at least as valid for the study of children and their pathways through development. Our current models are far from displaying a feeling for the growth of every individual child. The idea of the experiential child takes McClintock's approach as a model for rebuilding our theoretical understanding of development in childhood. In this model each individual child and pathway speaks to the general case. Our theories are not about "normal" or "modal" children or children from a particular place in time, space, or class, but about how development takes place in the wild and on the ground in each individual case. For this reason we cannot ignore the necessity for the close study of individuals over time in different environments.

I do not mean to imply that we should look to some ancient, ideal hunting-gathering society to try to understand how childhood is composed. We must take our children in whatever diverse, complex, technology-driven society we may find them, while at the same time recognizing the importance of diversity in both the experience and the outcomes of what we find. Wherever the child is situated, she is engaged in experiencing and thereby acquiring meaning and knowledge. She is also surrounded by a variety of social figures who speak (or sign) about many things of both personal and social or cultural interest, and who, most important, take care of her during her many years of dependency.

The Experiential Child

Throughout this volume I use a number of concepts and terms that constitute recurring themes. They each require a brief introduction in terms of the roles they play within the framework of the experiential child. Following their introduction, I describe the interpretation of the processes of development in the context of this book.

Experience

Experience is basic to the analysis of the developing child because nothing psychological happens without it. Experience is a transaction of the person with aspects of the external world. It is pragmatic and local, oriented from the self and its concerns, dependent on motivation and attention. Experience is subject to both change and continuity over development. Change is inevitable because both the internal and the external conditions of experience change over time. The infant grows into a child, the brain and nervous system grow and develop, consciousness expands, past experience forms an increasingly complex background, social partners treat the child differently and offer different kinds of experience at different ages, language becomes a source of vicarious experience, and new parts of the cultural world are introduced. Thus what the child sees of a given scene at age one month, one year, or four years is likely to be very different at each age (and even more different than what an adult sees of the same scene). Some of the same cognitive processes are at work each time, but the content differs—hence the strong claim that there is *no neutral information* for the infant or child to process. Experience is all subjective and all at least potentially meaningful.

Meaning

Meaning is the crux of the matter. Meaning is defined here as whatever is perceived as relevant to the individual (person or organism) on the basis of needs, interests, present context, or prior history. I recognize that the word *meaning* has many meanings, one of which pertains to words and sentences; others to speakers and texts (Nelson, 1985, p. 8; Lyons, 1977). But I take the basic meaning to be that which has meaning—significance—for the individual. In this sense many in the cognitive tradition would substitute the term *information*, but I think the difference between the two terms is critical. When psychology set out to be an objective science, it left meaning behind (Bruner, 1990). Later, "information" was substituted for meaning. Information was presumed to exist in the environment in the form of possible distinctions to be made: this versus that, 1 versus 0. But these distinctions are not neutral points—they depend on the ability of the individual to discern differences. For that, the difference must be in some sense meaningful; that is, there must be a reason for making the distinction. The claim here is that it is not information that is taken in and processed but only meaning relevant to the individual.

Meaning thus applies across the biological spectrum, as well as across development. What is meaningful to an earthworm, a crab, or a robin is unlikely to be meaningful in the same way to an infant, a child, or an adult human. In part meaning is dependent on biology, that is, on what is essential to the organism; these are strong interests, and they may become satisfied without conscious effort because of biologically provided modes of pursuit. Processing of the patterns detected in the encountered world—including patterns of speech—results from the automatic application of biologically determined sensitivities residing in perceptual mechanisms or in the neural specifications of the basic memory system. Patterns then become part of the memorial record, meaningful to the individual as part of the background of expected experience, but not meaningful in the sense of conscious knowledge acquisition or active "making sense." These basic processes and patterns help the child to see the world in a human way and therefore to carry on meaningful making-sense activities.

Given the presumed evolved nature of meaning, some meanings may be common across individuals, cultures, and even species (for example, dark clouds "mean" or "signal" rain), but in large part meanings are individually, experientially derived, and for that reason personal and private. This means that when individuals learn and use a language system to communicate with others, they must accommodate their personal meanings to those associated with the language forms (Chapter 5).

Meaning resides in different places. Meaning is in the mind and the brain; it is also in the body that recognizes familiar things and places. Meaning comes to reside in the child, but it also resides in the social world, in the affect-laden interactions with caretakers and others, in the symbols and artifacts of the culture, in the language spoken around the child. Much of this book is about ways in which the child comes to be conscious of more and more sources of meaning and to discriminate among them, eventually to accept as meaningful many things that would not have been recognized as such at an earlier point in development.

The major breakthrough in human development, the one I believe finally made us different from all other animals, was the ability to share subjective meanings. This capacity begins to develop through nonverbal social exchanges in infancy and early childhood, but it takes a leap into the stratosphere when sufficient language has been acquired to enable the child to participate in the talk of the social world, and to join in the sharing of minds through talk, narrative, and other modes of discourse.

Memory

One result of taking meaning seriously is the implication that personal meaning is essentially memory; that to a large degree memory is the conservation, organization, and transformation of meaning. Essentially this is a claim about cognitive content, in that it subsumes language and concepts as repositories of meaning. Concepts and categories, as well as scripts and schemas, are seen here as self-organized, meaningful constructions of a developing memory system.

Recognizing the close connection between experience, meaning, and memory also sheds light on issues of learning. From this view, learning depends entirely on its relation to meaning, and meaning is subjective by virtue of its relation to experience. These intertwined relations may provide the basis for a new look at the educational enterprise, from its beginnings in preschools through the lectures of college professors. More will be said of the unity of memory and meaning in what follows; it implies a central role for both in cognition and in cognitive development.

Development

A major theme of this book is the need to put *development* back into developmental psychology, where it has slipped away from much of the theorizing and empirical research of the field, and also to insert it into theorizing in cognitive science and other "mainstream" domains of psychology and related fields. There are two sides to this theme: one is the acknowledgment that development is not given the recognition that is its due, and the other is the value of considering development in understanding psychological processes and products.

Several factors have pushed development aside as a major concern, even in developmental psychology. These include the adoption of models from cognitive science, which was built on conceptions of cognition as a computing machine. Machines are designed and constructed by humans; they do not grow or develop as organisms do (although their designers upgrade them constantly, often to the consternation of their users). The mechanistic cognitive science models adopted by developmentalists valued continuity over time and devalued change in basic "components." Moreover, the nature of the research growing out of the highly valued experimental method, considered to be the gold standard of scientific inquiry in psychology, has resulted in a largely laboratory science organized around single problems identified at discrete ages. This singular focus tends to lose the sense of the person in an ongoing developmental flow coming from many sources both outside and within the individual child.

Interpretations

Interpretation, as the theoretical stance taken here, expresses the attitude that all knowledge is conditioned on the perspective from which it is viewed. This reflects a phenomenological approach to infant and child development, and it speaks to the pragmatic nature of knowledge as well. Indeed, *interpreting* is a useful term for describing what people do most of the time, beginning in infancy, in perceiving and understanding the minds of self and others (Bogdan, 2003) and in making inferences on the basis of observations in the physical, social, and symbolic environments. Interpretation in this context is generally from the perspective of both biology and culture, as the two systems come together in the development of the individual child. The child's interpretation of the world is strongly pragmatic; she seeks knowledge in relation to her own interests, whether biological, social, or cognitive, and constructs new meanings therefrom. But the child is also always having knowledge thrust upon her in the guise of teaching. The relation between the child's interests and the teacher's is a classic conundrum from this perspective.

That all knowledge is perspectival—that is, based on what can be known from one position in time and space—does not necessarily imply a radical relativism because, as the feminist philosopher Sandra Harding (1991) argued, strong objectivity in science emerges from the contradictions and eventual agreements of observers in different positions. The theoretical discussions in this book are therefore characterized as "interpretations," but not only because my take on some of the issues examined is neither well documented empirically nor well substantiated in existing developmental theory. This book is an invitation to all who tend to think about development—even if they do not agree with any of my specific interpretations—to build the supportive theoretical structures that will make us all smarter and more successful in this joint developmental enterprise.

Social and Cultural Surround

Development must be considered within its social and cultural context. The mainstream view in cognitive development seems to be that culture is an important conveyor of social knowledge but that it is not a significant factor in the development of mind, which is or should be our concern. On the other end, those who write from a cultural perspective often emphasize the importance of the cultural contribution to knowledge but are less interested in the workings of the individual mind. I aim to bring these concerns together to consider how cultures, through their social agents, ensure mental development via different pathways and toward different endpoints.

Culture surrounds the child even before birth in the practices of prenatal care. The social figures in the child's life are essential to well-being, even to life itself. They provide the supportive structures that enable the child, in whatever conditions of culture and ecology, to enter into the life of the social world, as well as to acquire specific aspects of cultural knowledge and practice. Among the most important of these, certainly, is basic oral language, acquired through sharing meaning with others in speech. Language carries culture within it (Chapters 7 and 8). The members of the child's social world—family, friends, teachers, and so on—serve as cultural carriers through their speech, and through their behavior as well, which reflects the habits of the particular culture within which the child is growing up. Child-rearing practices are designed, consciously or not, to impart aspects of the culture.

A "community of minds" is the designation that I prefer for the symbolic culture within which children are raised, and into which they are gradually inducted as they become participants in the discourse of their community (Nelson, 2005b; Nelson et al., 2003). This label serves to identify both the institutional character of culture and its role in supporting the acquisition of the essential tools and techniques of "mind sharing." In an important way, the knowledge and skills that children acquire over the first five years of life are directed toward achieving entry into the symbolic community of minds that surrounds them. (Chapters 8 and 9 explicate this relation in more specific terms.)

Individual Pathways

Can emphasis on individual development coexist with emphasis on social and cultural construction? It not only can, it must. If children were being raised in a vacuum, or in a homogeneous environment, like rats in a cage, we would not necessarily need to be concerned about their individuality—although of course as McClintock taught us, even each ear of corn develops differently (Keller, 1983).

The important point is that each individual child develops in terms of particular experiences (which are conditioned on inheritance as well as experiential history and social and cultural conditions), and that the result is differences in patterns of development as the individual, self-organizing system puts together its puzzles in its own sequences and with varying components. Because of these complexities, no modal child exists, although we can locate statistical means on any measure we care to take. The extremes of the distributions may be as "typical" as those in the center, although they are likely to be considered "delayed" or "advanced" and to be treated as such.

Experience and Meaning as Process

The lifelong adventure of gathering meaning from experience is in the service of two overriding motivations: to make sense and to make relationships. At the outset of postnatal life, the latter—relations with others, critically with a mother figure—is most important, but sense making is equally built into the human cognitive structure, and the two proceed in tandem. Toward these ends, experience and meaning work together within a "meaning-memory system" that begins as simple memory for guiding action and interaction but over time is transformed into a complex knowledge system from which concepts, schemas, and episodic memories emerge (Chapters 4 and 7).

Experience occurs as a transaction of the individual with some part of the physical or social surroundings through perception and action. Events are the basic units of experience. Events may also include actions, reactions, and interactions within large-scale activities. This con-

ception contrasts with the idea that objects or features are basic units of
the mind. Objects and features are components of events. Events range
in size from small-scale momentary happenings to temporally extended
components of large-scale activities. Familiarity with events enables
the comprehension of large "slices" of experience. Experience is motivated and directed by meaning (Is Mommy pleased?), and meaning
sensors evaluate the experience and coordinate it with what is already
"known" in the system.[4]

Personal meaning must be considered in terms of three functions:
motivation, discernment, and conservation, each integrally connected
with experience. Meaning motivates the person to seek experiences
relevant to current or anticipated meaning structures. Meaning senses
and evaluates relevant content of experience in light of preexisting
memory, organization, and interest. And these experience-derived
meanings are conserved through organizing and reorganizing processes.
Memory and meaning are each central cognitive constructs: everything
in memory—what is known, believed, or remembered—is meaningful
content, not neutral information. What is meaningful in this sense is
what is relevant to the state of the organism, whether biologically (Eat
this, don't eat that!) or psychologically (Mommy is pleased; no, she is
angry). Memory preserves meaning for future use. Meaning is derived
from experiential transactions by distilling, as it were, what the transaction affords the existing memory system in the form of new knowledge,
confirmation of prior experience, or information of possible future significance. These processes may be thought of as making sense, knowledge gathering, or learning.

The Nature of Experience

Experience is in some sense continuous during wakefulness, thus it is
impossible to place a time boundary on what constitutes "an" experience. Major developmental changes in early life arise in response to the
emergence of levels of consciousness ranging from simple awareness to
the rich complexities of cultural consciousness, which I will discuss
later. But awareness can exist without attention, and it is attention that
keys experience. Attention varies continuously, from brief and fleeting
to total absorption in a task. Established meanings may direct attention, but so may novelty, attested by the well-known orienting re-

sponse. Meaning is in its most basic form highly personal; it is not made nor acquired but derived from experience in coordination with preexisting residues of prior meanings. Cognitive processes—association, categorization, analysis, differentiation, integration—are ways of organizing new and existing meanings in memory. Common, social, or communal "shared meaning" emerges either through similar experiences and shared processes and principles or through iterations of interactive communication, especially through language and other symbolic exchanges. Moving from solely personal meanings to shared meanings is a crucial part of the developmental process in human childhood.

Sharing meanings and experiences is not a simple, automatic process: whenever two or more people observe or participate in the same ongoing event they experience it from different perspectives, with different histories, with different background knowledge. These differences are most glaring when the individuals involved include an infant or very young child and an adult, although an adult arranging an event for an infant may find it difficult to keep these differences in mind. When giving a bath, for example, a parent whose experience with water play has been fun, whose knowledge about the source of the water and its disposition provides confidence, and whose body control ensures that the baby is safely held and not in danger, expects the infant to enjoy splashing water. Yet the baby may make it clear (perhaps by terrified crying) that her perspective is quite different from that of the adult. The two share an experience, but not a meaning.

The parent may attempt to *manipulate the meaning* of the bath experience for the infant, and to set up a sequence of experiential histories that will provide background for the next and subsequent bath experiences. Verbal and gestural expressions (including the embracing hold) convey a meaning that may come to be shared (the bath is fun and safe), but the overall experience itself remains quite different for each, given the different roles that the two play in the activity. The point to be emphasized is that experiences are different for people engaged in the same activity or event because experience is felt as an internal component of the transaction in the world.

Experience is at least partially the effect of directed attention, so if two people are directing their attention to different aspects of an event, their experiences of the event will be different. Thus *sharing attention* is a first step toward minimizing the difference between experiences.

Sharing attention emerges between infant and parent in later infancy and is a unique property of human experience. (Tomasello, 1999). Sharing attention ensures that some aspect of the event is experienced by both participants, but the constituents of experience nonetheless ensure that the experience is different for each.

Intersubjectivity established in shared activities is an early step along the road toward shared meaning, and it is a necessary step toward language, but it is limited. Language is the primary tool that humans use to go beyond attention to the *exchange of meaning*. Sharing the meaning of experience appears to be a unique motivation of human cognition incorporating the intertwined motivations of making sense and making relationships. It is the means by which sense making becomes a communal process. The enlargement of the boundaries of experience and meaning is at the heart of cognitive development, and it begins in the first year.

Encounters and Experience

To say that experience is directed by meaning is to say little about experience itself, except that it is identified as the interface between meaning and the world outside the self. Experience results from an encounter of the organism in the environment, involving perception, action, and interaction via communicative processes, broadly speaking, including language.[5] Whereas experience is often directed from within the organism (by meaning seeking), the encounter is as determined by the state of what is outside the individual, social and physical, as by what is intended by the experiencer. The encounter is the active drama, the experience is the receptive result for the individual. The interpreter (the meaning sensor) derives meaning from the experience in relation to what is already in memory (the meaning conserver). Consider a child's encounter with a new toy being demonstrated by an adult (perhaps a parent or a researcher). What influences come to bear on the child's reactions and on what is carried away (in memory) from the experience?

Constraints on Experience

Experience is directed by meaning, but it is constrained by a constellation of influences that determine what *may be* experienced at any given time. These influences include the evolved and developed state of be-

ing a human person, embodiment, ecological setting, social embeddedness, cultural and symbolic systems, and the history of prior experiential knowledge already conserved in the action/perception/
cognitive/memory system (see Figure 1.1). The point is that there are
many person-specific constraints on what is experienced in any given
encounter within a particular environmental context. Experience for
any given person in an "objectively" viewed situation is always different
from another person's experience in the same situation—and thus the
meaning derived from it will also be different. A brief look at each of
these constraints illuminates the point.

Evolved constraints affect experience no matter what the type of organism and no matter what the age of the person. Evolved constraints
reflect general characteristics of the species. The human body plan is
similar across people and ages, but size and proportions change radically in infancy and early childhood. Thus there is both continuity and
change over time. The specific set of perceptual and action systems
that all humans inherit as part of their evolutionary history determines
whether a sound wave will be heard, a voice will be interpreted, a face
will be recognized, and so on. A particular constraint of this species-
specific kind is the fact that human infants are born in an unusually
helpless state and are dependent on the care of mothers and others for
many months before they become even marginally mobile, and it is
years before they can be expected to care for themselves in basic ways,
such as by getting and preparing their own food. This implies that in
many situations infants are not able even to see the same aspects of the
situation as adult caretakers are, and that in most situations their
"meaning director" is focused on very different possibilities than that
of the adult.

In infancy and childhood *embodied* influences are of special significance, because during some periods (infancy, preadolescence) changes
in the body proceed at a rapid pace. The meanings derived from environmental encounters at one time may cease to be relevant after the
body changes. For example, knowing the angle of descent of a slanted
surface relevant to an infant's crawling skills is of little or no help when
that infant becomes upright and starts to walk (Adolph, 2000). Neural
systems (a crucial embodiment component) also continue their development for many years after birth, to a large degree in response to experience, with implications for the different meanings that the same
"objective" context may yield for infants and children of different ages

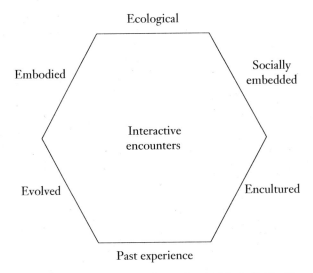

Figure 1.1 Constraints on experience and meaning within individual interactive encounters.

(see Chapter 3 for more details and discussion). The two-year-old child with an attractive new toy may find that her size and strength are inadequate to carry out the manipulations that her three-year-old playmate can, and so each has a different experience.

The *ecological* setting of experience may range in scale from geography to the furnishings of the infant's own room. The ecological "niche" of humans is highly variable, unlike that of other primates that live largely in tropical, well-bounded, thickly forested areas. Human infants are born into a specific cultural ecological niche and require attention, learning, and guidance from older members of the society to acquire the social ways and technological skills that support existence within their particular ecological setting. General dispositions, including especially the disposition to attend to and imitate the surrounding social figures, provide the basis for accommodating to the conditions of life that may constrain experience, either by presenting novel conditions to be examined or by masking relevant potential meanings in old, familiar surroundings. A child who occupies a particular ecological niche such as rural poverty, for example, would rarely be faced with the challenge of a new toy, and if she were, her action on it would be distinctively different from that of a more advantaged agemate, with concomitant differences in experience and meaning derived from it.

The *socially embedded* constraints on experience, deriving from the long and intimate dependence of infants and children on the care given by parents and other members of the social group, cannot be over-estimated. The assumption that early and extended social intimacy and dependence have especial significance for the cognitive as well as the emotional development of human children is now widely accepted (Byrne and Whiten, 1988; see Chapter 3). The very young infant (lying prone, for example) is totally at the disposal of his or her parents or caretakers, even for the opportunity to see things from more than one perspective. Experience for this infant may be very narrowly confined or widely available, depending on the conditions of care, and research suggests that such differences are important, not just for immediate experience but for the long term. Whether the child with the new toy is left to explore it on her own or is shown how it works by a parent or an older sibling, and how the toy is treated by those others, changes the experience and meaning of the encounter.

Encultured influences surround the child. Human language is a crucial component of culture that enables the child to become a full member of the group, privy to its customs, concerns, and concepts. Cultural differences affect the specifics of what the child may experience, and how they are experienced. Is the new toy one that replicates a functional artifact, such as a car? How does that fit with other artifact replicas in the child's experience, and with the relations of the functional artifacts themselves? Is the child encouraged to act out cultural routines with the toy ("driving" to a store, for example) that will have possible residues on "real" experiences in the world?

Finally, the history of *past experience*, in meaning and memory, plays an important role in determining the meaning that will be derived from any new encounter, whatever its nature. Thus this factor has the potential to multiply the influence of the other constraints on the child's (and the adult's) experiential meaning.

Figure 1.1 is meant to capture the different sources of influence on any given experiential encounter. It may be noted that the personal constraints reside on the bottom left, from memory through evolution to embodiment, and the "outside" constraints are those from the top and right, ecological, social, and cultural. The rate of change in each varies—making the "same" experiential conditions different from one time to the next. Memory history changes from moment to moment; physical growth—including neurological change—while constant, is more rapid during some periods of development than others. Although biological heritage may seem unchanging, it takes on different guises at different periods, for example at puberty. Social conditions change constantly during interactions and with different people, while cultural and ecological conditions may appear constant but are accessed differently as development proceeds, and of course in some historical periods, such as the present, they change rapidly in some aspects but not in others. Perhaps the most dramatic change—symbolic access, including language, literacy, and numbers—is not specified in this diagram; it draws on all the other sources—memory and meaning, biology and neurology, social and cultural settings—to form an experiential compound of its own, an outcome that I consider in the second half of this book.

Becoming a Different Kind

How much of experience and meaning is devoted to the *being* of everyday life as an infant or child, and how much is devoted to the *becoming* of a different kind of person—a toddler, a preschooler, a schoolchild, an adolescent—is a matter of some significance to theoretical conceptions of the process of development. Is developmental change simply a matter of piling up small steps, or does it depend on sudden shifts in some basic constituent of the overall system? What perturbations might be involved in the change from one developmental state to another?

Models of Change

Developmental psychology is charged with two missions. One is to understand processes of psychological functioning in different problem areas at different ages and stages of development, such as the ability to grasp the concept of numerosity in infants, toddlers, schoolchildren, and adults. The other is to understand how individuals change from one developmental stage to another. The contemporary field is more concerned with, and better at, accomplishing the first mission than the second. Volume one of the fifth edition of the *Handbook of Child Psychology* (Damon, 1998) includes twenty-eight chapters on developmental theory, and there are several more theory chapters in the second and third volumes on cognition and social-emotional areas, the majority of which provide accounts of psychological processes but not of major change. This proliferation of theoretical stances implies that there is no overarching conception that has won the minds of those who study development of psychological processes, nor is there a small set of strongly competing views. Instead the field is populated by those who hold to one of the thirty or so variants represented in the *Handbook*, and by others—probably the majority—who pay little heed to developmental theory but work within a single paradigm on a single problem and age or stage of development. Those I characterized earlier in this chapter as theory theorists certainly speak with a strong voice, but they do not represent the whole field. A different contender for broad acceptance is a version of systems theory, which is important to the ideas expressed in this book, as discussed in Chapter 2. However, systems theory does not in itself provide a way of thinking about major transitions or a distinctive solution to them.

The ways that change and continuity are conceptualized differently by the major developmental theories can be characterized in fairly general terms that provide perspectives on the views put forward here. The stalking horse of most cognitive theorists is a version of general process theory associated with learning theory, or its cousin associationism. Any general process proposal is tainted with the remnants of Skinnerian behaviorism and by the British empiricists, whose concepts of learning are held to have been at least inadequate. In a general process model, each bit of information (whether a feature, a symbol, a node, or some other mental entity) floats freely, finding and connecting to similar bits or to those associated in some other way such as contiguity; no further structure is envisioned, and change is continuous over time.[6] In any version of general process theory, a separate theory is necessary to explain major developmental changes.

Modularity has been proposed as the alternative to general processes. In this approach the various kinds of knowledge (linguistic, spatial, object, social) are clearly divided from all others, walled off into segments wherein different processes produce different kinds of outputs. The segments are prevented from talking to one another by their isolation and differing organizations (Spelke, 2003). Development takes place within but not across domains. Modularity implies a neural basis for development, and generally an innate basis, although in some models modularity may emerge later in development, at least for some functions.

Domain-specific models are related to modularity but may take a less strong nativist stance. One type of domain structure is represented by theory theories, already discussed, wherein each domain is organized in terms of a theory. Each theory is organized in terms of specific concepts and causal relations. It is not clear whether domains "talk to each other" easily or with difficulty or at all, as theory theory work is done within domains and not in a larger developmental context. We can think of modular and domain-specific theories as "vertically" organized, partitioning the mind in a similar way at all points in development.

In a general stage theory like Piaget's, structures change over time as entities at each stage become more complex and reversions to a lower stage are blocked, and at higher stages there are more complex connections with other entities. This type of architecture is "horizontal," in that operations change permanently with the move to a higher level, in contrast to the "vertical" architecture of modular arrangements where both mechanism and content remain separately compartmentalized over time. Ironically, in the modular case the only developmental mechanism appears to be learning.

None of these schemas appears satisfying. Associationism is too unfettered, modularism is too rigid; theory structures require too much and overly rigid innate differentiation; stage structures are too wholistic and unidirectional. Such quick and dirty judgmental comments hardly substitute for serious analysis, yet they encapsulate much of the critical literature.

Developmental Change as Movement to New Levels

The developmental alternative proposed here relies on a concept of levels, horizontal like a stage theory but without restrictions on reversion to earlier levels. Indeed, in the version preferred here, all levels, once achieved, continue to be available for different functions, and in adulthood all coexist in what Donald (1991) calls a "hybrid mind." The same processes that underlie the experience and meaning dynamic of continuous change through organism-environment interactions and self-organizing processes lead also to the emergence of higher levels of complexity. These psychological transitions each lead from a level of currently possible experiential encounters to a new level that expands the domain of consciousness. The transitions involve multiple changes, such as those of physical growth, neural development, and learning that set up enabling conditions for advancement to a new level. Additionally, each transition involves the perturbation of social or symbolic encounters, or both, which provide different perspectives on the previously established meaning system. Each transition then eventuates in a significantly different "kind" of individual: a baby, a toddler, a young child, and so on, with distinctive psychological as well as physical characteristics. We recognize these changes easily in individual children, and often they are attributed to growth and the passage of time in terms of age. Psychologically, they need to be explained in terms of self-organization, which enables smooth adaptation to such rapid and radical change.

This version of development is tied to different levels of organizational complexity. Structures and operations proposed in the different models noted above may apply to one or more levels of development as conceived here. For example, the general process model might be appropriate to the lowest level of development, whereas the modular organization might apply for some areas in some levels and the theory structure might be seen at higher levels of functioning. A structure of levels allows for the development of organization as well as meaning (content), and at the same time it retains advantages of flexibility across domains of functioning. What remains is to determine for each level of functioning exactly what additional operations, if any, apply. This is the conceptual framework that underlies the present proposals, which converge on the "hybrid mind" in a "hybrid culture" as delineated by Donald (1991, 2001) and Nelson (1996). The notion of a hybrid mind incorporates the idea of a number of systems operating in concert as appropriate. Thus at any level, all previous levels—but not those not yet achieved—are available for analysis and action.

Levels of Consciousness

The particular concept of levels illustrated in Figure 1.2 is based on the idea of the expansion of consciousness that accompanies (and perhaps instigates) major psychological, and specifically cognitive, changes. Two

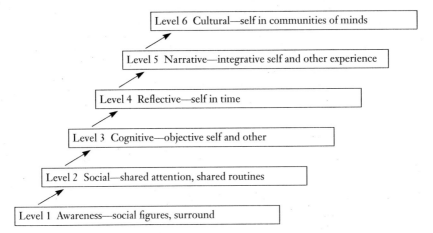

Figure 1.2 Course of development of levels of consciousness in infancy and early childhood.

characteristics of the shifts in functioning that take place are important to note. After the base level (level one), each movement to the next level comes about in response to new *social* experiences that reveal new ways of acting and understanding in the world. The second level, for example, is entered into with the emergence of social exchange and shared attention. This movement in turn reveals potentials of social interaction (such as imitation, routines) that were not in play previously. Next, experience with those social activities reveals a new perspective on the self in relation to the other, which, as it is enriched with use of words and other symbolic forms, uncovers the vast new territory of a named world shared with other people. Further experience with language in use brings the child into a new confrontation with the difference between self and other experiences and between self in the present and the past. This all-encompassing understanding then benefits from the integration provided through the psychological and physical causal structures incorporated in narratives of this and other worlds, and opens up the possibility of endlessly extended and shared cultural knowledge systems attainable through the written language and symbolic systems.

This quick summation of development in terms of experience and meaning indicates its endlessly circular nature, fed by encounters with the world, social and material, that through self-organization of meaning enable movement to new levels, which in turn lead to new organization. I emphasize that there is no implication that one moves *on* from one level to another. Rather, all levels already achieved are available for derivations of meaning and awareness in any further encounter. Thus this is a dynamic cognitive system, always in motion. I do not expect such a brief introduction to this conceptualization to be convincing or even sufficient for understanding, but I put it on the table here as an outline to be filled in in the chapters to follow.

Looking Forward

The themes outlined thus far resonate in the rest of the book along a roughly chronological and functional path that examines experience-based cognitive development from birth to school age. Chapter 2 diverges from this plan by expanding on some of the theoretical issues opened up in this chapter, identifying historical roots and contemporary connections to the ideas presented. In particular, it addresses the issue of the logical and rational mind versus the pragmatic and strategic mind, arguing that our evolutionary roots provide reason for accepting the idea of "psychological pragmatics" as a basic cognitive framework. Psychological pragmatics as a cognitive paradigm has roots in the theories of John Dewey in American psychology and in European phenomenology. How to integrate the pragmatic/experiential view with the semiotics of culturally based human cognition is a problem for cognitive theory at all levels. The issues involved are woven throughout the remaining chapters, and I return to them in Chapter 9, with its focus on developmental perspectives.

Chapters 3 through 8 address specific aspects of the developmental course of infancy and early childhood and illustrate the movement from basic awareness in early infancy through cultural consciousness as the child approaches school age. In Chapter 3 I consider the implications of the experience and meaning perspective for understanding infant development and the contemporary research in infant cognition, with emphasis on the constraints of biology, the necessity of social care, and cultural interpretations of the infant world and experience. I explore there issues of attachment, physiological and neurological maturation, perceptual and motor development, and social and communicative processes from the experiential viewpoint, revealing the confines of private minds in the context of the social milieu, as well as the emerging sense of self, conceptual development, and protolinguistic communication.

Chapter 4 focuses on the transition from infancy to early childhood, involving critical developments in mobility, symbolic functions, concepts and self-understanding. I examine there processes of mimetic externalization as an impetus for cognitive advance, including gesture, play, imitation, and early words, with a specific focus on toddlers' use of nonlinguistic symbols and representation. Overall the focus is on how children manage in a world of "hidden meanings," symbols that have meaning for older people but not for the toddler or young preschooler. This offers an essential clue for answering the larger question of how children develop within and eventually become part of the community of minds.

Chapters 5 and 6 trace the move from pragmatic communicative language to representational and cognitive functions of language, with the child's experiential meaning first leading and then conforming as language comes to restructure the child's cognitive repertoire. Language acquisition begins as a social pragmatic game, embedded in shared activities. Slowly it moves on to give voice to shared meanings, going beyond the strictly private meanings of infancy. The limitations of current word learning theories that rest on a mapping paradigm are contrasted with the pragmatic alternative based on language in use. Variations in the learning process across children, families and social-cultural groups are important to the understanding of these developments. Chapter 6 concentrates on the dramatic shift that occurs with the mastery of representational language, which provides the boost to cultural childhood and narrative consciousness.

Chapter 7 relates the emergence of narrative to the emergence of autobiographical memory through collaborative reconstruction of shared experience. Narratives incorporate time, social and cultural roles, motives, cognitions, the coherence of groups, other children, other worlds, other communities. This chapter emphasizes that the practices of narrativizing memory enable the understanding of self-continuity— past, present, and future—and the identification of knowledge source, including self-experience as distinct from the experience of others.

Two themes are addressed in Chapter 8. The first is the child's entry into a community of minds, an alternative conceptualization to the achievement of a theory of mind that situates the child in a social world where "minds" are significant. The second theme takes up one of the main topics of contemporary cognitive development, how conceptual knowledge is organized and reorganized in the child's knowledge schemas. The pragmatic, social point of view finds collaborative construction is a necessary process involving representational language and cultural knowledge structures. Again, the community of minds holds the key to "mind sharing" of cultural knowledge.

Finally, Chapter 9 returns to the process of development in terms of "experience in the wild." It recapitulates basic themes—experience, meaning, internalization and externalization, the biocultural conditions of development—and considers implications for methods. The idea of levels of consciousness becomes more explicit as the basis for a theory of development in terms of experience and meaning within a community of minds.

2

Perspectives on Meaning

So let us return to the question of how to construct a mental science
around the concept of meaning and the processes by which
meanings are created and negotiated within a community.

~ *Jerome Bruner, 1990*

$\mathcal{B}$RUNER'S CALL FOR constructing a mental science
around the concept of meaning implies two central ideas: that meaning
is crucial in understanding how human minds "work," and that meanings are created by communities and not only by individuals. These are
powerful suggestions that point toward a new foundation for developmental cognitive psychology. Bruner was of course one of the pioneers
of modern cognitive science and a major contributor to studies of infancy and language acquisition from the 1960s through the 1990s. In
the work quoted above he also notes that contemporary cognitive science has left "unexplained and somewhat obscured the very large issues
that inspired the cognitive revolution" (p. 10). Many of those issues involve the social and cultural bases of cognition, toward which much of
Bruner's own work has been devoted.

In this chapter I begin by noting the failings of cognitive science in
the eyes of its critics. I then consider some of the roots of a different,
more pragmatic and cultural-theoretical approach, connecting those
strands to contemporary work, evolutionary, developmental, and cultural, with an emphasis on the systems approaches to theories in developmental psychology.

How Cognitive Science Missed the Meaning

While Bruner, like many others, embraced cognitive psychology at its
outset, his expression of disenchantment reflects the sense that its ini-

tial promise of uncovering the "thinking machine" behind human activity has been betrayed by its strict adherence to the computational models of mechanics and operations. From its beginning in the 1950s, cognitive scientists adopted the model of the digital computer, along with information theory and theories of information processing that take "inputs" and produce "outputs" through mechanical operations. Both computation and information are meaning neutral, and deliberately so. With this model, the processor passes information from one state to another, but it cannot determine what is worth processing. Meaning must therefore be imposed on the basic model from outside; it cannot be derived from it.

The computational model is suited to the "solipsistic mind" (Fodor, 1981), that is, the mind as a unit to be studied independent of its context in the body or its situation in the world. The underlying assumption of cognitive theory has always been that of a real world of preidentified objects, properties, and situations, independent of any individual's specific point of view. This assumption supports the belief in the correspondence between the real world and internal universal concepts. The ideal research goal in this paradigm is the discovery of general operations that apply to any problem.

This model of cognition is flawed, however, and especially so when it is applied to the problems of cognitive development (see Clark, 1997; Hutchins, 1996, for general critiques). The computer model is not suited to natural cognition in a number of ways: its assumption of universals does not take into account different perspectives and positions with respect to perceptions and concepts of things in the world; it leaves meaning and content outside its neutral operations, to be added on; it does not allow for the influence of social and cultural conditions on its operations, nor does it take account of embodiment. Moreover, the computer model is a "top-down" process requiring the a priori stipulation of rules and representations, but work in robotics has demonstrated that knowledge of the environment can be assembled in a "bottom-up" process through action in the environment. Much of human cognition takes place in terms of social problem solving, where shared or situated knowledge processes are in play rather than individual rule following.

The "closed mind" view is often defended on methodological grounds by those who argue that to determine the parameters within which the mind operates, it is necessary to strongly constrain sources of variability. But in the end the variability that appears in the world and in the mind is not explained, it is simply ignored. The most serious problem, though, is that this model lies outside the natural world; there is no explanation of its biological evolution in the form of symbolic representations (Bickhard, 2002) or computations (Hendriks-Jansen, 1996), and there is no explanation of its development. Computers do not grow or change, but children do. For all of these reasons the computer model is particularly ill suited to developmental purposes, however well it has served research to date and continues to do so, now enriched with neurocognitive imaging techniques.

Analysis of the psychological and sociological reasons for relying on computational cognitive science models of cognitive development, as well as its theoretical appeal, would be a worthwhile project, but one I cannot undertake here. These developmental issues have been addressed insightfully by Bickhard (1987, 2002) and by Hendriks-Jansen (1996), and from a more general perspective by Clark (1997) and Hutchins (1996). I will return briefly to the developmental implications at a later point in this chapter.

Looking Back: Is Pragmatism a Meaningful Alternative?

Some critiques of contemporary cognitive science look back toward ideas that flourished before the advent of cognitive science and even before behaviorism took over psychology and much of social thought. They remind us that the quest for an experiential psychology is not unprecedented; it has strong roots from which to graft a new plant, roots that go back more than a century.

American Pragmatism Then and Now

Philosophical pragmatism, the legacy of William James, C. S. Peirce, and John Dewey at the turn of the twentieth century, incorporated key ideas of nineteenth-century Darwinian evolution. Pragmatists viewed human knowledge as deriving from the practical goals of everyday existence, and rejected the classical idealism of Plato, Descartes, and Kant. From the pragmatic perspective, knowing derives from action and remains action-oriented, expressed in the pragmatists' aphorism "knowl-

edge as use." Knowledge is "not a copy of something that exists independently of its being known," but "an instrument or organ of successful
action." It follows that things "are what they are experienced as" (successive quotes from Menand, 2001, p. 361). This aphorism places concepts in the meaningful center of human goals and activities. And because human activities are situated in communities of actors, meaning
belongs to the community as well as to the individual. More than a century later, pragmatism still appears radical in its opposition to repre-
sentationalism and the dualisms of subject and object, mind and body,
nature and nurture or genes and environment, all still present in current theories and debates.

For the developmentalist, John Dewey is a critical figure in this tradition. Dewey asserted that experience is the basis for thought. In modern cognitive terms, this might be restated as a claim that procedural
knowledge (or implicit memory) precedes the capacity for the declarative or metarepresentational knowledge (explicit memory) useful in
conscious thought processes such as problem solving. However, the
distinction between conscious and unconscious processes was not significant for Dewey; thinking was presumed to be a characteristic of
consciousness. Reflective thought, Dewey asserted, is not an apriority
to knowledge but a "vital activity" (Dewey, 1981, p. 200; original text
1910). In writings that seem to prefigure twentieth-century phenomenologists, Dewey took note of the "psychologist's fallacy," namely, the
"confusion of experience as it is to the one experiencing with what the
psychologist makes out of it with his reflective analysis" (p. 165). This
fallacy—assuming one's own interpretive perspective to be the same as
that of one's research subjects—is all too attractive, even to developmental psychologists today who are tempted to impose their own interpretations of reality on the children they study.

William James introduced the term "radical empiricism" for the idea
that knowing is "a functional relation in experience" between a knower
and what is known, including relations as well as objects (Heft, 2001,
p. 37). The concept of experience in Dewey or James is equivalent to
the role that "activity" plays in some modern works; the older term has
the added advantage of emphasizing subjectivity, with the admitted disadvantage of deemphasizing action. C. S. Peirce, the third member of
the pragmatist group, is most notable now as the American founder of

semiotics, the science of signs, and his work in this area remains alive today, often quoted if not widely read (see Chapter 5).

To sum up the pragmatist's creed: knowing is derived from experience, not a copy of something independent of the experiencer but a function of action, carrying meaning for the individual because of its relation to his or her goals. This relation precedes reflective thought directed to what is known. This orientation is consistent with the Darwinian evolutionary theory that reigned among scientists of the early twentieth century, and it remains so today.

Looking for Meaning in Phenomenology

Ideas not dissimilar to those of the American pragmatists emerged in Europe during the first half of the twentieth century in the philosophical phenomenology of Husserl, Heidegger, and Merleau-Ponty, among others. Heidegger's explication of the everydayness of "being in the world," in contrast to the objective theoretical stance assumed in classical philosophy, mirrored Dewey's theme of experience as prior to reflective thought. Heidegger also placed great emphasis on the embeddedness of experience in culture and the social practices of human life. Dreyfus (1991, p. 23) paraphrases this theme in Heidegger as follows: babies "begin to exist as they are socialized into the understanding of what it is to be a human being that is already contained in social practices." Heidegger viewed the basic mode of being human as "inhabiting" the world. Inhabiting implies that the world is not an object but is part of the self, and thus transforms the relation of self to objects in the world. This mode of "being" in the world avoids the very idea of a relation between a separate subject and object, as both are part of the same phenomenal position.

Nonetheless, Dreyfus comments, "if we step back from involved activity and become reflective, detached observers, we cannot help seeing ourselves as subjects contemplating objects" (Dreyfus, 1991, p. 45, on Heidegger). As the involved subject, the object is part of the involvement; one must remove oneself from the involved activity in order to view oneself and the object as separate. In contrast to the experiential knowing of inhabiting, the reflective stance results in a mode of theoretical knowledge—the mode that traditional philosophy (and psychology) has attempted to explicate. However, as Heidegger, Merleau-Ponty, and Dewey all insist, theoretical or reflective knowing *presupposes* practical "involved" knowing. This claim is basic to the foundation of an experiential or pragmatic psychology, with a special application to development.

The French philosopher Merleau-Ponty elaborated similar ideas in terms of the "primacy of perception": "The experience of perception is our presence at the moment when things, truths, values are constituted for us; . . . perception is a nascent *logos;* . . . it summons us to the tasks of knowledge and action" (Merleau-Ponty, 1964 p. xv). This proposition is illuminated by Merleau-Ponty's description of the development of the layers or orders of consciousness in the infant and child. In this vein he proposed an early order of organized experience constituted of whole configurations rather than or prior to an assembly of parts. "What classical academic psychology calls 'functions of cognition'—intelligence, perception, imagination, etc.—when more closely examined, lead us back to *an activity that is prior to cognition* properly so called, a function of *organizing experiences that imposes on certain totalities the configuration and the kind of equilibrium* that are possible under the corporeal and social conditions of the child himself" (pp. 98–99, emphasis added). Here Merleau-Ponty, like Dewey and Heidegger, makes it clear that a level of organization precedes that of reflective cognition, and he invokes the constraints of both the body (corporeal) and the social world on what the child may make of the whole of an experience.

At the same time that the pragmatists and phenomenologists emphasized the basic level of direct perception and knowing that comes from dwelling in the world as given, they also emphasized that for humans, the world as given is constituted by culture realized through social practices. The culture and the world are there before the individual experiences them.

The later philosophy of Ludwig Wittgenstein, whose intellectual roots were in pre–World War I Vienna but whose mature linguistic philosophy emerged in post–World War II Cambridge (Wittgenstein, 1953), centered language and meaning in social practices. Unlike the phenomenologists and pragmatists, he emphasized the futility of gaining meaning through introspection or private thought. Grasping the meaning of a word, from Wittgenstein's perspective, is a matter of organizing experiences of language *as it is used by other speakers* (Chapter

5). But to grasp meaning in terms of the use of a word is in some way to deny the personal meaning that a word might have for the individual. Herein lies a dilemma that reverberates in the development of the child. Each of the philosophers cited here confronted and ultimately rejected the subject-object problem of classical philosophy that serves as the foundation for studies of cognition in psychology—including developmental psychology—up to the present time. Each also attempted to reconcile the place of humans within the biological evolutionary scheme and, at the same time, within the cultural milieu and social practices that constitute the "world" for humans. These are hallmarks of pragmatism, with its basis in experience.

Is there a Remnant of Pragmatic Psychology Today?

Although pragmatism fell on hard ground when behaviorism took over psychology during the early and middle years of the twentieth century, remnants survived. G. H. Mead, a follower of James and Dewey at the University of Chicago, wrote as a "social behaviorist" during the 1920s and 1930s (see Mead, 1934). His conception of the natural and social origins of the concept of self has continued to be influential through most of the succeeding years. The roots of the ecological psychology of J. J. Gibson and his followers also appear to lie in James's pragmatism (Heft, 2001). Gibson's (1979) theory holds that the visual and other perceptual systems are designed to directly detect structure in the world; thus perceptual knowledge of the environment needs no intermediate representation or categorical interpretation. Roger Barker's psychology of everyday life and Fritz Heider's social psychology, both worked out in the 1930s and 1940s, also reflect influences of early pragmatism (Heft, 2001). Although Heider's work continues to be cited by social psychologists, Barker's studies of the minutiae of daily life among children in the Midwest have largely vanished into time.[1]

With these partial exceptions, the psychology that might have flourished in the wake of James's and Dewey's call for psychological pragmatism was aborted in the early decades of the twentieth century. Behaviorism, the new ruling psychology, rejected the dualisms of classical philosophy simply by ruling the mind out of psychology (Watson, 1913). In contrast, when cognitive psychology won out over behaviorism in the 1960s, it took a different route by ruling out the body and keeping only the mind. More recent calls for an "embodied cognition" or "situated cognition" have attempted to keep the mind in place while adding to it the body and its functions, as well as the environment. However, simply adding the body and the social or material environment to a preexisting mind is insufficient for a developmental psychology. Evolutionary theory also disappeared from psychology after the early years of the twentieth century and did not reappear in force until sociobiology emerged, in the form of a radical evolutionary psychology during the 1980s.

Its contemporary absence in psychology notwithstanding, pragmatism has experienced a revival over the past twenty years in the social sciences and humanities, as both philosophy and social movement (Dickstein, 1998). Despite the difference in emphasis between the original propositions of James and Dewey and those of today's pragmatism, which has strong connections to postmodernism, they do share common themes and great strengths. Kloppenberg (1998, p. 111) characterizes these as pragmatism's "denial of absolutes, its admission of uncertainty, and its resolute commitment to the continuing vitality of the ideal of democracy as a way of life." Whereas historians, political scientists, sociologists, humanists, and philosophers of science, art, politics, and language are all represented in the Dickstein (1998) volume on the reemergence of pragmatism, the absence of psychologists is striking. Equally striking is the almost complete absence of references to pragmatism in contemporary theoretical discourse in psychology.[2]

Nonetheless, despite the absence of a coherent theoretical movement and the continued dominance of the solipsistic-mind model of cognition, there are clear signals of a renewal of interest in experiential ideas within psychology. Emphasis on the embodiment of cognition, first asserted by Varela, Thompson, and Rosch (1991), has gained new interest from neurocognitive research connecting cognition to emotion (Damasio, 1999), action (Clark, 1997), consciousness (Edelman and Tononi, 2000), and self (LeDoux, Debiec, and Moss, 2002). Robot designs enabling the establishment of "knowing" without representation, through action in environments, and the relation of this work to dynamic systems in general and human development in particular, have had quite a wide impact, in part at least through Clark's (1997) presentation of the evidence. Indeed one can find intricate connections in the renewed interest in evolutionary biology—whether from a sociobiological perspective or a more comparative and cultural one—with a broadened idea of cognition that emphasizes the place of the cognizer as agent in the ecological world.

Preceding these recent trends are several strands of "contextualism" (e.g., Bronfenbrenner and Morris, 1998; Lerner and Kauffman, 1985), citing the relevance of social contexts for development, learning, and thought. Contextualism rests on the presumption that behavior is modulated by its context, where context may be very small-scale, in terms of a particular discourse, or as large as a cultural milieu. This perspective provides an important constraint on the universality of behavioral rules, but it does not reach into the actual construction of thought, of concepts, categories, rules, relations—all of the cognitive baggage that people carry with them across contexts. Contextualism has now been adopted into the larger world of cognition in the idea of "situated cognition," with roots in a number of different traditions.

Several other revisions of the cognitive model have been put forth in recent years. The ecological position taken by followers of Gibson places emphasis on the structured environment and the perceptual systems that are designed to "pick up" its structure (Heft, 2001; Reed, 1996). In a related view, Barsalou proposes that "a perceptual theory of knowledge can implement a fully functional conceptual system" (1999, p. 577, abstract; see also Prinz, 2002). Others put emphasis on action (Glenberg, 1997; McClamrock, 1995). These proposals address basic issues brought out in Hendriks-Jansen's (1996) critique of contemporary computational cognitive science, as well as Bickhard's (2002), but they do not converge on developmental solutions to the general cognitive problem.

In brief, the many proposals for "fixing" the contemporary field of cognitive science all tend toward a situated, embodied pragmatics. My contention is that such a move must involve a full-bodied experiential developmental psychology wherein perception and cognition are the evolved tools of adaptation to varied environments. Human self-interests are conditioned on the realities of ecological, social, and cultural experience. Following the lead of Hendriks-Jansen, Bickhard, and others, a developmental psychological pragmatics must emphasize experience from the perspective of the individual agent (child or adult), providing an integrated perspective that is missing from cognitive development theories that follow the perspective-free principles articulated in mainstream cognitive science. Insofar as experience is the source of knowledge of a variable world, the function and structure of the child's experience must be accounted for in any model of cognitive development. Most important: experience-based knowledge—perspective-based, not "reality-based"—precedes reflective thought in development.[3] Current models that view cognition from "outside" or within a universal frame inevitably miss this dimension of meaning.

Are Evolutionary Models in Psychology Meaningful?

Pragmatism and experientialism in the nineteenth and the early twentieth century drew broadly from Darwin's theory of evolution, with its strong functionalist assumption that traits are established through natural (or sexual) selection to the extent that they contribute to the survival and reproduction of organisms. In this way psychology in its formative years in the nineteenth century had a strong footing in biology. Although pragmatists recognized that individual human experience takes place in the confluence of a biocultural system, the cultural aspects were set aside by experimental psychologists such as Wundt,[4] on grounds that they were not open to experimental investigation. In turn, for the past forty years the biological side of the equation has tended to be ignored by cognitive developmentalists to the same degree as the cultural side, as the focus has been on the abstractly conceived internal structure of the child's mind. However, the perspective of developing systems promises to provide an avenue for the cultivation of both biological and cultural sides.

Developing Self-Organizing Systems

Developmental systems theory (DST) is a broad conceptual framework for thinking about the development of organic systems and the emergence of new forms, applicable to long-term evolutionary change as well as short-term ontogenetic change. The theory approaches the question of how systems originate and develop by analyzing the developmental process itself, in the same way that developmental biologists do. Susan Oyama (1985, 2000) brilliantly articulated the concept of DST in evolution and development, stressing that ontogenetic processes are as crucial in evolution as DNA. The key to understanding in this framework is the analysis of *process*, in terms of multicausal contributors to the system, rather than the *product* (the organism) of the presumed interaction of static genes and unchanging environments. Interaction is crucial, but it is interaction within a system of continuous multicomponent processes that leads to further developmental phases of process, not through some overarching plan but through continuous self-organization.

Many others have similarly proposed that a version of dynamic systems theory is the appropriate mode of analysis for development. Gottlieb's (1997) long-term research program in biopsychology emphasizes probabilistic epigenesis as the basic underlying process. Thelen and Smith (1994) use dynamic systems concepts from mathematical analysis of physical phenomena in an extensive program of theory and empirical research. Others with similar models and intent include Fischer (Fischer and Rose, 1993) and van Geert (1998). The core ideas of these theories has been summed up, in terms of the process of "soft assembly," by Gershkoff-Stowe and Thelen (2004, p. 16), as follows:

> Biological dynamic systems . . . are composed of multiple, heterogeneous elements. Under specific conditions, such systems *self-organize* [emphasis added] to produce complex patterns that change over time . . . Self-organization means that the organized patterns arise strictly from the interaction of the constituent parts. The hallmark of dynamic systems is a kind of circular causality, where no component part has causal priority over the others: the behavior of the system depends on all the constituents, including those in the physical world in which the system is embedded. Thus development is the product of multiple and co-dependent elements or subsystems cooperating within a single system (Oyama, 1985). New developmental patterns arise in a self-organizing fashion as a function of the changing interrelations between internal processes and contextual factors.

While this quotation provides a good summation of the prevailing theories, it should be noted that in the developmental processes with which I am concerned, it is not just the physical world within which the system is embedded but also and preeminently the social world.

Development based in self-organization has the capacity to lead to the emergence of new forms, much as the migration of cells in embryonic development leads to the emergence of organs such as the liver or the heart. The reliable interaction of forms and their environment at one level (the cell) produces the higher level of organization (the organ). In the postnatal development of human infants, new organs are no longer emerging, but self-organizing systems of interaction lead to the emergence of new kinds, for example new modes of locomotion (e.g., walking, Chapter 4) or new kinds of memory (see Chapter 7). The systems implication is that the development of organs and species is not radically different from the development of new modes of locomotion in its transformation of prior states into new emerging levels of organization.[5]

The process of evolution proceeds by reorganizing existing states to accommodate changes brought about by any of a variety of sources, whether environmental catastrophes, genetic mutations, or ontogenetic innovations. Successful self-reorganization in the face of change enables the survival of the organism and eventually the survival of the species. Analogously, successful self-organization at every point in the development of complex organisms enables survival and, at higher levels, increasing applications of intelligent action.

Emergence is an important concept in this approach, closely tied to the construct of levels of organization. For example, in the ontogenesis of the fetus, the emerging level of the organization of the heart is demonstrably more complex than that of the single cells that compose it, whereas the whole organism emerges as a product of organizing processes that eventuates in the newborn infant. At each point in this process self-organization is ongoing, and there are distinctive emerging levels of complexity of organization and growth as well. Previous levels do not disappear as they are integrated into higher levels. Processes of cell function remain critical and may be studied, as well as those of organs and organisms. In just this way, new levels of psychological development may emerge while earlier levels continue to function.

The DST biocultural perspective centrally involves the idea of the organism-environment as an interpenetrating system (Oyama, 2000) where development takes place in the interface. Human development is seen as a self-organizing system involving brain, body, and mind functioning together in interaction with both the internal and external environment, with successive periods of organization arising from this process. In this perspective, the individual and the social world form an interdependent transactional system that is constantly in the process of self-organization. We can consider the "elements" of the system separately at any point in time, but only with the caveat that they are not in practice separable, that the context, especially the social context, is always part of the process. The position that human minds are emergent products of interactions, beginning in infancy and developing within the environment of communicating adults, as argued by Hendriks-Jansen (1996), is consistent with the DST perspective. Schneirla (1957) was a pioneer in emphasizing the complexity of developmental processes and rejecting the "blueprint model" of the genes. The common misunderstanding of these processes is captured in the following quote from Lehrman, a colleague of Schneirla's: "The interaction out of which the organism develops is *not* one, as is so often said, between heredity and environment. It is between *organism* and environment. And the organism is different at each different stage" (Lehrman, 1970, p. 20, quoted in Hendriks-Jansen, 1996, p. 225). This view of the evolutionary developmental process emphasizes the significance of the behavior of organisms in the environment as the locus of selection.

Because complex systems are made up of many different subcomponents that may recombine in different ways, a mature form may initially appear as a small kernel of something else that eventually finds itself co-opted as a function into a system that takes on new powers (Fischer and Bidell, 1991). Any change must be "incremental and congruent with existing morphology as well as existing behavior to stand a chance of survival" (Hendriks-Jansen, 1996, p. 109). For the same reason, hunting for the origin of a particular capacity is likely to fail because the original version of that capacity will not be found in a recognizable form. Under these conditions it is imperative to study the development of the system on its own terms, recognizing transformations and the emergence of new capacities from the combinations and recombinations of old forms and functions. Just such a process is now recognized as essential in phylogenetic evolution (Depew and Weber, 1997). The essence of this conception of development is the movement from a less complex to a more complex organization that functions effectively for the individual in a social environment at a particular moment in time, and that in turn also leads to new levels of organized function.

This construction of the general systems approach to development provides for an account in which the biology of human development is not independent of culture and the social environment. Nonetheless, biological development has its own directedness and telos, and understanding its processes provides insights for understanding the larger complexities involved in psychological development, of which the biological is an essential part. Toward this end, the lessons from developmental systems theory (Oyama, Griffiths, and Gray, 2001), the dynamic systems theories of Thelen and Smith (1994), the dynamic development of Fischer and Rose (1993), and the probabilistic epigenesis of Gottlieb (1997) serve as the foundation.

Developmental psychologists have been remarkably cautious in embracing this view and applying it to their own work. The implications for all developmental studies are serious. Instead of attributing single causes, parceling out influences on an outcome (e.g., genetics versus environment), or searching for single origins of a trait in early development—all common practices in developmental psychology—under this theory, one studies the *process* of development in an area as it unfolds, noting how different internal and external influences enter into the process and contribute to development over time. Such is the practice in contemporary developmental biology. As Oyama and colleagues (2001) have noted, biologists never say they are nativists because there are no developmental biologists who attribute causality solely to the genes; thus "innateness" has no obvious meaning.

Evolution, Genes, and Environment in Contemporary Psychology

It seems somewhat odd, but it is no doubt to their credit that developmental psychologists have for the most part stood aloof from the resurgence of interest in sociobiology, neo-Darwinism, and the rise of evolutionary psychology as a reductive and deterministic discipline. Sociobiology emerged as a separate field with the publication of a book of that title by E. O. Wilson (1975), whose main field of research is the social insects, ants in particular. Wilson's intent has been to emphasize the complexity of social organization that is possible under genetic determination. His writing extended this premise to other social animals—including primates, humans among them—with the strong implication that genes keep the behavior of humans and other animals on a "short leash" in social contexts as well as in such contexts as foraging and predator responses.

Whereas many psychologists read *Sociobiology* with interest, its influence on theory and research in developmental psychology was initially modest at best. With the emergence of its offspring; evolutionary psychology (Barkow, Cosmides, and Tooby, 1992), many psychologists, developmentalists among them, found that its claims fit their own views of genetic influence on psychology. Steven Pinker is perhaps the best known and most prolific adherent to this brand of genetic determinism (Pinker 1994, 1997, 2002). A main claim of evolutionary psychologists is that psychologists have in the past ignored the vast influence of genes on human behavior, instead assuming the view that human behavior is infinitely plastic, open to social and cultural influence through learning impressed on the "blank slate" of the infant mind. Against this presumed vacuum, evolutionary psychology theorists focus on traits that they presume were found to be adaptive for human life in the so-called environment of evolutionary adaptedness (EEA), identified as the Pleistocene Era, 1.7 million to 10,000 years before the present (BP). In the view of evolutionary psychology, genes were "set" during the EEA, when conditions of life revolved around hunting and gathering, and they may prove to be maladapted to present-day life.[6] Critics point out that genetic variation in the species over the succeeding time span is plausible, that no one knows exactly what the EEA conditions were, and that the genetic leash is not nearly so determinative in human behavior as evolutionary psychology theorists imagine, citing empirical research in anthropology and social psychology (Laland and Brown, 2002). To these persuasive criticisms I would add the weaknesses of the gene-environment interaction assumption in general, as found in the field of behavior genetics.

Like evolutionary psychology theorists, behavior geneticists focus on the genetic determinants of human behavior. Their interest is in the partitioning of effects of genes and environment on individual traits, which they study by analyzing statistical correlations among twin pairs, sorting out the differences between identical twins (100 percent shared genes) and fraternal twins (siblings with 50 percent shared genes), among other methods. This practice emphasizes the contribution of genes to variability within the population in such traits as intelligence and morality. Whereas it would be possible, given the methods used, to emphasize the influence of environment on the expression of different traits, or to consider the effects of environment-gene interaction, behavior geneticists in general appear to agree with evolutionary psychology theorists that genetic influences have been underemphasized in psychology in the past, to the detriment of understanding basic causes of psychological variables. It should be noted, however, that neither group has actually identified any genes that are presumed to influence the outcome of trait distribution; rather the conclusions drawn are based on inference from mathematical analyses. The particular weakness of behavior genetics from a systems perspective is the dichotomous partitioning of genes and environment, which violates the assumption of interdependent processes of development, and of the role of the organism in behavioral interactions with the environment.

As a result of these and other trends in empirical research and theory related to evolution in psychology, its study or even its consideration in psychological theory has tended to be avoided by those who hold less deterministic views, including most developmentalists, who have long accepted the conclusion that there is no conflict between nature and nurture and that their interactive processes must be understood. However, the problem with evolutionary psychology is not one of accepting or rejecting evolutionary influences for fear of genetic determinism. Rather, the issue is how to effectively incorporate knowledge of our biological evolutionary inheritance into the study of psychology, and particularly into developmental psychology. One advantage of developmental systems theory is its insistence that many different influences enter into the organization of the organism; thus the phylogenetic inheritance incorporates epigenetic influences, including the inheritance of environments—particularly the social and cultural environment—as well as the collectivity of human genes.

One point that such considerations bring out is the commonality in early behavior and development among primate infants, including humans. Should we assume that human infants have built-in conceptual structures similar to those of chimpanzees (such as concepts of permanent objects or theory of mind)? Or can our theories of cognition and development adequately account for both the similarities and differences found among related species? The principles of DST and other dynamic systems theories allow us to understand these issues more deeply than other current theories do. From this perspective, the essentially static genetic determinism of both evolutionary psychology and behavior genetics are ill fitted to developmental analysis.

The Nativist Turn in Developmental Psychology

Beginning in the 1960s, research on visual perception indicating that infants at birth were already active seekers of things to look at, in spite of their relatively poor visual acuity, began a virtual stampede of research showing that infants know more about the visual world than had previously been believed. These studies formed the basis for the proposal that newborns are in possession of theories about the physical world that enable them to make sense of otherwise confusing and confounding environmental displays (Spelke, 1988; see Chapter 1). This position is consistent with the view that infants and young children are endowed with the same kinds of computational "hardware" that adults have, and that adult models should thus be applicable to developing minds with little or no modification. This "no-change" structural-continuity assumption supports the concept of the "wise child" who is capable of intellectual feats (logical reasoning, theory building) that are usually attributed to educated adults.[7] Ultimately these claims fall back on the position that basic structures and competences are innately specified. The structural-continuity position thus belongs to the nativist side of the eternal nature-nurture debate in developmental psychology.

Defending their nativist views, Spelke and Newport (1998, p. 276) argue that it is crucial for developmental psychologists to "tease apart the constant from the changing, the rigid from the flexible, the universal from the variable, and the inborn from the acquired." The constant, universal, and inborn are viewed as providing foundational knowledge for the child's use, in contrast to the inevitably variable interactions with the world. They therefore propose that research should aim to identify the "core capacities" that "(a) emerge *in anticipation of their function*, (b) are *constant over development*, (c) reflect evolutionary adaptations providing for phylogenetic continuity, and (d) serve as building blocks for the development of culture-specific actions . . . providing a universal vocabulary from which culture-specific skills are assembled" (p. 283; emphasis added). Hidden inside the child's mind is a "representational vocabulary" that supplies the basic formats for knowledge about the world, to be elaborated as children become exposed to culture-specific demands. These formats anticipate needs that arise later in life; they may serve no immediate function. The continuity assumptions in this view of the computational mind appear to support the idea of an infant cognitive system that is fully capable of reasoning and judgment, although constrained in communicating those judgments by immature response systems. An agenda is thus set for locating the origins of adult cognition in the conceptual givens in the minds of babies, justifying the goal of uncovering those representations that are inbuilt and those that must be built later.

Some of the debatable implications of the developmental continuity position must be noted. Whatever the core capacities are assumed to be, the assumption that they emerge prior to their function is in direct conflict with a dynamic systems theory, which views capacities as "assembling" in the course of their functioning (Thelen and Smith, 1994). Similarly, the idea that core capacities are constant over development is strongly challenged by social theories of, for example, language development (Tomasello, 1999, 2003). In any theory of human development, language must be considered a "core capacity" but not an unchanging one. The view that core concepts are established first, and that it is only later that culture-specific demands are added to the child's store of competences, is consistent with the cognitive model of the isolated (solipsistic) mind. The idea of building blocks that first structure the mind and *then* turn to cultural and social knowledge variations is vulnerable to the evidence that cultural variations in experience shape infant development even in such basic capacities as modes of locomotion, with effects on cognitive change (see Chapter 3).

Spelke and Newport (1998, p. 276) promise a "new view of human nature" to be derived from experiments with infants that shed light on "cognitive development, human knowledge, and human nature," allegedly revealing the contributions of innate structure to human knowledge. From the perspective of the experiential child, the premises of this nativist program are unable to fulfill this promise because they (a) ignore the embodied condition of learning and knowing; (b) ignore the social conditions in which babies develop and learn; and (c) ignore the cultural origins and nature of human cognition and human knowledge. Without taking account of these conditions, any new view of human nature would be bereft of what makes us human. A larger view of human knowledge and human nature—especially its social and cultural dependence—and a deeper view of the biological dependence of human cognition—especially its embodiment—provide a very different interpretation of the evidence for infant "knowing" that Spelke and others have uncovered in the first months of life.

Naturalistic Cognition

The trend toward a naturalistic cognitive science viewed from philosophy and neurocognition (Einstein and Flanagan, 2003; Flanagan, 1992) is consistent with this deeper understanding of our phylogenetic background. Here innateness is understood in terms of the structures that have evolved in the phylogenetic history of the human species; in particular, how the brain has evolved in ways that are both similar to and different from those of other closely related species. How brain processes relate to cognitive and behavioral processes becomes an empirical question, and as brain imaging has become more feasible, the possibility of making fairly direct inferences from one level to another has opened up. For the developmentalist, this approach offers a number of advantages. For example, comparative neuropsychological studies of other primate infants will enable us to make inferences about what kinds of structures and processes may be "built-in" in the infant primate brain, our own as well as those of our close relatives. This perspective makes it appear unremarkable that human infants may build up expectations about the structure of the object world fairly early in development, as this may also be observed in infant chimpanzees, for whom such knowledge is crucial in order for them to move about on their own as they do.[8]

The naturalistic approach, however, implies more; it implies that the classic epistemological assumption—that infants, children, and people in general are motivated to understand the true nature of the world—is deeply misleading. Human infants, like other infants and mature members of other species, seek knowledge relevant to their place in the world. Their concerns are pragmatic; they are not interested in knowledge for its own sake. By this I do not mean to deny curiosity or the urge to explore the world around them; what I am suggesting, rather, is that there is no urge to construct an abstract or coherent theory of what is discovered. Validity and truth inhere in what is useful in rela-

tion to the interests and goals of the actor, not in some abstract objective truth. Infants and children are not scientists or theorists, and to
analogize their problem-solving efforts to those of scientists is misleading on both ends of the analogy. However, human infants, like other
animals, are prepared to pay attention to certain kinds of experiences
and to ignore others. These premises are in accord with those of the
early pragmatists.

Where Is Meaning in Phylogeny and Ontogeny?

In the late nineteenth and the early twentieth century, G. Stanley Hall
(1904) and other psychologists proposed several ways in which child
development recapitulated the supposed evolution, biological and cultural, of the species. Biologists and psychologists alike have attacked
these proposals as superficial and misleading, with sufficient strength
to ward off further attempts along the same line over the next century.
Gould (1977) cast what seemed to be a final blow against any analogy
between phylogenetic and ontogenetic biological sequences, and indeed there are good reasons for caution in this regard (Nelson, 1996).
Nonetheless, the stricture can be taken so far that homologies of developmental sequences in related species are ignored and clues from the
conditions of phylogenetic sequences are overlooked in development.

As a case in point, the comparison I made in *Language in Cognitive
Development* (1996) between developmental levels and those identified
by Merlin Donald (1991) in the evolution of the human mind has been
criticized as recapitulatory. I discussed this issue in some detail, noting
that the sequence Donald projected, of four levels in human evolution
emerging through three periods of radical transformation of mind,
bore an intriguing resemblance to the levels I had been finding in early
childhood development. I explored this issue in discussions of the developments concerned and concluded that the levels existed in development, but with considerable overlap in their timing and unfolding. I
revisited this issue more recently, focusing on memory development
(Nelson, 2005a).

Donald's (1991) account of the evolution of the human brain, cognitive system, language, and culture is in my view the best documented
and most provocative of the many different proposals on this topic.
Donald begins his account with a description of the level of memory

and cognition humans share with other primates (and probably most mammals) in terms of event memory (large or small). Three transitions follow during the evolution from general primate to *Homo sapiens*. The first transition supplements the primate mind with a level of social representation that Donald terms mimesis, involving imitation, movement in time with others, rhythmic movement, and the capacity to recall and operate on one's (action-based) representations. The mimetic level sets the stage for the emergence of complex human language and the movement to the symbolic/linguistic/narrative level, which again is social in nature and provides the basis for myth and other cultural and social narrative forms of expression, interpretation, and explanation. This oral, directly communicative, and cognitive-symbolic level eventually gives birth within human history (that is, not through biological change) to the external-representation level of writing, graphic forms, literacy, mathematics, logic, and science. This level Donald refers to as theoretic.

Donald's theory has attracted much deserved attention. He recognizes that speculation about the evolutionary basis of cognition and language is subject to the problem of unknown and in many cases unknowable "facts," as well as to constantly changing estimations of important dates and fossil interpretations, and competing theories based on the same facts (e.g., Bickerton, 1990; Mithin, 1996; Noble and Davidson, 1996). Regardless, the theory is especially provocative from a developmental perspective, as it projects a sequence in the evolution of human cognition that has resonance for the appearance of particular clusters of skills and competences in early development, especially those that are related to Donald's levels of mimesis, event knowledge, and narrative representation. The fact that Donald projected these levels without reference to development but on the basis of the emergence of competences as revealed in the fossils and archeological evidence for hominid evolution makes this sequence especially interesting.

A major contribution of Donald's theory is its conception of levels of cognition that in the mature "hybrid" mind operate on different aspects of experience. The emergence of a later competence, such as theoretic thought, does not override prior levels of cognitive processing, such as oral narratives or basic event representations (e.g., scripts), but applies to different functions of the cognitive process, while also impinging on and thus modifying the range and operations of the earlier capacity. Donald emphasized especially that mimetic skills and processes permeate modern human life and minds to a degree that generally goes unrecognized in cognitive psychology, for example in the practice of manual skills, sports, and group activities such as dance and music making.

After examining the developmental evidence, I concluded (Nelson, 1996) that the levels or layers that Donald identified served analogous functions in early childhood, but that rather than forming a clear sequence, they appeared to be developing more or less simultaneously. In the end it appeared that Donald's work, implying a hybrid human mind that operates sequentially or simultaneously in parallel on different levels, was supportive of my hypothesized developmental proposal, and that the latter lent strength to his proposals as well. The weak form of the recapitulation hypothesis was fruitful in making the comparison (see Nelson, 2005a, for an update). However, the outcome of the comparison led to an increasingly complex developmental hypothesis, as is evident in this volume.

A different take on the evolution of cognition and language was laid out by Terence Deacon in his 1997 book *The Symbolic Species*. As the title suggests, Deacon believes that the key to the unique capacities of human minds lies in the particular neural adaptation that enabled the use of symbols. Many have claimed that language is the attribute of humans that makes us unique in the animal world and that serves as the fulcrum of culture; however, Deacon makes a particularly strong case for the unique cognitive demands of symbolic representation. In addition he emphasizes the special neural circuitry required to enable precise cortical control over vocalization. His theory of language evolution specifically invokes the developmental demands of language learning and the adaptation of neural structures in response to phonological and symbolic processing demands as proto–language use gave rise to these adaptations.

Deacon's conception of the evolution of these abilities involves the notion of "niche construction" in which (in this case) hominids established an advantageous niche that relied on symbol use. He emphasizes, however, that rather than requiring a strong genetically determined structure, these language bases demanded increased learning capacities. "The evolutionary dynamic linking language behavior and brain evolution has the opposite effect [from genetic determinism]: the *de*-differentiation of innate predispositions and an *increase* in the contribution by a learning mechanism" (Deacon, 2003, p. 92, emphasis in original). Thus although Deacon's conception differs from Donald's in the timing and mechanism of language emergence, it provides another developmental perspective for the coevolution of language, culture, and cognition.

Throughout the following chapters I refer to aspects of these theoretical foundations in the different areas concerned: infant cognition, language, and symbolic development. Two areas that are particularly relevant to our understanding of our biological evolutionary heritage are the full suite of capacities and the demands of early infancy. These have led in different directions (see Chapter 3), the first of which emphasizes the social support and attachment of infants and parents, discussed insightfully by the sociobiologist Sarah Hrdy (1999). The emphasis on innate knowledge was discussed above (Spelke and Newport, 1998). The other direction leads toward examining the competencies and development of human infants in relation to those of other primates, a topic that draws attention to the relation of phylogeny and ontogeny, as well as to the development of unique aspects of human development (Tomasello and Call, 1997). One of those unique aspects is clearly our dependence on culture (Tomasello, 1999).

The Promise of Developmental Theories

A theory of development is generally assumed to presuppose an endpoint, a telos or an equilibrium plateau. The endpoint is presumed to shed light on the proposed course of development, and thus on distinctions among theories. For example, both Piaget and Vygotsky considered the logical, scientific thought that dominated the intellectual world of the early twentieth century as the telos of human development, which raised the issue of how the presumably illogical, unknowledgeable child could attain the intelligent status of the adult scientist. They each asked, as others do, "how to get here from there," where "there" was the state of the infant or preverbal child. These two towering theorists of the mid-twentieth century perceived different routes toward the goal because they viewed the "same" end state in different ways. In Piaget's view, scientific thought is a characteristic of individual minds, although resting on historically established scientific progress. Indeed, his basic metaphor for cognitive development was the progress of scientific thought over human history, a genetic episte-mology. Individuals who reached his highest level of formal operations might engage in whatever scientific thinking was in progress during their lifetime, but the structure of such thinking would not differ from one era to another.

In contrast, in Vygotsky's Marxist view, scientific, logical thought is a product of cultural-historical forces that shape individual development differently in each cultural and historical context. Thus some individu-als might benefit from specific cultural environments that emphasize scientific thought while others might engage in art or literature, and those within the same cultural milieu but without the benefit of mod-ern education would remain at a less developed, pragmatic level of thought.

The difference between Piaget's telos and Vygotsky's—the structural model of logical adult thought at its most developed state versus the functional model of culturally achieved knowledge and thought—un-derlies many theoretical differences in developmental psychology to-day, although they are not always attributed to these historical deriva-tions. In particular, as indicated at the beginning of this chapter, much of present-day developmental theory is based on variations of cognitive psychology and cognitive science, where the endpoint model is that of the logical, symbol-processing, modular computational machine. The most general answer to the question of how one gets "here" (to the ra-tional adult model) from "there" (the infant mind) is that the necessary modular computational machinery is in place from the beginning, but it needs to be supplemented with learning or training before it can op-erate most efficiently and in an integrated mode. These theories devi-ate from the developmental course mapped out by Piaget, presuming a much greater degree of innate structure supplemented by learning, al-though their endpoint assumptions are similar in their emphasis on the rational structure of individual minds.

The distinctive quality of Piaget's theory in relation to our concerns here is his reliance on action as the source of knowledge—a link to the pragmatism of James and Dewey (through James Mark Baldwin), as pointed out by Bickhard (2004). In this respect Piaget was a true ex-perientialist. However, the weakness in Piaget's account is his ignoring of the social context and the social practices that surround the individual's action in the environment. It is puzzling to note that in Piaget's detailed accounts of infant development there is rarely a mention of another person (for example, a parent); the actual parent who is the experimenter remains unacknowledged.

In the Vygotskian biocultural view, development is derived from cultural conditions of the transactions of persons in the social, symbolic, and cultural environment; the "natural" constitution of thought is thus nourished and tuned by the symbolic resources of the social and cultural world (Vygotsky, 1962). The adult mind is assumed to be fully enculturated, mediated through symbolic systems, its structure largely determined by the conditions of its development. Thus how to get "here" from "there" is mainly a question of how the social and cultural world interacts with the potential inherent in the developing individual infant and child.

These two contrasting paradigms have given rise to very different research lines. On the one hand the questions are, what are the bases or origins of particular components of the adult mind, and when can they be identified? On the other, those questions are seen as a will-o'-the-wisp, in that development changes the characteristics of the mind as it encounters new potentials for action and activity and is nurtured by social practices and cultural scaffolding. It is these opportunities for experience and meaning that are at the heart of the developmental process.

Biocultural Developmental Psychology

To the great advantage of the field of developmental psychology, over the past thirty years both cross-cultural research and cultural theory have emerged as important contributors to our understanding. Indeed, a variety of approaches to the theory of development from a cultural perspective have emerged, most prominently Cole (1996), Rogoff (1990, 2003), Valsiner (1987, 1998), and Wertsch (1985, 1991). Each of these theorists situates cultural developmental psychology within the general theory originally proposed by Vygotsky (1962, 1978). Activity theory derives from the same source (Scribner, 1985; Stetsenko, 2003, 2004), and like the pragmatic theories of the past, it places special emphasis on the derivation of knowledge from action. Cross-cultural comparisons of cognitive development reveal differences in both the content and the structure of thinking (Cole, 1996) and have raised the question of how such differences emerge in practice. This question is obviously of central interest to a pragmatic psychology, one concerned with experience as the basis of knowledge. Vygotsky's theory, based in cultural-historical analysis, seems positioned to provide answers, as well as to apply to practical problems of education and intervention.

Within American psychology, internalization of knowledge that is originally external is often presented as the core of Vygotskian theory, based on what is now his most famous dictum: "Every function in the child's cultural development appears twice: first, on the social level, and later, on the individual level; first *between* people (*interpsychological*) and then *inside* the child (*intrapsychological*) . . . All the higher functions originate as actual relations between human individuals" (1978, p. 56). An important point to note in this passage is Vygotsky's equation of higher-order mental functions with cultural development. This principle has been taken to mean that the child internalizes the structure or content of the cognitive capacity (e.g., memory) or skill (language) from exposure to and with the support of the adult's model. The construct of adults' "scaffolding" of the child's problem-solving activities by way of appropriate hints or Socratic queries supports this idea.

Unfortunately, the scaffolding idea tends to lead to the interpretation that the child is dependent on the input of adult teaching for the acquisition and learning of concepts and skills, and that the resulting contents of the child's mind are in some sense *copies* of what is presented by adults. Variations on the scaffolding theme, such as Rogoff's (1990) idea of the child as an apprentice acquiring skills through guided participation, are subject to the same misinterpretation. As Rogoff and other theorists well recognize, this is a distortion of Vygotsky's intent and also of the intent of contemporary scholars. However, this facile interpretation of Vygotskian theory is quite widely disseminated, among other places in educational practice. The actual intent of the "interiorization" idea expressed in the above quotation involves the child's activity in interaction with adults; it could be rephrased as a social version of Piaget's constructionist approach. It is consistent as well with the collaborative view of development implied in the biocultural model (Nelson, 1996).

Vygotsky's concept of internalization (or interiorization) brings out an important relationship between the internal and the external that will play a role in the discussions to follow. Vygotsky's formulation ap-

pears to place the external in the hands of the social Other, the interacting role. In Piaget's conception, the external is the world of objects
that the child may act upon. But there is an important missing piece
here, in that one of the distinctively human characteristics that develops early in the child's life is the capacity to externalize mental contents. That is, to a significant and important extent, the external is in
the hands of the child; making the internal external is the key to communicating with symbols, but it also has manifestation in activities such
as play, imitation, music, art, and narrative. Because of their important
roles in the social-cultural process of cognitive development, internalization and externalization can be viewed as two sides of the same developmental process: the inside-out process of development. This idea
is elaborated in Chapter 4.

Coming from a different perspective, that of comparative psychology, Tomasello's (1999) exposition of the cultural origins of human
cognition provides a comprehensive contemporary biocultural view.
His account includes comparisons with other primates, the central role
of language and its acquisition, and the importance of the "ratchet
effect" both in cultural evolution and in individual development in
culture. The so-called ratchet effect refers to the fact that in human
society cultural advances are transmitted over generations, so that in
each generation culture is "ratcheted up a notch," providing a different
artifactual base for individuals to begin with and move on from as they
make their own contributions to the next generation. The ratchet effect is produced as each new level of knowledge or technology sets the
child—or the culture as a whole—on a new trajectory toward what is in
effect a different telos. Thus, for example, the child born in 1900 (just
becoming acquainted with the telephone and electric light) was in a far
different place in terms of cultural development and knowledge from
the child born in 1950 (in a world of radio, movies, airplanes, automo-
biles, and the atomic bomb) or the child born in 2000, surrounded by
television, computers, and electronic toys. (The social, political, and
artistic aspects of cultural change are of course subject to similar effects
but not always viewed as clear advances.) Tomasello's work points the
way for an integration of contemporary studies in developmental psychology with those of cultural psychology. He considers both learning
and intentionality as key concepts in the development of individuals in
the culture.

The idea that cultural cognition is symbolically saturated appears as the most significant point to emerge from cultural psychology from varying positions. Both within language (as in metaphor) and without (in images and signs), in internal and external representations, human cognition is symbolically constituted. Indeed, this is why the evolutionary theories of Donald and Deacon are so relevant to developmental cognition; they address issues of how presymbolic thought relates to symbolic thought. Of course, human thought is never truly presymbolic; human infants are born into a symbolically organized cultural environment, as Hendriks-Jansen (1996), among others, has emphasized. Nonetheless, the infant does not interpret the symbols as conventionally intended, and meaning inheres in the interpretation, not in the sign (Chapter 5). Infants have years ahead of them to acquire the signs and their meanings that will be incorporated into their cognitive structures and experiential knowledge. It is these processes that must be understood if cultural cognition and cultural development are to be fleshed out as psychological theory. Most current theories barely touch on this process, although Vygotsky himself led the way in his studies of signs as tools, inner speech, and spontaneous and scientific concepts (Stetsenko, 2004).

Conclusion

Weaknesses in the old cognitive-science models of the mind of the infant and young child have been addressed by the alternative formulations briefly summarized in this chapter: by pragmatic theories in psychology and philosophy, by evolutionary and comparative analysis, by a range of classic and contemporary developmental theories, especially those that place the developing mind in its cultural context. The summaries presented offer only a glimpse of the contributions to contemporary thought made by various theorists. They are meant not as a guide to the theories cited but as a compilation of some of the significant ideas that can lead to a better understanding of cognitive development in situ, and especially of the place of meaning in that development.

My own orientation is indebted to Tomasello's analysis of the joint biological and cultural origins of mind, as well as to many of the other developmental thinkers noted here. However, my aim is to get inside the process, to view it from the child's perspective and from that of individual developmental change. These two aspects may be thought of as the twin constructs of simultaneously *being* and *becoming*. In Chapter 1 the state of being was described in terms of experience and meaning. These processes must lead to "becoming" something different—older, wiser, bigger, more knowledgeable—all accomplishments of the developmental process, which remains to be fleshed out in the following chapters.

3

Being an Infant, Becoming a Child

In Mother Nature's great gallery of creations, human infants are both
masterpieces and connoisseurs—connoisseurs of mothering.
~ *Sarah Blaffer Hrdy, 1999*

Most of our species-typical activity patterns are uniquely adapted to
bootstrap the infant into an intentional world.
~ *Horst Hendriks-Jansen, 1996*

*E*VERY THEORY OF COGNITION and its development is
obliged to propose an account of its beginnings in infancy. Piaget undertook his painstaking studies of his three children, using both detailed observations and naturalistic experiments, to build a theory of
sensorimotor stages prior to the emergence of representational
thought. As discussed in Chapters 1 and 2, these studies have been
challenged by research in recent decades that supports claims of representational thought in early infancy. In this chapter I consider what
alternative a naturalistic, pragmatic theory based on experience and
meaning may offer on the beginnings of development in infancy.

First, an account of the natural history of infancy speaks to the six dimensions of experience outlined in Chapter 1, with a special emphasis
on embodiment and the role of social support and interaction. I also
note the dramatic changes in activity and sociality observed in the last
few months of the first year and the beginning of the second, and consider how these relate to the earlier developments and prepare for the
coming toddler period of transition to early childhood. Second, I will

discuss research that uncovers the process of development in different areas within a developmental systems framework. This research illustrates the point that it is problem-specific knowledge, not domain-specific theories, that is the basis of infant intelligence and knowledge. In everyday life, infants seek pragmatic solutions to problems in the context of social and cultural scaffolding.

Conditions of Infant Development: Being and Becoming

Being an infant means adapting to the requirements of being in a particular unfinished developmental state within a particular social/physical/cultural environment, while under conditions of rapid physical and mental growth, total dependence on others for survival and care, and relative immobility, among others. Looking, touching, and hearing are initial ways of experiencing the world, which is at first totally novel but rapidly becomes familiar over small bits of space and time. Because human physical and cultural conditions are extremely various and thus unpredictable—beyond a small set of universals, such as the existence of people and objects in space—the particulars of the environment must be discovered through experience. While being requires continuous adaptation, *becoming* a different person (a crawler, a walker, a talker) is ongoing at the same time.

Culture

The most basic universal condition of infancy is that all children live in culture; that is to say, humans are a cultural species (Donald, 1991; Klein and Edgar, 2002; Tomasello, 1999). In this sense culture itself is a biological given. Human infants do not survive outside of culture any more than they survive outside of a social group. This reality impinges on our understanding of the relation of infant knowing to later development. Infants must be open to culture, as they must take what they get, whether it be a tent in the desert, a hut in Bali, a mansion in Hollywood, or an igloo in the Arctic Circle. Infants must deal with the specificity of their worlds, both social and physical, not with the generalities of "world" and "epoch." And both the social and the physical are shaped by cultural realities.

Cultures in turn, of course, are shaped by other forces, such as in their geographical settings: a Balinese hut would not suffice in an arctic climate. They are shaped as well by their history; each generation begins anew with a new cultural surround.[1] As many have noted, the influence of culture does not begin at birth but long before, in the prenatal conditions of life in the womb, including, for example, maternal diet and health care. Cosmopolitan infants of today find themselves in a world of spaces defined as rooms, furnished variably to suit their special functions: rooms for sleeping, cooking, eating, watching TV, and so on. They grow up with telephones, computers, video screens, and much additional technology. They wear special clothes and have special objects (toys) to interact with in their special beds (cribs, or cots). Outside the home they ride in carriages or strollers and often in special seats in cars. Theirs is a cultural world of infancy that even includes special foods. Their activities are determined by parents "in cultural mode": listening to music, reading, playing, feeding, visiting other homes, going on errands, and so on.

Embodiment

The vulnerability of the very young infant, and the ongoing growth and development of the infant's biological systems, places strong constraints on how this creature may experience the postnatal environment. Unlike other primates, human infants are born in what is essentially a fetal state, that is, a state of development that most other primates complete prior to birth. Physical anthropologists have identified the intertwined constraints of upright locomotion (with the accompanying smaller pelvic girth) and the expansion of infant head size to accommodate a large brain as being jointly responsible for the increasingly altricial status of human neonates in the course of human evolution.[2] Postnatally, human infants continue to develop physiological, neural, and motor systems that in other species are well developed or at least better developed at birth. Newborn Macaque monkeys, for example, cling to their mother at birth and gain independent mobility by the end of the first week (Poti, 1989). In contrast, neonatal human infants lie helplessly on their back or stomach (depending on which posture is chosen for them by attending adults) when they are not picked up and carried by an older person. Looking and sucking are the primary means by which they interact with the environment for the first two to four months. However, hearing sounds coming from outside the womb is possible even before birth, and the human infant's hearing may be especially sensitive to certain classes of stimuli, most important, the range of the human voice.

A great deal of neural-system development takes place after birth in the context of experience, at a dramatic pace during the first two years, and the system remains plastic not only through childhood but into adulthood (Johnson, 1993, 1998). The human brain at birth is about twice the size of the chimpanzee infant's brain, and continues to grow at a fetal rate for two years, whereas the chimpanzee's brain reaches a plateau of development shortly after birth. At maturity the human brain compares with the chimpanzee brain on a ratio of about 7 to 2.5 in terms of the encephalization quotient, or EQ, which expresses the relation of brain to body weight. In the human's first year of postuterine life and throughout the second, synaptic pruning of neural connections proceeds vigorously, which is strongly indicative of the essential role of experience in the normal development of the infant brain. At two years the chimpanzee's brain has completed its development, whereas the human brain continues developing throughout the preschool years, and in some processes (for example in myelinization and the formation of new synapses) throughout the developmental period of childhood and adolescence as well. The most prolonged postnatal development of the brain in humans involves the cerebellum, hippocampus, and cerebral cortex. Ongoing development of these structures, particularly the last, according to Johnson (1998), places major limits on cognitive functioning in infancy and early childhood. The hippocampus is centrally involved in memory, and its functional immaturity during the early years may account for delayed development of specific aspects of memory (Carver and Bauer, 2001). We can expect to learn much more about these systems in the future as brain imaging in infants and young children becomes more feasible and widespread as an investigative tool.

The human newborn lacks control of motor activity. Because the first few months are mostly spent in a prone or supine position, unless propped or held in a more upright posture, the infant's view of the world is highly restricted; even parts of the self, such as a hand or foot, await further motor development before they can be held in view and examined. So also the infant's view of other people depends on those others to make themselves seen in particular perspectives. Some dimensions of experience appear to be particularly salient to the infant, such as the mother's smell, sweet tastes, and phonetic and prosodic features of speech. Over the first four months the visual system develops from a very limited focus to one that approximates that of the adult. The neonatal visual system is drawn to facial configurations as well as to salient contours, such as black and white bull's-eye targets. Recent research, however, suggests that what draws the infant's attention to faces is not a face schema per se; rather, the attraction is the result of nonspecific perceptual biases that, with experience, allow the emergence of specialized processes devoted to faces (Turati, 2004).

Social Dependence

The evolved "expected experience" of human infant environments (Greenough, Black, and Wallace, 1987) has two major components: the physical environment of spaces and objects, and the social environment of interaction and communication. The infant and young child are always in and dependent on the social world, defined by the cultural choices that particular social others have made in terms of dwellings, furnishings, foods, friends, toys, activities, and a myriad of other things. Without the provisions of social relations, infants would be (and sometimes are) severely damaged or even doomed to an early death (Spitz, 1945; Bowlby, 1982). Although the infant's experience from the beginning depends totally on the social arrangements of the cultural world, the social world and its choices also change with the child's own development, both guiding experience and leading the way, sometimes blocking particular pathways as well. For example, contemporary practices may dictate that a three-month-old infant is removed from the full-time care of the mother and placed in a group-care arrangement while the mother is employed outside the home. The roles of the father and other family members (such as grandparents) are part of this selection process over which the infant has no control. Thus the child's experience in the world is almost completely under the selective control of social others in the early years—primarily, of course, parents and other family members, but in different cultures and social arrangements a variety of people may serve in as guides and caregivers.

Adaptation to the complexity of social and cultural experience from the infant's perspective, as imagined by the primatologist and socio-biologist Sarah Hrdy, provides an uncommon but striking picture of infant development (Hrdy, 1999, p. 388), reflected in the partial quotation that heads this chapter and that continues as follows:

> In Mother Nature's great gallery of creations, human infants are both masterpieces and connoisseurs—connoisseurs of mothering . . . Infants memorize her scent and assess her glances, her warmth, her tone of voice. Above all, infants are exquisitely sensitive to signals of maternal commitment. Will she stay close or (most dreaded prospect!) disappear?
>
> If human mothers were automatically nurturing, their infants would not need to be so attuned and keenly discriminating . . . If a baby finds a rubber pacifier soothing it is because for at least fifty million years, primate infants so engaged could feel secure, because a baby sucking on a nipple is a baby likely to have a mother close at hand . . . as Darwin remarked, each touch, intonation, and expression, as well as how long it takes the mother to respond to signals of distress, contribute to an accumulating internal dossier on her "thoughts and intentions."

Hrdy emphasizes that the infant-mother bond is not inevitably a smooth or strong one; unlike other primates (and mammals in general) human mothers lack the instinctive patterns that ensure immediate bonding. She adds: "Of course human infants are born connoisseurs: over generations, those that were not so savvy were more likely to miss cues critical for survival in an already hostile world" (p. 389). Infants are equipped with behavioral systems that promote attachment. For example, their visual focus is initially limited to about seven inches, typically the distance between the nursing infant's eyes and the nurser's face, and, as already noted, the visual stimuli that neonates prefer (curves, light-dark contrasts, acute angles, and movement within a frame) are characteristics of the human face (cheeks, eyes, lips). In Hrdy's view, the kind of "innate knowledge" that infants are equipped with is designed to ensure the continuing care of the mother (not, as the contemporary cognitive approach presumes, specialized domain knowledge for the infant).

As Hrdy also emphasizes, during the period of human evolution,

natural environments underwent extreme changes in climate and related conditions that called on different survival responses from infants
as well as adults. Having a flexible repertoire of behaviors would allow
for differences, such as different attachment styles, that might be bene-
ficial in some rearing environments and not in others. Certainly, cultural practices in infant care today are highly variable. For example, in
some cultures infants adapt to being carried day and night, in others,
they learn to sleep alone and to nurse on a schedule.

As physical growth proceeds, the infant must expend energy to adapt
to different postures, to explore different parts of the body (e.g., by
bringing hands into view), and to respond to the playful activities of
others, such as being tossed into the air. In addition, infants must tune
their emotional and physiological expressions to the environment's response, for example, by ceasing to cry when picked up. This line of
responsiveness merges into reciprocal communicative exchanges, and a
newly discovered vocalizing ability may be brought into play effectively
to engage the other. How these social exchanges develop over time between mothers and their infants has been explored by a number of
researchers during the past decades (e.g., Fogel, 2001; Stern, 1985;
Tronick, Als, Adamson, Wise, and Brazelton, 1978).

There are two main messages to be drawn from Hrdy. First, infants
are prepared at birth to survive *as infants* (that is, as being). Sooner or
later they will become adults, but for the time being their main task is
to get through infancy, to grow, to tune their perceptual systems to the
world around them, to exercise their muscles, and, by all means, to see
that they are firmly and securely attached to someone, typically the
birth mother. Second, the most important of the "built-in knowledge,"
or learning patterns, of infancy are those connected with maintaining
social contacts. These are indispensable. Objects are there, but they
can wait for the day when they can be handled and used independently.

Private and Changing Experience

An important implication of the course of early development is that the
infant's experience changes from day to day, week to week, and month
to month as neural, perceptual, and motor systems mature and the infant gains a history of experiences, conserved over time, that make
some scenes familiar. A view that was familiar at one month of age

ceases to be so as vision and posture change in the succeeding months. Being a newborn or a two-month-old must be very different from being a six- or nine-month-old. But the infant has few ways of communicating this; the infant's experience remains entirely private while being totally social. The infant's experience is totally social because of the child's utter dependence on others, especially for nurturance and safety. His or her investigation of the world (through perception, emotional responses, and action) is thus continuously open to observation. These social conditions represent an extreme form of intimacy, enhanced by the human tendency toward attentive intersubjectivity, such that caregivers may expend considerable efforts to discern what the infant thinks and desires. Such intensive concern would be felt as intrusive if it were directed toward another adult.

Yet in spite of such attentiveness from the other, the infant's interior experience remains totally private, inaccessible to probing. Only through the crudest kind of emotional expressions—smiles, frowns, laughter, cries—can the infant present her view on a passing scene.[3] And that the scene is literally passing is an important aspect of the infant's experience. It is passing in the sense that the infant for several months after birth has little or no control over its content or its temporal duration. It is passing also in the sense that its temporality is always of the present, without the experiential depth of past or future.

In summary, what we can say about the infant's experience in the first few months of postuterine life is that it is wholly social but also private, of the present while undergoing constant change as embodiment changes within a more or less stable, socially composed background. These life conditions are important to the interpretation of the findings from scientific experiments. What matters most to the very young infant is mothering.[4] Of course anything encountered could be significant to what matters, and so attention should be paid. It is the latter condition, presumably, that leads the child beyond the circle of mothering.

Preparing for Change

To this point the demands of *being* an infant have been described, but surviving implies *becoming*, the necessity of preparing to take one's place as a participating person within a cultural world. Action systems and social-cultural interactions play essential roles in this process, with social-cultural guidance taking the lead. Gaining familiarity with the arrangements and activities of one's initial family environment is necessary, as it sets routines and patterns that are essential characteristics of all cultures, and makes available cultural artifacts that enable exploration and identification as similars or familiars (through mouthing, handling, dropping, and so on). These routines also provide the social interaction and protocommunication and play activities that set the stage for later participation in language.

Becoming thus includes the infant's attachment to caregivers, attention to and sensitivity to linguistic patterns, engagement in joint attention and imitation, attention to objects and their potential for engagement, and engagement in social play and games. Of course, experience in the social-cultural world is essential to all of these developments. As Hendriks-Jansen stated:

> The species-typical activity patterns of newborn infants are adapted for development rather than for ultimate use by the mature individual. The natural environment of the human infant is a cultural environment consisting of man-made artifacts and adults who interpret their own and other people's behavior in intentional terms . . . most of our species-typical activity patterns are uniquely adapted to bootstrap the infant into an intentional world. (Hendriks-Jansen, 1996, p. 203)

The important cognitive developments in *becoming* are those that essentially involve coming to take one's place in the cultural world through vital social and cultural experiences.

The psychological demands of infancy include adapting to a social environment of unpredictable characteristics, to the physiological and muscular strains and pains of physical development (consider teething), to the emotional stresses of absent mothers, strange intruders, weaning, and other crises. All these present challenges that the infant must take on. Some of the ways that the infant adapts during his or her first half year in the world will serve to support further learning, and may even be retained into adulthood. But most will be covered over with different kinds of knowing. Biological preparation for engaging with the psychological world may be absorbed into social and emotional schemes that in turn become part of other kinds of knowledge in later development.

Research on the Natural Course of Infancy

Infant Motor Activity

Esther Thelen[5] and her colleagues have carried out a program of research on motor system development based on dynamic systems theory that demonstrates convincingly how biological systems develop in different ways in the context of varying environmental conditions. Their premier demonstration was a series of experiments on infant walking behavior, from the first "instinctive" stepping of the newborn to the competent steps of the one-year-old (Thelen and Ulrich, 1991). Close analysis of the stepping movements of newborns, the disappearance of this response at about two months, and its reappearance over the last part of the first year revealed to these researchers a complex picture of the components involved in the walking pattern. Through careful experimentation they first discovered that the newborn's muscular step pattern when the baby is held erect is identical to the infant's later kicking pattern seen when the baby is lying down. That is, the initial stepping pattern does not disappear, but it is no longer sustained when in an upright posture. Further experiments with stepping on treadmills indicated that the infant's step movements (not yet employed freely) are perfectly coordinated for mature walking.

In explaining these findings Thelen and her colleagues pointed to one of the hallmarks of systems theory, that a seemingly unitary behavior is composed of many subcomponents. Stepping on the treadmill was shown to be independent of supporting weight on the feet. They concluded that "locomotor development can only be understood by recognizing the *multidimensional* nature of this behavior . . . in which the organic components *and the context* [emphasis added] are equally causal and privileged." They went on to argue "that cognitive development is equally modular,[6] heterochronic, context-dependent, and multidimensional" (Thelen and Smith, 1994, p. 17).

In related work Adolph (2000) has demonstrated the influence of motor development on perception of the environment. Adolph's studies involve the infant's estimation of the angle and depth of a surface in the course of the development of sitting, crawling, and walking. In this case, the organic development in one dimension (muscular-motor) and the activity context are jointly components of the perceptual system that enables eye coordination with locomotion. They have shown that accurate estimation by the crawling infant of a gap in support or of the descending angle of a supporting surface must be relearned when the same infant begins to walk. The infant's perceptual "knowledge" is initially tightly bound to the context of the body's posture and perspective on the surface.

A classic example of motor development in relation to depth perception comes from experiments with the "visual cliff," a table-height, flat surface construction with a drop of three feet or more visible through the transparent support surface, first designed and studied by E. Gibson and Walk (1960). When placed on the transparent surface over the deep portion of a visual cliff, infants who have not yet begun to crawl show no fear. Moreover, when they first begin to crawl, infants of six or seven months, when placed on the center of the drop-off portion, are as fearless as noncrawling infants. But after a few weeks of crawling experience, infants draw back from the edge of the visual cliff, displaying distress. Spelke and Newport (1998) explain these differing reactions from their nativist position, as follows: "Infants may show no fear when placed on a cliff because they *fail to realize* that their propensity to avoid crawling off drop-offs functions to protect them from danger" (p. 287, emphasis added). In other words, they attribute the discrepancy to a dissociation of perception from reasoning. They imply that after a few weeks infants come to *understand* that their avoidance of drop-offs protects them from danger.[7] Spelke and Newport's interpretation appears to take cliff-avoidance as instinctive knowledge, but knowledge that must be incorporated into a broader range of actions and situations and related to possible adverse consequences.

However, caution about crawling over an apparent cliff depends on depth and distance perception, and, as Adolph (2000) has shown, this perception changes with the experience of different modes of posture and mobility, sitting, crawling, and stepping. Thus, when the new crawler does not show fear when supported by the glass over the visual cliff, it is not because the perceptual system does not access the *reason* for avoiding cliffs but because the postural-perceptual system has not yet integrated depth perception at different removes from a cliff into the overall organization of that system. The two explanations may sound the same, but they are quite different: the first is all in the head, in the form of knowledge; the second is in the body, in the form of perceptual-motor-context adjustments. Further, the perceptual-motor "knowing" system is subject to change as the body changes, a very important consideration for an organism that is growing rapidly.

Social Interaction and Communication

It is now well established that a constellation of social developments that begin to emerge around nine months and continue developing over the following three to four months appear to form an intersubjective revolution in the life of the infant. To understand these revolutionary developments in the last quarter of the first year, it is necessary to take account of the long and intimate relation of infants and their caregivers over the first nine months of extrauterine life (Hobson, 1993). As suggested earlier, infants are apparently designed to first try to "make sense" of their mother and her activities, using built-in and developing perceptual capacities, learning mechanisms, and rhythmic adaptations that, at least in most cultures in which infant patterns have been observed, are met with reciprocal interaction patterns on the part of the mother. Videotaped observations have revealed the "tuning" of mother and infant that takes place in minute steps as they become more practiced at turn taking over the early months (as when the mother "sings" a phrase such as "good girl," and baby responds by cooing or gurgling). The infant's dependence on the adult's role in such exchanges becomes vividly apparent in the laboratory when the mother, following a laboratory protocol, presents a blank face (looking away with a neutral expression), which results in the infant's distress, accompanied by efforts to reengage (Tronick et al., 1978).

A number of authors have begun to emphasize an early "intersubjectivity" on the part of the infant, as displayed through reciprocal turn taking (Braten, 1998; Gergely and Watson, 1999). Although the mother clearly interprets the baby as engaging in a communication game in such contexts, it does not seem necessary to attribute a general construct of intersubjectivity to the infant. Such practices, however, do set up a familiar interactive sequence that emerges in a fuller and more meaningful form as language begins to become part of the exchange.

The development of social relationships and communicative practices are essential to the development of language. Other developments in infancy lead in this direction as well.

As is now well documented, there are many precursors to speech apparent in early infancy. Even before birth, infants are capable of hearing voices and are particularly attentive to their mother's voice; as proof, hers is recognized and distinguished from those of other women after birth (DeCasper et al., 1994). Newborns also distinguish between the language spoken by their mother and other languages (Mehler and Dupoux, 1994). By eight months, infants are tuned to the phonetic properties of their native tongue and no longer respond to phoneme distinctions that are not part of their own language. In controlled experiments they respond to phrase boundaries in ongoing speech passages (using prosodic contours) and may identify word segments, although such passages and the words within them have no content meaning for the infant (Jusczyk, 2000). Thus it is clear that infants are specifically attentive to the contours of the speech they hear, and that their perceptual-cognitive systems actively analyze the speech stream into its discernible parts. Of course, such analysis is dependent on being surrounded by social speech.

All of this is of obvious utility in preparation for later speech acquisition, although it will be many months before the child is capable of producing connected speech on her own. At around ten months the child's vocalizations turn into discernible babble, with consonant-vowel reduplicates such as *ba-ba*, *ma-ma*, and *gu-gu*. Also at about this age, the infant responds to particular words or phrases as meaningfully associated with action (e.g., *peek, give me, thank you*), objects (*doggie*), and people (*daddy*). These harbingers of language use to come provide a new depth to communication in the infant's social world and provide a new experiential domain for the child to explore. Most children, however, produce few if any words and short phrases before the second year. The entry of meaning into this developing system is of profound importance; its course is the main topic of Chapters 4 and 5.

Representing Object Knowledge

Currently the most contentious topic in infant cognition is probably that of object knowledge. Piaget took the position that infants do not have representational thought; that mental representations arise with the semiotic function, toward the end of the second year. Most British and American cognitive developmentalists have rejected this aspect of Piagetian theory, and this has been a strong motivation behind infant cognition research and theoretical development for the past fifty years. In Piaget's theory, the focus was on how the infant constructed a concept of three-dimensional, permanent, independent objects from initial evanescent visual scenes. In countering Piaget's constructivist view, experiments have been interpreted as demonstrating object knowledge of this kind in the early months of life (Baillargeon, 2004). Spelke, Baillargeon, and their colleagues and students adhere to the principle that infants represent objects in a certain way; this principle goes beyond perceptual specifications to provide the content that specifies that the object they are viewing is a three-dimensional solid and is permanent; other objects will not pass through it, and it will not disappear when they can no longer see it. Infants are believed to reason about objects on the basis of these principles.

Interpreting infants' responses in mentalistic and emotional terms applicable to adult thought and language is characteristic of this work. Experimenters interpret infants as making decisions about the meaning of visual scenes, displaying their knowledge by duration of eye gaze (Baillargeon, 2004). For example, infants are said to interpret the movements of animate and inanimate beings in terms of the "goals" of "agents," and when looking longer at one stimulus display than another, they are said to show surprise (e.g., Luo and Baillargeon, 2005). In my view, the abstract notions of agents and goals are not warranted by anything in the behavior of the infant but are representations in the experimenters' minds, and the attribution of surprise lacks evidence that its expression can be differentiated reliably from any other reaction, such as a basic orienting response. This is not to argue that the experiments in question do not reveal differences between conditions, but that the basis for the interpretation of the differences is open to question. The same is true for many other experiments said to reveal adultlike thought processes for which there is little or no evidence in the infants' conscious or unconscious response. Other observers have questioned the meaning of object knowledge in early infancy, specifically. If the studies of infant representations of objects indicate an established object concept at four months, why do children of eight or ten months of age behave as though they have no such concept and as if for them objects follow the rule, "Out of sight, out of mind"?

Thelen and Smith have analyzed a number of object-representation studies and have shown that a dynamic systems account provides a more complete interpretation within an understanding of the infant's developing activity patterns and interactions with the environment (Thelen and Smith, 1994; Smith and Thelen, 2003). A particular task that has received extensive focus is the paradigmatic test of the independence of the object from the infant's action, represented in what is now known as the A-not-B error. This error is quite regularly observed in the infant's responses at about nine months, when the child is presented with a hiding task involving a choice between two hiding places, A and B. The experimenter first presents an attractive object, then covers it with a cloth or other screen at place A, allowing the infant to uncover and retrieve it at that place on several trials. Next the experimenter hides it at place B while the infant watches; when allowed to retrieve it, the infant reaches to uncover it at A, not B. Many variations on this task have been carried out, and many theoretical hypotheses have been tested over the years, without resolving the difficulty that infants have, whether it is owing to memory, object concept, inhibition of response tendencies, or something else (see Wellman, Cross, and Bartsch, 1986).

Most recently Thelen and Smith and their colleagues have analyzed the A-not-B task in a dynamic systems framework in which the mechanics of the body as well as the spatial arrangements are considered as part of the overall system (Smith, Thelen, Titzer, and McLin, 1999). In a series of experiments, they demonstrated that failure in the standard task depended on the convergence of system conditions that, when altered, produced success. For example, one such condition involving body mechanics is the infant's height. Experimenters found that raising the infant to a different height than experienced during the hiding resulted in the infant's correctly reaching to the B hiding place. Among the many conditions discovered to affect performance on this task is the onset of self-locomotion; infants who have begun to self-locomote (by crawling or cruising) perform better than those who are more passive, and when infants are given artificial means of self-locomotion (with wheeled walkers) they soon succeed in the A-not-B task.

(See section "Locomotor Experience and Psychological Change" for a discussion of related studies.)

The classic studies of the object concept, beginning with Piaget's, assume that the problem concerns how infants conceive of objects in some abstract universal sense. The results of Smith and Thelen's work within dynamic systems theory imply a need to reconceive the theory of the object concept, not in terms of a principle of object permanence but as part of a continuously adapting, self-organizing action system. This theoretical stance, however, does not answer the question about the origin and existence of object concepts.

Concepts and Categories

The formation of categories and concepts of kinds of objects, such as those that are named at the basic level of object categorization (cats, dogs, cars, trucks)[8] has been of interest to researchers from this perspective: Do *preverbal* children have concepts that can serve as the basis for word learning and later language acquisition? Current theories of word learning that assume a mapping relation between words and the objects referred to rely on the availability of object concepts suitable for this purpose (P. Bloom, 2000). For many years, category formation in infancy was held to be doubtful at best; distinguishing within groups of things and forming categories of similar things was assumed to be an advanced cognitive ability (Piaget, 1962; Vygotsky, 1962). Forming concepts of those things categorized, or forming categories based on a conceptual criterion, goes beyond the perception of similarity to attribute a meaning, or an "essence" or "core," to the group of similar things.

It is now known that infants are able to form categories—that is—to make categorical distinctions, from a few months of age. Researchers have found that four-month-old infants can distinguish between categories of cats and dogs, for example, when pictures of items from one category are presented in a habituation paradigm followed by a member of an alternative category. If dishabituation is observed (an increase in visual fixation time) when the new category member appears, it indicates that the infant is discerning a categorical difference. As Mandler (2004) has argued, the ability to make such distinctions is based in perception, and what the research indicates is the categorizing capacity of perceptual systems. This is not a trivial outcome, but it raises the question: Do these experiments indicate that young infants (e.g., four-month-olds) have concepts of dogs and cats, concepts that they carry away with them when they leave the laboratory, or do they simply exhibit categorical processes "online" and fail to establish knowledge about what they have perceptually distinguished?[9]

Mandler (2004) argues that early categorization results do not indicate concepts but only perceptually based categories. She believes that infants are actively engaged in forming concepts of the object world through perceptual analysis, extracting image schemas as "conceptual primitives" of the kind that Lakoff (1987) proposed, such as "containment" and "path." This powerful theory provides the experiential basis for representational thought in infancy. It takes the active infant epistemologist of Piaget's conception and shows how this can lead to conceptual knowledge at a young age. However, the conceptual constructs of infancy are not the concepts (logical or not) of adults. Mandler's (2004) work has the potential to reconcile the claims of nativist thinkers about infant cognition with those of followers of a more pragmatic path.

Mandler and her colleagues have tested older infants in a more active paradigm that allows the infants access to sets of small replicas of vehicles and animals. Using a measure of sequential touching (Ricciutti, 1965; Sugarman, 1983), they have found that infants categorize not at the basic level (e.g., dogs and cats) but at a global level (animals and vehicles). They also have shown that children distinguish the behaviors, or actions, that can be attributed to the different global categories, suggesting a conceptual basis for the categorization. Mandler maintains that the studies of older infants that she and McDonough have carried out using interactive measures, including examining, or touching and handling, indicate that infants' concepts of the world, based on their experiential interactions with things, are more general than the basic-level concepts that characterize the "thing words" that they tend to acquire first (Mandler and McDonough, 1998). This claim, based on an extensive series of studies, raises the pointed question: Do children have basic-level object concepts before they learn words? If not, do they acquire basic-level categorization from the process of word learning? I defer this tempting question to the following chapters.

Social Understanding in Transition

Experience in infancy was earlier characterized as social but private, inasmuch as the infant, like nonhuman animals, is very limited in her ways of expressing her perspective on events or her understanding of them. Moreover, the differences between her own perspective and meaning and those of her caregivers are not apprehended by her. In many respects and for many dyads the reverse is true as well: no matter how well intentioned, caregivers may have little insight into or understanding of the infant's perspective on events. Observations of mother-infant chimpanzee dyads reveal a more extreme form of this situation. In an ant-fishing situation, for example, a mother chimpanzee uses a stick to fish for ants through a hole in a tree trunk, while her clinging infant watches. The mother chimp dips the stick in and then brings the prize food to her own mouth, unattentive to the infant's fixed attention on her actions. The mother appears oblivious to the infant's interest in sharing either the ant-fishing activity or the food treat. This pair has no way of communicating desires or needs other than through physical manipulations.

The situation is different for human infants. Typically, human mothers attempt to communicate with their babies from birth (although the degree to which they engage in such behaviors varies across cultures). Parents replicate and encourage their infants' cooing, smiling, and babbling, setting up protoconversations and engaging in explanatory talk about the events the infants are experiencing. Physical closeness (which is part of the chimpanzee's infancy as well as the human's) is accompanied among human dyads by a communicative imperative. Nonetheless the human infant's experience of these and other shared events remains essentially private.

This situation starts to change as the infant begins to employ the tools of imitation. As Meltzoff and Moore (1985) established, a kind of imitation can be observed from the very first moments of life outside the womb, as newborns may respond to tongue protrusion in an adult model with an effort at tongue protrusion themselves. But it is in later infancy that imitation begins to be established as a regular means of extending the repertoire. Again, research by Meltzoff and his colleagues (Meltzoff and Gopnik, 1993) provides evidence for the readiness of nine-month-old children to engage in imitation and to incorporate their imitated actions into their own repertoires. For this reason imitation has become a useful tool in the study of memory in the last part of the infant's first year and during the second (Bauer, Hertsgaard, and Dow, 1994; see Chapter 4). Imitation is considered by many theorists of the evolution of human language and cognition to be a key element in the expansion of social knowledge sharing among hominids (Arbib, 2005; Donald, 1991).

In the last quarter of the first year, further steps are taken toward the sharing of experience that are of particular significance to the transition from infancy to childhood. At about eight to nine months, infant and mother begin to share engagement with an object in an active process of *joint attention*. An indication of the process is the infant's disposition to follow the mother's gaze when it shifts to a new target. Much attention has been given to this development by theorists, on the grounds that it represents a new understanding of the intentionality of another. The experience involved differs from that of the younger infant, who attends either to the mother or to the object but not to the interaction of the three together (Hobson, 1993). Earlier, the infant appears to take for granted the mother's attention to the self, and views an object in the mother's hand as something to be regarded, perhaps reached for and mouthed, but not as an object of shared interest and engagement.

Tomasello and his colleagues (1992, 1999; Carpenter, Nagell, and Tomasello, 1998) propose that joint attention on a target between adult and infant is a critical social development necessary to the later development of language and cognition. Expanding on the construct of joint attention, Tomasello (1999) views the ensuing social developments as the beginnings of the child's understanding of intentionality, an essential basis for language. Carpenter and colleagues (1998) studied a set of indicators of related developments over the nine- to fifteen-month age range that together form a system of communication and social relatedness. These include: following the mother's gaze, following and using a point, gestures, and imitative learning, all of which group together in correlational analyses. In their longitudinal analysis, they found that joint engagement preceded the onset of following a point and gaze following (attending to the shift in mother's attention as indicated by the direction of her gaze). These later indications of attention following tended to emerge around the end of the first year. There was considerable variability among children as to the timing and progression of the five social behaviors that Carpenter, Nagell, and Tomasello studied. Although the behaviors tended to emerge in a similar order, they emerged at different times for different children. In particular, referential language tended to emerge after the onset of all of the other social behaviors, including the use of communicative gestures.

These correlated social-cognitive developments have provoked a variety of interpretations in addition to Tomasello's (1999). For example, Trevarthen (1980) sketched a progression from a primary interrelatedness of self and other early in infancy to the secondary intersubjectivity that he saw as arising at about nine months. The infant's growing sense of self in relation to the mother is the center of Stern's (1985) account of social/self development in a cognitive framework, which resonates with Bowlby's (1982) idea of the infant's internal working model of the mother. In Moore and Corkhum's (1994) model, the infant's developing attention to another's goals is attributed to cognitive mechanisms, an individualistic position tied to the infant's independent development. Carpendale and Lewis (2004) argue that social interaction must be made central to the interpretation of these developments, rather than the cognitive state of the infant. However, as Carpendale and Lewis point out, Moore's later (1999) interpretation fits what they term the epistemic triangle of mother-infant-object (see also Hobson, 1993). Each of these authors in different ways emphasizes the continuity of the self-other relationship over the months of infancy, eventuating in a more dualistic intersubjective relation at about nine months.

Carpendale and Lewis (2004) propose an account of the construction of the child's social understanding as emerging within triadic interactions consisting of communications with others within experiences of the world. This theory not only looks back to earlier social interactions, as do the others noted here, but also looks forward to the kinds of interactions that lead to the later achievements termed "theory of mind" in the current literature (see Chapters 7 and 8). Carpendale and Lewis's view is largely consistent with my own take on the significance of the social-cognitive transition that occurs over several months during the last part of the first year and into the second. This

interpretation recognizes the profound significance of the human capacity for sharing attention, but it attempts to put it into a slightly different natural developmental frame.

In this frame, the young infant, privately experiencing, expects and
indeed demands attention to the self for fulfilling her needs. The infant
habitually experiences the attention of the parent focused on herself
when the two are together in an activity. She does not imagine the parent attending to other things. However, as she gains control over her
own movements, and especially when she becomes self-mobile, she becomes aware of both her own attention directed to places other than
those affirmed by the parent, and the divided attention of the parent. In
other words, it is not joint attention that propels the infant toward the
new phase of intersubjectivity, but awareness of *divided* attention on the
part of the infant as well as on the part of the mother figure. It is the
contrast in social relations that elicits new awareness; expected attention to a target is contrasted with a shift of attention to an unexpected
target, evoking interest and possible concern. Subsequent differentiation of the states of shared attention and nonshared attention lead to
the emergence of strategies for interpreting the intentionality of the
other.

For the infant, directing attention to the shifting of the mother's
gaze from the self or from the object of joint engagement to a different
target is a new development in the interaction experience, which hith-
erto consisted of the mother's either attending or not attending to the
self and to their shared activities. The new meaning of this aspect of experience is the realization that the mother may attend to targets other
than the self, with the attendant implication that these targets compete
with the infant for the mother's attention. By following the mother's
gaze, the infant can maintain a hold on the mother's activity involvement. If both mother and infant are attending to the same target, they
remain in tune. Therefore it becomes important to the infant to track
the mother's attention, in order to understand and to anticipate new activities, including the possibility of the mother's leaving the infant's
scene. (Previously the mother's leaving might have brought forth pro-
tests of varying kinds from the child, but the leaving was not anticipated through attention to cues and signals of shifting attention.)

The infant's new interest in tracking mother's attention also draws
attention to the appearance of new people on the scene, met by the

child with anxiety as to the meaning of the person and a reference to the parent's reaction to determine whether this is a safe or threatening occurrence. This latter reaction is referred to as "social referencing," which appears in the child's repertoire at about the same time as joint attention and following mother's gaze. This interpretation suggests how the documented changes in the infant's repertoire of social behaviors during the last half of the first year may be accounted for in a developmental framework, without assuming that a cognitive maturation program is at work. Recent findings on the relation of locomotor development to psychological change in these dimensions are in general accord with this interpretation as well.

Locomotor Experience and Psychological Change

Given the interpretation outlined above, it is of singular interest that the social-cognitive behaviors emerging at the end of the first year have been found to be related to the broadened experience gained by the infant through independent locomotion. This perhaps surprising connection has been documented by Joseph Campos and his colleagues (Campos et al., 2000) in a paper aptly titled "Travel Broadens the Mind." It is important to note that from the perspective of domain-specific development, there is no reason to expect that a mode of independent locomotion would have an effect on any process except the neuromuscular system involved in it. Such approaches expect specific changes within discrete domains but do not expect relations between domains, and do not anticipate synchronous changes or sequences of unrelated domain developments (Spelke, 2003). From the experiential perspective, however, we would expect that moving on one's own would open up a variety of experiences that were previously unavailable to the infant, with perhaps major consequences for psychological development.

The focus of the Campos research program is the nature and effects of experience gained by infants subsequent to the onset of independent locomotion in the last months of the first year. On average, infants begin to crawl between seven and nine months of age; typically, this involves crawling on hands and knees, but some infants creep on the belly instead, a more effortful attempt at moving on their own. In addition, some infants today gain experience in independent locomotion prior to the usual age of crawling through the use of wheeled walkers that enable them to sit and push with the feet to move about.

Campos and colleagues have compared the development of a number of different social and cognitive skills with infants' experience in locomotion by holding age constant and examining the effect of locomotion and degree of experience on the skill in question. Campos's studies usually include infants of eight and a half months, some of whom have not yet begun voluntary locomotion, while others have been independently mobile for five to nine weeks. They have also been able to compare infants who are abnormally delayed in crawling for one reason or another with those who have normal crawling experience. They argue that locomotion "changes the intrapsychic states of the infant, the social and nonsocial world around the infant, and the interaction of the infant with that world" (Campos et al. 2000, p. 151). The specific changes investigated in this research include social and emotional development, perception of self-movement, distance perception, search for hidden objects, and spatial coding strategies.[10]

The crawling infant needs to keep track of his or her own position as well as that of the caregiver, requiring an expanded version of social signals—signals at a distance from the parent, on the part of the infant as well as the parent. In contrast to the immobile infant, the crawling infant can control her own distance from the mother, and by the same token she can engage in proximity seeking, the hallmark of attachment behavior. Such changes in infant and parent behaviors are related to experience with crawling. In addition, a notable change in emotionality takes place, particularly the onset and increase in the expression of anger on the part of infants as well as parents. Campos and colleagues (2000) have also found a relation between infants' responses to referential gestural communication—for example, pointing to a distant object—and the onset of and experience with locomotion. Thus locomotor activity, distal perception, and social cognitive development are found to be developmentally intertwined.

The interpretation of joint attention developments is consistent with these findings. Experience gained through exploration independent of the parent's immediate proximity and oversight is accompanied, as Campos emphasizes, by the infant's checking of the parent's position and attention. Such checking is understandable given that, prior to independent locomotion, infant and parent were in fairly continuous close or at least predictable (from the infant's perspective) positioning in relation to each other, and thus there was no need for checking or for distal communication. There is a reciprocal effect on the infant's part as well, a recognition that one's own attention is separate from that of the parent's attention to a target. This recognition of the separability of attention motivates the infant's focus on tracking attention and following the parental gaze to establish joint attention, the beginning of understanding intentionality. The argument here is that the early, incipient understanding of intentionality emerges from the relation of self and other together, not from one or the other direction.

In addition to the social cognitive behaviors characterized as intentionality, Campos and colleagues (2000) have found relations between self-produced locomotor experience and the onset of fear of heights, the perception of distance and of size and shape constancy, A-not-B search tasks, and spatial coding strategies. They also document socioemotional behavior changes related to independent locomotion such that "infants become more willful, more autonomous, more prone to anger and glee, more sensitive to maternal separations, more intense in their display of attachment behaviors, more likely to encounter the mother's wrath, more prone to begin social referencing, and more likely to initiate interactive games and processes" (p. 167).

The range of perceptual and cognitive skills related to independent locomotion, including the socioemotional and social-cognitive effects, more or less define the critical developments of the latter part of the first year of life. Thus these relations speak strongly against a domain-specific development program and for the developmental systems model. Normally, developing hands-and-knees crawling grants experiences to the infant that contribute to wide-ranging developments in social, communicative, emotional, perceptual, and cognitive skills that mark the transition from early to later infancy. In the months surrounding the first birthday, children are undergoing a dramatic change in their experiential transactions, extending their attention to include a configuration of participants in actions with objects that constitutes a self-determined joint engagement space rather than an experiential space that is totally dependent on the arrangements of the adult other. Responding to the cues and gestures of others and engaging in gestural communication through which meanings can be expressed and independent goals can be manipulated become part of this loosening of the prearranged scenes of early life.

A caution must be entered, lest the claims of developmental systems theories be misunderstood. The claim here is not that attention sharing and intentionality would not come about without crawling (or would come about only in connection with crawling), but that the course of development would be different. It is interesting that experience with walkers is equivalent to experience with hands-and-knees crawling in most of this work, while belly creeping, which requires more intensive attention to the motion itself, does not have the same broad relation to development in other domains. Moreover, Campos and his colleagues have studied infants in environments where crawling is delayed or discouraged; the findings suggest delays in the associated social-cognitive developments but not a total eclipse of them. Other experiences may substitute for the developmentally "expected" or typical one. Indeed, characteristic of biological and psychological development is the buffer provided by multiple pathways to a common end, as self-organization processes incorporate different embodied and social experiences into the developing state of the organism. These developments of infancy are enlarged, expanded, and elaborated in the phase that follows, becoming a toddler, when the child takes the upright human stance and strides forth, using the lingo of the community.

Reflections on Infant Development and Research

By the end of the first year, or within a few months of the second, infants have become differently organized in terms of intersubjective social cognition, social understanding, mobility, and varying cognitive skills, all aspects of development that prepare them for the next moves into mimesis and symbolization. Yet while still being infants they have begun to experience their inhabited worlds in more complex ways, with broader personal horizons, greater experiential depth (that is, more memory), and more extensive social communication. These experiences presage the next moves toward childhood.

This chapter has presented a highly selective view of the research on infant cognition, neglecting large areas related to "core knowledge," "innate theories," and "representational infant" research programs.

Certainly the massive amount of work done in the past twenty-five years on infant cognition in the first six months of postnatal life has produced important new knowledge about the capacities of young infants in terms of perceptual systems organized to detect object boundaries, small numbers of objects, typical object movement patterns, and the persistence of objects in space over short periods of time. In addition, infants have been shown to be capable of discriminating similarities between objects and images that underlie categories based on shape or other salient perceptual features.[11] These are not small achievements for major research programs investigating nonverbal organisms, but they need not change our views of the basic nature of the immature human mind. So far as we know, some or all of these capabilities are common among other primate species, most of which mature at a much more rapid rate than do human infants.[12]

The relevant issue for a theory of infant development is how behaviors—such as showing fear on the visual cliff—should be interpreted, with different interpretations framed in terms of perceptual systems (à la Gibson) or in terms of built-in concepts and reasoning. The observational facts usually don't differ among theoretical schools, but interpretations do. Similarly with linguistic competence: Infants have been found to be sensitive to speech sound patterns, both phonetic and prosodic, that are related to basic grammatical phrase structures. Does this indicate an innate language module of the kind specified by Chomsky, or does the sensitivity rest on some more general analytic capacities recruited through evolutionary processes for language analysis? Some social characteristics of infants—being attentive to caregivers and responsive with smiles and other indications of positive feelings, and engaging in protocommunication with parents, including turn-taking and patterned vocalizations—are not shared by other primates. Are they indicative of a social module (possibly a theory of mind module) or are they specific to the attachment process, as Hrdy believes, but with generalized effects on social relationships that become reorganized through developmental systems processes?

The social cognitive research cited above is based on what I have termed the natural history of infancy—that is, close observation of what infants do and how they are supported in their doing by parental activities; an approach similar to that of ethologists. Research in this framework is designed to probe, observationally and experimentally, the source of these behaviors and activities in developing perceptual, motor, neural, cognitive, and affiliative capacities. Some of the research cited has roots in ecological theory (Adolph 2000); other research comes out of psychodynamic (Stern, 1985) or ethological theories (Fogel, 2001); some is closely related to Piagetian theory blended with a version of cognitive science (Mandler, 2004); while research in memory (Bauer, 1996; Carver and Bauer, 2001) branches out to contemporary neuro-cognitive science. None of these approaches presents a comprehensive theory of infant development, although Mandler's theory promises to be a comprehensive theory of the development of object knowledge.

Beyond the nativist modularity theories (e.g., Spelke and Newport, 1998), the dynamic systems theory of Thelen and Smith (1994) comes the closest to an emerging theory of infant development that bridges motor and cognitive development. As it stands, however, the dynamic systems theory has not encompassed the scaffolding of social partners in the development process. This is a necessary part of any theory of human development; it is especially so in the first year, but the more complex developments that succeed this period are no less in need of a theoretical resolution of the social support system with the biological-psychological system. Campos's project, in its reach across social, motor, and cognitive domains and its explanations in terms of dynamic systems, demonstrates both methodologically and theoretically the promise of this approach.

However, I would caution that the application to human developmental psychological processes should not be restricted too closely to the physical, mechanical dynamics of the original source theory. A developmental systems theory must be open to many social and cultural components that are not located in the individual and that change over time. Nonetheless, what is especially well illustrated in Campos's work is the feasibility of carrying out a program of research that in its essence is experientially defined.

Conclusion

Insight into consciousness in infancy requires imagining the perspective of the infant in his or her first encounters with the world. Of greatest interest throughout the first year are the sights, sounds, touches, and movements of people. Over this period the infant's consciousness increases rapidly, from fleeting levels of awareness interspersed by long periods of sleep to sustained periods of engagement with the physical and social world. It is generally agreed that the first level of experiential awareness is that of a physical self distinguishing the boundary between self and not self (Damasio, 1999; Neisser, 1997). We cannot know what the newborn infant's experience is "like," although we can note that most of her time is spent in either nursing or sleeping. More important, it is clear that experience widens constantly over the first months of life as the regularities of existence become background to change. Encounters then become occasions for registering and organizing regularities and differences, in what the body senses and what it can do. These experiences constitute activities of "making sense," foremost of the people on whom the baby depends, additionally of the nonhuman environmental surround. Infant experiential activities can be divided into the two goals of making sense and making relationships, which sometimes alternate and sometimes work together, but in no way are they different domains of conceptual knowledge, object and social. Rather, they are different foci of attention within a unified field of events and activities from which meaning is derived and conserved.

Midway in the first year, a new level of consciousness begins to emerge, as almost all students of infant development agree. The physical boundary between self and other and self and object is now extended to a three-way relation between self, other, and object, where self and other may share attention to the same object. Thus a new consciousness of self and other comes into play, where the tracking of the other's attention (that is, attention to attention) is of interest. Tracking attention merges into tracking intentions, of both self and other. Sharing attention to objects leads to drawing the other's attention to objects through pointing and other means of gestural communication. Expressing one's own wants and needs, for example by raising arms to indicate a desire to be picked up, becomes part of the repertoire. A newly emerging ability to use imitation as a learning tool, as well as an enjoyable activity, comes into play. Tracking the sequence of routines, games, and caregiving experiences, such as a bath or a feeding, provides the basis for predicting and reacting to change, as well as for taking reciprocal roles in the activity. This capacity also indicates an expanding working memory that is capable of encompassing a sequence of actions and interactions, keeping track of where the point of action is at present and what is to come next.

All of these well-documented developments make it clear that a revolution in consciousness takes place in the last six months of the first year and the first few months of the second, instigated by the social disruption of the original togetherness of infant and adult and its reestablishment through more complex social means. As new shared experiences become available, the infant moves closer to the possibility of responding to and reproducing the sounds of language in ways consistent with the acquisition of words, an achievement transitional to the next level of development.

4

Toddling toward Childhood

> Mimesis was a new system of self-representation . . . cognitive
> features usually identified exclusively with language were
> already present in mimesis.
>
> ~ *Merlin Donald, 1991*

*P*ERHAPS THE MOST DRAMATIC transformation in the human life span is the transition from infant to child that occurs between the ages of nine months and three years. A list of just some of the changes involved suggests the ongoing drama: increasing mobility, from crawling to walking to running; learning first words and making sentences; weaning from breast or bottle to regular family meals; gaining control over excretory functions; participating in social peer groups. The most overtly obvious changes during this phase are in physical size, mobility, and dexterity; but equally dramatic is the acquisition and use of speech. As the developing system reorganizes to accommodate these changes, the balance between being and becoming appears to skew toward the becoming side. The infant and toddler must continue to maintain stability within change as during the first half year, but changes from without as well as within increasingly press toward the transition to childhood.

There is no sudden shift in either embodiment or environment that marks these changes from day to day, no obvious hurdle over which a child must climb. Neither the first nor the second birthday signifies the end of infancy, and wide individual differences in the timing of specific milestones are the rule. Some infants at one year are already well launched into word use while others remain virtually wordless until the second birthday. Some are veteran walkers at twelve months while others continue to stay close to the ground. And so on. How a particular child and family constellation manages these transitions of embodiment, socialization, and enculturation is subject to the contingencies of system organization—pulling together routines and habits in conjunction with ever-changing environmental conditions. The infant-becoming-child must have some secure base of support and internal stability to safely navigate these challenges. Social awareness is important, and so is reliance on event schemas to guide action and to anticipate the actions of others in familiar routines. These work together, in that the familiar can be anticipated by the child with reliability, while the unfamiliar is navigated with reliable social partners. Event schemas must be flexible enough, however, to allow for change over time.

It is during this period of development that specific modes of *human* activity and knowledge emerge. Because the emergence of language during this period is so compelling and presents so many interesting problems for theorists to address, it is tempting to view the toddler age primarily in terms of phases in the acquisition of language, and in previous publications that has been the major emphasis in my own work. However, the period can be most fruitfully viewed as one in which *mimetic cognition* comes to dominate children's everyday functioning (that is, being), while oral language is slowly working its way into prominence in the becoming narrative period to follow. In the process, both the making sense and the making relationships functions take on new meaning.

Meanings in the Transition to Childhood

Mimetic cognition, proposed by Donald as a specifically hominid capacity for exchanging social knowledge and establishing cultural practices, is an enhancement of the capacity for imitation, applied in social learning and intentional memory recall (Donald, 1991; Nelson, 1996; Chapter 2). The emergence of *intentional representation* is at the heart of mimetic cognition, with major consequences for human cognition and cognitive development, as well as for varying kinds of social collaboration and collective action. This critical transition to the modern human mind in phylogeny, as envisioned by Donald, is replicated in the developmental transitions of the toddler period. In the sections that follow, I argue that the representational advances in cognition in this period require a different conception of representational development than that usually assumed (one that turns out to be closer to Piaget's theory than to that of contemporary cognitive developmental theories). Backing this argument is the evidence of new representational activities in this period—in memory, gesture, play, imitation, categorization, and words, with repercussions for the self and social understanding. To provide a base for the understanding of these developments, I first review infant memory and its development.

Infant and Toddler Memory

Thirty years ago even psychologists doubted that an infant could retain a memory for more than a few seconds. This idea was challenged first by experimental studies that indicated that recognition memory for faces and other forms might last for a period of weeks (Fagan, 1984). Later the programmatic studies by Rovee-Collier and her students traced the retention and loss of memory by babies over time, under different conditions of learning the relationship between kicking a leg (that was connected by a ribbon to a mobile) and activation of the mobile (Rovee-Collier and Hayne, 1987). What is important from these studies is not only that memory in the first half year of infancy is established, but also that it decays after nonuse over relatively short periods of time. Such decay is no doubt functional for a rapidly changing organism in a world that is also changing in its physical conditions as well as its social offerings. As I have argued elsewhere (Nelson, 1993), if the basic function of memory is preparation and support for future action, single or nonrepeated experiences should be overridden by updated constructions of what is of significance to the organism. Of course, for adults many things are of lasting interest and significance, and children learn over time to hold on to memories whether or not they relate to action programs. However, infancy and toddlerhood are still governed by the basic system that discards or overwrites memories that are no longer relevant (Nelson and Fivush, 2004).

The toddler's simple games and songs, and "scripts" (event schemas) for participating in caregiving and other social routines, are evidence of the patterned organization of repeated experiences. Children learn to anticipate sequences of repeated actions in feeding, bathing, and dressing routines, among others; indeed, they become adamant that actions must occur in a specified order (Bauer and Wewerka, 1997; Lucariello, Kyratzis, and Engel, 1986). These meaning structures of everyday events form a background of basic knowledge about how the world around the infant works, much as scripts, scenes, and schemas of everyday life function for adults. They constitute an important portion of the early memory system, which is focused on the dynamics of events in preference to the static features of specific objects (Nelson, 1986).

Most researchers agree that infant memory is implicit rather than explicit, not accessible to voluntary recall. Neurological development in the infancy period (Carver and Bauer, 2001) and the dissociations found in aphasia that first led to the distinction between implicit and explicit memory both generally support this conclusion (Schacter, Wagner, and Buckner, 2000). Because implicit memory is not accessible to voluntary recall out of context, it is not available for intentional representation. However, recent studies using delayed imitation of action sequences with infants as young as nine months indicate that explicit memory may emerge in the latter part of the first year (Carver and Bauer, 2001). This timing accords with neurological evidence indicating the maturation of the hippocampus and related neural pathways that underlie the brain circuits serving memory in older individuals.

Nonetheless, such explicit memory is not long lasting in infancy, with a limit of about one month for event components presented to the infant at nine months of age. With rare exceptions, specific infant experiences are not retained into later life. It appears that any very long-term effects of early experience may result from the continued relevance of those experiences rather than from their independent retention over time. This way of viewing the infant's cognitive system in terms of meaning and its organization is consistent with the proposal in Chapter 1. At this early point in development, much of the organization of meaningful components takes place at a nonconscious, implicit level derived from experiences that are not remembered as such but only in terms of the meanings derived from them.

Mimetic Representation

The main distinction between implicit and explicit memory is that the former is not available to consciousness and is not accessible to intentional recall, whereas explicit memory may appear in consciousness and can be recalled in the absence of specific external cues. That is, it may be represented in the mind or in the world. The important assumption here is that neither perception nor implicit (nonconscious) memory is representational. The (perhaps radical) claim is that basic memory conserves meanings from prior experience but it does not represent those experiences; it does not represent anything. In this view representations are *constructed* from the contents of memory for internal or external use. Which aspects of memory are accessible to intentional representational processes is open to question. This construal is implicit in the construct of mimesis in that intentional representation articulates the contents of memory and may be used to externalize meanings and thus make them available to others, as well as to reveal the meaning in a new way to oneself. Henceforth, the term *representation* is used here exclusively to indicate potential or actual intentional representations.

In prior work I referred to the young child's event schemas, such as lunchtime, bedtime, and so on, as mental event representations, or MERS (Nelson, 1986, 1996). I now recognize that this terminology is inconsistent with the position I just articulated. The construction of an organized event schema may be carried out through unconscious cognitive processes similar to those postulated for the formation of implicit categories and concepts of objects. Some organizations of this kind may be accessible to intentional internal or external representations through action, as in play, or speech, as when a three-year-old responds to the question, "What happens when you have dinner?" with a statement such as, "You eat and then you go to bed" (Nelson, 1986). But these schemas are initially formed and may continue to exist in an unconscious, unreflective mode that nonetheless serves to guide participation in everyday events. This suggests that some implicit contents of memory may become explicit, a process described by Karmiloff-Smith (1992) as explicitation.

Another important assumption with respect to mimetic processes is that representations have communicative and cognitive functions. Representations in action—such as imitation—may serve cognitive functions, but they may also serve social functions, enabling joint activities as in play, dance, music, and so on. And they may also be used in mime to convey knowledge from one person to another. Using vocal representations takes this function one step farther, first in onomatopoeia or vocal gestures, next in words acquired through imitative processes. Imitation is in fact at the root of all of these mimetic representational processes.

Recalling memory through internal processes of representation is in effect an internal imitative and reconstructive process. Similarly, Donald emphasized practicing skills as an element of mimesis, such as perfecting a throwing motion, noting that practice is a specific human behavior (Donald, 1991). Practice requires building a model in the mind that guides one's action toward an internal goal of "goodness."

Of particular interest is the use of representation to externalize meaning for self or other, a process that results in a circle of meaning sharing. The circle begins with imitation, through which the actions of one member of the group become the internalized memory of another, later replicated through the externalization process of intentional representation. When this process is reversed, a person produces an intentional display of the external contents of one mind for the benefit of another, through action, graphics, or vocalization. These processes together may have constituted the origins of social mimetic signs, conventionalized meaning carriers. A similar basis for signs in action appears in toddlerhood in the form of gestures.

The emergence during late infancy of shared attention (Chapter 3) is essential to these developments, as well as to the development of language. The mimetic development of intentional representation and its externalizations goes beyond shared attention to establish the beginnings of *shared meanings*. I emphasize externalization here rather than simply expression; the latter term connotes making one's internal thoughts and feelings public, but I am arguing that intentional representation also has important reflective functions for the individual who makes them public. Thus "expression" does not quite serve the purpose; externalizing implies that the public form becomes available for contemplation and manipulation both by others and by the self.

From Infant to Toddler Mind Sharing

In the characterization of the infant mind in Chapter 3, the emphasis was on its private interior and social surround. Beginning with the move toward intentional representation and externalization, mental privacy is broached and social sharing of mental contents is opened up. Language is the quintessential mode of realizing the possibilities for sharing meaning, but language is not instantly available to the very young; its culturally determined symbolic forms must first be acquired.

The mimetic mode serves an intermediary function by both providing a medium of meaning sharing and simultaneously supporting the acquisition of the more complex, general, and abstract symbolic language instrument that later takes over the mind.

In any shared experience between two (or more) participants, the experience for each is double-sided, both internal and external at the same time. Experience always has an inside component derived from the transaction of the person in the environment; it also has an outside component, the active or inactive (e.g., observational) involvement in the activity. Often there is a third component, as well, that exists in the relational space between the participants. For example, in the context of the infant's bath, this space might include terrified crying (or, more happily, laughter) on the part of the child, and soothing words from the parent. These relational expressions, simultaneously external and internal to both, become part of the experience, constituting "comments" on the shared experience. They *externalize* "inside" aspects of the experience for one or more participants, with or without intention. In the bathing case, it is the affect aroused by the experience that is expressed in the infant's crying or laughing. For the very young infant these expressions are involuntary (not representational), but increasingly they come under greater voluntary control as the infant uses them intentionally to communicate and thus to bring about the sharing of the experience to a greater or lesser degree. The deliberate use of vocal and motoric signals to externalize meanings and emotions may serve as both intentional communication and as intentional self-directed representation.

Early forms of intentional externalization may be transitional between spontaneous expression and deliberate representation; these include imitation, gesture, play, and early word productions. These various modes reconstitute the memory organization of an event in different forms: play may encompass an attempt to reconstruct the whole event, whereas imitation reconstructs a focal segment of the whole, and gesture and single words break the whole into parts.

Imitation and the Acquisition of Knowledge

In the latter part of the first year, infants delight in imitating the novel actions of other persons and observing others imitating them. Meltzoff and Moore (1999) documented the use of imitation in infancy in the acquisition of new how-to knowledge, showing that infants of nine months could imitate an observed action by someone else not only immediately after the observation but also after a delay of a week or more. Bauer and her colleagues used the capacity for delayed imitation to track the development of memory for an observed action sequence over the first and second years. They focused on accuracy and extent of retained knowledge and on the length of delay, which ranged from one month for the youngest subjects (nine months of age at the start of the trial) to well over two years for the eldest, who were two years old at the first observation (Bauer, Wenner, Dropik and Wewerka, 2000). The now extensive body of research on this topic indicates that imitation is highly functional for the infant-becoming-child in the acquisition of knowledge of what people and things do and how those actions are accomplished.

The basic paradigm in delayed-imitation studies involves the presentation of a series of three- or four-step action sequences by the experimenter (usually each sequence is demonstrated more than once). Children return to the laboratory on a later occasion (weeks or months later), where they are shown the original props used in each sequence and are allowed to play with them; they are encouraged to show what they can make with them if they do not do this spontaneously. Even the youngest children tested tend to repeat some part of the action sequence after a month's delay, as evidenced by their relevant actions on the target objects compared with those of a group of naive subjects. Age differences in reproducing the temporal order of actions are considerable. The youngest children do not demonstrate a better-than-chance performance after intervals of three months or longer, whereas children who were twenty months old at the start of the experiment can reproduce the order of actions in the sequences as much as two years later.

These imitation studies have shown that in late infancy and early childhood children retain memory of observed actions that may later serve as the basis for an external reconstruction of the observed event. Of course, the memory may be partial or degraded (or may have never been complete), and its reconstruction may be muddled. However, as is also true for adults, a partial external reconstruction of something not fully understood or remembered may bring to mind pieces of a sequence that are initially missing or serve to represent the original even though it is not complete. This is an important aspect of the externalization of knowledge: one is better able to observe and reflect on an externalized representation of a remembered event than on its internal memory form, perhaps because one can manipulate it in ways that reveal its internal structure more effectively. Adults experience this effect when they are impelled to draw a diagram, take notes, or write out their new theories. Recalling and reproducing a previously observed action sequence may thus be the first step toward reflective cognition and consciousness.

In a further demonstration of the function of imitation in this period, Meltzoff (1995) showed that, at least by the middle of the second year, toddlers are not simply imitating the form of actions observed but are focused on the goals of the action as well. In a series of studies, Meltzoff allowed toddlers to watch another person attempt to accomplish a task (such as pulling an object apart) but fail to bring about the desired end. When the children were then presented with the same materials, they spontaneously tried to achieve the apparent goal result—and succeeded in doing so. However, if the original observed model that fails is not a person but a robotic machine, toddlers will not attempt to pull the object apart, presumably because they do not interpret the action as a failed attempt at a goal. This result implies that the child's meaning system for persons is distinctive from that for artifacts and that (as Meltzoff argues) it incorporates the idea of intention.[1]

Piaget (1962) emphasized that imitation played a crucial role in the emergence of representational intelligence, a role that modern theorists typically dispute as they deny the developmental sequence implied. However, as both Donald and Tomasello have argued, neither language nor culture would be possible without imitation (Donald, 1991; Tomasello, 1999). Imitation by infants and toddlers is a ubiquitous tool, a mode of adopting cultural means and ends, and of fitting in in the surrounding social world, as well as a way of mastering the affordances of artifacts. Imitation does not *cause* language or culture, but it is a necessary enabling condition. From the perspective of the experiencing and meaning-acquiring young child, it is an essential means of matching one's own understanding of things and people in the world with that of the adult, whether in the same time frame or after a delay. And it enters into all of the externalizing modes that humans use.

Gesture

Gesture is usually considered as a nonverbal communicative system, in some cases equivalent to verbal language in its symbolic quality. Indeed some theorists speculate that human language began as gesture, before speech (Arbib, 2002, 2005; Hewes, 1976). Other theorists (e.g., McNeill, 1992) emphasize that gesture is a parallel component of human verbal communication, sometimes used unconsciously to accompany the message conveyed by words (Goldin-Meadow, 1997). In some contexts, gestures are used intentionally to express meanings that the speaker cannot convey in words, implying that for hearing speakers, gesture is a different communicative system than speech. Even among deaf users of American Sign Language (ASL) the use of gesture is distinct from the use of ASL signs. The latter are products of a socially constructed symbolic system of discrete signs used with conscious intent, whereas gestures may be quite standard within a culture but are often acquired and used without conscious intent. To the extent this is the case, it verifies the continuing existence of a mode of unconscious meaning unconsciously expressed, such as that hypothesized in infancy.

The use of gestures to express pragmatic needs or wants is quite common among older infants and young toddlers. Such gestures often derive from natural action schemes, such as holding up the arms to indicate a desire to be picked up. Such a gesture externalizes simultaneously a felt need and a meaning that inheres in the movement. At the same time, it is a move toward intentional communication using conventional signs—that is, signs whose meanings are shared by two or more people, at least the signer and the interpreter. Late in the first year and into the second, infants also appear to use personal gestures to express knowledge, for example in lifting a cup to the lips in a "drinking" gesture or in stirring in a container with a spoon (Piaget called this a "recognitory gesture"). The action used in this externalization of knowledge gained from routine practice may help to cohere and stabilize a concept of the object for the child in a way similar to words (see Chapter 5). Recognitory signs thus manifest an important function of externalization, making apparent to the self in the world what is somewhat disparate or disorganized in the mind and thus enabling, through action, the organization or stabilization of knowledge that may have been previously only partially grasped.

Other uses of gesture include the sometimes repetitive pointing that one-year-olds may engage in to ensure the shared attention of the adult. Efforts at pantomime can also be observed in the toddler who attempts to reenact or direct the parent to some activity. "Baby signs" that parents teach their infants for expressing wants and needs before they learn to speak have been studied by Acredolo and her colleagues with surprising results (Goodwyn and Acredolo, 2000). Baby signs are not the symbolic system of ASL used by the deaf, nor are they spontaneously generated by infants, but they are modeled on natural iconic gestures and are reported to be fairly easily acquired by infants. Researchers have found that early baby-sign users make an easy transition to oral language and that positive associations of cognitive achievements with signing are found as late as the school years.[2] Other researchers report that, prior to about eighteen months, infants are as willing to acquire gestures as to acquire words for referring to novel objects, but that once they have embarked on the spoken-word learning game in earnest (usually midway through the second year) they are no longer interested in using gestures in this naming way (Namy and Waxman, 1998).

It may be that gesture, beginning as an intentional externalizing system, subsequently goes "underground" as an expressive communicative system, substituting for lexical items or for emerging knowledge or nonverbalized aspects of cultural messages. In some ways it resembles play in its action-knowledge form, while in others it resembles language in its communicative function. In both ways it seems to be a precursor or undifferentiated system that then becomes more defined in its own terms as the later systems—play and language—emerge as different modes fulfilling some of its functions.

Play

Many young animals play, but human children stand out in the degree to which they use toys and other objects to play out adult activities and games. Play is in fact characteristic of humans throughout life, whereas other animals (including other primates) do not engage in play in maturity, when the serious demands of adult life take over.[3] Theorists have speculated endlessly about the function of play for children as well as adults, citing practice of skills needed in adulthood, learning and problem solving, creativity and imagination, narrative practice, socialization, peer relations, and self-development (see Sutton-Smith, 1997, for a review). Many developmental psychologists (following Piaget, 1962) identify the onset of *symbolic* play as occurring in the second year, when the toddler can be observed using a toy or another object to stand in for something in an activity that is being "played out," such as feeding a doll. The role of the accompanying adult in these play-games has been less well studied, but it is speculated by some (including myself) that symbolic play of this kind is first initiated by adults and then taken up by the toddler.

Recently a number of developmentalists have questioned whether toddlers or even young three-year-olds are really engaging in symbolic play, that is, whether the activity they are playing out "stands for" something else. Indeed, the complexities of representation and symbol use confound the easy equivalence of play with symbolic functioning. There is a good deal of evidence that young children have difficulty keeping two things in mind simultaneously, as is allegedly necessary in maintaining action in pretense and in the real world simultaneously (DeLoache, 2004; Tomasello, 1999; Nelson et al., 2003; but see Leslie, 1987, for opposing views). Research by Tomasello, Striano, and Rochat (1999) found that toddlers do not readily engage in symbolic play when encouraged to use objects as stand-ins for real things unless an adult models the play. Harris and Kavanagh (1993), however, found that two-year-olds readily engage in play actions such as "spilling" pretend tea, a finding seemingly at odds with Tomasello and colleagues' claims. However, in play situations such as tea spilling, the children may be invoking familiar action scripts, and they may be following the adult's action cues as they would in real life. Admittedly, discerning when the child is entertaining two different versions of reality, one of them in pretense, is a difficult theoretical and methodological problem that has not yet been sorted out, but it has important implications for our theories of early cognitive development.

It is plausible to conclude that below the age of about three years children are not engaging in symbolic play even while deeply engaged with realistic toys. The alternative interpretation is that they are engaging with what for them is a version of the "real" thing. Let me be clear about the argument here. Children do play out "driving" cars into toy garages, and putting dolls to bed in toy cribs. But as Huttenlocher and Higgins (1978) argued, this activity does not establish that the child represents the toy car as *standing for* a real car; rather, the argument goes, he treats the toy as a *version* of the real thing. If we take this perspective on the activity, many peculiarities fall into place, including the research cited here.[4]

Another anomalous observation that speaks to the issue of symbolism is the fact that toddlers frequently behave *as though* the toy version were the real thing. Activities of this kind by toddlers younger than two years of age include situating a toy chair so that they can lower themselves into it and then struggling with their own bodily size and position and the position and size of the chair as they attempt the maneuver (unsuccessfully of course). Psychologists tend to be swift in dismissing such observations, suggesting that the child is simply using an action scheme (sitting) to represent the chair. However, this explanation does not account for the struggle that the child goes through. Fortunately, DeLoache and her students have subjected these observations to experimental test by videotaping toddlers in a playroom equipped both with normal-size toys and, in one of five different scenarios, with a larger-than-usual toy version of an object (but clearly not the real thing), such as a chair or an auto (DeLoache, 2003, 2004). The children's efforts to use the "representations" as real are dramatic, especially the effort a child makes to climb into a car that is clearly much too small to allow that possibility.[5]

In earlier work DeLoache (1990, 1991) showed that children younger than three years are not able to engage in "dual representation." This finding is based on a series of studies in which children are shown a furnished room and a small scale model of the room and its furnishings. Children are shown a small toy to be hidden in the model and a larger version of the toy that is then hidden in the same location in the full-size room. In this task children below three years of age fail to use the model as a guide for finding the toy in the full-size room. DeLoache (1991) explains that these very young children see the model as an object in its own right and cannot consider it simultaneously as a representation of the room and thus cannot use the relations among items in the model to guide them in finding a similar item in the room. This conclusion is consistent with DeLoache's later findings on the treatment of the large-scale replicas as versions of the real things rather than as representations of them. It is also consistent with the results from Tomasello and colleagues, casting doubt on the representational nature of play with objects.

Although there is no agreement at present on the interpretation of these findings, the idea that children treat all artifacts as "real" objects whether toys or not indicates that the toy version is just that: a version of the real thing, something that can be manipulated in ways that the real cannot, but not something that stands for it. Playtime may be seen by children as a separate activity from other "real" activities without requiring that they hold in mind two world models at the same time, just as bedtime may be seen as different from lunchtime.

Vygotsky (1978) came to a related conclusion with his claim that, before the age of three years, children were not able to engage in symbolic play. He reasoned that symbolic play involves invoking a different world, with cultural rules that apply in that world. Thus it involves suspending the rules of the real, present world but keeping both in mind, so that the players can move back and forth from one world to the other through verbal directions. He claimed that children younger than three years cannot engage in this kind of dual reality.

The assumption that play is used by toddlers as a mode of externalizing activity knowledge, similar to the way gesture and imitation are used, is not at risk in this nonsymbolic interpretation. In many ways these three activity types are difficult to distinguish in their early forms, and they may even be simply different perspectives on the same activities. For example, one kind of early playful activity consists of filling containers with blocks, sand, or other materials and then emptying them out, often over and over again. This is not different in kind from the use of a spoon to stir in an empty container, or from lifting the container to the mouth as though to drink, considered previously as gesture. Whether these are symbolic of the real-life object actions is less important than the recognition that they are ways of exploring the functional relations among objects and the self, relations that have been observed but whose components are not immediately accessible to the child simply through perceptual means. It is thus a way of extracting meaning from functional relations. This meaning can then be projected from the play activity to the real working activity engaged in by the adult. Thus this kind of externalizing in play may become a move toward meaning sharing.

More complex use of toy replicas of real-world objects to play out everyday activities, such as putting a teddy bear to bed, giving a doll a bath, or driving a car to a garage, may be viewed as an externalization of everyday event knowledge, organized as scripts for routines. Experiments have indicated that children of less than two years are reluctant to vary the play script from its real-world model, for example, by reversing the bath or bedtime routine in some way (Bauer and Mandler, 1990). Many early play routines appear to be externalized versions of internalized event schemas, and they are no more to be tampered with than are the actual routines themselves. Group play among toddlers also often resembles the playing out of events (Seidman, Nelson, and Gruendel, 1986). Such play imagines variations on routines not as symbolic but as semireplicative, making external what had been private. The external representation then can be further explored.

Late in the second year, children at play often appear to be sorting toys into classes, sometimes putting all the horses in one pile and all the cars in another. Sorting activities of this kind are another way of externalizing the meanings that are being organized around toddlers' experiences in the world, thus making them more available to further explicit exploration. It has been noted that some young children appear to focus more on these kinds of activities than they do on make-believe or symbolic play (Wolf and Gardner, 1979), a "style" preference that appears to be related to styles of early language (see Chapter 5). In addition, Gopnik and Meltzoff (1996) found that children who were more advanced in sorting objects in the second year (i.e., by making complete sets) were also more advanced in acquiring object words. In their studies, Mandler and McDonough found that the first conceptual categories are not "basic level"—distinguishing cats from dogs, for example—but "global"—distinguishing animates from nonanimates (Mandler and McDonough, 1998; McDonough and Mandler, 1998). Children's spontaneous sorting behaviors may also indicate awareness of the discrepancy between their own categories and those of the words being learned for object classes.

In summary, these various action modes—imitation, gesture, object and event play, category sorting—allow toddlers to represent their meanings, their knowledge of things and how they function in events in the child's world. The representations are external, "in the world" and available for reviewing. They are also available to others, adults who engage with the child and who may attempt to interpret or to share the child's meaning, Often, parents and others make available their own meanings by using the objects (or through conventional gestures), showing the child how to play with the objects. Either way, these are social steps toward shared meanings that become more precise as language enters more fully into the picture.

Words

Without a doubt the most exciting development in meaning sharing between babies and their parents usually begins toward the end of the first year as the infant becomes responsive to particular words used in familiar contexts, the beginning of language comprehension. The kinds of words that children respond to include action games, like "patta-cake"; directives, like "no" and "stop"; and phrases that reoccur in distinctive contexts, like "bye-bye." It has sometimes been argued that such understanding is little different from that of the pet dog who rushes to the door when his owner inquires "Walk?" Yet the infant, unlike the dog, quite rapidly builds a repertoire of meaningful words and phrases and typically by one year may carry out simple directives, such as "Throw me the ball." Such responses do not necessarily indicate that the infant discriminates between the individual words used, but rather that he or she is able to interpret the request in context.

Responsiveness to language may be viewed as the child's recognition of the meaning of a *parental externalization* of intent. That is, the infant interprets the parental verbalization as an expression of her internal desire state. I do not mean this literally; that is, the infant does not believe that the adult has a "mind" or an invisible place where commands and directives are stored. Rather, the infant responds in terms of the attention sharing that has been established, a level that points to meaning but does not guarantee it. Responding selectively and appropriately to verbal directives at ten to fifteen months indicates an association of some specific components (words) of parental speech with aspects of their shared activities. This responsiveness may carry over to other contexts, or it may be quite context specific. Both patterns have been observed in the word learning process.

Comprehension of words usually precedes the infant's own production of words by several months. An initial discrepancy between the infant's meaning system and the categorizations of the world that are embedded in the language as used by adults may hinder the child's attempt to use the parent's words. For example, children often begin to produce words that appear to belong to a whole context or scene, such as the use of "car" in the context of going out or watching the street through a window (Bloom, 1973; Nelson, 1973). Piaget (1962) and Vygotsky (1962) both provided numerous examples of this kind, and the earlier literature on early word learning referred to these uses as "holophrastic," to indicate that the single word was used to stand for a whole expression or sentence or situation. These uses alert listeners to the child's attention space, but observers may misinterpret the boundaries of that space, assuming that the child is focused on a particular kind of object rather than on the whole scene.

The child's early efforts to join in the use of the language heard around her have the potential to reveal differing perspectives on experience, as well as personal meanings that may be shared. From this view, the early understanding and use of words adds an exciting dimension to the externalizing processes for sharing experiences and establishing meaning. The child who points to a variety of objects, animate and inanimate (such as real dogs and stuffed toys), and delightedly declares "doggie!" is using a new-found tool for sharing her understanding of the world, externalizing her knowledge, and finding that others can respond to it, validate it, or modify it, or simply accept it as part of their shared worldview. This brings forth a new dimension of experience, one that is uniquely human.

My belief that before learning words one-year-old children are constructing concepts of objects (e.g., dog, car) around their experiences with these things, and are extending the concept to new prospective category members, often on the basis of what things do, grew out of observations of mothers and toddlers at home, taking part in a longitudinal study of word learning (Nelson, 1973). This conclusion was formulated in terms of children's *functional core concepts* that fit their experiences with events (Nelson, 1974). The proposal accounted for many discrepancies between the lexical meanings of words and the way that children over- and underextended their early words. The potential mismatch of children's early concepts and those of the language being learned is considered in more detail in Chapter 5, in relation to the process of lexical learning.[6]

Self and Social Implications of Externalizations

During the second year, gesture, imitation, and play are all emerging and developing as ways in which the infant-becoming-child begins to make evident, to self and other, the way in which she understands her inhabited world. The crucial significance of these expressions is that the same representations are accessible to both viewers, child and adult, are thus shareable in the sense that they hear or see the same production, which may be a first step toward conscious reflection on action knowledge. The action form of these representations differs from linguistic forms in that the latter are abstract symbols that have no iconic relation to the things (or internal contents) for which they stand, whereas the production of gestural and imitative representations, as well as play, is readily interpretable by both child and adult. They can focus on their meaning together. As with all experiences, background knowledge, experiential history, and so on make even the interpretation of gestural representations different for the two participants. Their externality, however, provides clues that help the parent or caregiver tune in to the child's meaning system at the same time that they help the child to formulate her meanings and make them evident to others around her. Words, in contrast, must first be established as mutually interpretable representations before they can be used communicatively as such. Because of its conventionality, a word may not incorporate the personal meaning of the gesture or play; meaning sharing is always an incomplete enterprise.

The toddler may operate more independently in the second year than in the first, but parental (or caregiver) scaffolding and responsiveness are bound up in the developing system and are central to the solving of the many problem areas that arise in emotional and motivational systems, related or not to the cognitive and communicative skills that are under development.[7] The process of development is affected by the mother's attitude and actions and, importantly, by the joint interaction between the mother and child. I attempted to capture this in sketches of cognitive-linguistic matches and mismatches, based on interaction styles (Nelson, 1973). Some mothers and their toddlers in the 1973 longitudinal study seemed perfectly in tune, others seemed to be completely off-key, singing different songs or even screeching at each other, literally or metaphorically. The point here is that different children face different problems cognitively and emotionally in moving through the developments of the toddler period, differences that result in varying patterns of achieving developmental milestones like language.

Because of these variations, there are dangers in making broad generalizations about developmental patterns across populations of children. One needs to go at least one level higher than that of mean values to discover a level of generalization of process that would explain the variations as well as the means. One higher level is the process of interaction patterns, which has been the focus of other kinds of research (e.g., Bruner, 1983; Fivush, 1994). One more level up from the child adult dyad is the cultural context of the interactions, and this level remains basically unexplored, although valuable insights have emerged from anthropological studies (Ochs and Schieffelin, 1984; Heath, 1983). Some cultures routinely provide the scaffolding that toddlers need, others maintain rigid controls, and still others keep hands off. Again, the child's experience, meaning, and developmental strategies will necessarily vary within these different contexts.

Experience, Meaning, and the Emerging Self in the Second Year

The cognitive and communicative functions of externalization in the second year include one of the toddler's most significant developments: possible representations of the self. The development of intersubjectivity toward the end of the first year entwines the self and other in a new relationship wherein the two are recognized by the infant as distinctively separable and interactive. By the middle of the second year a firmer representation of an objective self appears to emerge. The child may begin to think of herself as an actor in the ongoing drama of her world, a coequal with the other players in the family and elsewhere. The sense of objectivity is part of the meaning system; thus we can speak of the "cognitive self," a self that can be referred to as "I" or "me" or by name when the appropriate language forms are acquired. Even before this, the child responds to her name and provides responses to queries addressed to her, such as "Do you want an apple?" "Where's Amy?" and so on. As discussed in Chapter 2, Dewey and Heidegger both emphasized that the objective self becomes visible only when one can stand back from the original participatory engagement and take the stance of an observer of events and participants. Although children of less than two years of age may be able to take a partially objective view of themselves as a physical object, it seems unlikely that they are capable of distancing themselves from the participatory activity.

The achievement of an objective cognitive self has been conceptualized in terms of the test of the "mirror self" (Lewis and Brooks-Gunn, 1979; Lewis, 1997). The question posed in this test is whether the toddler recognizes her (objective) image in a mirror. Prior to the second year, infants tend to be fascinated by images in the mirror but to treat the image as that of a generic baby, not of the present self. The mirror-test paradigm is simple and highly replicable (although, like most developmental milestones of the first and second years, its achievement is highly variable from the ages of sixteen to twenty-four months). A mark (a bit of rouge) is surreptitiously placed on the child's forehead or nose prior to showing the child her image in a mirror. A child who touches the mark on her face is held to "pass" the test, while those who touch the mirror or ignore the mark do not. Passing is held to indicate that the child has attained a sense of an objective self.

As Lewis (1997) has pointed out, the onset of an objective sense of self, one that can be externalized and viewed in a mirror, has consequences in the social world. It reveals the fact that the self is observable by others; everyone can see "me" and what "I" am doing. This appears to be the impetus behind the onset of a cluster of behaviors that constitute self-consciousness: shyness with strangers, shame, inhibition, embarrassment. These behaviors are external manifestations of some new understanding of the relation of self to social others, although such understanding is still very limited. The implication, for our purposes here, is of a wider sense of shared meaning: everyone can see me (and, perhaps, know what I am thinking). It is also a sign of the new reflection that the child is capable of, reflecting on behavior as well as external representations of knowledge. This reflection is still limited, in that it refers to what is manifest in the world, not to what is in the mind. Although the mirror test may be passed early in the second year, the developments involved in the full realization of the cognitive self may be extended over months and into the third and fourth years.

I gained some perspective on this process in recording and analyzing the bedtime monologues of a child (Emily), beginning when she was twenty-one months old and continuing until she was three years old. My purpose was to uncover her perspectives on the events of her life and how they entered into her memories (Nelson, 1989c).[8] Emily was an early talker and habitually talked to herself after her parents left her in her crib at night and naptime, before she fell asleep. Her parents were crucial participants in both the recordings and interpretations of Emily's monologues and their meaning in her life. Subsequently, analyses of her monologues and pre-sleep dialogues with her parents, conducted by several colleagues and myself, revealed much more in the way of developments in language, narrative, self-understanding, and knowledge structures than originally anticipated. Relevant to the present topic, they revealed the slow development of an independent self (Nelson, 1989b).

One indication of Emily's emerging sense of an objective and subjective self came in her use of first-person forms, alternatively "I," "my," and "Emmy" in different discourse contexts (Gerhardt, 1989; Nelson, 1989c). An example of a monologue from when she was not quite two years old indicates the use of language to externalize a struggle of self-concept in contradiction to her father's characterization of her. In this sequence, Emily had begun crying whenever her father began to leave the room, and he had several times attempted to quiet her by insisting that "big girls don't cry." For example: "Big boys and girls don't cry . . . [baby brother] cries when he goes to sleep because he's a little baby, but Emily and Carl . . . Carl's a big boy and Emily's a big girl! They don't cry . . . You're such a good girl." Although she continued to cry until he left the room, she then quieted and began a monologue based on his account of what they would do the next day. Then, switching the subject, she murmured, "Big girls don't cry. I a big kid but I, I, I . . . ahh ah ahh kid . . . I big kid but I do cry [said very slowly and softly]." This externalization in language allows her to make the contradiction explicit, but the slow and difficult expression suggests her difficulty in coming to terms with it.

Further analyses of Emily and her world, as seen through her presleep monologues, indicated that her sense of self became more firmly established over the course of the year, as indicated by her more conventional use of self-reference and her representation of self in relation to other children after she started preschool (Nelson, 1997). A major form of monologue from the beginning was the recitation of what happens at different times and on different days. The later versions are impressively extensive. She also produced narratives of her past self in adventures such as buying a doll. In other reports she struggled to account for the distinctive actions of parents and children, to establish causes for actions, and to evaluate the behaviors and likes of her peers. If any proof were required of the social and cultural context of a child's life and her cognitive concerns about it, these monologues would provide it. Emily's self during her third year was, like the first two years as described here, thoroughly embedded in the social world of interactions and activities.

Variations in Self-Organization during the Transition to Childhood

At various points I have emphasized the variability of the ways in which developments are manifested and the age at which children come into a different phase in the overall scheme. This is evident particularly in the age at which children begin to use language, but it is also characteristic of the achievement of the cognitive self, as reflected in the mirror test. The age at which subjects pass this test ranges from about fourteen months to about twenty-four months. We also see this variability in the degree to which different children engage in different activities, for example in whether they are "analytic" categorizers or "wholistic" dramatists in play (Wolf and Gardner, 1979). Individual differences in the rate at which different milestones of development are achieved, and the ways in which they are constructed by the child in conjunction with the social and ecological environment, are reflections of the process of developmental systems organization. Development is not linearly progressive. Different components must be transformed and reorganized in different ways, depending on how the system is composed and organized at any given time. What has gone before constrains but does not determine what is possible as a next step.

The child's temperament, as well as parental personalities, may impinge on the disposition of a child to follow one pathway or another. Each is subject to contingencies. In addition, the numerous different developing parts of the self may compete for attention within the system. It has long been observed, and has been verified in recent studies, that early walkers tend to be late talkers and the reverse, that early talkers tend to be late walkers. In fact, each of these activities requires practice and concentration on individual skills; accomplishing one requires directing significant attention to it that may then not be available for practicing of the other. However, in the long run they are both accomplished, and the system may never be, as it were, unbalanced. Of course sometimes it is out of balance; at least a few late talkers that I have observed have appeared to be frustrated in their efforts to communicate.

I emphasize these different progressions and different rates because parents and professionals, as well as researchers, tend to use the average (mean) age of achievement of some important milestone, such as first words or first sentences, as "the" age or the "normal" age. This tendency gets in the way of understanding processes of development, as much as it interferes with understanding the development of individual children. For example, the use of different externalizing modes may be influenced by experiences in dyadic interactions or by experiences with different action patterns, such as gross motor play in contrast to play with sets of small animals. The point to keep in mind is that the developmental system, while consisting of different realms (or domains), develops as a whole, maintaining stability in the face of change, balancing rapid development in one area against relative stasis in another.

Reconsidering Representation and Meaning in Development

In this chapter I have laid out the mimetic view of the representational forms that appear in the second year, emphasizing especially what the possibilities of external representation may reveal for the child and for the meaning-sharing system that is emerging. It may serve well to review here the construction of representation and its implications that I have been working with, and to review early memory and its development from that perspective.

Representation tends to be viewed very broadly in cognitive science, which usually considers all mental contents, including perception and memory as well as spoken and written language, to be representational. Although not all developmentalists agree, current work in cognitive development also generally assumes that perception and memory are representational. Thus, for example, researchers describe what happens when an infant sees an item revealed from behind a screen that is different from the one she saw going behind it in representational terms: the infant "represented" item A and is "surprised" to see item B. But a representational description of this result is not necessary. It can be agreed that the infant remembered something about item A from having seen it that is different from what she sees in item B. The fact that perceptual memory lasts for as long as seven seconds (or however many) may be notable at a young age, but it says nothing about representational or nonrepresentational thought (even round worms have memory).[9]

Most theorists are satisfied with terms such as "procedural" and "implicit" memory that do not imply conscious formulation or explicit representation, and they also may accept (if reluctantly) the view of perception as nonrepresentational. However, if denying mental representation to infants also involves the denial of concepts and categories, evidence for the existence of such mental constructions can be brought forth against the claim. Mandler (2004) draws on this evidence to counter Piaget's (now radical) position on nonrepresentational thought in infancy, which he termed the sensorimotor period. It is also true that Piaget's position does not adequately account for how representational thought might arise from nonrepresentational thought. On these and other grounds, Mandler argues that representations in the form of concepts are part of the infant's mental armamentarium from the beginning. As I stated at the start of this chapter, I now prefer to reserve the term *representation* for intentional representations that emerge with mimetic processes. This preference brings out the questions, unanswered by Piaget, of what precedes representations and when such processes emerge.

Memory has been typically studied in psychology without regard to its content or meaning. Similarly, in developmental psychology memory is traditionally considered to be neutral with respect to content and is studied in terms of "information processing," a way of ducking the question of meaning (as suggested in Chapter 2). The perspective here is quite different; it holds that making-sense processes derive meaning from experience, relating elements of current experience to self-interest and goals and to past experience conserved in memory. These ongoing dynamic processes organize memory in terms of meaning structures. The processes do not copy anything from the "outside" into the "inside," nor do they create a model or a representation that repro-duces the so-called outside real world. Rather there is a functional but inevitably incomplete and fragmented memory of experienced events and situations (including spaces, objects, persons, actions, and other sa-lient conditions) that has *personal significance.*

The event is considered to be the basic unit of experience and thus of memory (Donald, 1991; Nelson, 1986, 1996). Over time events may be combined to form generalized, meaningful wholes that are termed schemas or scripts, concepts, and categories, and they may be broken down into parts that are then made available for further organizing into other concepts and categories (see Schank, 1982, on dynamic memory). These organizations of events again do not represent anything; their potential function is in guiding both physical and mental action and in interpreting perception. They are presumed to be potentials of hu-man neural systems; that is, they are *processes* for structuring in differ-ent ways the meaningful content of pragmatically encountered scenes. Through these processes, memory is the repository of meaning derived from experience; meaning also emerges from organization and con-struction within the memory system.

Two points here may be obvious in this interpretation of memory but may also strike readers as odd. First, everything that enters mem-ory is defined as somehow meaningful to the individual. Thus memory *is* meaning. Similarly, mental content derives from its experiential rela-tion to the individual experiencer. There is no neutral, "objective" in-formation waiting in memory until it is recognized as fitting into a con-cept or otherwise related to the knowledge structures that memory organization delivers. These propositions reflect a basic claim about the subjectivity of cognition. Later in development, shared and cultural meaning will become part of the encounter with the social and cultural world, but these must nonetheless retain subjectivity as well.[10]

In distinguishing among different views of representation, it is im-portant to distinguish between representations *as* mental constructs (e.g., perception, image schemas) and representations *of* mental con-structs (e.g., gestures). Representation, in the present view, is a *func-tional* mode of cognition, but it is not a *basic mechanism* of the cognitive system. It is a function of human intelligence that is characteristic of our most advanced capacities for rational thought. Representation here implies intention; it implies representation for some purpose. In con-trast, basic mental constructs (memory, perception) belong to the natural world of biological systems, and it is misleading to suggest that nature represents anything for any purpose. When theorists amplify mental functions by attributing representation, they suggest that a visual image or a memory stands for or is a copy of something else (something outside the mind) for someone, evoking the dreaded problem of infinite regress (see Bickhard, 2002, on this point). Intentional representation avoids this trap; it is a developmental achievement, just as it is assumed to have been an evolutionary achievement in Donald's (1991) framework.

My position on this is influenced by the hybrid mind concept developed by Donald (1991), proposing different functions that have emerged during the evolution of the human mind; the mimetic level centrally involves the capacity for intentional representation. Previously evolved levels allow cognitive processing, generalization, specific memory, and other manifestations of intelligence, but do not allow intentional representation, which is, however, required for uncued recall of memory contents, or for the external representation of memory for self or social uses. In my developmental interpretation of this mental progression, the mimetic function emerges in the course of later infancy and the toddler period and is manifested in the various uses of imitation, gesture, object play, and early word learning. My view is thus aligned with Piaget's idea about the emergence of representational thought at the end of the sensorimotor period and its manifestation in terms of imitation, play, and symbolic functions. But I do not deny—in fact, I endorse—the idea of infant concept and category formation more or less as Mandler (2004) characterizes it, although I do not ascribe representation to this level of cognition. I view these infant constructs as "implicit" in the same way that memory in this period is implicit.

To clarify my position, the following layers of mental contents and operations are assumed:

- processes of perception and action schemes, including organized schemes evolved to achieve adaptive functions;

- schemas, scripts, categories, concepts, and conceptual frames organized from experience on the basis of evolved processes designed to anticipate and organize action and interaction in the world;

- representations constructed from mental contents (memory) for specific purposes to represent a particular experience, to convey an idea to someone else, to organize a knowledge structure, to solve a problem, or to create a new conceptual or imaginative construction;

- symbolic representations constructed from symbols for communication or for mental operations, often with the aid of external forms and props.

The first two levels are involved in the basic process of making sense of the world scene encountered by the child. Memory for individual experience and the schemas, scripts, concepts, and categories that constitute aspects of semantic memory are meaningful, organized components of general memory (more will be said on this in Chapter 7). These are seen as a resource for constructions and representations but not as representing anything. They contain potential components of representations, to be called on when a representation of some experience or specific memory is required for some cognitive or communicative purpose. Such a representation might be mental, providing the basis for conscious thinking. Early in development, however, it appears as an external representation in play, in action, or in language. Indeed, its very construction is a developmental achievement. Briefly then, memory is a conservatory of meaning. What gets constructed, reconstructed, and represented externally are products of the overall meaning system, drawing on memory as its source.

That there are experience, meaning, and memory without representation, however, does not mean that there is not thought. Nonrepresentational thought is possible in the sense that memory is activated in contexts and can enter into processes of cognitive manipulation within those contexts. The term *representation* is confined to the deliberate composition of a representation of some specific part of the remembered world—an event, or a memory or idea or extended theory or story, in language or other symbolic form. These could be termed "constructed representations," but I am proposing that it is *only* these that are representations. This claim follows from the layered nature of cognition. Representations are ways that individuals have of reconstructing memory to better represent meaning for the self and for others.

The implication I am drawing (still tentatively) from the several forms of external representations considered in this chapter is that these external representations—imitation, gestures, play, words—begin to develop before intentional mental representations are formed. Indeed it is the externals, in particular the language, that make the internal representations possible.[11]

Cognitive Consciousness

The developments of externalization described in this chapter are symptomatic of the emergence of a new level of cognitive consciousness as the child moves outward from the private mind of infancy. Cognitive consciousness is the first level at which the child begins to take an objective view of the self in relation to others and the world. This level has been recognized as a significant advance by many theorists, as discussed earlier, and has been seen as the beginning of the autobiographical self by the neurologist Damasio (1999). The onset of this level of consciousness is gradual, becoming apparent over the course of the second year in externalizing activities. It is usually coincident with the learning of first words and the construction of simple sentences. Delayed imitation, sequential knowledge of familiar events and causal relations, and construction of well-organized categories of objects all speak to cognitive organization. Understanding the objective status of the self is deeply interconnected to that of others, as is revealed in the evidence of a new self-consciousness, embarrassment, and sense of shame or guilt that becomes evident at around two years of age (Kagan, 1991; Lewis, 1997).

Most of these cognitive and interpersonal developments can be seen as resulting from the new awareness that emerged at the prior level of social consciousness, compounded by new contrasts made possible through the externalizing modes of mimesis, including gesture, play, and word use. The social, communicative, cognitive, and linguistic abilities to some extent proceed along different lines, reflected in the strong individual differences in paths through the transition period, but in the end come into convergence.

We can think of the two-year-old as a mimetic child, capable of replaying in consciousness, as well as in external play with toys or substitute objects, the actions of herself and others. Thus a certain degree of reflection on states of self and other can be achieved through the imagination, either in thought or in play. As Emily's monologues demonstrate, for some children this may be possible in language as well. But this is play with what is and what can be, not with what was and what may yet be. It is not using objects in play to stand for real things, or to symbolize the self in another place or time. Moreover, there is no evidence in all of these new skills and capabilities that children at two years have a sense of self in the past. The bulk of the evidence indicates that one- and two-year-old children are not yet tuned in to the significance of the specific past or the possible future, and have no sense of themselves in past experience. While the cognitive consciousness of the toddler years is an advance over the unselfconsciousness of infancy, it is still a consciousness that is confined in space and time and retains the essential privacy of the infant mind, even while displaying some of its contents in externalized representations.

Conclusion

This chapter traces the transition processes of later infancy that gradually change over to the processes of early childhood. The interconnectedness of the developments involved, from social-communicative to cognitive-linguistic, has been emphasized, but at the same time it is important to recognize the individual paths by which different children find their way. Our theories of development must account for both the commonality and the variability. The developments of the toddler period described in this chapter bear a strong resemblance to Piaget's descriptions of the end of the sensorimotor period and the beginnings of representational thought in his book *Play, Dreams, and Imitation in Childhood* (1962). The consideration here of imitation, gesture, play, and first words brings in contemporary research findings, but the model might be seen as simply an updated version of Piaget's account. However, this coincidence does not actually reflect a return to Piaget's theory; rather, it indicates a reconsideration of the meaning of these ubiquitous activities of late infancy and toddlerhood, which also fits in with proposals of a mimetic stage in the evolution and development of human cognition and language (Donald, 1991; Nelson, 1996). Piaget focused on the semiotic function and the emergence of representational thought, specifically the idea of the permanent object. These ideas are important to theorists but not, I argue, to the child who is developing.

My interest is in exploring how the phenomenology of experience and meaning may shed light on the theoretical constructs used in our field as we seek to explain development, particularly cognitive development. Thus far we have come toward the understanding that meanings, like experience, are dynamic, loosely organized around experience, barely stable enough to be considered concepts, and not accessible enough to conscious thought to be considered representations. But we cannot do without some such terms for subconscious mental processes and organized thought, even in the earliest stages of postnatal existence. I prefer the idea of "dynamic memory" (Schank, 1982), which continuously organizes and reorganizes experiential residues in the subconscious cognitive system. Such a construct is more in line with neurocognitive research than the static ideas connoted by our usual terms, and because it is, it also allows us to focus on the immaturity of the neural system as well. This focus keeps researchers ever alert to such factors as the slowness of processing in infancy and early childhood and the limits this places on the amount of information that can be absorbed from any experience, as well as the developing status of the central nervous system, which may limit the range of what are thought to be the child's theoretical projections.

Finally, the developments traced here, with their interdependencies and interconnectedness, argue strongly against the modularity view of development and strongly for a social, pragmatic view in which children use their emerging biologically enabled skills (locomotor, categorical, verbal, imitative, gestural, playful, memorial) to advance their experience and find and share its meaning with others. This enterprise increases in intensity as language becomes a major mode of communication and cognition.

ॐ 5

Experiential Semantics
of First Words

Once a lexicon has been established the speaker hears the same
word as the listener . . . the crucial factor in escaping from
the private worlds of thought into the shared social
world of spoken language.
~ *Esther Goody, 1997*

Human beings have a need to "tune" their conceptualizations
to those of others.
~ *Ray Jackendoff, 2002*

LEARNING TO USE WORDS launches the toddler into a
social world of a different kind than she experienced previously. Using
language enables the child to "escape" the private mind of infancy and
begin to join the communities of mind that surround her. In this chapter I consider the processes involved in this move and the pros and cons
of theories that have been proposed to explain children's almost universal success in making this leap forward, as well as significant individual
and cultural variations in the pace and style of word learning in the second year. Along the way I discuss the concepts that infants bring to
words and the problem of tuning these to conventional word meanings
and symbol systems.

The infant constructs a beginning lexicon in collaboration with at
least one other user of the language, in shared activities wherein the
two may interpret each other's communicative intentions. This view of
word learning is referred to as a "social pragmatic theory" (Tomasello,
2003) or, in my terms, "the acquisition of shared meaning" (Nelson,
1985). In this context a major problem faced by a learner is deriving

117

from the uses of a word the meaning that users intend to evoke, and thus identifying clues to conventional meanings—meanings and concepts that may be novel to the young learner. Many current theories stop with the problem of intended reference, specifically what object a speaker intends to name. However, this is a very limited view of the process; from the beginning it is the child's effort at discerning meaning that determines what and how words are learned and used.

I begin this chapter with an overview of some of the "natural history" research on children acquiring first words and of the characteristics of the process that have been uncovered. Next I examine the search for theories to explain how children learn words, and the research that addresses those proposals. The social pragmatic theory includes a concept-tuning approach to meaning that addresses a wider range of related phenomena and offers solutions to more identifiable problems than do the cognition-linguistic alternatives. Finally, I look at how social symbol systems become part of the child's mental representations.

Early Word Learning in the Wild

Long before the point at which the infant responds to parents' language use in a meaningful way, parental talk frames their jointly engaged activities, highlighting the actions and attentions of the child.[1] Even in families and societies in which parents do not engage in naming things or in other kinds of direct tutoring, immersion in a language-using community contributes to the child's learning patterns, patterns that may also draw on the contributions of siblings and a broader range of family members (Heath, 1983; Ochs and Schiefflin, 1984).[2] In contemporary Euro-American families, infants typically begin the word learning process in partnership with a parent or other close caregiver, a person familiar with their individual habits, routines, likes and dislikes, and other characteristics relevant to the way that language is used. Parents usually speak in a particular register of the language—called child-directed speech (CDS)—in which prosody is exaggerated, sentences are short, and words are simple and repetitive, among other characteristics. For example, a mother may say, "Do you want some JU—ICE [high, rising tone]? JUICE?" The question is produced in a higher than normal pitch, and the key word is stretched out and given a louder emphasis. Speech of this kind typically forms a background to the infant's interactions with parents and others from birth, and even before; it is a significant part of the infant's experiential history. Infants and young children attend to CDS in preference to characteristic adult-directed speech, and the exaggerated emphases of this speech register may aid in the child's ability to parse words and phrases used in parental and sibling interactions (Fernald, 1992). This background of communication and language experience prefaces the child's entry into the complexities of actually engaging in word use, which begins sometime around the end of the first year and the beginning of the second.

Pathways to First Words

Longitudinal studies of first word learning, which began to appear in the 1970s and 1980s, tracked children's word usage through maternal diary records, tape-recorded sessions, and observations in the home: Nelson (1973), a study of eighteen one- to two-year-olds; L. Bloom (1973), her daughter's word uses; Greenfield and Smith (1976), functions of first words by two children, one Greenfield's son; Bowerman (1982), word meanings in uses by her two daughters; Benedict (1979), word comprehension in eight children; Rescorla (1980), overextensions in twelve children; Bates, Bretherton, and Snyder (1988), a study of twenty-seven children; L. Bloom (1991), context of uses by twelve children. The methods and focus of these studies differed; all but Benedict's (on comprehension) focused primarily on children's own early word production. Together they included observations of about seventy-five children during their second year, and on the whole the data showed remarkable agreement. The studies that included more than one or two children emphasized variability in both rate and style of word acquisition. Striking individual differences have been confirmed in large-scale studies based on the maternal checklists of the MacArthur Communicative Development Inventory (MCDI) (Fenson et al., 1994).

These studies indicated that children's first forays into using words or short phrases for communicating with others usually begin toward the end of the first year and during the second, with children using an average of 10 words by about fifteen months. Comprehension of words and phrases precedes production, usually by several months. Most children comprehend 100 or more words and phrases prior to acquiring a productive vocabulary of 50 words, achieved on average by about nineteen months. At the end of the second year most children know and use about 50 to several hundred words and have begun making two- and three-word combinations. Many (but not all) children experience a "vocabulary spurt" in the middle of the second year, during which new words are added at a newly rapid rate (often 1 or more a day, in contrast to the earlier rate of 1 or 2 per week).

These modal patterns conceal a broad variation in rate and type of word learning that reflects individual, family, and cultural ways of entering into the speaking world (Heath, 1983; Nelson, 1973; Bates, Bretherton, and Snyder, 1988). For example, meeting the first "milestone" of ten productive words may vary from as early as ten months (rarely) to as late as twenty-four months (also quite rare but within normal range). There is considerable variability in the content of vocabularies, as well (Fenson et al., 1994). Conventional wisdom and earlier literature on children's language emphasized that infants focused on learning the names of things. It was therefore surprising to discover that object names were not prominent among the first words learned by many of the children I studied (Nelson, 1973). Some children produced as few as ten nouns among their first fifty words, which included short phrases or social expressions (e.g., "night night," "where's it?") as well; I termed these children "expressive." At the other end of the spectrum, children I called "referential" learned as many as forty nouns among their first fifty words. Notably, none of the eighteen children I studied learned *only* object words during this early phase.[3] Different learning "styles" of this kind have been observed in numerous studies (e.g., Bates, Bretherton, and Snyder, 1988; Hampson and Nelson, 1993; Lieven, Pine, and Dresner Barnes, 1992), and they need to be accounted for among the phenomena of first word learning. However, most empirical research and most theories of word learning focus on children's learning of nouns—specifically, object names—which is assumed to be the normal route into language. This restriction is unfortunately misleading.

Overall, studies of language learning in natural environments highlight three separate problems faced by the child entering into language use: achieving comprehension, achieving production and use, and achieving conventional meanings. Each is a different problem that requires a somewhat different explanation.

Achieving Comprehension

Why does comprehension appear easy for the infant, beginning as it does many months before production? To a large extent, these are different processes. In displaying comprehension of what a parent says, the child may simply be responding to some part or the whole pattern of a phrase, such as "throw me the ball" in the context of playing with a ball. The phrases responded to often involve actions or games in routinized and highly familiar activities. In other cases they involve *identifying* specific objects in specific places, for example the names of toys or pictures in books. It is notable that, among English speakers, early comprehension and production vocabularies do not greatly overlap—comprehension is much more likely to involve actions (e.g., "sit"), routines, and games, such as "peek-a-boo," than object names (Benedict, 1979). In early comprehension infants are engaged in one side of social communication with language, but it is questionable what they learn about the *meanings* of words. They may identify certain actions or things that have certain sound patterns, but they are not necessarily building a vocabulary of word-concept relations. Experiments with young toddlers have focused on receptive learning, but there is as yet little detailed analysis of the characteristics of comprehension at this period and little or no comparison between the two kinds of learning.

Achieving Production

Variability in the rate of productive acquisition of words, as well as in word kinds, implies that beginning language use is not a simple process of single mechanisms and invariant stages; rather, it depends to a large extent on many factors in the child's past and present experience. Tomasello (1999) argues that children's capacity for interpreting communicative intentions is the critical factor that enables children to begin learning words at the end of the first year, when the ability to share attention has matured (Chapter 3). While certainly necessary, this capacity is not sufficient to explain the wide variability found among one-year-olds in building a working vocabulary. Consider, for example, that the range in age of achieving a vocabulary of fifty words is about one year (thirteen to twenty-five months) among normally developing children (Nelson, 1973).

In comparison, the age of beginning to walk varies from nine to fifteen months, about half of the age range for the beginning vocabulary. A full year of developments in other domains—physical growth, neural development, cognitive and social development, and development of self (Chapter 4)—may ensue before the slower word learner acquires the level of lexical expertise of the faster one. It might be expected that these vocabulary measures index relative degrees of brightness or dullness, but they do not; very few relations between early language rate and later intelligence measures have been found. Rather, what the variations imply is that word learning is a complex process that integrates contributions from several different systems, including those that involve parental interactions, as well as the capabilities and disposition of the child learner. The amount of parental talk that infants and young children hear is related to the early growth of children's vocabularies (Hoff and Naigles, 2002; Huttenlocher, Haight, Bryk, Seltzer, and Lyons, 1991; Tomasello, Mannle, and Kruger, 1986). A mismatch between the mother's style of interaction and the child's may also affect the child's pace in acquiring words (Nelson, 1973).

Variations in both rate and style of learning have been found to be related to the mother's style in interaction with the young language learner, measured in terms of focus on objects (referential) versus social (expressive) aspects of situated words and phrases (Hampson and Nelson, 1993). Hampson (1989) found that there was greater consistency of style between mother and child and less differentiation at twenty months than at thirteen months, supporting the idea that word learning is a collaborative process involving negotiations between parent and child. Style of learning is also related to the child's subsequent progress in acquiring both vocabulary and grammar (Bates, Bretherton, and Snyder, 1988). Few theoretical explanations of word learning have addressed the wide ranges of rate and style of learning during the second year, assuming, rather, a "modal learner"; almost all focus on object naming.

Achieving Conventional Meaning

How can the infant understand the adult's meaning in using a term? This question goes beyond the interpretation of reference that is usually the focus in word learning research. Toddlers are quite good at interpreting the reference of a speaker, relying on their ability to interpret the intention of another, even when the object referred to is out of sight (Baldwin, 1993; Tomasello, 2003). However, homing in on the same referent, as important as it may be to further communication, does not ensure that the two persons are accessing the same *concept* for the agreed-upon referent. Some children who are slow to launch into the use of words on their own may have difficulty in relating their own, private, experience-based meanings to the words that parents use.

Children's uses of words in nonstandard ways are well documented in studies of children in natural, home environments, supporting the suggestion that the child's preverbal object categories are rather different from the adult's. Some of these errors involve "overextension" to items that are not category members in the adult lexicon (Rescorla, 1980; Bowerman, 1982). An extensive literature and theoretical debate as to the basis for children's overextensions or category errors grew during the 1970s and 1980s. On one side, Eve Clark's (1973) analysis of parental diary studies found that most overextensions were based on perceptual similarity with the target item; for example, many children call all four-legged mammals "doggie" for a time. In this view, "four-legged" is considered a necessary and sufficient feature for the semantic representation of "dog" in the child's lexicon. A different view regarded overextended terms as "holophrases," words that expressed a functional meaning that would normally require a sentence—such as using the word *car* to express the idea of an expedition—or that referred to a whole scene or situation by a word for an object seen there, such as using the word *cow* to refer to a visit to a farm. Barrett (1986) showed that in some cases first words are confined to a single example in a familiar context, as when the word *duck* refers only to the toy duck in the bath, and then later are extended and perhaps overextended to a large category of objects (see Anglin, 1977). For many words this may be a common strategy used by most children at times (Nelson, 1996). In the case of either under- or overextension, the child's idea about what a word refers to diverges widely at times from the adult meaning and changes from one situation to another, as both Piaget and Vygotsky documented. Some contemporary researchers discount this evidence, even going so far as to deny that it exists ("Children do not make mapping errors," P. Bloom [2000, p. 53]), despite its extensive documentation.[4]

My proposal of a "functional core concept" (Nelson, 1974) was partly motivated by the overextension errors. It was based on the idea that children form concepts around relations and functions that they experience in their own lives, and use this "core" in extending the category to items identified on the basis of the (perceptual and functional) features of the core members. The functional core concept aligns with contemporary ideas about adult concepts as well as children's categories (Miller and Johnson-Laird, 1976; Kemler Nelson, Egan, and Holt, 2004). Many psychological theories of concepts and categories today also assume a more functional and pragmatic basis of categorization than the logical constructions that were previously attributed to them (e.g., Barsalou, 1989).

The functional core proposal also fits rather well with current research showing that young children will extend a name for an object to a different item that shares shape or other key perceptual features and will project "nonobvious" characteristics of the original onto the new item (sometimes known as the "induction problem"). For example, shown a novel stuffed toy with a rattle inside, the toddler will identify a similarly shaped stuffed toy when asked to choose another with the same name, and will shake that toy as though expecting it to have the same "function" (or the same nonobvious feature).[5] The functions that infants and young children might organize conceptual knowledge around are likely to be different from those that adults agree on, however. The young child's functional concept is based on private experience, different from the adult's and from the conventional meaning of the language established through communal use.

Moreover, function and perception are often held to compete, and a contentious literature on perception versus function continues to rage today, although with new proponents on each side. Landau, Smith, and Jones (1988) claim that shape is the basis for extending a word to new instances for both adults and children, but new evidence shows that children base concepts on events (McDonough and Mandler, 1998) and extend words on the basis of function (Kemler Nelson, 1999), and P. Bloom (1996) argues that "intended function" forms the core of adults' and children's concepts of artifacts. However, perception and function actually work together, and their dominance may change with the context of word use (Labov, 1973; Nelson, 1978).

In summary, ethological studies of children's word learning have emphasized the child's contributions to the process, including those stemming from his or her orientation to the social world and from the child's own world of shared activities and reference. Children's association of words with perceptual characteristics of objects is clear in terms of their extension of words to other like objects, but so is their preverbal conceptual understanding of objects, including especially the events and actions they participate in. Children's routines support their understanding of words used therein and their participation by using some of those words themselves. Individual differences imply different orientations to the function of words, whether for interpersonal, expressive, or referential purposes; they also imply that children vary in the degree to which expressing these functions is a goal or not. Lois Bloom (1993, 2000) emphasizes that children's motivation in using words is to express their ideas, a cognitive function, but for some children the social function of word use appears much more compelling, and other children appear unmotivated to begin word production at all during most of the second year.

The Word Learning Problem: Theoretical Proposals

How does a child identify a word and its reference? How does the child attribute meaning (sense) to the word? What conditions are necessary for word learning to occur? What conditions influence learning, for better or worse? Answers to these questions have come from several different theoretical orientations.

The Naming Game

Early in the modern "cognitive period," researchers tended to assume that the child's problem in word learning was a well-defined task of decoding language by mapping the reference of words onto things in the world. An early example of such a task description was provided by Roger Brown (1958), who is rightly considered the father of modern child language research, the initiator of the first modern studies of children's early sentence grammar (1973), and a mentor to generations of child language researchers. His contribution to the word learning process was the identification of a point-and-name routine now sometimes called the naming game:

The tutor names things in accordance with the semantic customs of his community. The player forms hypotheses by trying to name new things correctly. The tutor . . . checks the accuracy of fit between his own categories and those of the player. He improves the fit by correction . . . . We play this game as long as we continue to extend our vocabularies and that may be as long as we live. (Brown, 1958, p. 194)

There are many good things about this description, including the fact that it is a two-person game with more than one trial, in which the "tutor" helps the "player" by correcting category errors. But a weakness of the description is the assumption that naming "things" is the critical first step toward language. The naming game has since been adopted by many researchers as an experimental paradigm, but without Brown's inclusion of multiple trials. Rather, most of what has been retained today from Brown's account is the assumption that the learner follows rules of category discovery—or an induction process—by forming hypotheses and testing them against new items.

LAD and the Quine Problem

Soon after Brown proposed the naming game paradigm, Quine (a Harvard philosopher and colleague of Brown's) included a passage in his book *Word and Object* (1960) that subsequently took on a strange life of its own in the word learning literature. Quine accepted the idea that the basic first step into learning a language was to acquire the names of things, but he brought out a paradox, in the form of the indeterminacy of reference, that seemed to render the task virtually unsolvable. He presented the imagined scenario of an anthropological linguist (AL) doing fieldwork on a language with which he was previously unacquainted, taking notes while listening to a native speaker (NS). NS utters the word (sentence?) "gavagai" as a rabbit runs across the grass near where the two are seated. Is the AL justified in concluding that "gavagai" is the term for rabbit in this language? According to Quine the answer is, "By no means." The word might mean "rabbit running," the color of the rabbit, "undetached rabbit parts," or a host of other exotic possibilities.

Quine's linguist, of course, was not a *first* language learner, and thus he of necessity imported some of his prior linguistic knowledge to the situation, but even so, he could not be certain of the reference of the word offered. Whether the problem is thought to be perceptual, conceptual, or linguistic, with only a single opportunity to attach a name to a moving target the task appears unsolvable, as it requires entering this single word-referent hypothesis into a mass of other such ambiguous pairs and attempting to sort them out into a coherent system. Quine's analysis implied that a child not knowing the language would be at an equal disadvantage in attempting to rule out an infinite number of incorrect but possible referents for any given word. To astute students of child language, it also seemed to imply that, as Chomsky had argued with respect to grammar, the child must be given help through an innately specified language acquisition device (LAD).[6] To learn a word, the child would need guidance as to what words can refer to, in order to narrow down the infinite number of naming possibilities.

In general, psychologists have ignored the Quine paradox on grounds analogous to those applied to Zeno's paradox of infinity, illustrated by the unwinnable race between the fox and the tortoise. Just as, in the real world, the fox does always win the race, so the child always ends up with a vocabulary of object words. Moreover, if the child is given the opportunity to apply a term to new instances, as in Brown's naming game, and receives feedback, the difficulty might be expected to disappear or at least to diminish considerably. Thus when the game is considered to involve two persons and to allow for many trials, the child need not be lost in a sea of irrelevant hypotheses, but when the child is assumed to have concepts similar to those of adults, the game devolves into one of mapping a word onto the "right" concept.

Quine's problem took on new life, however, with the question of what constrains the child's hypotheses to enable her to determine the correct reference for a word. This line of questioning led to new research on early word learning formulated around the mapping problem, conceived as the problem of mapping words to the world and ruling out the infinite number of possible incorrect mappings (e.g., Markman, 1987). Markman's rule—words refer to whole objects—was proposed to help narrow the field to a category of things that are legitimate candidates for naming. For example, faced with a cat and hearing "see the cat," the child assumes "cat" refers to the animal, not the animal's whiskers. Later refinements specified that the child understands that the correct referent is the object that does not already have a name, or is the one the tutor is gazing at. These rules are not about just words but also the categories and meanings accessed by words that indicate the correct extension (or scope) of the word. The "taxonomic" constraint was proposed to rule out thematic categories of things that belong together, such as a dog and his bone, and to restrict the choice to "kinds" of whole objects (Markman and Hutchinson, 1984).

Following in this line is a broad experimental program supporting the idea that a set of *principles* emerge during the last part of the first year and over the second year that enable children to "break the word learning barrier and learn their first words" (Golinkoff, Hirsh-Pasek, and Hollich, 1999, p. 305). These principles begin with reference to objects and move on to categories and conventional naming practices. The typical experiment in this and other research presents a child with a novel word in association with a novel object, then tests its extension to other objects from the same category or a different one. The question is whether the child is able to "fast map" the word onto the category that the object represents. "Fast mapping"—picking up cues for word-referent mappings from a single exposure—is assumed to be responsible for the acceleration in children's word learning late in the second year and into the preschool years (the latter being a period in which children apparently acquire seven or more words per day). A late addition to the principles set in this "emergentist coalition theory" is the use of social cues that emerges at about two years of age. Of course from a social pragmatic perspective, one must account for the social component of the word learning system from the beginning, as the next line of research assumes.

The LASS Alternative

Bruner (1983) adapted a form of Brown's naming game, placing more emphasis on the contribution of the tutor, in this case the mother, in making words accessible to the child. In an extensive analysis of the longitudinal observation of one mother and infant engaged in looking at pictures in books, Bruner distinguished several different "rounds" of the naming game, with the mother first pointing and naming a pictured item, then asking the child to point to the named item (comprehension), then pointing and urging him to name the item ("What is that?

Can you say *X?*"), and finally expecting the child to point and name the items on the page, while the mother supplies encouragement and approval. These rounds could extend over many months, and, as Bruner emphasized, they depended as much on the mother's role as on the child's learning of his own role. Bruner used this and other examples in which a mother consistently "upped the ante" as the child acquired the rudiments of word using skills, to exemplify the process he termed LASS (for language acquisition support system). This designation was a deliberate counter to the LAD proposed by Chomsky (1965).

Bruner was not concerned with Quine's paradox. He assumed that parents and children were "in tune" and that mothers possessed insight into the capabilities of their children, which expanded over time as more of the skills of identifying and naming things were mastered. In this paradigm mothers "scaffolded" their children's progress in the way that Vygotsky (1978) described for cultural learning in the "zone of proximal development." Thus Bruner brought the child language-learning problem into the realm of modern social and cultural learning theories, providing the basis for further research on child language to compete with the linguistic-cognitive views of "principles" and "constraints" (e.g., Tomasello, 1992, 1999; Snow, 1986, 1999).

Recently, the contribution of the social partner to the word learning game has been supplemented by recognition of the role of the child in interpreting the intention of the adult. In countering the need for "built-in" rules or derived principles, Baldwin (1991) and Tomasello (1999) have provided experimental evidence that children are able to interpret the parent's intent, even when the object is not in sight and the adult is not gazing at it. For example, a researcher pretends to look for a "dax" among a set of toys but does not find it; later she sees a new object among a group of toys and exclaims, "There it is!" Two-year-old children are able to choose the correct object when asked to find the "dax," although it was never named as such. This line of research rests on the child's ability to interpret the intentionality of the speaker—to answer why is she saying that, as well as what is she referring to?

A "Nothing Special" Proposal

How Children Learn the Meaning of Words, Paul Bloom's (2000) book, aims to give a definitive answer to how children learn words. Bloom provides an extensive review of the literature in support of his theoretical claims, which rest on the premise that nothing special is needed for learning words—that is, nothing linguistic or innate. What is needed, in his view, are two general cognitive and social capacities. The child needs at least a primitive state of theory of mind, adequate to interpret the intentions of another, and the child needs some cognitive abilities, such as are required in interacting with the environment (e.g., induction). Bloom rejects the proposals of the principle theorists, arguing that no principles restricted only to word learning are needed. However, Bloom also denies that social support or input is necessary or even effective. In this regard he states (p. 84): "Adults' attempts to teach children words might help speed up the word learning process. But they are not necessary for word learning and, even when they are present, do not substitute for the child's own ability to infer the referential intentions of others." (It seems strange to recognize the infant's cognitive contribution but not the adult's, putting all of the burden of learning on the child.) Bloom's is a "bare-bones" proposal that may appeal to many across a broad range of theory sympathizers. In my view, however, this is an inadequate integration, for reasons that follow.

Left Out and Unaccounted For

Theories focused on the child's cognitive formulation of rules or principles for decoding references, including the "emergentist coalition model" (Golinkoff et al., 2000; Hirsh-Pasek, Golinkoff, and Hollich, 2000) as well as P. Bloom's (2000), are fatally flawed for the simple reason that they focus almost entirely on the problem of learning object names. This restriction fits the assumption that the child's problem is a simple mapping task, to be solved by finding the correct referent of a word in use. The other end of the mapping is the concept or category (or other mental representation, such as a perceptual feature) that represents the word in the child's mind and enables her to extend the word to new instances that belong to the category or share the feature (and so on)—to make an induction about the scope of the word. The single focus on object names allows this model to work, but it does not work successfully for other kinds of words, as many researchers have pointed out in the case of verbs or adjectives (Merriman and Tomasello, 1995).

Acceptance of the experimental "fast mapping" paradigm as a model of learning in natural contexts is one of the blinders that prevents researchers from moving beyond object terms. A major deficiency of that paradigm is that it cannot account for the social conditions of language and its use. Notably, it is people who refer, not words, and they may refer to an infinite number of things in any given context, real and imaginary, whole and in parts, as well as nonthings such as actions, events, properties, attitudes, ideas, and emotions. A child who operated on the assumption that words are names of visible, whole objects, and only objects, would be stuck at the very outset in attempting to interpret such messages as, "Are you done? Do you want to get down?" at the end of a meal. (Perhaps this is what Hollich, Hirsh-Pasek, and Golinkoff [2000] mean when they speak of "breaking the barrier" to language learning.) That children do not operate on this principle is evident from analysis of the varied composition of early vocabularies. Nonetheless, many researchers (unlike the children they aim to describe) believe that early word learning is mainly about object names, and that solving this problem will enable them (researchers and children alike) to go on later to solve the more complex problems posed by the whole range of word types. This strategy is doomed to failure, because it does not conform to the data: many different types of words are learned and used from the beginning.

Before we consider a more complex social-communicative proposal that aims to account for the learning of all kinds of words at all stages of development, the question of what is being learned needs to be probed further. Two sides of the problem need to be addressed. First, do object names account for most of the words learned early in development? And second, what accounts for successful learning and use of nonobject words?

Objects, Nouns, and Other Words

Words for objects may be referred to as object names, but many times researchers use the general term *noun* in the same context. Although not all nouns are object names, it is true that across languages and cultures, terms for objects are almost always nouns, and because it is assumed that most nouns that children learn are object names, the use of noun in this more restricted sense appears acceptable. A deeper analysis, however, reveals the fallibility of this exchange.

Many researchers claim or have concluded that nouns are dominant in early word learning, reflecting a universal bias that enables the child to "bootstrap" into other kinds of words and more complex language (Caselli et al., 1995; Gentner, 1982; Pinker, 1984). The argument from generative grammar is that the child's problem is to identify noun and verb classes in order to identify sentence structures in the language; having an easy identifier for nouns (object names) would help to solve this problem. However, in addition to the individual differences indicating that many children do not learn mostly nouns, cross-linguistic studies have reported significant variation in the proportions of nouns and verbs learned in early vocabularies, in comparison to those of English learners. For example, Mandarin Chinese (Tardif, 1996) and Korean (Gopnik and Choi, 1990) learners acquire a larger proportion of verbs than nouns (Tardif 2006). Nonetheless, all children in all languages learn some nouns as well as other words. Thus if knowing nouns is essential to learning the structure of grammar, no children, whether learning English or Chinese, whether expressive or referential, are at risk. There is a risk for researchers, however, in relying on an assumed noun bias in early lexicons.

Consider some of the complexities that surface when the data are analyzed with a focus on variability. For example, a large number of very common words in toddlers' receptive and productive vocabularies have dual uses as either nouns or verbs (Nelson, 1995a). Some of these in their noun forms are objects (e.g., dress [noun], dress [verb]), while most are nonobjects either denoting the exact same action in both forms (drink, hug, kiss), or related (walk, a walk) or unrelated referents (park, a park) (Nelson, 1995a). Toddlers use them alternately in both roles. This raises the question of whether children have separate "entries" for the two forms in different parts of their lexicon, or whether the overlap is noted by children at all; perhaps they simply attach the word to whatever cognitive construction is associated with the object or action in context.

To evaluate the dimensions and consequences of reliance on the noun bias, we (Nelson, Hampson, and Kessler Shaw, 1993) analyzed the vocabularies of forty-three toddlers whose mothers filled out a vocabulary checklist (Bates, Bretherton, Shore, and Snyder, 1984) when their children were twenty months old. At that age the cumulative number of words in the children's vocabularies ranged from 13 to 579.

What is of particular interest in this analysis is not the ratio of nouns to verbs, which like most analyses reveals a "noun bias"; of the words learned, on average 70 percent were nouns and 15 percent verbs.[7] Rather, of interest is the variety of semantic kinds of nouns appearing in early vocabularies. First, object names learned constituted only 38 percent of all words learned and just over half (53 percent) of all nouns. These were separated out, together with proper names and substance terms (mass nouns). The remainder—common count nouns that are not object names—made up 31 percent of the nouns learned and 22 percent of the total number of words. On average for each child there were 35 of these among 200 nouns learned, compared with 31 verbs and 38 other types, neither nouns nor verbs. Together these three nonobject word categories accounted for half of the total words learned, on average. These analyses indicated that the assumption on the part of word learning theorists that names of objects dominate early vocabularies is false, and thus any description, explanation, or theory of word learning by toddlers that is confined to object-name learning is incomplete at best and at least inadequate.

Table 5.1 shows the varying nonobject kinds of words in the count noun category, with examples of words of these types that children learned during the first word learning period, prior to acquiring grammar. Each of the words in this table comes from the child's everyday life experience. With few exceptions, the *meanings* of these words cannot be learned in a simple word-to-world mapping format as exemplified in the naming game. How, then, do children acquire their meanings? This is the crux of the matter.

Concepts, Categories, and Word Meanings

The mapping metaphor assumes that reference identifies meaning. The child identifies what object the speaker is naming and thus learns the word's meaning and can use it himself (Brown, 1958; Markman, 1987). In exploring the critical distinction between reference and sense, Gottlob Frege (1892) emphasized that what a word is used to refer to may not be adequate for identifying its meaning. The apparent assumption in most word learning research is that infants come to language with a supply of categories and concepts of objects, organized in accordance with innately specified conceptual structures. In this way

Table 5.1 Nonobject noun types and examples learned and used by children (N = 45) at twenty-month assessment

Semantic type	Examples	No. of children in sample using the type
Place	Park, kitchen	24
Action	Kiss, drink	14
Generic	Toys, animals	14
Event, activity	Party, lunch	12
Social roles	Doctor, brother	10
Nature	Rain, wind	9
Time	Day, morning	6
Part	Button, wheel	3
Material	Wood, play dough	1

Source: Nelson, Hampson, and Kessler Shaw, 1993.

Note: Nonobject nouns used by half or more of the sample at twenty months: bath, home, kiss, money, outside, park, toy, walk.

words may be mapped to objects, which unproblematically map to internal concepts. The implicit assumption here (rampant in linguistics, psychology, and philosophy) is that all people have the same "built-in" concepts about the things in the world, based on the same built-in perceptual and cognitive processing systems. It is therefore assumed that the child's concept matches (is the same in critical ways as) the adult's.

The majority of researchers of word learning apparently assume that the infant has available "basic-level" object categories to fit the object names typically used by parents. That this basic level is the one most salient to infants prior to their learning language is under challenge, most directly by Mandler and McDonough (1998), who have shown that infants and toddlers naturally categorize objects at a global level (e.g., animals) and ignore the categorical distinctions at the basic level (dogs and tigers; see Chapter 3). McDonough (2002) found that word-learning toddlers show a similar disposition, extending category labels to other members of a taxonomy such as animal (for example, using "cat" for raccoon as well as for cat) in both production and comprehension tests. These findings corroborate the studies of overextension cited earlier (Bowerman, 1982; Rescorla, 1980) and present a challenge to theories of word learning that rely on the ease of mapping object names onto basic-level object categories.

The issue of *universal* conceptual meaning arises because it is assumed that lexical items (words) specify meanings in the lexical component of a language. As Jackendoff (2002) points out, Chomsky's (1965) theory located language (phonology, syntax, semantics) in the brain, as part of psychology. Thus if meanings are "in the head" and meanings are part of a semantic system that is at least universal across a given language, then individuals must all possess the "right" meanings, whatever these are. This has become accepted dogma in the sense that words may be used to name or express concepts but not to form concepts (P. Bloom, 2000). Most problematic is the implicit assumption that children come to language with concepts that fit the meanings of language and are waiting to be given words so that they may be expressed. Bloom endorses this assumption in his book, with claims that children do not make mapping errors and that children must have concepts prior to learning the words for those concepts (P. Bloom, 2000). This assumption is endorsed by many other theorists as well, or is simply accepted implicitly. The question of meaning is rarely if ever addressed in the spirit of asking how children attain meaning; rather, researchers tend to ask how children learn the words for the meanings that they have.

What Do Words Mean?

Words are different from earlier forms of communication between the infant and those around her because they are part of a system of symbolic communication that rests on conventionalized form-meaning pairings that are reciprocally understood. Both speaker and listener, and indeed all speaker/listeners of the language, must use the word in a way that means roughly the same thing to each, even though their individual conceptual contents may differ (Jackendoff, 2002). Having the "same meaning" may be loosely interpreted and does not indicate no difference. I prefer "shared meaning," which indicates that each speaker/listener expects the other to interpret the words in the message in the way intended, however distinctive their extended personal meanings of the individual words may be. How the child's meaning system becomes coordinated with the meaning system of the language being learned, and how that affects both experience and meaning for the child—aspects that were previously individual and private—are major issues from this perspective.

Of course, children's meanings must relate to the words used, and in the end they must relate to conventional uses and meanings of words shared by all users of the language. The conventional relation traditionally assumed between the word, the referent (e.g., an object), and the concept or meaning is depicted in a semiotic triangle (Figure 5.1A). In this triangle the line from the word to the object reflects reference, that from the word to the concept reflects the relation termed sense. The concept may be interpreted in terms of the semantics of the language, but the concept must belong to the individual users, both speaker and listener, if language is to do the job of communicating. In an experiential meaning framework, however, we cannot make the assumption that the concept associated with a referent is the same for all speakers; this is especially true with regard to the toddler's concepts, because the toddler's experience differs radically from the adult's. Figure 5.1B illustrates the situation: there are two intersecting triangles sharing the same referent and word, but with different concepts. Dotted lines indicate that the problem is to coordinate the child's and adult's concepts so that the child may use the word for the same referents as the adult does. But this difference between adult and child is only one of degree in comparison to the difference between adult speakers.

The conceptual theory of lexical meaning presented by Jackendoff (2002) recognizes some of these issues, albeit from the perspective of generative linguistics and the adult speaker. He begins with the point that the accepted assumption in linguistics today is that language structure, including meaning, is part of mental structure. This is in contrast to the claim that language is an ideal object outside of people's brains, a communal product, like Saussure's (1915) proposal of *langue* in contrast to *parole*, language in use. But, Jackendoff notes, concepts of the same thing may differ from person to person, which poses the problem: "If conceptualization is essentially personal, how can we communicate?" He then proposes the solution: "Human beings have a need to 'tune' their conceptualizations to those of others—to have a common understanding of the world . . . adapting oneself to the community's conceptualization" (p. 330).

Thus, importantly, Jackendoff accepts the reality of the variation in conceptual content and structure among people who speak the same language. If concepts constitute meanings of words, to communicate people must "tune" their concepts to the community conceptualiza-

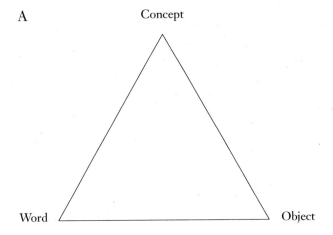

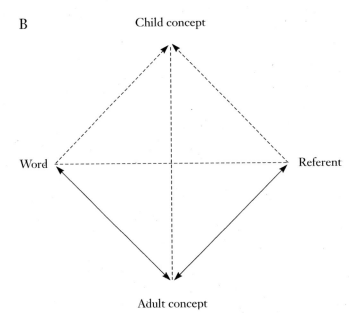

Figure 5.1 A. Semiotic triangle indicating the abstract relation of word, object, and concept, or meaning (Ogden and Richards, 1949). *B.* The conjunction of two semiotic triangles represented in the mother-child word learning situation, where the word and object relation is apparent to the mother but must be established by the child. In addition, the child's concept of the object differs from that of the mother and the two must be coordinated through use, indicated by the dotted lines.

tion. To interpret the meaning of a word, they must use the community consensus. However, this does not mean that all excess sense meaning is sanded away by communal use; some may remain as idiosyncratic edging around the central core. This view merges nicely into the philosopher Wittgenstein's (1953) doctrine of meaning from use and is also coherent with a Whorfian perspective on the effect of language on thought (Whorf, 1956; see Chapter 6). The construction theory of grammar and language acquisition provides detailed backing for this approach (Tomasello, 2003). These proposals have important implications for the child's pragmatic progress in word learning.

To summarize: to learn a word's meaning the child must have or must *construct* a concept or category that the word accesses as its meaning. Mapping theories assume that this process is accomplished by mapping from word to world under principles of reference such as the whole object and taxonomic constraints. The unexamined assumption of the mapping theories is that the child's presymbolic concepts or categories are the same as the adult's. The problems with this assumption are clear in the word-learning and concept forming processes discussed.

Progress in Shared Meaning: Experiential Semantics

How *do* children solve the problem of learning words? The child, situated in a specific social-cultural, interactive, experiential niche, becomes more aware of his or her own meanings, as well as those of others, through various means of externalizing and sharing experience (Chapters 3 and 4). From this perspective, word learning may be reconceptualized as a process that begins with joint engagement that externalizes the intentions of the adult partner (e.g., mother) through verbal expressions, eventuating in communicative comprehension. The process broadens as the child begins using some of the same sounds to externalize some parts of *her* meanings that fit similar "slots" in these joint engagements. The next moves involve tuning the meanings of these word and phrase sounds as they are shared in different contexts and, finally, sharing words and meanings with a wider world of language users. The first part of this sequence is illustrated in the comprehension and early production of words. The last part of the process, sharing meanings of words, assumes the likely misfit between the child's perspective, the uses of language, and the meanings of words as they are used by practiced speakers.

Children's Private Meanings

Private meanings do not assure understanding of public language uses (Wittgenstein, 1953). But private meanings are surely useful in solving the public meaning problems. We can assume that infants begin with private meanings within a dynamic memory system that varies from that of the adult system in a number of ways. The meaning structure of late infancy provides the basis for knowing about and understanding everyday life, always from the distinctive perspective of the small, young, naive child. The infant's ongoing organization of routines, scripts, and scenarios, as well as conceptions of mother and mothering, of family members and others, her familiarity with things experienced and ways of experiencing, and so on, are formed within this private, dynamic system. Much of the infant's experience may be inconstant over time, so that the content of her meaning structure is likely to come and go as everyday life reveals new things and events, new aspects and perspectives.

The infant's meaning structure is thus not like a static store of hierarchically organized concepts (such as Fodor's 1975 "language of thought" or as assumed in current cognitive theories), nor is it likely to correspond to the adult's conception of things, or to the conventional meanings of words in the lexicon of the community language. The meaning structures of infancy do not appear to be like the adult categories assumed in cognitive theory, whether these are defined in terms of features, networks, or theories. Infants' concepts and categories are based on individual experience and meaning and are more general, looser, less stable, and more fluid than adults'. Evidence for "looseness" and fluidity of the child's meaning structure as it is brought to bear on word learning comes from the large literature on toddlers' overextending of their known words to items deemed "inappropriate" by adult standards (see Mandler, 2004, for additional research and argument). The claim that children do not have the "right" concepts available with which to acquire their language is of course at odds with the assumptions of contemporary word learning theorists and appears to be a handicap, but as we will see, in fact the problem dissolves through the pragmatic interaction that provides *continuity of process*, from infant meaning structures to word meanings and adult concepts.

Toward the end of the first year, the infant and parent come together in focusing their attention on an object, forming a triadic relationship; in the second year the triad expands to a quadrangle with the addition of a word that demands attention (Werner and Kaplan, 1963). The triadic relation here is that described in Chapter 3 between mother, child, and object. When the word is added to the triangular relation of shared attention, a quadrilateral or double triangle, similar to that in Figure 5.1B, is formed. Again, the problem is to coordinate the perspectives of mother and child, including the word as well as the meaning already established for the object, which will combine with the word as symbol. At first, from the infant's triadic social-consciousness perspective, the scene no doubt appears complete without the word; the word "belongs" to the parent-speaker, but it also "belongs" to the scene, object, action, relation, or property. For the child, the word has no meaning of its own in the way that the toy or other part of the scene does.

When the mother uses the word to draw attention to some interesting sight ("Look! A bird!") or to direct the child's action ("Get the teddy") the word may become associated with an established (preword) meaning for the child. But for the child the word may still "belong" to the mother in her relation to these things. Not until the child is able to see that she can accomplish similar acts (e.g., directing attention) through the use of such words will independent word production seem rewarding and useful. Children's arrival at this point apparently varies widely, as the varying age at which they begin to use and accumulate words indicates. (The folk belief that some children are delayed in talking because all their needs are fulfilled without using language may have some truth in it.)

Tomasello (2003) asserts that social pragmatic theory includes two constraints on word learning: the structured social world that includes patterned cultural interactions, and the child's social-cognitive capacities that enable "tuning in" and participating in the patterns there. These constraints explain why learning words does not begin until late infancy, when the child has developed these capacities and engaged in these practices. They also may explain the variability in children's beginning of and progress in the word learning process. The social-cultural interactive context and social-cognitive interpretation are essentially relational conditions that are interdependent; some relationships undoubtedly elicit earlier and more active verbal expression from the child than do others.

Children Must Learn the Meaning of Words

How does shared meaning for words, and thus messages, become established as a general rule and not just within a preestablished context? This is the job of *conventionalization*, parceling out meanings among candidate words, a job that is accomplished over historical time by large groups of speakers who tune in to one another's meanings in multitudinous contexts. The end product is a system of symbolic relations. Each individual language user learns to interpret the meanings of thousands of words and to use them in constructing messages for others. Very seldom does someone actually invent a new word for a new meaning, toss it into the cultural pot (so to speak), and see it become established in the broader community.[8]

How, then, do speakers of a language come to understand each other? Wittgenstein (1953) addressed the general issue of how meaning is established, asserting that reliance on one's own conceptual knowledge is insufficient to establish word meaning; that is, a private language does not assure one's understanding of a public language. He argued that the meanings of words do not exist in some ideal form (as in a dictionary), nor do they exist in private mental lexicons. Wittgenstein insisted that the meaning of words resides in their use in discourse within particular "language games" or cultural activities. In Wittgenstein's language game, the problem of meaning is that of learning the criteria of use of words in discourse contexts. In the child's case, the problem is to discover the criteria of parents' (and others') use of words in joint activities. Wittgenstein's aphorism that "to learn a language is to enter a way of life" seems profoundly applicable to the child's first forays into the acquisition of word meaning. Equally insightful is the quotation that heads this chapter: "Once a lexicon has been established a speaker hears the same word as the listener . . . [this] may [be] the crucial factor in escaping from the private worlds of thought into the shared social world of spoken language" (Goody, 1997, p. 391). The essential privacy of the child's mind prior to his becoming capable of using representational language as both speaker and hearer is a crucial component of the view put forward in this book.

Wittgenstein's kind of language game is quite different from Quine's (1960) single-turn game and Brown's (1958) multiple-turn game, and from the experimental paradigms derived from them. It depends on consideration of the context of the word use, as well as the inferred referential intent of the speaker. It thus depends on building or rebuilding concepts to fit words "from the outside," attending to multiple sources of meaning in multiple uses. In the situations in which language is used between parent and child, the burden of interpretation is shared, as the subculture (i.e., the family) has its own rules of use for the subset of language forms used therein. Within this accepted-language game, parents attempt to clarify the child's understanding of what is meant, if confusion is evident, and they are often quite good at guessing the child's meaning of a word, even when it is used in an anomalous way. This process is likely to be very slow for some words, but it may be rapid for words that draw from shared perspectives and activities. This process will be considered further in Chapter 6, where more complex language forms are discussed.

The problem of learning word meaning is seen here as one of *matching* infants' meaning structures with those of adults through the use of words in discourse within activities; this contrasts with the stated problem in cognitive theories of mapping words to the world. The goal for the child is sharing meaning, not the successful solution of a lexical acquisition task. Words are assumed to be tools for meaning sharing, for advancing the process of being with others in shared endeavors. Lexical acquisition follows from this process. As it succeeds, the child's interest in and progress in acquiring and using more of the language increases exponentially.

Matching Concepts: The Pragmatic Move

When adults use words to communicate something using *their* concepts or word meanings, the child's problem is one of matching—or constructing—a meaning that *fits the context* of the adult's use (where the context includes the communicative situation and the activity of engagement). Assuming that the context is such that the child understands that the adult's word refers to an object, the child may have available an unnamed concept—or an object or a picture of an object—that seems to fit the adult's use of a new word, or she may not. If not, the child must *construct* a meaning that fits the adult's use, on the basis of evidence from current context, ongoing discourse, and general background knowledge. The same process holds if the word appears to be one referring to the action or other properties of the activity of engagement. In any case, a basic assumption that guides the process is that the word is relevant to the ongoing situation, including any discourse taking place within it (see also L. Bloom, 2000). Recognizing that language is based on shared conceptual meanings and that individual concepts differ, the problem becomes one of aligning different concepts (those of the tutor and the learner, or the speaker and hearer) to the same words. Once aligned, the differences must be resolved, and it is the child's problem to make the relevant adjustments on the basis of the adult's use of the word in this and other contexts, with whatever help the adult offers.

In summary, the problem of learning word meaning entails coordinating meanings that are consensual in the language system with those that exist individually in the mental contents of language users. The conceptual meanings of infants are organized around the infants' experience and thus are different in many ways from those of adults; adults' own conceptual meanings, in turn, may differ in some ways from those of the language but tend toward the conventional conceptualization of the community (Jackendoff, 2002). Thus, rather than a problem of mapping from word to concept, the problem of word learning is one of attaining shared conventional meanings.[9]

Usage-Based Language Acquisition

The general process just outlined is compatible with Tomasello's (2003) theory of usage-based language acquisition, within which he situates the social pragmatic theory of word learning. He emphasizes that children "learn what they hear." They acquire "items" of language that they hear in use, which vary in size from grammatical morphemes (e.g., "-ed" or "-s" on word endings) to words to standard phrases and idioms, and subsequently build constructions by combining those items. Tomasello argues that "the pragmatics of the situation in which the child learns a new word structure the learning process" (2003, p. 49).

The different kinds of words that children learn from the beginning suggest that children learn words that are used in situations in which they can read the communicative intentions of the adults. Children then use their observations of language in use as a resource for further understanding and construction.

Both Tomasello and Paul Bloom view the child's interpretation of intentionality as a foundational component of the word learning process. The difference between their theories is that Tomasello considers what infants hear and the cultural situation of learning to be just as critical as their own social cognitive processes. For Tomasello, intention reading is part of cultural learning. In addition, although both theorists assume that children interpret the intentions of others, Bloom's theory holds that the child maps what is displayed onto a preformed conceptual system; Tomasello proposes that the child actively constructs new meanings and new forms from what has been observed in an interaction. Tomasello's theory is nested within a social pragmatic theory of language that applies across all words and phrases as well as larger constructions of language; Bloom's is by definition confined to words, and largely to the class of object names.

Are They Symbols?

Children's early words have often been identified as part of the move into symbolic functioning, the prime characteristic of human cognition. A different view is taken in the semiotic analysis originated by Peirce (1897), who identified symbols as one of three kinds of referential signs used in intentional communication, the others being icons and indexes. Deacon (1997) has built on Peirce's theory in proposing a different claim about the uniqueness of human cognition, expressed as the "symbolic species." Deacon views human languages as symbolic systems that require a high level of neural complexity and that evolved as a unique specialty of humans. In this view, symbols build on icons and indexes, which are both tied to the concrete, visible world of things, to constitute abstractions that characterize human thought processes. These claims raise the questions: Can the words that children learn and use in the second year correctly be thought of as symbols in this sense? And what might be the consequences of considering them in this way?

Icons are closest to natural associations of things that are based on similarity. Icons are widely used worldwide to communicate with people who speak different languages (e.g., the signs on doors of men's and women's toilets). An index does not resemble its referent but is associated with it in some way. For example, smoke may signify a fire. However, unless it is intentionally used as a sign for fire or for some other purpose, an index is not a communicative sign but is simply a clue of some kind to the target of attention. Symbols are signs that incorporate *intentionality, conventionality,* and *reciprocity.* In addition, symbols belong to systems of arbitrary signs—neither iconic nor naturally indexical— that need bear no natural relation to the things signified. All communicative signs involve intentionality; some may involve conventionality as well. A child's gesture of raising arms expresses the intentionality of being picked up, for example, and is conventionally interpreted by the parent. However, it is not a reciprocal sign; the parent does not usually use the same sign to express the same meaning (i.e. "I want to be picked up") but rather interprets the child's personal iconic sign as intended. Different people may use different gestures for individual purposes. In contrast, linguistic signs (words) are used by both speaker and listener for the same conventional meanings.

Natural languages are symbolic systems, as are numbers, computer languages, and other artificially derived systems. A symbolic system imbues the abstract symbol with a level of sense meaning derived from the structure of the system itself beyond that of its reference to things in the world or to psychological concepts and categories (Frege, 1892; Quine, 1960). The lexical system embeds words in networks of related meanings that go beyond that of the referent-sign-concept relationship; dictionaries reflect these lexical relations, providing definitions of words in terms of other words. In semiotic terms, *symbols are social, intentional, conventional, reciprocal, arbitrary, and system-dependent.*

Deacon (1997) argues that the unique characteristic of cognition in humans in comparison with other species is the mode of learning that is involved in acquiring systems of abstract symbols. He believes that it is the system that is key, in contrast to other sign types; for example, icons indicate referential relations between sign tokens and objects in the world in a one-to-one relation, while indexes refer to categories (e.g., dogs and cats). Deacon argues that learning a single referent-word relation may be learning an index or an icon but does not qualify as learning a symbol. Of course in the language as a whole, each word is part of the symbol system in its relation to other terms, and typically even young learners are able to recognize at least some of these relations (e.g., dog and cat are both animals).

Deacon proposes that the symbolic system depends on cognitive recoding at successively higher levels of *relationship patterns*. He claims that these relations depend on the learning of indexical tokens, initially, and that the learning of large numbers of indexical relations is necessary before the symbolic system can be discovered by the individual learner; it cannot be learned by itself from the outset. Thus the child's initial matching of words for objects to his or her own experientially based concepts at the indexical level is a necessary step. This is a critical point: the symbolic relation is not accessible to learning from real-world relations but must be discovered in the pattern of *tokens* (in this case, words) that represent the pattern of items being named. Crucially, for understanding children's progress in this domain, the analysis implies that learning a word is not equivalent to learning a symbol but is necessary for moving to the stage of symbolic acquisition.

Emphasizing this point, Deacon states that symbol learning "depends on significant external social support" and requires "counterintuitive learning strategies" that focus on relations among names rather than on the real things named (1997, p. 379). Once in command of a word, its place in varying levels of relationships (indexical, symbolic) may become salient in the uses of the word by others in natural discourse, or the new level may emerge from nonconscious analysis of the previously acquired words. Thus, according to this analysis, not all word learning and use is symbolic; what is learned initially as an indexical word-object association is not a true symbol but an index masquerading as a symbol. The "mapping" metaphor in its simple associative sense may fit the indexical use of words but not the symbolic. An indication of children's understanding of words and meanings as indexical rather than symbolic is found in Piaget's (1929) evidence that for young children the names of things are considered to be as indispensable to the thing as any other feature; the word *cow* belongs to the animal cow, which could not be called by another name.

In summary, becoming a symbol user appears to be a complex developmental problem. The indexical relation is a referential one, experiential and pragmatic, while the symbolic relation is systemic and representational. The developmental solution must involve the child's discovery of conventional meaning within a symbol system. This construction of the problem is compatible with aspects of the system envisioned here and will be considered again in Chapter 6.

What Changes When Children Learn Words?

At whatever age children acquire a large supply of words that they use to communicate needs, wants, affect, beliefs, knowledge, or other concerns, they change from the infant state (literally, "without language") to that of the language user. They are thereby launched into a new state of consciousness that has enormous consequences. These first emerge with the beginning vocabulary, but the really radical changes come over the course of years. Inevitably the child's meaning system is no longer so personally, privately based in experience; it becomes more enculturated through language use. Words may cause underlying conceptual meanings to acquire permanent status where earlier they were fleeting, evanescent. Concepts are likely to become less fluid, more stable, and more generalized. Like objects in action, words may be manipulated in thought (Vygotsky, 2004). Words may be used where heretofore actions and emotions bore the communicative burden. Instead of pointing, or fetching, a child may simply use the word to refer to what he wants. These consequences for thought and social interaction are amplified as language gradually becomes the medium of thought as well as of the expression of self.

As meanings and words come together, the effect is to propel the child's consciousness into a new level of awareness where the child's meaning and the adult's meaning come to be shared through the use of words. The effect wrought is not simply a laying on of words on preexisting concepts so that the concepts can be expressed by the child (as Paul Bloom and many others claim). Rather, as Vygotsky saw it, the effect is of a merging of word and concept into a single whole. The child's concepts become changed, become "tuned" and enlarged—or in other cases contracted—by the uses of the community. Becoming a word user is, then, the child's first step into the larger cultural community; with words, the child's meanings can be shared with anyone who speaks the same language, and the child can participate in the meanings expressed by anyone else in the community. A dramatic change indeed.

Conclusion

In this chapter I have begun to address the issues involved in how the child's mental world and lived-in world are changed by the new resource of language, and how the words of the language come to be "owned" by the child. The process is more complex than typically described, and more variable than usually assumed, as revealed in naturalistic studies of children engaging in early language learning in their homes. Laboratory experiments, which rarely include the interaction of parent and child and often "teach" nonce words for odd-looking (or simplified) novel objects in paradigms of comprehension, lend themselves easily to the interpretation of the child as hypothesis tester. Hypothesis testing poses a question about the applicability of a word to an object, taken from a presumed large set of possible words and objects, with the implication that if this object is wrong, some other can be brought forth that is right. In contrast, I propose that the child does not generate hypotheses but rather seeks to *match* his or her understanding of a situation with the words used by others in that situation. Meaning matching is an externalization of the child's interpretation of the situation and its contents. The child's correct matches, as well as errors, including both the under- and overextension of words and their resistance to easy correction, can be accounted for in this way.

The process is a pragmatic one. The child does not begin with a preset structure to be filled in, either linguistic or conceptual. Instead the merging of word and concept comes about through activity, through experiencing the word in contexts that bring concepts to the fore and where interpretable others, such as family members, use the words that fit the child's understanding of the situation. Chapter 6 continues this discussion of meaning matching in terms of words that come into play with more complex language and linguistic representation.

6

Entering the Symbolic World

When the symbolic gateway is opened . . . a whole new universe
of cognitive and learning opportunities opens up.
~ *Philippe Rochat, 2001*

CHILDREN OF TWO TO FOUR YEARS ask and answer
questions, listen to stories, report on their activities, remember episodes from their past lives, plan for coming events, engage in dramatic
play and storytelling, and learn about the natural world and about adult
activities such as work or religion, among the myriad linguistically dependent experiences of modern life. These various enterprises require
more complex *minds* than those that supported their activities in the
first two years of life, including that of word learning. Although there is
no direct way to observe how minds change during this period of life,
we can examine the more complex ways that children use language and
look at the contexts in which they learn and use its critical parts and
functions, and thereby chart the ways that language changes thinking.
In this chapter I open the topic of language use in conversation, play,
and stories. In the next chapters I will look at the cognitive changes in
the domains of memory, theory of mind, and conceptual knowledge
that both reflect and benefit from language use.

Chapter 5 revealed how using words opens the possibilities of *sharing reference* to things present and not present in the immediate scene,
and of engaging the attention of others—not just one's near and dear
but potentially all speakers of the language. This ability confers social
power of a new kind and, however slowly and subtly, tunes the meaning system of the child's mind toward that of the cultural community.
Words by themselves can be used to refer to objects, events, situations,
activities, people, and relationships, and when combined with other

149

words they can draw attention to aspects of special interest, for example, "rabbit running," "Daddy home," "stove hot." This referential function of language use is basic, important, and powerful, but it is still limited.

The truly extraordinary power of language lies in its *representational* possibilities. Representation in language supplements "in the world" experience with linguistic experience that may evoke past and future, far-off places, times and events, unknown people, and imagined realities. Everyday language representations are prototypically public narratives representing experiences of the narrator or of other people. As Donald (1991, p. 257) put it, "Narrative skill is the basic driving force behind language use . . .: the ability to describe and define events and objects lies at the heart of language acquisition." Language representations also include discourse genres such as descriptions (i.e., states of the world), arguments, explanations, and theories, and expressive forms, such as poetry and humor.

By about two years of age children begin to enter into the use of these functions of language, first by participating in family conversations in which they may introduce topics or comment on others. When children have grasped some of the complex grammatical uses that enable them to construct accounts of events, they may advance slowly but surely toward full participation in the oral culture around them. This advance is a major step toward the possession of the symbolic powers that humans employ, and it is captured well in the following passage:

> When the symbolic gateway is opened . . , a whole new universe of cognitive and learning opportunities opens up . . . The child . . . can now . . . contemplate the world, reenact past events, imagine virtual realities, and generate logical inferences about future outcomes. She can exchange abstract ideas with others within conventional symbolic systems using words, gestures, drawings, or mathematical formulas, or express love, hate, bliss, boredom, or blues via songs, poems, movies, symphonies, dance, books, drumming, or a simple eye exchange. All these abstract and often obscure processes that make us human rest on the ability to function symbolically . . . That is what makes us different from any other animal. (Rochat, 2001, p. 193)[1]

Because symbols and symbolic structures are conceptualized in different theories as having different implications for development (Chapter 5), a straightforward accounting of my view is called for here. I concur with the views of Deacon and Donald in the claim that symbols are abstract *learned social and cultural systems*. Natural languages are symbolic systems culturally designed to communicate representations between people, including ideas and thoughts that are difficult or impossible to convey in nonsymbolic ways. Further, language takes over and profoundly changes the experiential meaning systems that have been growing in the child's memory from birth. Thus representations in language, such as narratives, are made possible by acquired systems of meaning that take us beyond ourselves and beyond present time and place, into abstractions and imaginary spaces, private or shared. Here and in the next two chapters, I examine the consequences for the child of becoming a participant in representational language, and the ramifications of its symbolic functions in social life, in mental constructions, and in thinking with language.

Everyday Representational Language

Language allows speakers (and writers) to represent temporally unfolding situations that involve different characters and multiple events causally related to the goals and mental states of their protagonists; in other words, it enables the construction and communication of narratives. Skill in using language in this way is especially significant for the child for two reasons: it allows the child to connect with others' meanings, that is, with their knowledge and experience; and it provides a way for the child to represent his or her own knowledge and experience in a mode that allows conscious contemplation of its meaning. It is also through language that the child has access to conceptual systems that are embedded in and thus only accessible through linguistic forms, not through direct experience.

Reference is an essential part of the system of representation. It is rooted in the joint attention to objects and events that is a key development in the last months of the first year of life and that leads to the acquisition of first words during the second year. Words (and larger constructions of language) may establish reference, but their most significant use is accessing meaning. In composing sentences and engaging in conversations, as children usually do by the age of two years, a child uses words in representational formats that display one person's meaning (memory, speculation, inference) for another's consideration. These representations may impart new knowledge through the use of familiar words whose meaning is manifest in the immediate perceivable world. But the most radical breakthrough of representational language is its potential for moving *beyond* the perceivable world to abstract, hidden, or imagined constructs and relations, a development that takes the child into a world of cultural knowledge that is outside the realm of direct experience.

Because we adults use representational language in this way all the time, and because our modern technologies make travel into time, space, and abstraction commonplace, it somehow has escaped the notice of many developmental psychologists that such a move must have a profound impact on the life of a child. Learning a language is one thing, using it in its most powerful ways is another. Here I consider the consequences for the child's understanding of self and the world around her when she ventures beyond first words into these transformative functions of language.

Understanding Representations in Language

By the end of their second year, the great majority of children have acquired a beginning vocabulary of object words, verbs, a few adjectives, and other useful words and phrases. These include a variety of words used to refer to events, actions, roles, places, and other phenomena, learned on the basis of the child's experience (see Chapter 5, Table 5.1). Children then move on to construct word combinations that express grammatical relations: verb-object (e.g., "eat toast") and subject-verb combinations ("Daddy eat"), and soon more complex constructions (see Bates, Bretherton, and Snyder, 1988; L. Bloom, 1993; Bloom and Lahey, 1978; Tomasello, 2003).[2] These moves constitute the essential developmental beginnings of the ability to use language in both comprehension and production as a representational medium.

While the rules of grammatical constructions are vital to the child's success, the *meanings* of the content words and the function words that connect them (prepositions, conjunctions), as well as grammatical morphemes (such as the plural -*s* and tense markers such as -*ed*), provide the main substance from which the interpretation of the representation must be derived. This is not to deny the importance of the grammatical possibilities for making different representations with the same words. For example, the simple exchange of subject and object in the sentence "Jason pushed Janice into the pool" would introduce a different scenario leading in a different narrative direction. Nonetheless, as has been noted by many others (of both a nativist and nonnativist bent), children tend to learn the basics and most of the complexities of their grammar rather quickly and easily in the years from age two to four.[3] They continue to learn words and their meanings, however, for decades to follow.

Beyond grammatical competence, the move to a symbolic level of language that enables the interpretation of and participation in conversation and narrative requires, for the construction and reconstruction of representations, the ability to learn, understand, and use words that refer to nonpresent, unknown, and nonvisible entities. That is, it requires the acquisition of a large vocabulary of abstract terms. This problem has been relatively neglected in the literature on word learning and on the construction of language in general (e.g., P. Bloom, 2000). It is apparently generally assumed that once children learn the names of object categories, they can easily go on to acquire the words for the more abstruse topics that people talk about. At the end of his book on how children learn the meanings of words, Bloom admits that his theory is incomplete, in part because the research has focused on learning words for artifacts, and he suggests that words for abstract entities, such as the activities involved in games, and moral terms like *fair* and *wrong* are ripe for investigation. I agree, but Bloom's strong assumption that children learn words only for concepts that they already possess places a roadblock in the way of this investigation. How language aids children in acquiring concepts not accessible through direct experience, and in evoking and tuning concepts that are already implicit in their experiential meaning systems, is a central issue here. Some of the abstract words that children hear and learn in the early years that are crucial to their understanding of the general discourse around them have been studied and discussed at length in the literature. I review some of them here to illustrate the processes involved.

Temporal and Causal Terms

Temporal and causal terms express relations among actions, states, and events. The terms *before* and *after* and *because* and *so* are of particular interest because of their importance to constructing clausal relations in grammar, as well as for their temporal and causal meanings (L. Bloom, Lahey, Hood, Lifter, and Fleiss, 1980). Their meanings are vital to narrative representations, which take place through time and in which the sequence and causal relations of actions are important to comprehension. It has long been observed that these terms are generally used by children *before* their logical meanings are fully understood. Earlier studies in the Piagetian tradition placed this understanding as late as the early school years (Clark, 1983).

Very young children are good at maintaining the sequence of action in events that they participate in, and they also appear to have an implicit understanding of many physical and psychological causal relations (Nelson, 1986). But it is not safe to say that they have concepts, or fully established meanings, of such relations as *before, after, because* and *so*. Rather, studies of temporal and causal terms suggest that the word meanings and the concepts emerge together from their use. Specific instances of the general relations expressed in temporal and causal terms are implicit in the relations of specific actions and events (e.g., sequences of one thing before another) in a child's organized knowledge of everyday events, such as bedtime scripts. The use of the words to express specific instances of these relations may aid in making the relations salient and thus precipitate the child's conceptual understanding.

In the process of collecting and analyzing children's accounts of familiar everyday events—scripts for activities such as having lunch, a birthday party, going to a restaurant—we noticed that children were using the terms *before* and *after* to denote sequential relations at an age when other experimental studies suggested that they were confused about the meaning of these terms. Some examples from young four-year-olds (French and Nelson, 1985):

Child A (birthday party script): "Blow out the candles. I eat cake, but *before* I eat it, I just take out all the candles."

Child B (restaurant script): "Then you tell the waiter what you eat, what you wanna eat, and then, then you eat *after* the waiter gives ya it."

The point of these examples is that when a relational context is familiar or logically constrained, or both, children as young as three and a half years are able to deploy the terms *before* and *after* to express their relational meanings. In an experiment following up this finding, three- and four-year old children were asked to respond to the terms *before* and *after* to locate an action within a familiar pictured event that was either arbitrary (e.g., playing in the park) or logically constrained (paying for groceries) (Carni and French, 1984). In this task all but the three-year-olds responding to arbitrary sequences answered correctly at above-chance levels. Even the three-year-olds could solve the problem when the sequence was both reliable and familiar. This finding points to two separate issues. One is how the relational meanings of terms of this kind are learned through relational event understanding. The second is how the relational terms themselves aid the child in constructing representations of the events.

Fast mapping is the general fall-back explanation for how preschoolers acquire the vast number of words that they do (seven or more each day, according to many accounts). In this process a child is alleged to notice the odd word in a construction and enter it into her lexical store for future reference, together with information about its meaning derived from context. The proposal for the acquisition of relational words like *before* and *after* and their meanings begins in a similar way, with one difference: the beginning point is the *activity context*, including the discourse in which the verbal context of the use of a word is embedded. Young children often ignore speech that they cannot interpret (Nelson, 1996), and a new or unknown word might not be attended to at all if the child is able to make sense of the discourse without it, perhaps relying on familiarity with the sequence of the activity. When such an interpretation fails, the child may take note of the word and, over subsequent uses, come to interpret its role and to use it herself in clarifying expressions such as those above ("*before* I eat it;" "*after* the waiter gives ya it"). In such uses, the relational word actively helps the child to produce a representation that satisfies his own understanding of the situation and enables him to make it clear for his listener.

Three-year-olds in the Carni and French study accurately used the temporal marker *after* to identify the order in both sequence types, arbitrary and logical, but failed to interpret reliably the order of actions and propositions in arbitrary sequences (e.g., pet a dog + go on a slide + swing) using the temporal marker *before*. These findings suggest that the familiar, logically constrained sequences supported the children's gradually increased understanding of the connective terms. By four years, children were able to construct statements that accurately represented both constrained and free event types.

The event-representation studies analyzed children's natural speech naturally as they responded to requests to represent their knowledge of familiar events that varied in terms of conventional and logical order. The Carni and French study employed an experimental paradigm to pursue children's understanding of the relations marked by temporal and causal terms in a more constrained way. Another opportunity for examining the use of temporal and causal terms arose with the analysis of representational monologues by the child Emily, whose bedtime speech to herself was recorded and analyzed over the course of her third year (see Chapter 4; Nelson, 1989c). Emily's monologues have been analyzed with a number of different goals and have yielded a rich store of information about the private world of a two-year-old. Elena Levy undertook a detailed examination of Emily's uses of causal terms, in relation to her parents' use of the same terms in context, to trace the relations of use by parent and child (Levy and Nelson, 1994). She found that the two-year-old's first use of '*cause* (for *because*) was anomalous both semantically and grammatically: "broccoli soup carrots 'cause rice." Thereafter, Emily began to use the word appropriately in grammatical constructions, but only in the same context as that of her father's dominant use in bedtime talk, in relation to sleeping ("you have to go to sleep because . . ."). For example, at two years, "Now Emmy go to sleep '*cause* Emmy kind of sick." She next extended the word to other social-psychological contexts that were observed in parent talk, and finally used it quite freely in conjunction with other words such as *but* and *so*. Thus the idea of '*cause* appeared to expand with its use in a wider range of contexts.

Levy and I termed this a process of moving from "use without meaning" to "meaning from use," and we think of it as a general process apparent at any point in development when words are learned "en passant" (as Johnson-Laird, 1987, put it). The practice of acquiring meaning from use builds on the experiential basis of word meaning to achieve the criteria of use, as argued by Wittgenstein (1953; see Montgomery, 1997; Nelson and Kessler Shaw, 2002). Recognizing children's practice of using new words in contexts in which they have been observed in use by others clarifies why children are so rarely observed to use words inappropriately,[4] even though they make errors in interpretation when tested in experiments in which novel contexts are deliberately chosen (Clark, 1983).

This proposed sequence of use and understanding, however, goes against the usual assumption that comprehension precedes production, and thus it demands a modification of such expectations. It also raises an issue for the theory that meaning is the basis on which memories are made; in this case (and many other contexts), a "meaningless" form seems to enter before meaning is identified. However, when it is understood that the *context* of the word itself has meaning, thus framing the meaningless form and setting it up for analysis, the sequence is no longer anomalous.

Mental-State Terms

Emerging uses of mental-state terms provide other examples of this process of acquiring abstract words and concepts. Mental-state words (e.g., *know* and *think*) are abstract in the same sense as temporal and causal terms: they have no concrete visible referents. In addition, mental states denote hypothetical entities and processes that are constituted through discourse about actions, events, and the goals, motivations, and emotions of the people involved in them.[5] Children are attentive to the language of the mind from about two to three years, but the meanings of the words are obscure at the outset and only gradually become clarified and distinctive. Many studies have focused on children's acquisition of the lexicon of mental states, especially words for beliefs—*think, know,* and *guess*—but also words for perception—*see, hear*—and emotion—*happy, like, sad, angry* (Bartsch and Wellman, 1995; Bretherton and Beeghly, 1982; Furrow, Moore, Davidge, and Chiasson, 1992; Johnson and Maratsos, 1977; Moore, Bryant, and Furrow, 1989;

Kessler Shaw, 1999). Overall, these studies indicate that children begin to use a variety of mental-state terms as early as two years, especially emotional and perceptual terms. At three years, most children studied produce the focal cognitive terms *think* and *know* at least occasionally in the course of everyday conversations, but it is not until about four years that children appear to use these terms to indicate specific mental states, distinguishing between the meanings of *think* and *know* on the basis of certainty. And it is not until the early school years that tests of comprehension show clear discrimination between the terms *think*, *know*, and *guess*. Even in the late elementary years children do not demonstrate understanding of the full range of distinctive meanings of *know* (Booth and Hall, 1995).

To track the uses of the terms *think* and *know* in discourse contexts, Kessler Shaw carried out a study of parents' and children's uses of these terms in the home during joint interactive activities, when the children were between two and a half and four years old (Kessler Shaw, 1999; Nelson and Kessler Shaw, 2002). This analysis revealed the beginnings of uses of *know* and *think* by both mother and child within specific activity and discourse contexts for pragmatic as well as mental-state purposes, and it also showed that the uses of the terms by parents were restricted to certain sentential functions and discourse contexts. That is, their use had a kind of ritualistic sense. Both of these terms have more than one meaning in English; only some uses of the terms make reference to mental states, while others refer to procedures (e.g., "knowing how" to ride a bike) or to pragmatic relations among activities (Booth and Hall, 1995).

The children in this study tended to adopt one or two uses of each term specific to the discourse context and function, months before they extended the word to other contexts or functions. Each child first adopted one of the discourse functions modeled by the parent (e.g., guiding, naming, or guessing in a particular activity, such as eating or playing with a dollhouse). For example, in response to the mother's question, "Where do you want to put it?" two-year-old I.K. responds, "I think—right here I'll put it." "I think I'll . . ." and "I think it goes . . ." were among the more common uses of *think* in the study. Only one child by four years had achieved a broad general meaning of *know* that was used to refer to nonpresent as well as present activities and to novel relations among events.

As with temporal and causal terms, the acquisition of meaning of mental-state words is best conceptualized in terms of the "Wittgensteinian" process of acquiring meaning from use in discourse contexts (Levy and Nelson, 1994; Montgomery, 2002; Nelson and Kessler Shaw, 2002). This gradual process begins with appropriate uses in contexts in which they have been used by adults, but the use by the child is simply pragmatic (without meaning). Subsequently, this use is extended to other contexts, and other uses by adults flag the attention of the child, who then gradually builds up an inferential understanding of what the term implies.

Superordinate Terms

Superordinate (hypernymic) category terms, such as *food, furniture, tools,* and *clothes,* are also abstract terms, although they are not abstract in the sense of denoting hypothetical constructs or logical relations. Instead they are abstract in the symbolic sense discussed by Deacon (1997), in that they relate to other terms of the language rather than directly to categories of concrete things. Thus *food* stands in a superordinate relation to all edible items and *animal* is superordinate to all animate living things, established through the symbolic relations among the terms. The relation is one of inclusion (an apple is a kind of food). These kinds of categories have been studied extensively over many years, with researchers almost always finding that young children have difficulty forming categories of this kind (see Nelson, 1985, 1996). The abstract inclusion relation appears to be difficult for them to understand, although they do not have difficulty thinking in terms of collections of items; indeed they appear to prefer to treat categories as collections (Markman, 1981). This is not surprising, as everyday categories such as food, toys, and clothes are often referred to in collective terms ("eat your food," "put on your clothes," "pick up your toys"), so that "all these things together" are food or clothes or toys, a different relation than that of inclusion.

In addition to the collective use of the terms, their acquisition as superordinate terms is facilitated in the child's everyday experience and representations of events. Event representations may be viewed as composed of syntagmatic and paradigmatic relations in a way similar to such relations in sentence structures. Syntagmatics determine the hierarchical linear structures of sentences in speech and writing—the syntax. These structures (e.g., noun phrase and verb phrase) create open slots to be filled by specified kinds of words and phrases. The lexicon, in turn, specifies the particular items that can fill such slots, in terms of verbs, nouns, adjectives, and other categories of speech.[6]

In its application to the experiential construction of conceptual organizations, the syntagmatic dimension is assumed to be composed of a hierarchy of event representations, such as actions, events, scenes, and narratives, causally connected. The paradigmatic dimension is composed of items that can fill open slots in these structures. For example, in an event script of a meal such as breakfast or lunch, the actions of "serving" and "eating" both provide "slots" for types of food and drink. Thus food and drink come to serve as hierarchical categories that subsume particular food items that can enter into the meal event. Paradigmatic relations produce "slot-filler categories" that consist of items that fill a particular slot in activities and discourse contexts (e.g., "put on *pants, shirt, socks*, etc."; "eat *apple, egg*, etc."). I have hypothesized that these interconnected relations are basic constructional processes of the human cognitive system that enable the symbolic structures of language to emerge, and that also characterize the child's spontaneous structuring of hierarchical conceptual structures (Nelson, 1982, 1985).

Evidence for this kind of experience-based conceptual organization was found in studies of children's event representations, or scripts (the syntagmatic component), summarized in Nelson (1986). The paradigmatic component was evident in a series of studies of slot-filler categories that indicated that young children, school-age children, and adults all revealed experiential organization of everyday categories, such as food and clothing, as well as the less personal category of animals (Lucariello, Kyratzis, and Nelson, 1992). We had predicted that the youngest children (four-year-olds) would produce and use only experiential (slot-filler) categories, while older children and adults would move toward and use both experiential and conventional taxonomic categories, a prediction borne out by the data from category productions.[7] More recently Nguyen and Murphy (2003) have reported that all ages, including young children, can classify food items in both experiential and taxonomic orders on alternative occasions, when required to do so in experimental contexts.

Together, these studies have shown two important things. First, children do categorize things in the world spontaneously on the basis of their experiential encounters with them, and they use the structuring principles of syntagmatics and paradigmatics to draw out these categories.[8] Second, categories are organized at least in part in the process of collaborative construction, and through that process move toward the conventional taxonomic or "logical" structure favored by the culture. Acquiring the abstract rather than pragmatic sense of superordinate terms is more difficult for children and is often delayed until the primary school years. The general point is that children quite readily learn words from their use in everyday discourse and associate the words with their place in experiential contexts, but in many cases they do not move to a more abstract symbolic level until later.

Abstracting Word Meaning from Experience

Research on types of abstract language terms has revealed the significant interdependence among learning relational and abstract terms and their use in pragmatic contexts, the child's acquisition of the form in these contexts, and the gradual extension of their use to other contexts, where similar relations within and outside language in the social, psychological, or material world are in question. Studies of temporal and causal terms, mental-state terms, and superordinate category terms have shown that children quite readily adopt the *uses* of terms for pragmatic meanings that they can grasp in relation to ongoing present activities. This finding led to the proposal of a general model of word learning (Levy and Nelson, 1994) that assumes that most words are learned in terms of the context in which they are used by others, including the activity context, the discourse context, and the linguistic or grammatical function context.

The child's first exposure to a new word (actually the first realization or attention to the word) takes place in an experiential complex of the kind described in Chapter 1 that includes the child's perspective, the ecological context, social interactors and speakers, cultural knowledge, and experiential background knowledge. Together these may support the child's attention and elicit an inference as to the word's reference (Fernald, 2005). The child's inference is based on a number of assumptions—about the topic of the discourse, the relation of reference to other words, slots to be filled in in the construction (e.g., object of a verb) or in the discourse (such as reference to an object or person). Inferences of this kind may be strong enough to support identification of the new word in a different context as much as a week later.

Yet many new words are not central to the topic of discourse, do not fill obvious slots, and may be ignored on first hearing or unconsciously entered into the ongoing pattern analysis that lies behind all language learning (Tomasello, 2003). Some of these words, like the temporal words *before* and *after*, and the causal '*cause*, turn up in many constructions and begin to appear in the child's constructions as well. To explain these observations, Levy and Nelson (1994) proposed the following steps toward word knowledge (summarized in Nelson, 1996):

- New language *forms* are acquired, together with their distributional relations with other language forms, on the basis of the discourse and sentence context.

- Discourse patterns are interpreted in terms of the child's experiential knowledge and meaning system.

- Following adult uses, the child forms a discourse notion of use and produces it in closely constrained syntactic formats and in the context of specific topics.

- Use of the form (externalizing) alerts the child to further uses by other speakers and to inferences about its meaning.

- Comparison of the use by self and others may lead to a resystematization of the form and other forms that are semantically closely related.

- The child's uses indicate at least partial control in productive speech, but comprehension tests reveal gaps in the child's meaning.

- Full control of the meaning of some forms may be delayed for years after they are first acquired and readily used, requiring further reorganization of the meaning system.

This description is meant to apply to the acquisition of most words, but it does not assume that all words go through the same or all of the steps outlined. Object terms are considered a special case of the general rules. Some object words, for example, may remain at the first step, although many go on to respecifications of meaning (e.g., the term *doctor* that may be used first for one person only and without knowledge of its general cultural meaning). This description of word learning in terms of a word's use, and the gradual acquisition of criteria for its use, aligns with Wittgenstein's (1953) claim that meanings depend on their use by community members in the context of activity (Montgomery, 1997).

Symbolic Systems

The Levy and Nelson (1994) proposal implicates a symbolic system within which words take their place. For example, the system of temporal sequence locates a reference symbol to which the terms *before* and *after* are related in a specific order. This abstract relational system may then be used for representing relations in the world. As outlined in Chapter 5, Deacon's (1997) interpretation of Peirce's semiotic analysis of symbols assumes that learning natural languages results in the acquisition of abstract symbol systems, not simply independent lexical items attached to single concepts or categories. But the abstraction of the symbolic relations is built on the underlying initial relation of words to things (or activities) in the world.

Deacon's analysis of symbolic systems raises several points that are critical to the development of language and cognition. First, language as a system grows in the brain in response to the uses of language as the child experiences them. As it grows, connections and organizations among words and language structures develop (word classes, synonyms, categories, and so on). Understanding symbolic relations requires moving to an abstract level, a level that is not directly connected to real-world objects or relations. This requirement underlines the inadequacy of basing word-learning theories on the learning of object words or other concrete items, which may be learned as associations or indexes. In contrast, learning abstract words, such as words for mental states, temporal relations, and so on, which do not have referents in concrete reality, must rely on the relations of these words within the language itself. The symbolic level requires a move from concrete reference (index) to symbol, but for abstract words there is no concrete reference per se, only words in discourse use.[9] Complex representational language, relating abstract categories of elements to one another to form sentences and semantic relations and thus to establish new representations of relations in the world, is based on the kind of symbolic system described by Deacon. Passages of extended discourse must provide the context for understanding the words within them, as attested in the prior discussion of learning such words.

The process described is obviously similar to the grammatical construction problem, and the apparent solutions are similar as well (Tomasello, 2003). We need much more research on the way that children relate their experiential understanding to the linguistic representations they hear and seem to understand, and particularly to those they produce, in order to better understand and explain the growth of meaning beyond the beginning pragmatic stages of learning words.

Representing with Models, Pictures, and Objects

While representing in language requires the use of an abstract symbolic system, other conventional means of representation exist, including visual art, photography, graphics, drama, play, film, and video, television. Often these are referred to as symbolic, but they are symbolic in a different sense than is language. All of these modes involve some aspect of iconicity or mimesis, and it is this resemblance relation that dominates, rather than the abstract-system relation, even when the symbol alone is not immediately interpretable (for example, in the case of the cross that symbolizes the Christian church and religious doctrine). In such cases, convention fuses iconicity with abstract symbolism within a cultural institution. When visual representational media (such as pictures) are referred to as symbolic in the same sense as language, it obscures the distinction between them that might explain differences in children's understanding and use.

For example, DeLoache's (1990) studies of the use of pictures and models as representations of a room where a toy figure is hidden have been interpreted in terms of symbols and signified objects. However, from the Peirce and Deacon perspective, the picture or a model has an iconic relation to the room where things are hidden, not a symbolic one. Nonetheless, the fact that in DeLoache's studies children younger than three years have difficulty using an iconic representation suggests that they do not understand the "stands for" or "represents" relation. But in learning words, which have a much more abstract relation to the signified than the iconic picture or model, one-year-old children seem to have no problem with the "stands for" or "signifies" relation. In fact, when two- to three-year-olds verbalize the hiding place in the model, they are able to solve the problem (Homer and Nelson, 2005).[10]

The puzzle of how children understand the representation of words and pictures and other iconic forms is complex and not easily solved. Words are not iconic like models, objects, and pictures but are components of abstract arbitrary symbol systems (or in first learning, indexical relations). They are presented in a mode different from the things for which they stand (aural speech rather than visual and tactile material). On the surface, it might seem that the symbolic status of objects is more primitive, in many senses, than that of speech. Objects, after all, are concrete manipulable items, and most researchers view toys as symbols of objects in the "real world."[11] If in human evolution people began using objects as symbols (a stick standing for a tree or a person, a rock standing for a predator) then one might expect objects to be at least as interpretable to children as words when they are used as symbols, but that does not appear to be the case. In the studies by Tomasello and his colleagues, words are accepted for use in a "stand-in" function in a way that objects are not (Tomasello, Striano, and Rochat, 1999; Chapter 4).

Here is a possible resolution of these puzzles. The symbolic relation found in language and other human, culturally constructed systems (e.g., mathematics) is indeed special, as Deacon claims, and young children are cognitively capable of converting their initial indexical relations of words and reference (essentially associations) to the abstractions of the symbolic system level while retaining the relations to concrete and pragmatic context. However, children view the iconic relation in mimetic terms, that is, as a reproduction of form, not as a stand-in for the original. The replicas are then conceptually, but not symbolically, understood. The latter proposal finds support in some of DeLoache's later work, specifically on children's attempts to use toy replicas in real, functional ways, and in the unwillingness of three-year-olds to use a doll or a drawing as a representation of their own body to demonstrate where they have been touched, for example.[12] This resolution suggests, counterintuitively, that the symbolic relation is an evolved capacity of humans that is "discovered" by the child, as Deacon claims, but the iconic representational relation requires teaching, learning, and practice.

Entering the Discourse

Once children are able to use some language, parents typically begin to expect them to attend to and engage in conversational discourse in the course of everyday events. Frequent references to episodes from past experience, or to those expected in the future, appear in these contexts, as well as talk about the here and now (Lucariello and Nelson, 1987). At two years, most children contribute little to such talk, but with growing language skills they begin to take an active part, as several studies of mother-child talk within the home have found (Lucariello, Kyratzis, and Engel, 1986; Hampson and Nelson, 1993; Kessler Shaw, 1999). Informal conversation between parents and children includes short narrative accounts of experience, explanatory talk, admonishments and negotiations, future plans, and sometimes stories based in fictional worlds, read from written works or told orally. Examples from two- to three-year-old Emily's crib talk included bedtime dialogues with her parents as well as pre-sleep monologues rich in talk about the there and then, revealing Emily's intense attention to her parents' accounts of what would happen in the near future, and her own recounts of what she had experienced in the recent past, as well as reference to psychological causation.

The many studies now available of children's memory talk are probably the most revealing evidence of their increasing competence with conversational reference to past and future, and to causal and temporal relations (Fivush and Nelson, 2006; Reese, Haden, and Fivush, 1993; Nelson and Fivush, 2004). These studies are considered in more detail in Chapter 7. They have but touched the edges of what conversation contributes to the child's language and to the child's understanding of the world she inhabits, a topic that has become of greater interest among developmental researchers in recent years (Blum-Kulka and Snow, 2002).

Receptive and Expressive Language Skills

Receptive language refers to how well a child can understand a passage of speech, while expressive language refers to how well the child can use speech to express her own ideas, knowledge, or memory of an experience. When a child controls a certain (not yet determined) level of receptive competence, she can begin to understand brief stories or recounts of events that other people construct in language, to retell them, and to construct her own. Achievement of competence in this level of language use is typically measured by one of the instruments designed to identify weaknesses in children who are not developing language normally. These test instruments, such as the Test of Early Language Development, or TELD, generally provide separate assessments of syntactic and semantic mastery and of receptive and expressive skills. The latter skills, essentially denoting the same dimensions as comprehension and production of words, are of particular interest to the issues of representational language.

Receptive and expressive skills are often involved in the same task (whether in a language test, in a psychological experiment, or in everyday life)—for example, when a child is asked to retell a story that has been read to her. However, the two abilities reflect somewhat different cognitive demands, as do the comprehension and production of words (Chapter 5). Receptive language ability requires attending to the speech of another person and interpreting the grammatical constructions used to construct the message, as well as the meaning of the words in the context of the discourse situation and the linguistic structure. In addition, interpreting the message involves sufficient short-term memory and attention to keep track of what is said, and to integrate it into the context of earlier speech and situations, as well as to relate it to any background knowledge that the speaker is assuming as shared and relevant. These are very demanding skills that require considerable practice. Beyond this, the child is expected to be able to remember the message or its gist; that is, to make it part of his or her own mental contents, whether through remembered words or in a nonverbal form achieved through some process of "translation" from verbal to imagery or conceptual meaning, or through some combination of these. As with real-world experience, such memory is necessarily meaningful, but not always in the way intended. We have little information about how these skills develop or how they are achieved in oral discourse in young children.[13]

In contrast to comprehension, expressive language skill calls on the child to transform his or her own ideas, knowledge, memory, or desire into verbal form "online," in conformance with the demands of the task, or the questions asked, as well as in relation to the total discourse

situation. In a test situation, the task may also require the child to interpret pictures or other materials in order to provide a verbal response.
Nonetheless, the cognitive demands of receptive language in terms of
attention, memory, linguistic knowledge—both syntactic and semantic—and conceptual interpretation on the whole appear to be greater
than those for expressive language.

Why, then, is receptive language, or comprehension, generally considered to be easier than productive, and to precede it in development?
Children's problems with receptive language almost always are accompanied by expressive language problems, but the reverse is not true. If
we differentiate "earlier than" and "easier than," the puzzle this poses
may disappear. Comprehension must be achieved at each level of language acquisition if production *with understanding* is to follow. This
does not imply that comprehension is easier than production; it simply
implies that it is a prerequisite, necessary but not sufficient. Nor does it
imply that production without comprehension is not possible. In fact,
production without comprehension is a common cognitive strategy on
the part of language learners, beginning in infancy with the onset of
babbling and the acquisition of prosodic contours derived from patterns of adult speech. As discussed in the previous section, studies of
the acquisition of abstract terms have documented that many forms are
used without full—or sometimes any—understanding of their conceptual meaning (Levy and Nelson, 1994). A reanalysis of the productions
in Emily's nighttime monologues revealed the many ways in which she
appropriated a form prior to using it for its conventional discourse
function, including oral narrative prosody and reported speech, as well
as word meanings and sentence constructions (Nelson, 2004).

The important function of mimesis in language learning is highlighted in these practices, as production of speech depends on the reproduction of forms heard from others' speech. But the infusion of
meaning into the forms learned depends in part on the interpretation
of the meaning *intended* by others' speech. The road toward meaning
may sometimes, perhaps often, be followed via *use* of the forms in the
child's own speech in ways that fit the same construction and context of
the others' production, as the study of causal and mental terms indicates. Indeed, as I have argued, externalizing the functional use of a
form puts the not-yet-comprehended form out into the social space
where it can be reflected on and responded to by both others and

the self. In summary, when comprehension is viewed as a prerequisite for *meaningful* production, its earlier achievement (in word learning, grammatical constructions, and discourse forms) is understandable. However, its prerequisite status also sheds light on the functional but nonmeaningful production of forms. Earlier competence does not imply that comprehension is easier than production; indeed it often requires more or different skills, including greater attention and memory, in addition to language knowledge and oral usage requirements. Of greatest importance to our present concerns, comprehension is vital to representational language functions in narrative, explanatory discourse, and other discourse genres. Young children clearly benefit from hearing stories and conversations (Dickinson and Tabors, 2001; Blum-Kulka and Snow, 2002), and the total amount of language they hear in the home appears to influence later school achievement (Hart and Risley, 1995). Yet the process of *understanding* discourse in early childhood remains a neglected area of research.

Narrative Representations in Play and Stories

Pieter Brueghel's sixteenth-century painting *Children's Games* illustrates a myriad of games and amusements being enjoyed by both adults and children in the public square of a Northern European town. Some of the games look familiar, most seem rowdy and athletic, all appear intensely social. Children today are unlikely to participate in such informal communal activities, although the traveling circuses, seasonal fairs, amusement parks, and various "lands" and "worlds" of today provide commercial simulations of carnival aimed at the young and also (often secretly) enjoyed by their elders. One way or another, over time, play with others introduces children to shared worlds beyond the bounds of personal routine experience. How does play contribute to children's entry into the symbolic world?

Narrative Play

The skepticism voiced in Chapter 4 about very young children's engagement in *symbolic* play has been reinforced by Lillard's (1993) work on young children's understanding of pretense. She found that before five or six years, children in her studies labeled "real" actions as "pretend." For example, when a person was hopping it did not matter whether the person intended to "hop like a rabbit" in pretending to be a rabbit, or just happened to hop that way. In both cases younger children stated that the person was pretending. It appears that for preschool children "pretend" indicates a mimetic action, not an intention to stand in for something else. To repeat this argument, mimesis is essentially the replication, with variation in a different context, of some form, whereas symbols use a different form to convey the meaning of what is being represented.

In contrast to Lillard's studies, Harris and Kavanaugh (1993) claim that their studies show that children understand pretense in the toddler years. However, children may mimetically interpret a "pretend" action as engaging in familiar routines with versions of familiar object types (Chapter 4). To reconcile these contradictory claims about pretend, children's engagement in and understanding of play can be viewed in terms of layers of participation, from initial understanding as a variation on familiar routine, where the variation signals "fun," to instantiation of an alternative reality maintained in parallel with the "real." Children of different ages and different degrees of narrative consciousness may participate in the same activities with different understandings of their own and others' actions and roles.

Along the road toward the understanding of what pretend means, children readily take up narrative play with peers of the same or different ages. In small societies, whether neighborhoods, villages, or streets, groups of children tend to gather to play out dramas ranging from the very simple (such as races or hide-and-seek) to the very complex (such as treasure hunts or "hospital" play), sometimes based on stories, movies, videos, or TV, sometimes made up on the spot. In North America such play usually begins in preschools, where the children tend to be same-age peers, which restricts the complexity of the overall plots. By three years of age children are usually engaging in group play with peers, but pretend dramatic play is typically delayed until age four or five in preschool environments (Power, 2000; Sawyer, 1997; Sutton-Smith, 1997).

Vygotsky (1978) viewed the development of imaginary play with rules (i.e., social conventions and norms) in the preschool years as constituting the background for a change in consciousness, specifically in the emerging possibility of voluntary intentions, unconstrained by real-life demands. He proposed that the child starts with an imaginary situation very close to real life, for example in carrying out activities with a doll that replicate those a mother carries out with a child. Here the rules "operate in a condensed and compressed form" (p. 103). This view is borne out by studies of the use of children's scripts in play (Seidman, Nelson, and Gruendel, 1986). This kind of play invokes an imaginary situation but one that is comprehensible because it is based on the real. At the youngest ages, "play is more nearly recollection of something that has actually happened than imagination . . . It is more memory in action" (Vygotsky, 1978, p. 203).

Whereas the play of toddlers includes turn taking, social responsiveness, and complementary roles, the pretend play of preschoolers goes beyond this in terms of complexity of content and structure. For example, Power (2000) quotes a segment from Ariel (1992, pp. 120–121) indicating the complexity of dramatic play among five-and-a-half-year-olds; the complicated direction quoted here is one "turn" in a particular game: "First, let's pretend the baby-girl is in front and the mummy is behind, and then let's pretend you allow your baby to get lost, because after all, you have a dog. Children, when they get lost, the dog gets them back. Come on! Let's pretend you arrived home. You told your little girl: 'Sweetie! You may get lost!' So, are you getting off? [Off a pretend horse]."

The play of these girls and of other older children is substantially advanced compared with that of the three- to four-year-old, in terms of the language used and the social pretense involved, which increases the number of possible activities, as well as enables the participants to engage in joint planning, negotiating play roles, and other complexities of the pretend social world. As Power (2000) emphasizes, pretense at this level reveals developing social perspective-taking skills as well as the acquisition of social norms.

The most significant of Vygotsky's (1978) claims about play is the point that pretend play involves rules, and that to engage in such play, children reenact the social conventions that dictate how to carry out particular roles—for example, what actions a mother must undertake in caring for a baby, or what actions a doctor must perform. In other words, in play scenarios the child externalizes in word and action shared *cultural* knowledge of how the world functions, what rules it follows, what roles are played and how. As previously proposed, such externalizing is a two-way street: it both reinforces knowledge already attained and opens it up for further reflection and questioning. Similar to the role played by conversation, but more open-ended in its involvement of situations beyond personal knowledge, play allows the child to escape the boundaries of everyday living and to externalize thoughts about others' roles and imagined worlds. It bridges personal memory and the narratives found in imaginative stories that most children experience both at home and in preschool.

Story Narratives

Listening to stories (read or told) has been shown to foster children's cognitive development as well as language development during the preschool years, as measured by school achievement and standardized tests (e.g., Heath, 1983; Dickinson and Tabors, 2001), but how stories have these effects is not known. I suggest that stories bear directly on the problems of different minds, different selves, and different times that are central to the child's emerging understanding of the world. Understanding how children begin to understand stories is the relevant issue. Children begin their exploration of the world from the position of ignorance, as a private experiencer without access to the experience of others except through shared activities and expressions of attention, attitude, and affect manifested through gesture and facial expression. In the toddler and early childhood years, the beginnings of sharing experience and affect through conversations opens up shared meanings, alternative perspectives, and temporal distinctions. These insights, however, tend to be confined to the family or a small social group, and to reveal the intentionality embedded in activities of two or a few well-known people.[14] Typically, the child also experiences some of the world of "others" through expeditions outside the home and may become entranced with certain aspects of that world (e.g., machines and people at work).

In addition to conversations about the there and then, in most American homes (and those of other groups as well) children of two to four years generally listen to stories that are read from storybooks as a regular part of their experience (Heath, 1983; Fontaine, 2002). Stories relate novel experiences, some in realistic worlds, others in fantasy worlds. How do these impinge on the child's experiential understanding? Although reading to infants provides experience with extended passages of oral language, infants are not expected to understand a story line as older children are. To follow even a simple fictional story, a child must interpret the meanings of sentences referring to unfamiliar people and places, including:

- reference to pictured scenes, actions, and people;
- representation of the relations in the story presented in linguistic form;
- representational relations to previous sentences, pictures, and their meanings;
- representations of the goals and problems presented in the story, retained until its ending.

The child must also retain in memory the ongoing actions, mental states, and causal and temporal relations, and call on them when needed to interpret other parts of the story.

How these matters are managed by children of two, three, or four years is still a research enterprise in promise only. On the face of it, these processes require high levels of attention, short-term and medium-term memory, and "translation" from complex verbal forms to complex meaningful relations not previously organized in conceptual or schematic forms. It would appear that pictures should help the child to make these connections, at least to establish reference. There is some evidence, however, that children's memory for simple stories is not aided by pictures and that pictures may even interfere with verbal memory (Nelson, 1996). Studies by Sloutsky and Napolitano (2003; Napolitano and Sloutsky, 2004) have supported this interpretation in part. They found that when presented simultaneously with equally discriminable but unfamiliar visual and auditory stimuli, four-year-olds processed only the auditory components (comparable to processing the text rather than the pictures).[15] The fact that, under many circumstances during the preschool period, language appears to dominate other sources of information, including the child's own memory (Chapter 7), may be related to these effects. Using language to represent relations in the world or in mental worlds requires an understanding of different abstract symbolic relations; understanding the relation of pictures to the things pictured requires a different kind of representational relation, an iconic relation. It may be that in story processing the two modes interfere with each other and that the child must learn, with practice, to integrate them.

On a different level, young children tend to remember the gist of a complex situation and lose track of details (Brainerd and Reyna, 1990). Because pictorial presentations do not typically represent the narrative form of the story, they are not remembered as story gist or as retrievable details relevant to the story line, and thus they may fail to provide support for story memory. Whatever the eventual explanation or causal relations may be, the relation between story text and pictures is another area that is ripe for cognitive development research during this age period.

Young children often insist on having the same stories read repeatedly over time, as most parents and developmental psychologists are aware. These are typically stories that the child is drawn to for their characters or the relation of the theme to their own lives (Miller, Hoogstra, Mintz, Fung, and Williams, 1993). It is equally plausible that children in the early years rely on repetitions of a story in order to make the connections that enable a full representation. Repetition may also be the most effective way for the child to encompass the relations between events as presented in the story. In the end, children sometimes memorize the entire verbal representation and can relate it to the pictures on each page, thus becoming able to "read" the story on their own. Repetition, memorization, and variation in retellings is typical of oral cultures (Ong, 1982; Rubin, 1995). It is natural to think of young children as living in oral cultures situated within a literate society, and thus their reliance on these modes may be seen as typical of their cultural situation.

These possibilities with respect to how children come to understand stories in early childhood are highly speculative, based on hypothesized relations among verbal representations and the child's own understanding of symbolic relations and events of the world. More will be said on these topics in the following chapters. However, it remains surprising that developmental psychologists have not thus far systematically addressed the problem of how young children come to understand stories.

Applebee (1978) attempted to explore some of these questions by interviewing young children about their knowledge of classic stories, such as Cinderella, to determine whether they made a distinction between the real world and the pretend world of fiction. His stance was consistent with that taken here, in asserting that at first children immersed themselves in the story, and that becoming an "observer" of the story and its representation of events was a developmental achievement. As a consequence, young children were expected to believe strongly in the characters in the stories. Surprisingly, he indeed found that a large proportion even of school-age children (seven to ten years) believed that Cinderella was a real person who lived sometime "long ago."[16]

Recognizing that young children absorb oral accounts of imaginary characters in imaginary worlds in the same way that they do accounts of happenings from a past time no longer remembered, or as experienced by someone else or projected into the future, makes such findings comprehensible in that the real and the not real are not yet distinguished; as documented in the next chapter, a similar lack of differentiation between past and future or self and other experience is common at this age. Fontaine's (2002) study of children's understanding of fantasy and stories from everyday life brought out this melding of reality and fantasy. She read two types of stories to three- and four-year-olds, those based on episodes that could occur in young children's real lives (e.g., "sleeping over" at a friend's house) and those based in fantasy (including a prince-frog, or witches). Fantasy stories were remembered better than "real" ones, perhaps because of the greater novelty of their characters and actions. In answers to questions about the characters involved in the different types of stories, four-year-old children did not make clear distinctions between the characters or their actions on the basis of their reality status (for example, in response to the question, "Could you meet him on the playground?").

Although some of the four-year-old children in Fontaine's study were relatively sophisticated about stories, story characters, and books, most appeared to retain many confusions about what is "real" and not "real" in stories. They were most definitive about clear fantasy characters—for example, about a character who took off her head—but in other cases they might distinguish real and not real on the basis of emotional responses or preferences. It appears that story narratives may have the same status in the young child's meaning system as personal-experience narratives, and may remain in the same limbo of an unspecified location of time and space.

Beyond content and beyond literacy, what cognitive skills might children be extracting from stories? Even the simplest and shortest story makes demands on the child's attention span and ability to hold together extended bits of representational language in order to later unwind an extended passage and reconstruct it into a meaningful whole. It is probable that the youngest listeners do not manage this from a single listening experience, although they may pick up a few phrases and some allusions to familiar things. Miller et al. (1993) analyzed a beautiful example of one two-year-old child's developing understanding of the story of *Peter Rabbit*, which became a favorite and was read and reread to him many times over the course of a few months. After a number of readings he began to articulate his association of the actions in the story with his own experience with gardens and perhaps with his own disobedience, "retelling" the story from this personal perspective, with himself as the protagonist. This example supports Applebee's idea that younger children inevitably situate themselves in the story, and it provides a useful frame for understanding the process that many children experience when they take on the identity of a story character alone or in group play.

Another example comes from Wolf and Heath (1992), who studied one young girl's extended identification with Rapunzel and other fairy-tale characters during a period (between age one and six years) when she was insistent on these as real (although shifting) representations of self. In their melding of reality with imagination, such self-representations are similar to those of other children who have imaginary companions (Taylor, 1999). This suggests still another area of the undifferentiated state of the preschooler's meaning memory system. An example from Emily's monologues at about the same age reveals ways in which she, too, melded a story with material from her own life experience. Emily "talked the story" while looking at a familiar book during naptime. She recalled many phrases from the story and interpolated material from her everyday life. She was not reconstructing the story as it existed in the book, although she was following the pictures in the book while reciting to herself (Nelson, 1991; see also discussion in Nelson, 1996).

Together these examples suggest that the reconstruction of verbally presented material is an ongoing process as it is interpolated, amended, or elaborated from experiential memory. Given the proposition put forth in Chapter 7, that in the early childhood period no distinction is made between experiential memory and memory derived from verbal presentations (or alternative indirect sources, such as TV), such reconstructions could easily merge into imagined realities, such as having an imaginary friend or of becoming Cinderella.

Two points need to be highlighted here. One, stories introduce young children to "worlds they never knew." Perhaps most important, they introduce characters in situations that children seem to have little problem relating to, even in the most fantastic animal stories. As Harris (2005) has noted, stories often include reference to the characters' mental states, which are elaborated in conversations with parents about the story. Because such stories represent examples of the very attitudes, emotions, and intentions that theory of mind is concerned with, especially with differences in knowledge and belief among different characters, experience with stories appears to be a likely source of the child's coming to understand the differentiation of others' memory and minds from one's own. Two, stories present examples of the continuing relevance of actions over time, making clear the consequences of action in the past for what happens in the present and future. Taking on story roles (e.g., becoming Cinderella) may be one way in which children are able to cut the knot of self and other and differentiate themselves from story characters and plots, and in the process stake a claim to the "selfness" of their own episodic memory. These speculations lead directly to the issues considered in the next two chapters, which concern developments in memory and mind over this time period.

Conclusion

In this chapter I have surveyed issues from a variety of experiential contexts, including learning complex concepts from words in discourse and the higher-order derivation of meaning from conversation, play, and stories. These verbally based representational experiences have the potential to advance the child's reflective consciousness through the process of reproducing representations in the mind and consciously considering their components and constructions. Through this process, dependent on social interaction, it is hypothesized that the child is able to extend his or her understanding of the self and other as distinctive persons. The language practices involved provide the grounds on which children find their way into human ways of knowing self and others within cultural groups.

Developments in infancy awake the initial sense of self (Damasio, 1999), but its further development at the reflective and later narrative levels is restricted by the use of symbolic representations among social groups. The child of two years, embarked on learning to use language in conversation and other representational formats, is possessed of a level of consciousness that I term "cognitive" (Chapter 4): the awareness of self as an object, a person among other people and objects. As the child emerges from the immersion in representational language toward the end of the fourth year, a new, extended state of consciousness is entered, wherein an awareness of states of knowledge—her own and others'—is both salient and accessible to reflection and transformation. This new *reflective* consciousness relies at the outset on the kind of social interactions made possible by simple language and gesture or mime. These in turn lead, in normal development in natural language-using environments, to more complex language use and abstract symbolic social interactions that construct concepts like "mind," and shared representations of past and future as well as facts and fiction.

These are the fruits of the developments observed in this chapter, and they will support the further developments to come. This interim level of consciousness is transitional; it does not enable children to distinguish well between sources of experience, nor to be aware of different states of consciousness in self or others. Nonetheless it opens up the possibility of entering the world of narrative, with all of its complexities.

♔ 7

Finding Oneself in Time

> Remembering past events is a universally familiar experience.
> It is also a uniquely human one.
> ~ *Endel Tulving, 1983*

$\mathcal{A}$N EXPERIENTIAL REVOLUTION is under way in the child's mind during the preschool years. The private mental life of the child is invaded by ideas, beliefs, and categories from other people, as well as storied accounts of the past and future, other times and other places. Of course these riches are not all taken in at once. Just as the infant, when she first encountered her private world, slowly accrued structure and meaning over months, so do children, as they begin to garner ideas, concepts, and knowledge about things unseen and unseeable from encounters with representational language, slowly shift meanings and conceptualizations from their prior self-perspective toward perspectives shared with the larger world. In this chapter I consider how the child's mind accommodates to these changes. I begin with some of the larger issues raised by the relation between language and thought, and then turn to the effects of language on memory and meaning, as revealed in research on autobiographical memory, self in time, and the source confusions of early childhood.

Thinking in Language

Adults who learn a second (or later) language usually find that the process of acquiring facility in the language takes many months or years, depending on the context of use—immersed in a culture where the language is being used or learning from books or tutorials. A final step toward mastery of the language comes when the learner finds that she is

179

able to "think in" the new language. What does it mean to think in a language? When are children able to do this, and what does this achievement imply for their thinking?

Some philosophers, past and present, maintain that thinking is something that takes place in language, and that those who do not have language are not thinking, at least not in the way that humans with language do (e.g., Dennett, 1994). The vast majority of psychologists, however, both past and present, do not or would not support this view, and many have reservations about claiming any impact of language on thought, preferring the view that the human capacity for thinking is a product of human cognitive structure (and ultimately brain processes), strictly derived from our biological evolutionary heritage. Language, in this view, is presumed to be a separate add-on to basic cognition that makes it possible for people to represent thoughts to each other.[1] By-products of using language for representing thoughts include specific cognitive effects, such as the use of words as labels, that improve performance on some tasks, a manifestation of the internal, or "intramental" function of language (Gentner, 2003; Jacques and Zelazo, 2005).

Children as well as adults benefit from labeling in certain tasks. In one type of experiment, for example, the child must identify the location of an object (on the top, middle, or bottom of a tower) by its analogy to the similar location of a different object in a different construction. Without a label (e.g., *top*) the child has difficulty making the transfer, but when the locations are labeled, very young children succeed (Gentner, 2003). Results of labeling tasks can be explained in Vygotsky's terms: the word's meaning is a generalization that simplifies the problem for the child. The label *top* is a generalization of a relative location that applies anywhere; the child does not need to recall the specifics of the first perceptual display (as using an image requires) but only the general relation to apply it to the next display. This is a stunning result, showing that by using general language terms even very young children may construct representations that identify a highly specific solution to a problem. Still, as Vygotsky pointed out seventy-five years ago (1962; first published in Russian in 1934), the experimental strategy used in this research separates the word/meaning unit into two parts and thus fails to address the essential question of how the form-meaning unity of language operates either intermentally (between people) or intramentally (within the mind of one person).[2]

An essential function of language is that of representing events previously unknown to the listener, thereby providing a new view of the state of the world and other minds for the individual, child or adult. To accomplish this, words that stand for general concepts and relations are used in constructions to produce specific descriptions. Representational language thus serves as a mode for communicating complex ideas between people; through this representational function, it becomes a language for thinking as well.

From the perspective of the "hybrid mind" articulated by Donald (1991, 2001), nonverbal thinking is a basic level of cognition, different in humans than in other animals, but also different in humans from verbal thinking, as well as from thinking supplemented by prosthetics such as writing, graphic presentations, electronics, and so on. When children are able to use language in thinking, they have moved into a different mode of thinking with different potentials—specifically, with potentials for abstract and communal thought and the articulation of components of ideas. Children without language are surely thinking, but they are not thinking in or with language.

Vygotsky worked and wrote before Whorf (1956) set out his ideas about the influence of language on thought, and indeed the two have different perspectives on this relation. Whorf's position was that different languages (e.g., Navaho and English) encode relations differently, in ways that affect people's habitual thinking. He was particularly interested in "covert categories" that require expression in some languages and not in others. In English, for example, gender is a covert category—it appears in English only when we use third-person pronouns (*it, he, she*)—whereas it is overt in most other European languages, where adjectives and noun endings require gender agreement. Early psychological research found little support for Whorf's hypotheses, but more recent research (Boroditsky, 2001; Lucy, 1992; Levinson, 2001) has probed the relations between language and thought more deeply and found considerable evidence that specific ways of, for example, structuring space and time in different languages influence the ways that people think about as well as speak of these relations.

Vygotsky was not interested in the structure of different languages but in the ways that people encounter and use language in different levels of thinking. In particular, he claimed that children begin using language as a pragmatic, social tool, and that only gradually, toward the end of the preschool years, do they begin to use language as a tool for

self-guidance, as private speech. In time, he believed, private speech—
at first overt—goes "underground" to become "inner speech," a more
elliptical language of mature thinking. Vygotsky connected these ideas
to the idea that children's spontaneous but not "logical" concepts later
become influenced by logical, "scientific" concepts learned in school.
In this way inner speech, influenced by both language use and cultural
teaching, becomes a reflection of cultural conceptualization.[3]

Slobin (1987) proposed a middle ground, allowing that people can
think "for themselves" in some nonlinguistic mode but that "thinking
for speech" requires attending to the particulars of the language that
one is using, for example in the ways that it permits expression of time
and personal relationships. A particularly important aspect of this position is that the distinctions required by the specific grammar of a language require the speaker to attend to specific details of experience that
may or may not be attended to by speakers of other languages. Slobin
emphasizes that this affects ongoing experiential processing, not some
invariant underlying conceptual frame. For example, children speaking
different languages include different details and perspectives in reporting narratives based on a picture story. A somewhat similar position
has been proposed by Bowerman and Choi (2001), who have studied
how children's acquisition of different languages reflects the grammatical and semantic differences among languages. They have found that
preverbal children in Holland and Korea already make distinctions in
perception and action—for example, the difference between putting
something "in" or "on" an object—that reflect the specific ways in
which their different languages divide up the spatial domain of attachment.

There are essentially two ways of viewing these and similar findings:
children come to language with several possible attachment relations,
and the language-appropriate one is selected in response to uses in the
prevailing language; or children's interest in attachment leads them to
attend to the ways that language encodes these relations, and their in-
choate cognitions about the domain are shaped to those that the language they hear uses. Essentially, the first view suggests that basic cognitive structures include a vast number of possible divisions of the
domain, while the second suggests that there are no preexisting divisions but only those that the language being learned provides. The fact
that adjusting to new prepositional domains is one of the most difficult
adjustments for second- and third-language learners to make lends

support to the latter possibility. Having once mapped the domain, later learning that overrides this mapping becomes more difficult. These disputes identify two clear alternatives: language affects cognition; language reflects cognition. A dynamic developmental-systems position offers the alternative of accepting a little of both, in the process achieving the symbiosis of mind and culture that Donald (2000) proposes.

None of the present explications of the relation of language and thought have made clear what "thinking in language" is and how it differs from thinking outside of language. In some sense, thinking implies working out some relationships that have not already been established in prior thought. It may also involve retrieving or reconstructing situations or problems from memory, and it may involve constructing a problem "space," or a story "space." It may involve planning. There is a strong phenomenological sense that much thinking goes on "unconsciously"—spontaneously or in response to conscious thought. Thus there is usually a basic distinction made between conscious and unconscious thinking. "I was thinking" generally refers to conscious thinking.

Considering that language evolved as a communicative system, and accepting Ong's (1982) distinctions between oral and written cultures, evokes the idea that conscious thinking derives from the oral use of language to talk with others about problems, plans, stories, and so on. From this perspective, when we "think in language" we are essentially talking with ourselves: dividing the self into two parts, one that maintains the topic, the other that proposes solutions.[4] Then "thinking for speech" is really no different from speech for thinking; it is just the other side, useful for composing overt speech to use in dialogue. This Vygotskian view of thinking allows for levels of cognitive processes—that is, for thinking before or without speech—but it is a view that highlights the different way, the conscious way, that human adults (in contrast to young children and other animals) direct their thoughts. It relates directly to issues of executive function as dependent on the maturation of frontal brain areas late in development (Jacques and Zelazo, 2005). Executive function is, from this perspective, but one name for one function of language in thought.

This view resolves the issue of why thinking in a different language is different from thinking in a first language; it is different because the languages are different, and, as Whorf pointed out, the languages are different because the cultures are different. This close connection between culture, language, and thought has yet to be accepted in much of contemporary psychology, but from the developmental perspective, combining Vygotsky, Whorf, Wittgenstein, and Donald's conceptions of cognitive science, it is compelling. (See Chapter 9 for further discussion.)

Developing Autobiographical Memory

The major transition in early childhood can be viewed as essentially a move from the self confined to one experience-based reality to the recognition of many possible realities, represented by others, viewed through media, and imagined alone, made available through social, cultural, and symbolic resources. The resulting expansion of experience and meaning brings about significant cognitive change and a new, expanded consciousness of time and the self. Two important changes are posited: the emergence of a new, uniquely human kind of memory, episodic (and thereby autobiographical) memory; and the bifurcation of experience-based memories into "my memory of the past" and representations from others (other people's experiences, general knowledge, facts, or fictions) that come through language or other indirect sources.

I suggest that the mental shifts involved in these developments lead to quite radical and complex changes in the organization of memory and meaning, involving differentiations between procedural, episodic, and semantic memory as these are presently conceived in neurocognitive theory. These complexities are multiplied by different modes of organizing: narrative and paradigmatic (or categorical or factual). Whereas each of these distinctions has a place in the cognitive literature, it is not at all clear how they are interrelated in cognitive structures and functions (much less in neural processing), and the developments involved tend to be viewed piecemeal, if at all. There is, however, a rich lode of research bearing on the developmental issues that provides a good basis for further work in this direction, and that I consider here in the context of the emergence of autobiographical memory.

Autobiographical Memory as Self in Time

Personal memories of the events of our lives constitute what is called autobiographical memory. In some ways this is the most natural reference for the term *memories*. Yet it seems that this is a kind of memory that infants and young children do not share. At the very least, they do not share in reminiscing about the past because they do not have the skills required to talk about it. But do they have the same kind of memories that adults have, memories that they share with others or simply savor themselves? If not, why not? These are questions that have been motivating a great deal of developmental research on memory over the past twenty-five years.

The well-established observation that most adults do not remember childhood experiences from earlier than about age three and a half years, the phenomenon termed childhood (or infantile) amnesia, provides a convenient starting point for thinking about this problem. When an adult does remember something from earlier than age three, it is usually a fragment or a brief scene, not a full meaningful episode (Nelson and Fivush, 2004; Pillemer, 1998). Overall, few memories from the preschool years are retained into adulthood; more begin to accumulate around age five or six years. Over the succeeding school years, the number of autobiographical memories retained by adults is about what would be expected, based on a standard "forgetting function" derived from the frequency of memories at varying distances from the present, as reported by adults (Wetzler and Sweeney, 1986).

These facts, accumulated in psychological experiments over more than 100 years, support the supposition that something dramatic changes in memory during the years from two to five that makes remembering specific events from one's past life both feasible and of value for the individual. They strongly suggest that autobiographical memory, as a specific kind of memory, emerges at the end of the preschool period (Nelson and Fivush, 2004). This poses the question for developmentalists: what changes during those years to make memories durable over time?[5] To address this question it is of course necessary to have a good understanding of the structure and function of memory prior to the emergence of what we know as autobiographical memory, as well as to understand the kind of memory we call autobiographical.

As argued in the earlier chapters, memory is a central function of the cognitive system, essentially a "catchment" for meaning in which different meaningful elements may be associated, transformed, set into new contexts, and in other ways organized and reorganized individually. Chapter 4 traced the development of memory from implicit memory in the infancy period to the increasing ability of toddlers to remember experienced or observed events over longer periods of time. As emphasized there, the memory system begins and continues for some time as a strictly private operation. For this reason there is no distinctive sense of self associated with the contents of memory. This might strike some readers as anomalous: the system is private but not of the self? The reason is that there is no necessity for marking contents as being *about* the self, as there is no contrast; there are no contents that are independent of the activities and interests of the self, therefore the self is implicit in all, but not "self-evident."

Infants and young children remember the general routines of their lives, the spatial arrangements, the ways of different people, and other aspects of their inhabited worlds, and they update these memorable context-setting particulars as needed on different occasions. Scripts for familiar events are one kind of such general knowledge that supports children as well as adults in activities of their everyday lives. Young children also note and retain memories of novel events, although their memory for the components of such experiences may be scattered and fragmented, reflecting the character of their experience in terms of the limits of short-term memory for connecting segments of extended experience. As situations change over time, remnants of earlier memory may drop out of the organization (see Bauer, 2006, for a review of the relevant research). Evidence that toddlers have memories of specific episodes has been available for many years, from parent diaries (Nelson and Ross, 1980) and transcripts of parent-child talk (Fivush and Hamond, 1990; Hudson, 1990), as well as from experimental studies (Bauer, 2006). But neither in records of past talk nor in delayed-imitation studies is there evidence that children younger than three years are "reexperiencing" a specific episode in the sense of thinking "I was there"; rather, the data can be explained simply in terms of recalling "things that happened."

Memory that incorporates an explicit sense of self is termed "episodic," to distinguish it from the sense of simple factual memory, the memory that "things happened." The belief that a remembered experience was uniquely mine, that "I" was there and observed or participated in what happened on that specific occasion, which Tulving (1993) calls "autonoesis," is the key component of episodic memory. There is considerable evidence and much theoretical backing for the claim that episodic memory is not available in the early years of life but emerges during the later preschool years (Perner, 2001; Wheeler, 2000). At what point episodic memory emerges in early childhood is a major puzzle. Tulving's provocative claim that episodic memory is unique to humans—that only humans can "revisit the past"—implies that episodic memory is an evolutionarily new kind of memory, the only memory kind that is "about" the past (Tulving and Lepage, 2000). Other memory kinds, like those of other animals and those of human infancy, evolved to preserve information learned in encounters with the environment; they are useful in predicting new encounters and taking effective action within them (Nelson, 1993, 2005). But these memorial contents do not include consciousness of self in the past encounter; they are not about the self in the past but only about the world and its happenings. To the extent that memory is not episodic in Tulving's sense—that is, not autonoetic (self-knowing)—it follows that noetic or semantic memory is not justified as its contrast; there is then only (recallable) memory.

Autobiographical memory, according to Conway and Rubin (1993, p. 103) "is memory for the events of one's life . . . it constitutes a major crossroads in human cognition where considerations relating to the self, emotion, goals, and personal meanings all intersect." It is generally agreed that episodic memories are major constituents of autobiographical memory, making up the stories of our lives that form the backbone of how we know who we are (Bruner, 1994). Inasmuch as episodic memories are characterized by two essential components, the subjective self and a definite sense of past time, to understand the course of development from early memory to the emergence of autobiographical memory, it is necessary to trace the course of development of these constituents of episodic memories: self and time.

Emergence of the Continuing Me

The emergence of the self in time—that is, the self with a history, a continuous "me" that extends from birth to death (or at least into adulthood)—is coterminous with the beginnings of autobiographical memory. This developing self history prototypically consists of many episodes that have apparent meaning within the whole, typically organized in terms of school, jobs, and relationships. It may include significant "turning points" that made a difference in the direction of the life course (Bruner, 1994). The self history is private, as all memory was in infancy and very early childhood, but it is also shaped by social experience and by cultural norms (Fivush and Nelson, 2004).

A new consciousness of self in time is involved in this new kind of memory, but is it a change in memory that brings about such consciousness, or the reverse? Is there an underlying catalyst that provides an impetus for both developments, as the experience of independent locomotion in later infancy provides the catalyst for several related social cognitive developments? In earlier work I proposed that the child's experience of representational language is just such a catalyst (Nelson, 1996). This idea suggests that verbal representations of shared experiences of the past expressed by parents and others evoke internal verbal (or perhaps imagery) representations of the self in the past on the part of the child. Memory serves as the source for the representation—internal or external—whether in action (i.e., imitation, play) or in verbal or pictorial form, but memory does not provide these representations as such. To talk about the personal past requires, first, the retrieval of some bits of memory—whether fragments or organized events—and, second, the ability to represent these bits—to rearrange and reconstruct them—in verbal form. Because the self is not at first overtly present in memory, it does not *initially* have a specific role in the child's representation.

Child's Time

Self and time are coindicated in episodic memory. To organize memory in terms of *self in time* requires a new sensitivity to the passage of time and to the placement of experiences in the specific past or the future, in relation to the present. It is generally taken for granted that memory requires locating events in time: things happened in the past, or will happen in the future. But it is necessary to suspend this assumption here and consider that the toddler or young child has only a sense of now and not now. The young child's focus (like that of nonhuman animals) is always on the present. Past and future must become established as specific "mental spaces" that are different from the present. Rather than simply living in the present with "knowledge" about what has happened in similar circumstances (in the past), the child becomes able to call up particular scenes from specific past experiences, including her own role in the events, to represent them in language, and to talk with others about them.

The experience of time is both very personal and very cultural (Nelson, 1996). It is symbolically regulated by cultural means, through technological tools such as clocks and calendars and through linguistic designations, such as days, weeks, and months. All of this we adults take for granted, but young children must learn these systems, and they do so with apparent difficulty. The problems that they have in mastering even such simple temporal concepts as before and after, or the order of yesterday and tomorrow, suggests that children do not come equipped with a natural understanding of temporal orders, or concepts, although their bodies are well supplied with a variety of biological rhythms that extend over days, months, and even years.

Talk with parents supplies a rich source of support for becoming aware of the past and future as distinct temporal locations relative to the present. The far past becomes more discrete when parents refer to "when you were a baby," "when we lived in X," or "when we were at the beach last summer," perhaps while looking at photographs or videos; the suggestion for the child is that growing up and having birthdays is part of an ongoing life. The future looms in the language that parents use to entice children to prepare for times to come, whether they are talking about the short range (e.g., "after your nap") or a longer time frame ("next week," "this summer," "when you go to school"). There is ample evidence that children receive just such introductions to the past and the future (Reese, Haden, and Fivush, 1993; Nelson and Fivush, 2004).[6] These introductions serve as scaffolding (in Vygotsky's sense) for the child's growing sense of a past life. Thus supported, the child begins to move from the "experiencing I" to a "continuing me," with a sense of being in the midst of a past and future (Nelson, 1997, 2001). This move requires a reorientation and a new conceptualization around time, a topic that has been quite neglected in developmental studies.

Research on time suggests that children are late to grasp both temporal order and duration, and do not master many cultural divisions of time until well into the school years.[7] Nevertheless, young children acquire verb tenses fairly quickly as they acquire basic sentence grammar, with basic past and future tenses appearing in their speech generally around two years of age (Bloom and Lahey, 1978). However, both past and future tenses tend to be used initially for very local time passages, for a just-completed action or an about-to-be-undertaken action (in English, *gonna* or *'ll*) (Bloom, Lahey, Hood, Lifter, and Fiess, 1980; Weist, 1986). Does this mean that the child's temporal space does not extend beyond an "extended present"? According to Weist (1986), very young children are unable to use the present as a reference time for referring to the past. That is, they are unable to maintain their stance in the present while at the same time reporting something from past time (beyond the ongoing present). This proposal implies that children are restricted to thinking in terms of one representational space at a time, a restriction in line with theoretical claims from other research domains (Perner, 1991). Weist's evidence is consistent with the conclusion that infants and toddlers live only in the ongoing present and have no concept of a far past or a far future. If children did have such conceptualizations at a time when they have acquired the language necessary to express them (i.e., past and future tense), the question would then be, why don't they use the available language for these concepts, or alternatively, how do language forms aid in the expression of or the actual acquisition of temporal concepts?

Children's script knowledge is relevant to this problem. In early studies of scripts verbalized by three- and four-year-olds, we were initially surprised to find that children distinguished general accounts of "what happens" (scripts) using present-tense forms from specific accounts of "what happened one time" that use the past tense (Hudson, 1986; Nelson, 1986). In script accounts, they used the present tense and the general "you" form; for example, "you eat and then you go home" was a script by one three-year-old for what happens when you go to a restaurant. In contrast, in recounting a specific birthday party the personal pronouns *we*, *he*, and *they* were used, together with the past tense of the verb: for example, "he opened the presents" and "we had cake." Thus by the age of three years children were making distinctions in grammatical formulas between the general and the specific past, between scripts and episodes. But what is of equal interest is that the three-year-olds did not distinguish general scripts from specific episodes in terms of the actions reported. When asked to tell "what happened" one time (e.g., at a birthday party), they tended to report the general script. These findings seem to indicate that, while children establish meaning and memory around the general event type, they use temporal markers on the verb to mark specific occasions. That is, the past-tense forms relate to past actions and events, but the child's grammatical distinctions represent the difference between general and specific memory, not past and present *time*. It happens that, in English, the general past is formulated in terms of the present tense, thus obscuring the basis of the child's use.

The specific question of children's understanding of self in the past was addressed in provocative studies by Povinelli claiming that three-year-olds are not aware of the self as existing through time. In a first study, Povinelli and his colleagues (Povinelli, Landau, and Perilloux, 1996) videotaped children engaged in a game with a researcher in the course of which the researcher surreptitiously placed a sticker on the child's head. When the tape was replayed for the child minutes later, three-year-olds showed no reaction to the sticker, although they could identify themselves on the tape. Four-year-olds, however, reached up to remove the sticker from their head as they watched the tape, and seemed puzzled by its appearance. Povinelli considers this situation as an analogue to the mirror test with one-year-olds, and suggests that it indicates that the three-year-old sense of self is of a present self, not of a self in time. That is, the taped record of what happened during the game is viewed as irrelevant to—noncontinuous with—the self who is watching the tape; therefore there is no point in observing or acting on the sticker.[8] In a later study, Povinelli and Simon (1998) found that four-year-olds who could pass the initial test in a similar situation failed to distinguish the past self from the present self after a week's delay.

It is not surprising that many are skeptical of the meaning of Povinelli's findings, as it is difficult to countenance the idea that the child might not recognize the self of a few minutes before as relevant to or "the same as" or continuous with the self of the present moment. But these studies do suggest that for children of three years and younger, simultaneous consciousness of self in the present and at some other time is very weak at best. In spite of having acquired tense forms appropriate to reporting on the past, they appear unable to locate or recognize themselves in the past.

Self and Other

Just as important as making distinctions of time perspective is making the distinction between "my" experience and "yours" (or someone else's). This is a critical point in early childhood that is related to but not the same as the distinction between episodic and semantic memory. The latter distinction crosscuts that between "my experiential memory" and memory from some other source; experiential memory may include both single episodes and distributed and organized elements that are included in semantic memory; similarly, both episodic and semantic memory may originate from different sources, including the self. Experiential sources may still be confused in later childhood and adulthood, as is evident in the now extensive research on suggestibility (Ceci and Bruck, 1993; Loftus, 2004). Such persistence into later years implies that although the two sources may become distinctive during the preschool period, they may require vigilant marking in order to make them so.

Making the distinction between "my" memory and "other's" memory requires an explicit representation of one's own memory as distinct from the other's. The claim here is that "my" mental contents—memory of past experiences, "knowing about," thinking—become personalized only *because* they are differentiated from that of others. When the "I" who thinks, knows, and remembers becomes a salient concept, the child may then become open to thinking of self over time, in the distant past (in "my memory") as well as in the possible future. Overall, three intertwined differences in young children's memory compared with that of older children stand out: (1) self-involvement is not a salient aspect of memory; (2) time is not salient in memory; (3) the source of knowing, whether verbal, from other or self, or directly experiential, is not distinguished in young children's memory. As we argued in Nelson and Fivush (2004), conversations about past experiences foster the child's attainment of these interrelated distinctions.

Let me be clear about this proposed relationship. I am not arguing for a direct transfer from adult to child of memory accounts or the structure of memory accounts, or of an understanding of self or time, through conversational exchanges. Rather, what I propose fits the general process of social-cultural learning that Tomasello has also emphasized in different ways (Tomasello, 1999, 2003). This process involves social interaction with a model pattern or structure more advanced than that already developed by the child and the developed capacity of the child to rerepresent parts of the model in memory, to be accessed in similar contexts at later times, either alone or in social interactions.

This general process is dyadic (or multipartied) and temporally extended. It involves not only cognitive preparation and development on the part of the child but also, and essentially, appropriate models from cultural partners (peers or adults). Partners may be more or less effective in presenting appropriate models; much of the evidence we have from studies of conversational interactions (e.g., Reese et al., 1993) is based on the variability of such effectiveness in changes over time by children. This model is implicit in the Vygotskian theory of scaffolding more advanced levels of learning by parents or teachers for the benefit of novice learners (Vygotsky, 1978; Wertsch, 1985). It combines at the level of verbal representations the mimetic process of learning and using imitated action constructions. Essentially the same process underlies the process of word learning presented in Chapter 6. In brief, children use the presentations of others as *resources* for constructing their own knowledge structures.

In the next sections of this chapter I present evidence for the effect of parental talk on the child's emerging episodic memory, as well as examples of the child's own memory constructions during the preschool years. This evidence supports the view that the distinctively human, autobiographical memory emerges from a collaborative construction created by the child and social partners (adults and peers) through verbal representations of past and future experience.

Conversations about Self in Time

From two to three or four years, conversational skills and the language forms used therein are consolidated (L. Bloom, 1991; Chapter 6), providing the child with increasing access to the experience and everyday knowledge of other persons—parents, siblings, peers, and other adults. Beyond this, conversation with intimate others provides expanded access to shared meanings, in addition to new awareness and new self-knowledge, and the possibility of reflection on the self as an active agent not only in the present but also in the past and the future. This process may highlight the contrast between unique self-experiences and those of other people. Seeing these contrasts requires one to remove oneself, decentering the self in the ongoing activity to reflect on differences—in the perspective of another who has experienced something different from oneself, and between the self in the present and the self at a different time or place. To reflect on these differences, it is necessary to represent them either externally or internally. Conversation is the main context within which the external representations of aspects of self and other, and of self in the past and future, become apparent. Conversations with parents about the past and the future highlight the role of the child as a person who has taken part in memorable activities with others at some other time than the present.

There is now a large and rich body of data from studies of how parents talk with children about episodes from their past (see Nelson and Fivush, 2004; Fivush and Nelson, 2006; Reese, 2002b). In general, when children are between the ages of two and three, their contributions to these conversations tend to be fragmentary and tenseless, without specific reference to the past. For example, in the following conversation initiated by a twenty-four-month-old child about a trip to visit his father, his contributions consist of single words or fragments (*M* stands for Mother, *C* for Child):

C: Mommy, the Chrysler building
M: The Chrysler building?
C: The Chrysler building?
M: Yeah, who works in the Chrysler building?
C: Daddy
M: Do you ever go there?
C: Yes, I see the Chrysler building\picture of the Chrysler building\
M: I don't know if we have a picture of the Chrysler building. Do we?
C: We went to . . . my Daddy went to work
M: Remember when we went to visit daddy? Went in the elevator, way way up in the building so we could look down from the big window?
C: big window
M: mmhm
C: ( )When . . . we did go on the big building
M: mmhm, the big building. Was that fun? Would you like to do it again? Sometime.
C: I want to go on the big building.[9]

Here the mother sets the child's reference ("Chrysler building") into the sequence of visiting Daddy at work. She provides the temporal and causal structure (using "when" and "so"), and emphasizes the high point of looking out the big window; she also supplies the evaluation ("Was that fun?") and connects it over time to the future ("Would you like to do it again? Sometime.") The child's mother would be labeled "elaborative" in Fivush and Reese's (1991) scheme, as she accepted the fragment indicating the memory of an expedition and spun it into a recollected narrative of the trip, supplying details and encouraging the child to contribute more. She ended with an evaluative question ("Was that fun?") and projected the child into the future with the possibility that they would do it again some day. Elaborative mothers have been shown in many studies by Fivush and her colleagues to be more effective in evoking more and more detailed memories in their children than nonelaborative mothers. In a three-year longitudinal study of mother-child conversations about past experiences, the mother's style significantly predicted the child's later memory recounts at three time periods, but the child's earlier contributions were not related to mother's later conversational style (Reese et al., 1993). These relations indicate that the direction of the long-term effects is from mother to child and not the reverse.

Narrative Talk

Parent-child talk about experiences that were meaningful because they were novel or unusual in some way, and that involved emotional reactions, lend themselves to narrative construction. The represented experience is formulated with a beginning and end, a temporal and causal sequence—this happened because that happened—and an evaluation—I was happy, sad, felt good, and so on. Narratives include what Bruner (1990) refers to as the Landscape of Consciousness, the features that provide the why and how of the episode, the motivations, causal chains, emotions, and other psychological states that underlie the actions observed. Routine experiences in which nothing special happens are not generally made into narratives to be shared with others, and when they are reported it is likely to be for purely factual reasons, such as, "What did you have for lunch yesterday?" ("Well, let's not have that again.")

As Nelson and Fivush (2004) argued, children learn what to tell and how to tell it in discussions with their parents about past experience. The thoughts and intentions of the individuals involved are as crucial to the unfolding narrative as the sequences and causes of the actions. It is relevant, therefore, to note that children who lack conversational experiences of this kind, for example autistic children, or deaf children of hearing parents who do not share a symbolic system, are delayed in autobiographical memory as well as in theory of mind (Goldman, 2003; Siegal and Peterson, 1994; Baron-Cohen, 2000).

Parental narrative-like representations of ongoing activities are powerful carriers of meaning for memory (Tessler and Nelson, 1994). In a study specifically aimed at uncovering the role of parental narrative in the child's memory for an event, Tessler categorized maternal styles in two types: paradigmatic, emphasizing the "what" of an experience, and narrative, emphasizing when, where, who, what was going on, and why (Tessler and Nelson, 1994). Tessler found that these categories distinguished among mothers who typically emphasized one kind of detail over another, either in reading a storybook or in talking about an event with their child, and differentiated their four-year-old children in terms of how much and what they remembered of an experience. The talk that accompanied the experience apparently structured the memory. Specifically, Tessler (1986) found that some mothers accompanied their expeditions (to the museum or on a neighborhood walk) with three- and four-year-old children with talk in a narrative style (providing background and meaning), while others were paradigmatic or categorical, pointing out what to look at and how to label it. Children of the first group of mothers remembered more about exhibits and sights and more of the contextual details than those of the other group. In addition, Tessler found that three- and four-year-old children tended to remember only those things about which both mother and child talked during the experience.

That what is jointly discussed is remembered later has also been found with younger children in a series of studies in which children were given specific kinds of verbal support by mothers that in turn influenced what they specifically remembered at a later time (Haden, Ornstein, and Didow, 2001). As in Tessler's study, the younger children (two- and three-year-olds) tended to remember only what they had discussed with their mother, not what either one verbalized alone. This is of particular interest because until a child is "tuned in" to the meaning of language used in a situation, it is primarily the most salient objects and actions that are remembered. Talking about particulars makes them more memorable. This finding reveals the powerful role of language at a very young age.[10]

These and other studies support the general finding from Reese, Haden, and Fivush (1993) that the way that mothers interact with their children during sessions of "past talk"—specifically, engaging in elaborative commenting on what the child is able to contribute (as in the "Chrysler Building" segment)—is associated with more memories and more detailed remembering by the child at later points in development. That is, the way that parents talk with children about things they have experienced together or separately, producing storylike narratives or more factually skeletal accounts (or none at all, perhaps), influences how children structure their own memories for remembering and telling, and what and how much they tend to recall of their experiences.

Future Talk

Parents tend to talk with children about the future as much as they do about the past, but it is not clear how children understand future talk (Lucariello and Nelson, 1987; Nelson, 1989b; Benson, 1994; Hudson, 2004). Representations of the future project something that does not yet exist and for which the child may have no preexisting schema or script to support understanding. The younger child may interpret the representation as something like a story, but as discussed in Chapter 6, researchers do not have a good idea about how stories are understood by young children. Thus it is unclear at the present time how children interpret the representation of an event not yet experienced, or whether the representation is called on in guiding the actual experience and the memory for the experience at a later time.

In bedtime talk with two-year-old Emily, her parents spoke about what would happen in the future as well as what had been experienced in the past (Nelson, 1989a). Typically her father told her a "story" of what they would do after her nap or the next day, and often she would request that he repeat the story ("tell again") many times. Emily listened intently to these accounts and often rerepresented them in her pre-sleep monologues after her father or mother left the room. When alone, she would attempt to recapitulate what her parent had said, inevitably misunderstanding or misrepresenting and often adding bits from her own knowledge store. One of the earliest of these recorded instances, subjected to several different analyses in Nelson (1989c) is reproduced here, with a single version of the father's account followed by Emily's monologue "reproducing" it (*F* stands for Father, *E* for Emily).

F: [before leaving the room—one of several versions] You know
what we're gonna do this weekend? We're gonna go to
Childworld, and we're gonna buy diapers for Stephen [newborn
brother] . . . and Emily . . . and we're gonna buy an intercom
system so that we can hear Stephen downstairs. It's neat, you're
gonna like it.

E: [alone after F leaves the room] And Daddy said
  Buy diapers for Stephen and Emmy
  And buy something for Stephen plug in and say ahhh
  And put the in
  On Saturday go Childworld buy diaper for Emmy
  And diaper for the baby
  And then buy something for the
  And . . . see . . . for . . . that . . . baby . . .
  Plug in . . .
  And get diapers for ANYbody.
  And buy more that that day at Childworld . . .
  And buy croutes [uninterpretable] . . .
  And maybe Childworld . . .
  Cause the one that broken at Tanta's.
  The one that's broken
  The one that's broken here
  The . . . the infant seat . . .
  Dada actually at home.

Clearly it is not simple for the two-year-old, just beginning to get control of extended conversational representations, to retain the details or
to understand explanations of things unknown, such as the baby moni-
tor. Yet much of the father's representation is reproduced in part, and it
is supplemented with a bit from Emily's own experiential knowledge
about the infant seat (not part of the father's Childworld recitation, at
least not in the recorded transcript).

    In a later monologue at twenty-eight months, Emily made a number
of changes and additions from the model presented by her father in her
rerepresentation of an anticipated experience of visiting friends at the
beach. His account included "hot dogs at the ocean," "a bunch of other
kids," "you can sit in the sand" "sit in the ocean," "you can splash." It
was quite clear from his repetitions that "hot dogs" and "ocean" are

projected as the highlights of the expected expedition to visit friends the following day.

Emily's monologue reconstructs Father's brief references into a full account:

> We are gonna . . . at the ocean. Ocean is a little far away. I think it's . . . couple blocks . . . away. Maybe it's down, downtown, and across the ocean, and down the river, and maybe it's in, the hot dogs will be in a fridge, and the fridge would be in the water over by a shore, and then we could go in, and get a hot dog and bring it out to the river and then sharks go in the river and bite me, in the ocean, we go in the ocean, and ocean be over by . . . I think a couple of blocks away. But we could be, and we could find any hot dogs, um the hot dogs gonna be for the for the beach. Then the bridge is gonna, we'll have to go in the green car, cause that's where the car seats are. Um, I can be in the red car, but, see, I be in the green car. But you know who's going to be in the green car . . . both children . . . I'm going to be in the green car in my car seat, he's gonna be . . . and nobody's gonna be, just . . . you know, these people, we don't know, and too far away from the beach, and two things.

Emily's additions to Daddy's account include: the ocean is a couple of blocks away, the hotdogs might be in the fridge, the children will go in the green car 'cause that's where the car seats are. These transcripts suggest that early in the third year (at twenty-four months) Emily attempted to repeat exactly the account that "Daddy" produced. By twenty-eight months she was freer with her interpretive version of what would happen.[11]

It seems clear that, for Emily, reciting accounts of what had happened and what would happen in the future had significant interest for her. One monologue at thirty-two months, an account of what would happen "tomorrow morning," extended for fifty lines (see Nelson, 1989a, 1996). This and similar accounts were based on both her father's continuing practice of telling about the next morning each night before leaving and Emily's own experience. It is very likely that such a controlled possession of the facts about expected events provides a sense of security and comfort to the young child. At younger ages, children rely on unvarying routines to provide security and stability.

Gaining control over routines through verbal means, as Emily did, externalizes and stabilizes experience in a way that is analogous to the use of words for symbolizing objects (see Chapter 5). When the routine becomes a memorized sequence, it acquires a representation that makes it "visible" to the teller and usable for purposes of storytelling, play, and categorization (Nelson, 1986).

We have no information about how such repetitions affected Emily's experience or her memory of an experience after the fact. However, we do have some information about somewhat older children who were told about what to expect in a coming event. Presler (2000) found that kindergarten children who had been given a verbal preview of an event in terms of the procedures that would be followed remembered the event later in terms of its sequential flow, whereas the children who had been given a preview of the kinds of things they would experience and learn about remembered more of the content of the workshop they attended. These differentiated effects appeared in delayed interviews weeks later, not in immediate memory on the day after. A more elaborate and controlled study of four- to eight-year-old children who talked with parents prior to a museum workshop similarly found a delayed effect of parental talk on the content of the child's recall. It appears that the pre-event talk influenced the consolidation of the memory, not its immediate contents. The children in both studies were considerably older than Emily was in the instances cited; we do not know at what age or in what way verbal representations before the event may begin to affect a child's experience or her memory of an experience.

Variations in Memory

One of the important but often overlooked factors in the literature on autobiographical memory is that not all rememberers remember in the same way; there are quite striking individual differences in when autobiographical memory begins (when the first memories of childhood appear) and in how many and what kinds of memories people retain over time. Some people report that they remember nothing before the age of eight or ten, while others report strong memories from the age of two years and many from four years and later. One way of understanding this is to consider functional types of memory. As Schneider and Weinert (1995) and their colleagues have found, memory is not a ge-

neric competence; it differs across materials and tasks for different individuals. People are not "good rememberers" in all domains, and they
vary in respect to which tasks they excel at or are poor at. Some adults
who have an excellent memory for academic material, remember com-
paratively very few episodes from their personal experience in adolescence or childhood. Also, there are both gender and cultural differences in autobiographical memory; for example, women tend to
have more memories and earlier memories than men do (Nelson and
Fivush, 2004; Fivush and Nelson, 2004). Cultural differences in age of
earliest memory and content of memory (such as emotional elements,
self versus interpersonal emphasis) have now been extensively documented (see Wang, 2001, for a review). For example, East Asian adults
have later early memories than European Americans and tend to focus
on more general and interpersonal aspects of an event.

The Who and What of Memory and Mind

Thus far, support for the influence of conversations about the past,
present, and future on children's memory has been documented, indicating the relative power of verbal representations to affect what is
meaningful and memorable from experience. A less positive perspective on this power, however, emerges from the accumulated evidence of
children's suggestibility and source confusion. Studies in these areas
implicate a dramatic result of becoming receptive to the verbal representations of events from others, namely that these are often not distinguished by the younger child from memory for the child's own direct experience. Such confusions imply that verbal representations
exchanged with parents, for example, may be incorporated into the
child's memory of an experienced event whether she experienced it
herself or someone else did. More dramatically, the child may take on
someone else's remembered experience and re-present it as his own.
There is evidence for precisely such an effect. Peggy Miller reports
that young preschool children sometimes adopt another's experiential
report as their own and retell it to someone else in the first person
(Miller, Potts, Fung, Hoogstra, and Mintz, 1990), suggesting that children make no distinctions in their episode memory between things that
they have personally experienced and those that they have only heard
about.[12]

This possibility has been explored extensively in the context of young children's susceptibility to the suggestions of interviewers in connection with the question of whether children are reliable witnesses in cases of child abuse or other judicial proceedings. There have been strong claims made on both sides of the issue, with some research indicating that children are highly resistant to the suggestions of interviewers while others emphasize the ease with which false accounts of entire events can be implanted in children's minds (for reviews, see Goodman, Rudy, Bottoms, and Aman, 1990; Ceci and Bruck, 1993). The resolution of this conflict must rely on identifying the underlying nature of the younger child's memory, its developing characteristics, and the contexts and conditions under which high suggestibility is observed at different ages. I aim here at the first part of this problem: understanding developments in memory over the preschool years. The fact that younger children are more susceptible to suggestions than older children and adults (but not always) is part of the background to be explained.

The confusion of personal experience with reported episodes is apparently well accepted by many adults as characteristic among young children, as indicated by the skepticism they express with respect to reports of very early memories, including their own. Indeed, reflective adults also not infrequently report that they are uncertain whether something from the more distant past was what they had actually experienced or had only heard about. This introspective reporting suggests a recurrent confusion between self-memory—that is, episodic memory—and general "episode memory," memory for episodes reported by others.

A most striking documentation of such a confusion was reported by Piaget (1962, pp. 187–188f):

One of my first memories would date, if it were true, from my second year. I can still see, most clearly, the following scene, in which I believed until I was about fifteen. I was sitting in my pram, which my nurse was pushing in the Champs-Elysées, when a man tried to kidnap me. I was held in by the strap fastened around me while my nurse bravely tried to stand between me and the thief. She received various scratches, and I can still see vaguely those on her face. Then a crowd gathered, a policeman with a short cloak and a white baton came up, and the man took to his heels. I can still see the whole scene, and can even place it near the tube station. When I was about fifteen, my parents received a letter from my former nurse saying that she had been converted to the Salvation Army. She wanted to confess her past faults and in particular to return the watch she had been given as a reward on this occasion. She had made up the whole story, faking the scratches. I therefore must have heard, as a child, an account of this story, which my parents believed, and projected it into the past in the form of a visual memory.

This account is of particular interest because it apparently had the feeling for Piaget of autonoesis, yet it had never happened. Of course it is likely that the young Piaget had had background (script) memory for the recurrent event and the scene of walking with his nurse in the Champs-Elysées that could have filled out the personal feeling of the episode. The research literature on suggestibility in adults as well as children lends credibility to this account; experiments have demonstrated the feasibility of implanting false details in eyewitness memory as well as implanting in memory quite extensive but false episodes from childhood (such as being lost in a shopping mall) (Loftus, 1979, 2004).

Suggestibility is a specific outcome of the more general phenomenon of the fragility of source monitoring (Johnson and Raye, 2000). Johnson and her colleagues have carried out an extensive program of research on adults as well as children to explore these phenomena and have attributed a cluster of constructive processes involved to the frontal areas of the brain, well known to mature late in development. It is now clear that young children are especially poor at source monitoring, often unable to distinguish whether they were told, they saw, or they inferred information (Roberts and Blades, 2000). Preschoolers may confuse their own actions with those of someone else in a joint project, as well as what action they engaged in—acting, speaking, or thinking—in a game designed to evaluate these confusions (Ratner, Foley, and Gimpert, 2000). These difficulties suggest that they have not yet begun to make critical distinctions about the sources of memory, whether facts, actions, stories, or personal experiences. These problems are consistent with their failure to identify a remembered episode specifically as one of personal experience. From a functional perspective, I suggest that these difficulties emerge during the transition from "private mind" to "open mind." The latter provides the possibility of representing one's own memory in verbal form and rerepresenting the verbal presentations of others, both residing within the same system of meaning.

When and Why Does the Self Appear in Memory?

The self is not salient in early memory, because all memory is self-memory; during the transition phase proposed, there is no distinction made between self-experience and another's report, presumably because it is not evident at first that such a distinction based on *source* of memory should be made. Memory is by definition about personal meaningful experience, whether that is of the most general, implicit, subconscious kind or explicit, declarative, and recallable. Until the distinction of "my experience" (not yours) is made, it is also not relevant to distinguish aspects of the memory that point to personal involvement, such as the particular time or place of the event. More significant, it is not relevant to retain a memory over the long term for its value in an emerging self-history. The distinction between one's own actions and those of others, of course, has been part of the child's sense of self since infancy.[13] The problem seems to be maintaining the uniqueness of the self-experience in distinction to the verbally reported experience of another.

The conversational data reviewed support the proposal that the sense of self in time emerges in interactions with social others. On the child's part, "raising memories" and reconstructing them for verbal representation takes practice, which is provided through exchanges with parents and others in conversations. It is not clear whether reminiscing practices enable the child to recapture the experience of the past or whether they rather make possible reconstruction and representation of previously dormant memory. It seems plausible that two developments are involved here: one is the accessing of the past in memory with the autonoetic awareness that Tulving talks about. The other is Bartlett's (1932) "turning around on one's own schemas"—that is, the possibility of reconstructing and representing from memory, making stories for self and others, with or without autonoesis. This dual developmental shift suggests the schism of personal memory into episodic and semantic as a source basis: mine versus yours. But as indicated earlier, the narrative/paradigmatic organization crosscuts this split.

Narrative Consciousness

Autobiographical memory is in an important sense the culmination of the development of the self in time. It is essentially private, but its structure and content are extensively influenced by social interactions and cultural norms. It situates the self within a cultural framework (e.g., school, work, home) that changes over time, but that through its continuity enables a person to understand the self as a continuing whole. That understanding, as seen in this chapter and the next (see also Nelson, 2001, 2003), depends to a large extent on how the external representations of the self are encountered and internalized. The substance and forms of such representations vary culturally and historically, with significant implications for how autobiographical memory is structured and maintained in relation to the ways that different social and cultural norms and institutions frame the roles of individuals (see Nelson, 2003, for further discussion).

Autobiographical memory emerges in the context of the child's interactions with social partners who talk about their experiences in the past, and who tell stories about other people's experiences (see Nelson and Fivush, 2004, for an extended argument). These same influences come to bear on the child's understanding of the differentiation of minds and memories, the sources of knowledge, and the intentions of people in the world. Through these verbal experiences, the child begins to move into a broader state of consciousness, a narrative consciousness that takes into account the motivations, goals, emotions, and beliefs of other people and differentiates the self from others, making a meaningful narrative of the remembered experience.

This proposal, that at the beginning, everything "known" or "remembered" is private and also phenomenally "real," begins to make sense of a great many of the puzzles observed in the transition from infancy to the school years. During this time, imagination elaborates on what is private but is no less "real" than anything else found in mind. The contents of memory are not "monitored," because the system "assumes" that anything there comes from experience. Although adults, too, experience some uncertainty about whose experience they remember, and whether an imagined incident (or a TV episode) is real, for the most part they live or try to live in the "real" world. The imaginative constructions of early childhood reflect the conditions of the developing meaning system; the undifferentiated system becomes vulnerable to the unrestricted impingements of ideas arriving from varied sources that are confusable with the experientially "real." It is to be expected that children exhibit evidence of these confusions, some seemingly benign, as in play and stories, or in the creation of imaginary characters and assumed self identities. Children's imaginations are clearly active during the early preschool years, but their "reality monitoring" is not yet in place. It is not surprising that children of this age may be deeply disturbed by frightening dreams; the monsters in their dreams may be as "real" as any other thought that enters their head. These are consequences of the one memory/meaning system that has its origin and strongest tie to reality in interactive experience in the world, but that becomes vulnerable to importations from tales heard from others, read in books, and seen on videos and television.

I propose that the child responds to a felt need for boundary setting by making an effort to block the "not-real," "not-my-experience," and the imagined from taking a place in the "known" realm of the mind's memory/meaning system, marking such content as "not mine." This produces a first differentiation that may evolve into the episodic/semantic memory distinction. In addition to differentiating memory into mine and others' and recognizing differences among characters in stories, the child must differentiate fiction from fact. These various "cuts" are not adequately covered by the episodic/semantic memory distinctions. Chapter 9 discusses these and further developments in more detail.

Conclusion

To recapitulate: The very young child inhabits a reality where all knowledge is individually attained through direct experience and is thus individual and private. It is difficult for us as adults to imagine the world as it may appear to the toddler, for whom what is known is only that derived from his or her own experience. Phenomenologically, the important transition is from a state of living in a singular reality, derived solely from direct experience, to the recognition of dual or multiple *simultaneously available* representations of reality, including one's own past and other people's experiences. In consequence of this move, development of mind and memory must involve radical changes in potentials for knowledge, belief, and self-understanding.

In the "one reality" view, the young child's mind and world agree perfectly: for the child, the habitat is as she finds it. The mind itself is transparent (in the way that air is for us and water is for the fish) and therefore not accessible to the child's reflection. Because there is identity between mind and world, there is no need and no place for a separate *concept* of mind or of belief, true or false, beyond the observed states of the real world in the present. As states of the world change over time, the record of how things are is simply overwritten—updated to accord with the present perceived reality. The idea of a specific past, in which previous experiences took place, and the idea of a specific future beyond the immediate present are inconceivable in the state of a single experience-based reality. This single view also projects the child's own view onto all others who share the child's current situation.

Once language is acquired as a representational mode, with which many different sorts of true, false, imagined, planned, or remembered states of the world and mind can be placed into the public realm, children experience these symbolic artifacts as representing real things, states, and events. The language representation from another person is able to pass over the internal-external barrier that initially exists between people; as a result, the internal representation of the verbal message enters into memory in much the same way that ordinary experience does. This situation has the potential to create confusion between one's own experience and the multiple possible realities represented in hearsay. There is a parallel here with the apparent confusion of toys in play with "real" versions of the objects (see Chapters 4 and 6). Toddlers apparently "see" at least some toy chairs, cars, and other objects as "real"; similarly, older preschoolers apparently "remember" an experience that they have only heard about as one that they have experienced. Such confusions seem inevitable unless others' reports are somehow made distinctive from one's own experiential memory. These related phenomena in early cognition require a developmental explanation such as I have proposed here.

In summary, language has a specific cognitive function in adult humans, an intramental representational function, that enables us to understand others' narratives, conversations, perspectives, and knowledge or belief representations, and at the same time to keep them separate from our own experiential system of knowing. When developed, this function makes it possible for the child to represent in her own mind what someone else has presented in linguistic form, and to keep that representation distinct from her own experientially based knowledge or memory. The picture presented here suggests a phenomenal world of the young preschooler that is both ontologically and epistemologically radically different from the adult's; our adult's view enables us to take an "outsider's" perspective on our own experience and thinking that is impossible for the young child. In the dynamic developmental perspective, experience itself changes when representational language becomes understood as instantiating different states in time and different personal perspectives.

8

Entering a Community of Minds

> Cultural mindsharing is our unique trait, linked
> as it is to our conscious capacity . . . our brain's
> evolving symbiosis with mindsharing cultures.
> ~ *Merlin Donald, 2001*

*T*HE IDEA THAT INFANTS and young children have "private minds" that gradually open up to the awareness of others' meanings as they become open to social and cultural messages through verbal and other symbolic means has been a major theme throughout this book. In this chapter I explore the ways in which the child's access to the beliefs and knowledge of the social-cultural world radically changes her perspective on the mental life of both others and herself, and the ways in which access to other people's knowledge, imaginative creations, and counterfactual speculations brings about a "symbiosis of brain and the mindsharing culture" (in Donald's terms). I think of these dramatic developments, taking place between about four and six years of age, as the initial entry into the "community of minds." I begin in this chapter with some background on the community of minds idea and then consider its relation to theory of mind as it is conceptualized in the current literature, both theoretically and in empirical studies. Later I turn to its application in contemporary work on children's cultural knowledge, such as concepts and theories of the biological domain. Together, these illustrate the opening of minds to what Donald calls "mindsharing," or, in the terms I used earlier, "meaning sharing." Needless to say, these developments involve a greatly expanded consciousness of the cultural world, the beginnings of cultural consciousness.

The Community of Minds

The idea of the community of minds emerged in studies of children's responses in theory of mind tasks (Nelson, Plesa, and Henseler, 1998; Nelson, Henseler, and Plesa, 2000; Nelson et al., 2003), which focused in part on children's drawing on their own experiential knowledge in making sense of the questions asked of them. See Table 8.1 for a sample of these responses. We interpreted the younger children's difficulties in terms consistent with those articulated in Chapter 7, namely that three-year-old children have not yet succeeded in escaping from the confines of the private mind and have not yet gained access to the concept that other minds have knowledge and beliefs different from their own. We believed that this move depended on experience with the language terms used to talk about mental states, which thereby introduced the child to a community of other minds (and in the process exposed the child's own mind). Conceptualizing the problem in this way cast unfavorable light on the narrow perspective of theory of mind based on a single milestone achievement in the preschool years, unanchored to any prior or subsequent developments. The community of minds construct broadens the perspective and situates the achievements in the social-cultural context that supports them.

The construct of "entering the community of minds" is viewed as an overarching conceptualization of the main developments of the latter part of the preschool period. It stands for the important aspects of "sharing minds" that Donald referred to. These include sharing the mental contents of one's own mind with others (e.g., "Daddy's going to take us to the zoo tomorrow"), interpreting other minds ("I think she doesn't like me"), sharing knowledge ("Mommy says you get colds from germs"), sharing beliefs ("Lying is a sin"), sharing counterfactuals and hypotheses ("Maybe the tooth fairy will come if I'm asleep"), and sharing imaginary worlds ("Mary Poppins can fly through the roof"). These examples are deliberately drawn from children's worlds to illustrate the prosaic nature of this powerful force. While these examples are childlike, they could be exchanged for more profound examples taken from philosophy, theology, and science or for the equally prosaic examples of everyday adult discourse.

Entering into a community of minds is a complex transactional process that takes place over a significant stretch of time (Nelson, 2005b;

Table 8.1   Examples of children's spontaneous reference to personal
experience in an "unexpected contents" theory of mind task

The child is shown a raisin box (with a picture of raisins on the cover) and asked
to say what she thinks is inside the box. Then the experimenter opens the box and
the child finds crayons inside. The box is then closed again and the child is asked,
"When you first saw the box, at the beginning, when it was closed, what did you
think was in the box?"

C age 3 years, 7 months
R: . . . what did you think was in the box?
C: There are crayons.
R: Didn't you say something else at first, at the beginning, when the box was
   closed?
C: But I have raisins at home.

C age 3 years, 3 months
R: . . . what did you think was in the box?
C: Raisins.
R: Right, but what is really inside the box?
C: A bakery store?
(Perhaps the child interprets the question as to where one finds raisins?)

C age 3 years, 5 months
R: . . . what did you think was in the box?
C: Hum, it's . . . I changed it . . . from raisins.
R: Why?
C: Because it's crayons.
R: But why did you think there were raisins in it?
C: Because I thought they were raisins and they weren't . . . in there was a
   magic trick.

C age 3 years, 9 months
R: . . . what did you think was in the box?
C: Crayons.
R: How did you know?
C: Because.
[R asks what a friend, who is shown the box when the box is closed, will say is
   in the box.]
C: I don't know.
R: What do you think, if he didn't look inside the box, what will he say is in
   the box?
C: I think he'll say cookies.
R: Why will he say that?
C: Because he likes cookies.

C age 3 years, 5 months
R: [On opening the box and revealing crayons] What happened?
C: Because we ate them all and there's no more.

C = child, R = researcher.

Nelson, Hensler, and Plesa, 2000; Nelson et al., 2003). The conceptual change involved is a product of social dialogical, linguistic experiences that lead children into a new experiential space, where mental activities are salient, enabling new access to previously uncomprehended sources of knowledge about the world around them. *Entering* involves coming into a new place, different from where one was previously; here the place is a *community*, that is, a space occupied by people who are related by common purposes and understandings. The community that one enters includes *minds* that communicate (thus the community). Minds differ—this is the point of communicating. Entering fully into a community where people evaluate actions on the basis of intentions, beliefs, goals, plans, and other mental properties, requires both experience with the social and cultural world—its people, activities, norms and values—and a means of communicating about these matters with other community members, who talk about them with each other, laying them open to public examination. Practice in representing the world in language, and interpreting others' representations of both action and consciousness are essential to making the move into this community, where knowledge of all kinds is available for sharing.

The central proposition of this chapter is that culture, linguistic discourse, narrative, conceptual knowledge, and human cognition are intersecting complexes that enter into mature participation in community life. The focus on communities invokes the importance of the cultural context of the child's encounter with the world of mind and language. Experiences in which the child begins to encounter and engage with cultural knowledge systems beyond the personal range also bear on the acquisition of the knowledge tapped in theory of mind tasks. Practices in cultural environments common to life in the preschool years may be particularly significant: symbolic play and games, and cultural narratives—stories, myths, folktales, fables, proverbs, gossip, and so on—all contribute to narrative consciousness and thus to becoming a member of the community of minds where these practices originate. It is obvious that these experiences depend on the use of representational language.

Indeed the community of minds depends entirely on the ability to talk about matters of interest to the members of the community—that is, to talk about things that are on their minds. Social relationships (gossip), political affairs, education, the natural world (weather, predators), economic affairs, literature and art, games and drama, reminiscences about the past, plans for the future, histories, myths, religious doctrine, and moral principles all enter into these discussions, and except for some taboo topics, such discussions are likely to be overheard by children. In other words, the kinds of matters that are on people's minds in the community are as broad as life itself. These matters are the various *contents* of belief, not the construct of belief itself. But it is precisely the fact that belief is always *about* something that is important; it is *not* a thing in itself. Children must come to understand the contents of belief, not the concept of belief. They acquire knowledge of procedures and actions that lead them to reason about whether someone could or does know about something that differs from their own state of knowledge about that thing. It is this differentiation of another's state of knowledge from one's own that is the key to success, according to theory of mind, but the differentiation can be made only on the grounds of particular contents, not on the grounds of abstract notions of belief (e.g., the child in the theory of mind scenario could have the same beliefs as the observer). Making these differentiations is a critical step in development, and not only for discerning false belief in theory of mind tasks.

Thus competence in representational language is essential for entering the community of minds (and for solving theory of mind problems). Moving between the external representations of others and one's own internal understandings, and externalizing one's own representations from internal sources, is perhaps the step that moves the child closest to full participation in the community of minds. This movement depends on engaging in the discourse practices in the everyday life of the child that are complemented by developments in the child's language, meaning, memory, and conceptual system.

Community of Minds Subsumes Theory of Mind

Theory of mind (ToM) is a shorthand expression for the knowledge that children of a certain age display about their own and other people's mental states, such as their beliefs. ToM studies attempt to determine the degree to which children discern that the belief in the head of another may differ from the reality that they themselves can see. Empirical research focuses particularly on beliefs that do not reflect the state of the real world—that is, when people entertain and act on "false be-liefs." The conception of ToM as an important achievement in chil-dren's social understanding and cognition, usually expected at four or four and a half years, is backed by an extensive body of research carried out over the past twenty years or so,[1] and to an amazing degree it has come to define social and cognitive development during this age pe-riod. The judgment as to whether a child has acquired a theory of mind or not is usually based on one or a few tasks, typically with the follow-ing structure: The child watches while a story character (doll, puppet, pictured sequence, or video) places a valued item into one of two or several containers and then leaves the scene. A second character moves the item from the original place (*a*) to a second location (*b*); the motive for moving it may be given or not. The original character returns to the scene "wanting" the item. The critical question is, Where does he or she look for it? If the answer is *a*, the child is said to display theory of mind; if the answer is *b*, the child does not yet "have" it. Children younger than four years almost always fall into the *b* category.

What exactly is involved in attaining theory of mind? As is the case with respect to the episodic memory problem (Chapter 7), children must come to understand that people's minds may differ in terms of the knowledge they have available in memory and the beliefs they enter-tain. For example, in the typical ToM scenario described, the first actor is represented as believing that his toy (or other possession) is in *a*, where he left it, whereas the observer child believes (knows) that it is now in place *b*. The observer must be able to simultaneously consider the two real places in view as beliefs of different people (self and actor). The understanding involved is based on memory for past experience, or often the lack of such experiential memory. Source of knowledge is again a major issue. Performance on source-monitoring tasks has in fact been related to success and failure on ToM tasks, as well as to memory.

The construct of theory of mind is now thoroughly established throughout psychology, and the findings from developmental studies leave little doubt that a developmental "milestone" is involved (Well-man, Cross, and Watson, 2001).[2] The interpretation of the phenomena reflected in the achievement of ToM is, however, another matter. The interpretation that I wish to challenge is the attribution of the develop-ment of a *concept* or *theory* of mind solely to the child's own increasingly powerful cognitive processes. Virtually all of the dominant theories make such an attribution, including modularity theories, theories of the development of executive control or metarepresentations, "theory theories" positing implicit theories in the child's head, simulation theories, and some versions of language theories (see Nelson, 1996; Astington and Baird, 2005, for discussion of these theories). Of course cognitive processes and structures become increasingly powerful over the course of childhood (in part because of the development of neural networks), but in my view, *by themselves*, they do not cause the child to form a concept or theory of mind that is then available for application to ToM tasks. Indeed, the fact that highly intelligent children without language experience, such as nonverbal autistic children or profoundly deaf children in hearing families, fail the critical tests at the standard ages implies that cognitive development alone is not the explanation for the appearance of ToM at the age of four years.

At the same time, as argued in Chapter 7, many developments of the experiential meaning system are of relevance to ToM, especially those of memory. Most have implications for the development of ToM, and the relations among them are therefore of interest in understanding how ToM emerges from other social pragmatic skills and what its influence is on future developments. Among these developments are the emerging distinctions among experiential self-memory, memory from indirect (mostly verbal) sources, and imagination. In the state of the original private mind, there is no awareness of "mind" because there is no distinction of mind/not mind or my self/mind versus another's self/ mind. It follows that there is no distinction made between the child's own knowledge state and that of anyone else. Awareness of these distinctions comes from the explicit contrast made possible through representational language. I argued in Chapter 7 that awareness of a past self establishes the continuity of self from past to present. Yet at the same time, distinguishing past from present may draw an arbitrary line that makes past actions irrelevant to the present, and thereby subject to "overwriting." With further development both states, past and present, may be entertained simultaneously.

Among the various theories of ToM referred to previously, "theory theories" appear to be gaining dominance. Theory theories presume that a novel cognitive developmental mechanism—implicit theory construction and revision, which was originally proposed to explain devel-

opment within basic knowledge domains such as physics and biology—
also explains social cognitive knowledge, including ToM. As I noted in
Chapter 1, there are serious problems with such proposals. For example, how an implicit theory could be constructed in infancy or early
childhood (i.e., what cognitive processes might be involved) and how it
might relate to explicit theory construction or explicit knowledge in
general (e.g., does the individual eventually gain conscious access to the
theory specification?) are not addressed. Some writers seem to take implicit theory construction to be essentially the same as general conceptual processes (and therefore a harmless metaphoric usage), but others
(Gopnik, 1993a, 1993b; Gopnik and Wellman, 1994; Wellman, 1990)
make the larger claim that a theory, implicit or explicit, is coherent
(noncontradictory) within a domain, is characterized by causal relations between concepts, is subject to revision in light of new data, and
that ToM is such a theory. These are strong claims.

Bogdan (2003) notes that interpreting the goals of others—his take
on ToM—is more like experimenting than like theory, and he argues
that there is little evidence that ToM is theorylike. What is going on in
theory of mind tasks, as well as in the everyday contexts that the tasks
are supposed to represent, is that one person is attempting to interpret
what is in the mind of another in order to predict what the other will
do, or to interpret the discourse within or about the situation. This is
not the same as mind reading, to which it is so often likened. Nothing
guarantees that one person can correctly interpret another, even in the
ToM paradigm. Every "reading" depends on the interpretation of external evidence from a person's behavior. For example, the protagonist
of the ToM scenario may have been told by someone where his toy had
been moved to, without the observer's knowledge. Some of the putative
cognitive bases of ToM, such as metarepresentation and source monitoring, may be necessary to successful interpretation, but they do not
guarantee success. If interpretation is the process involved in understanding the goals and intentions of others, the bases for interpretive
success deserve primary research attention.

Reinterpreting Theory of Mind

In his essay on the "interpretive mind," Bogdan (2003) rejects the "men-
talism" and "theorism" of mainstream discussions of ToM, noting that

they reflect a "spectator" view of one individual dispassionately looking out on the world and forming theories about the minds of self and others. He argues that interpreting others is not about the mind but about human practices and the social skills needed for participating in those practices. He proposes that ToM primarily involves skill in interpreting the goals of other people; in the first instance, the capacity to view the actions and expressions of others in terms of their goals *in relation to one's own.* From this pragmatic perspective of "involvement," Bogdan sees basic interpreting as a practice that was selected in the evolution of the species for its advantage in achieving individual goals. Like many others, including especially Tomasello (1999), who emphasized intention reading beginning late in the first year of infancy, Bogdan sees the development of the social-psychological skills of ToM as beginning in the intensive psycho-social conditions of mental sharing in infancy (e.g., shared attention). Experiences in language and culture take these basic skills beyond the interpretation of situated actions. This account is consistent with my emphasis on the role of language in ToM developments (Nelson, 1996, 2005b).

Although Bogdan begins the story with an evolved interpreting "module" available from late infancy (and probably shared with other higher primates), he continues it with two additional developments in human ontogeny. The first is what he terms "metarepresentation," but he uses the term in a different way than it is commonly used by ToM theorists (e.g. Perner, 1991). In Bogdan's sense the interpreter (the child) represents to himself observable clues (from seeing and speaking) about the observed other's representations of the state of the world. The interpreter's representing of representations thus constitutes metarepresentation. This level of interpretive skill serves in "situated interpretation"—that is, in the here and now of ongoing activities, such as those in typical ToM tasks. Beyond this level, Bogdan posits a stage of "reconstruction" of people's engagement in practices that requires thinking, planning, and anticipating the goals and actions of others outside the immediate situational context. Reconstruction thus involves social-cultural knowledge of the kind that is displayed in scripts, canonical actions, and social norms. Reconstruction is presumed to develop during adolescence.

Bogdan's pragmatic position stands as a welcome alternative to the reigning theories of theory of mind, and as a helpful perspective on its development. My position on ToM shares many of the same assumptions, specifically the pragmatic and experiential basis of the developing skills. However, I view the child's entry into the interpretive mind space of the later preschool years (the ToM complex) within a symbolic cultural context that embraces the child and sometimes engulfs him in confusion rather than clarity (as indicated in Chapter 7). The community of minds construct aims to set ToM into this framework that interconnects mind and culture. This view, from the child's experiential perspective, is complex and multidimensional; there is much for the child to muddle through before being able to move on to the joys of middle childhood and the further possibilities of reflective reconstruction that Bogdan envisions taking place in adolescence.

The Community of Minds Perspective on Theory of Mind

Any theory of ToM needs to be related to the overall course of social and cognitive development during the crucial toddler and preschool years, and to the preceding as well as succeeding developments, preferably in a developmental systems framework (Carpendale and Lewis, 2004). Theory of mind as a social cognitive achievement, however, has been studied mainly as a discrete accomplishment of the preschool years. As others have also argued (Bogdan, 2003; Carpendale and Lewis, 2004; Chandler, 1988), this achievement is but a symptom of a far-ranging and profound developmental change that permeates the child's social, emotional, and cognitive life and presages further changes to come. I argue that this change is fostered by, and is to a large extent dependent on, the emergence of the representational function of language that provides a new communicative bridge to other people's minds as well as a powerful alternative mode of representing the world to oneself. Thus, results from the studies of ToM are best viewed from the perspective of the expansion of consciousness that takes place between three and six years. Representational language—conveying and reflecting on knowledge, imaginative constructions, reminiscence, explanations, and other social and cultural discourse, as well as cognitive functions—leads the child into narrative consciousness and thus toward entry to the community of minds.

The assumption that during their first ten years children are developing toward membership in a human community of minds broadens the concept of theory of mind from something that children invent for themselves (but that just happens to agree with everyone else's theory) to a cultural conception of what it is to be a person within a human community. The metaphor emphasizes two facets of this development. First, that what is at stake is understanding—and thus basing predictions and explanations on—*minds*, in the plural. Rather than putting the emphasis on the universal Mind, the emphasis is on minds that interact with and also differ from one another, in addition to having certain similarities of structure and content. Ultimately, understanding differences among mind states requires understanding the sources of differences among people—their backgrounds, personalities, relationships, and histories. The main reason for "reading" minds is to interpret the difference between others' and one's own orientation to the facts of the world, based on implicit goals. Indeed this is the first step toward entry into the community, and it begins as children are exposed to what other people think and know in contrast to what they themselves think and know.

The second critical facet of development addressed by the metaphor is the place of the *community*. In work on theory of mind, typically the problem is posed as one of understanding the beliefs of other individuals on the basis of their actions, or interpreting their actions on the basis of their beliefs. This is surely a useful component of social life, but as Bogdan has argued, belief is a weak link in the causal chain of action. Still, differences in beliefs and the sources of beliefs are important. The truly critical sense of belief is far broader than transient mental states: it involves the myriad sources of beliefs and reasons for doubting beliefs; it involves beliefs that are broadly held, whether held to be wrong or held to be the truth or held to be immoral. These are often matters discussed among adults, and sometimes in adult-child conversations; they are the stuff of the cultural community. These matters are where minds interact and come to agreement and disagreement, and where matters of possibly great significance may result, for example, in the case of religious beliefs that bring one community into conflict with another.

As previously argued, to enter into the community of minds one must differentiate one's own private view of the world from others' view and join in the common but variable mind space there. The key question then is, how does that differentiation come about, in particular and in general? Early in development, memory is entirely dependent on individual experience for knowledge accumulation, but living in a world in which knowledge is symbolically shared requires establishing distinctions among the sources of knowledge (Chapter 7). Thus a more differentiated system must be developed, one that distinguishes between "mine" and "yours," imagined states (including future projections) and real states, past states and present states, direct experience and verbal representations. Practice in making these distinctions is critical. The individual's growing narrative consciousness, which incorporates these many differentiations, provides a basis for engaging in theory of mind problems and makes it possible for him or her to participate more fully in the community of minds. In turn, this enables the move to a new level of cultural consciousness and, in the process, to more completely differentiating states of the mind. Only when this process is well under way is the concept of "mind" likely to come into question, together with the salience of belief states such as "think" and "know."

The advance in understanding marked by success in ToM tasks hinges on experience with other people's reported experiences and the distinctions made between personal experience and others' experience or, in the case of third-person reports, between one person's experience and another's (Chapter 7). The differentiation of time in terms of past, future, and present, and the differentiation of memory into self (episodic) and other (semantic), must be extended to third persons as related in narratives or observed in life. Experience with these distinctions is found in personal narratives as well as in fictional stories, which provide a rich source of information about the complexities of characters, their actions, and their motives.

Even as adults, we often assume that other people with whom we are communicating share our beliefs and background knowledge; we are often surprised to find that we differ (Birch and Bloom, 2003). The very young child is different only in assuming that everyone has the same knowledge. Usually we discover that others' knowledge differs from ours when they tell us it does. Other times, their evident goals and actions may cause a breach and a resulting effort to think about what knowledge they may be acting on. Young children learn the same way, from what others tell them; thus they gradually learn the general principle that people differ, and they also learn to track such differences when there are salient clues to be followed.

Perhaps the most important distinction between the community of minds view and other current views of ToM is that the burden of constructing the model of minds does not rest on the child's individual cognitive powers; rather, it is a gift from the larger community, which incorporates the constructs into its language and its talk about the concerns of people within the community. The child must do work to unpack the gift, which consists of many layers of concepts wrapped within one another, but the rewards are there for the taking if the child is able to try out the ideas for herself. Thus the process of entering a community of minds is necessarily a collaborative one, enabling the child to enter fully into human cultural life. Its beginnings in the early years prepares the child for participation in as yet unanticipated cultural communities in the future.

Toward Cultural Consciousness: Conceptual Knowledge

The same collaborative, constructive process that applies to the concept of minds and their functions applies to the myriad other concepts that the child meets and acquires from the cultural surround of childhood, many of less significance but all of utility in becoming a cultural person. Cultural knowledge, like language, exists outside the individual, in other heads and in other places, such as books. The community of minds grants access to these sources and resources. As discussed in previous chapters, concept making begins in infancy and progresses with the acquisition of language, which combines individual experience and shared knowledge. What children absorb from parents and books is then reconstructed as personal knowledge and reappears in their own linguistic productions. Such a process is familiar in educational settings (even graduate school), as when students reconstruct ideas that they at first failed to grasp, and in the process come to think of those ideas as their own discoveries. I believe that such "discoveries" reflect a common cognitive process that begins in the preschool years.

Earlier chapters discussed "private" or "personal" concepts that emerge from meaning processes, beginning in infancy, and emphasized that these experientially based concepts were often—even usually—different from those held by adults. Concept making is subjective, yet language users home in on shared conventional concepts for the purposes of symbolic communication. For many concepts, such as the abstract concepts of beliefs, mind, and community, young children begin to construct personal concepts to match the conventional ones of the language from the language itself, as it is used. Although they use words related to these and other abstractions, young children often lack any concept related to those held by adults for the same words. The process by which they begin to use, understand, and construct concepts connected to abstract words was outlined in Chapter 6. The broader concern here is how children's spontaneous concepts are structured and what the source of that structure might be. Most investigators begin with concepts about the natural world (i.e., "natural kinds"), such as concepts of animals. A brief review of this research history and existing theories will set the stage for a discussion of how concepts emerge in the community of minds through collaborative construction, proposed here as the basic process of children's concept acquisition.

The toddler's spontaneous activity of sorting objects was noted earlier (Chapter 4), together with the results of Mandler and McDonough's (1998) research indicating that infants and toddlers form "global" categories based on the events that different items could take part in. Children's early conceptualizations about "kinds" are organized from two sources: their own action-based experience with natural objects, artifacts, and toy replicas, and their experience with verbal and pictorial sources. Children tend to meld these sources rather than keeping them separate. This melding has continuing implications for the development of conceptual knowledge in terms of what Vygotsky called spontaneous concepts and the conventional (or as Vygotsky termed them, "scientific") concepts acquired from the culture at large, especially in educational settings (Nelson, 1995b).

There are two basic questions with respect to the child's conceptual base: What concepts and conceptual structures are accessible to young children? And where do concepts come from? In pursuing answers to these questions, a standard experimental approach involves children's sorting of "kinds" (e.g., cow, elephant, fish) into category "types" (animal, vehicle). This practice has a long history in the investigation of children's (mis)understanding of concepts and their hierarchical taxonomic structures, beginning with Piaget and Vygotsky and continuing through the modern era (Nelson, 1996). Research on concept formation in young children, on logical concepts (Inhelder and Piaget, 1958), on similarity relations in abstract categories (Bruner, Olver, and

Greenfield, 1966), and on taxonomic relations (Rosch, Mervis, Gray, Johnson, and Boyes-Braem, 1976) indicated the apparent conclusions that preschool children were poor at identifying and using relevant properties for concept formation and flexible concept use. They could form complexes but not logical classes (see also Vygotsky, 1962); they focused on perceptual features rather than functional features, and on concrete-level categories (Rosch's Basic Level) rather than higher-order abstract taxonomies or subordinate-level differentiations. In all, they were not very good at categorization and conceptualization tasks.

Vygotsky was alone among theorists in maintaining that the groups that children formed in sorting tasks reflected organized cognitive structures, just not the same ones adults used (Vygotsky, 1962). They tended to relate things in terms of everyday functions rather than similarities. For example, they might put a spoon with a bowl rather than with a fork, or a hammer with a nail rather than with another tool. Indeed, in many cases in which free sorting of a variety of objects was the task used, it became clear that children did not prefer perceptual similarity over functional relations. However, often the tasks offered only perceptual features as a basis for sorting (e.g., color, shape, or size) and thus presented no opportunity for alternative, functional choices.

Conceptual Knowledge in an Oral Culture

Conversing with young children is carried out orally, not in writing. Unless they are among the few who become skilled readers during the preschool years, children develop within and remain members of an oral culture embedded within the literate one. Walter Ong (1982), a distinguished scholar of the humanities, considered the many ways in which an oral society differs from a literate one. He emphasized that in an oral society, all knowledge, true or false, that is not gained from direct experience in the world is conveyed personally, from one individual to another. Ong argued that the constraints of the oral world are such that sustained thought is tied to communication with others, through dyadic or group discussions. By virtue of this constraint, conceptual thought tends to be *aggregative*—assembling various pieces of related information over time—in contrast to the analytic characteristics of written texts that attempt to "spell out" meanings in complete, complex sentences and break down complex configurations and reassemble them in terms of logical relations. Aggregative thinking may incorporate numerous bits of personal experience that influence the perceived meaning of a word or phrase, and that are conveyed with the word in communicative contexts, rather than reflecting the assumption, in literate cultural contexts, that words have precise definitional meanings. Concepts are derived from *participatory* interactions in oral settings rather than from objectively distanced literate sources. In other words, oral cultures operate one to one, or in small groups; meanings are shared by participants in common situations.[3] This is the nature of the child's cultural world.

The child's participatory involvement in activity—in contrast to objectively distanced observation—is precisely what has been the object of analysis in this book. Children gather their experiential knowledge through participation in the activities of the world, including the verbal discourse about the world that swirls around them. What they make of what they hear is influenced by what they know from experience, as well as by the activities and circumstances in which they hear it. If it is not seen as connected with the interests of their lives, it does not take a place in their meaning memory. That said, I recognize that children's interests are far-reaching, especially where people important to them are concerned, and their interests are also affected by the accumulation of experiences that they have shared and have heard about in earlier experiences. It is the uninterpretable and the meaningless that leaves no enduring trace in the expanding meaning memory.

The aggregative nature of conceptualization may be thought of as a process of encountering concepts that are embedded in highly contextual and situated discourse. Concepts used only in speech rather than in the external medium of writing tend to be complexive rather than analytically composed and may be difficult for a child to grasp. Speech is a dynamic, evanescent medium; the listener must be quick to catch the meaning of what is said before it fades away. Although talking with others makes a necessary contribution to the child's acquisition of knowledge and developing conceptions of the world, much of what is meant to be conveyed by adults is not "heard" by the young child. These observations are related to Vygotsky's notion of the importance of scaffolding in learning. For example, in Bruner's (1983) analysis of a mother teaching her young child to name items in "reading" a book, it is necessary for the "tutor" to be patient in repeating lessons and advancing slowly up the child's "zone of proximal development" (Chapter 5). Scaffolding does not result in the child's internalizing of the adult's concept or skill; rather, it provides a structure that the child can hang on to while constructing his or her own understanding of the task or concept. In time, the child must kick over the scaffold and proceed to construct understandings on her own, using the acquired structure as an internal scaffold for further meaning.

The idea that the oral culture surrounds the child's learning experiences is also related to the significance of externalizing knowledge, which was emphasized in earlier chapters. When the child is able to produce an external representation of thought for another, the other person is then able to aid in the reconfiguration of the child's internal thought processes. This is an important aspect of the ubiquitous questioning that children often engage in during the two-to-four- or five-year-old age (or older). Such questions are strong indications of children's expanding universe of interest (see Callanan, 1992, for provocative examples and analyses). By four years, the world in the child's perspective of interest is no longer so narrowly confined to the child's own view as it was initially but is composed of a variety of things and events that pose causal puzzles to be investigated. Children's questions indicate that they are mentally instigating investigations of the causal structure of aspects of the world, both psychological and physical. The child's accumulating conceptual knowledge is amplified by access to the community of minds, where institutions devoted to their questions reside (e.g., schools, libraries, computers, experts). This leads us to the next question: what is the nature of the child's conceptual system that organizes new information of this kind?

From Conceptual Deficiency to Theoretical Facility

Despite the deficiencies found in concept-sorting studies, it was clear that children learned words for category members at different levels of taxonomic generality, for example, learning *animal* as well as *dog, cat,* and *lion.* Then what was the conceptual basis for their words? Keil (1987) proposed a "characteristic to defining shift" in children's understanding of categories, suggesting that younger children attend to the salience and relevance of characteristic features rather than "deeper" qualities, such as defining functions. The question of what is "deeper" and when children are sensitive to it, in contrast to "superficial" qualities, now drives the discussion. Three candidates for such deeper qualities are function, cause, and essence. Each has received considerable attention in contemporary research.

The functions of things that children focus on in their earliest concepts tend to be rather obvious actions and roles in events (therefore not "deep"?), such as noises that animals make or the movement of machines. These are functions from the child's perspective, a perspective that was beautifully illustrated in Ruth Krauss's (1952) children's book *A Hole Is to Dig*, a collection of preschooler's responses to requests for the definitions of objects (e.g., "What is a hole?").[4] The child's view of functions is not the same as the adult's, any more than the child's view of the world around him is the same as the adult's. In fact, function may be very apparent and concrete or very nonobvious and abstract. Young children's focus on function in word learning has now been newly demonstrated in a series of well-designed studies (Kemler Nelson, 1999), but only when the function is salient to the child.

The current focus on function among concept theorists, related to the idea that conceptual categories are organized in terms of theoretical structures, views function in a more causal, internal, mechanistic, design, or intentional sense (Medin and Ortony, 1989). P. Bloom (1996) claims that terms for artifacts are understood by both children and adults in terms of intended function or design, but for children's concepts this claim must be restricted to those intentions that they might be able to infer or understand. A young child might understand that a pitcher is for pouring milk without the accompanying insight that someone designed it for that purpose—although the child might understand that her mother uses it for that purpose. These diverse relations are important in understanding children's meanings and deserve much further investigation (McDonough, 2002). In the end, it still seems true that children often focus on the role of objects in activities—that is, their function—a "deeper" understanding of the meaning of the object-concept than its perceptual features may reveal.

Causal relations are often related to function in the sense of what an object causes to happen. For example, a light switch may cause the light to go on, and that is its function, but of course that is only a proximal cause. Tomasello and Call (1997) reviewed evidence that humans—including human children, but not other primates—focus on the underlying (nonobvious) causes of phenomena. That children are sensitive to causal relations is obvious in their persistent "why" questions, as well as in some scattered investigations in the literature. Most recently, Gopnik and her colleagues have shown that young children are very interested in causal relations among phenomena (what makes things happen) and are insightful in making connections (Gopnik et al., 2004). The idea that young children focus on function and causal relations (both nonapparent in static forms and two-dimensional representations) is very much in line with the experiential, pragmatic basis of children's knowledge and their search for meaning, as are essentialist theories (up to a point).

Much research and theorizing today has turned the tables on the traditional emphasis on conceptual deficiencies in early childhood and now focuses on early and deep conceptual understanding as revealed in function and causal relations. At present there appear to be two widespread general ideas about early concepts: they are organized in theorylike structures, and they are based on underlying essences. These suggest a basic cognitive disposition that may match or contribute to more mature conceptual structures, to wit: (a) theories are presumed to be adequate structures but need filling in and reconfiguration with new data; (b) underlying essences may be of different kinds; children's essences may not match those of adults' conventional concepts. I have argued against the theory position throughout these chapters, but the emphasis now is on the child's presumably spontaneous construction of theories within well-defined domains, for example, the domain of biology (Carey, 1985). This emphasis involves a shift from a focus on the *structure* of categories to a focus on the *content* of conceptual knowledge. We can understand this shift in terms of the historical shift from an emphasis on the logic of categories (Inhelder and Piaget 1958) to the cognitive organization of memory, language, and conceptual knowledge. In the course of this movement, the emphasis has turned to analyzing *domains* of knowledge, identifying children's theories within domains, and identifying their essential underlying causal components and relations.

The New Look: Induction and Essence

Susan Gelman's comprehensive studies of children's conceptual knowledge investigate their focus on the "essence" of natural kinds, such as animals. In her book *The Essential Child* (2003), she lays out the background and theory behind the extensive research she and her colleagues have done on this topic, as well as a clear analysis of the conceptual issues. As Gelman sees it, the major turn in studies of children's concepts came with the use of an induction paradigm, which replaced the sorting studies used in older work. She cites Susan Carey's (1985) work on children's understanding in the biological domain of natural kinds as the initiator of this line of study.

In Carey' research, a child was informed that some "kind" (e.g., a worm) had some part or performed some action, and then the child was asked whether another kind also had the part or did the action. For example, the child might be told, "People have 'odems' [nonsense word] inside their bodies. Here's a kitten [or a whale or mosquito]; does it have an 'odem' inside?" The task was designed to help researchers understand the relations within the child's putative theoretical structure of the biological world. How related to people are kittens or whales in the child's mental theory? The series of questions enabled the researcher to map out the relationships. Carey's conclusion was that the younger child's biological world was more like a psychological one, dependent on its relation to the characteristics of people, and that it underwent theoretical change during the elementary school years.

In Gelman and Markman's (1986) original work with the induction paradigm, children were first shown a picture of a target creature, for example a bird. They were then shown a different bird (one that did not resemble the first) and a different kind of thing, a bat (that did resemble the target). The child was told that the first bird builds a nest (or lays eggs) and then was asked if each of the others does this. The child was thus faced with a choice between the same kind that looks different and the different kind that looks the same. On the basis of much work that followed this study, Gelman was able to claim that children do not conceptualize natural kinds on the basis of appearance only, but on the basis of some nonobvious "essence" that determines their identity. There is some evidence that children believe that "innards" determine essence, but in any event they seem confident that just because it looks like a duck, it is not necessarily a duck (it might be an ugly duckling and turn into a swan). Gelman's claim, while fairly strong, must be restricted to older preschoolers, however. Children of five years or younger are capable of being persuaded that magic or an operation can turn one kind of animal into another. At the same time, younger chil-

dren believe that if a calf has a cow mother and a cow father, the calf
will grow up to be a cow. This assumption reflects a generative belief
system that overrides difference of appearance and social influence (e.g,
through being raised in a different family) for virtually all characteristics of the natural world of animals.

There is unfortunately a potential downside to essentialist thinking
in both children and adults. Gelman summarizes Hirshfeld's work on
children's understanding of race, indicating that children tend to treat
different races as "natural kinds" and to assert, for example, that a boy
born in China of Chinese parents but brought up in the United States
by American parents will resemble his birth parents in behavior as well
as in physical characteristics. But is it necessarily the case that children
will hold these beliefs? This depends in part on whether we believe that
essentialism is an innate cognitive disposition that extends to all natural-kind concepts, or whether it results from cultural learning.[5]

Astuti, Solomon, and Carey (2004) have addressed a related question
in a cross-cultural study carried out with children and adults in Madagascar. They asked children and adults directly about the traits that
children would have if they were born into one distinctive and familiar
group of people and raised in another group, using a number of adoption scenarios. The study and its results are too complex to summarize
here, but their conclusion may be stated as follows. Among the Vezo (a
social group in Madagascar) adults and children have different theoretical structures about these concepts. In particular, adults hold to a "social group identity" theory as well as a biological generation theory applicable to different traits, while the views of Vezo children are subject
to the "endogenous constraint" that species kind is fixed at birth, en-
tailing "essential" group characteristics; but among these essential characteristics, the children do not differentiate between biological and
other traits. At adolescence, however, they reconstruct theories closer
to those held in the adult community.

These alleged theories and constraints have consequences for how
people view members of groups outside their own, however identified,
and the prospects for social learning and relearning of social biases.
Astuti and colleagues propose that a "constrained conceptual constructive" process enables children to learn the cultural categories of their
group, under general cognitive constraints on categories. At this very
general level, this is a reasonable hypothesis, but of course the success

of the proposal rests on what is assumed as constraint and what the nature of the constructive processes may be.[6]

"Root capacities" underlying essentialism were identified by Gelman (2003) to address the question of whether essentialism is an innate constraint on concepts, and if so, on which concepts. She concluded that a collection of these root capacities contribute to the predisposition to essentialize, but that each is neither necessary nor sufficient in itself. These are reproduced in Table 8.2. This kind of analysis is helpful in differentiating what otherwise seems a rather opaque principle to expect the child to rely on in the acquisition of cultural knowledge about natural kinds.[7]

As Gelman notes, there is little evidence for essentialism before the age of four years, primarily because the research has not been extended in that direction, although children clearly have concepts related to the natural world prior to that age. The key question that Astuti and colleagues were asking was, what does the child bring to the acquisition of concepts of the natural world? And yet they were not able to include children younger than five years in their study (most were of school age, up to twelve years). The limitations on age, together with the dimensions of essentialism and the identifying characteristics of knowledge that contribute to them, suggest a different developmental hypothesis. Fascinating as the results of these studies may be, they cannot tell us whether a child is "bringing" to the acquisition problem "endogenous constraints," and of what kind. Children have been developing in a social, cultural, and historical context for four or five years by the time they come to participate in the researchers' tasks. They have been talking for two to three years. Critically, for two or three years they have been listening to the talk of their elders and participating in conversations; listening to stories; watching TV programs and videos; attending preschool; going to museums, Disney World, and other "worlds" and "lands"; having pets; growing flowers; visiting friends and relatives. And probably much more. This is what a child today brings to the research lab. It is probably not very well organized, not well sorted out between "my" knowledge and "your" knowledge, and very "gappy," but there is a lot there to draw on in addition to any endogenous constraints that may help them to organize knowledge. And as we found in analyzing children's responses to questions about their answers to ToM inquiries (Table 8.1), children often spend a good deal of

Table 8.2 Root capacities underlying essentialism

Root capacities		Essentialist instantiations
Appearance/reality distinction	→	Nonobvious properties as core
Induction from property clusters	→	Inferences about the unknown
Causal determinism	→	Causal properties as core
Tracking identity over time	→	Importance of origins
Deference to experts	→	Acceptance of category anomalies
Above, collectively	→	Realist assumption about categories and names
		Boundary intensification
		Immutability; stability over transformations
		Importance of nature over nurture

Source: Gelman (2003), Table 11.2, p. 314.

time and effort in organizing their prior knowledge for public consumption (Nelson et al., 2003).[8]

The implicit assumption behind the goal of determining what a child brings to a concept inquiry is that, whatever that is, it is not a product of learning. This assumption is often put to an experimental test, as it was in Gelman's research. Analysis of mother-child interactions around a specially designed picture book found that there were next to no references to kinship, origins, and so on in the mothers' talk. The conclusion seemed clear: children don't learn those ideas from parent talk. Of course, Gelman and other researchers are well aware that this situation does not represent the whole of a child's socializing experience; still, the implied conclusion is that the child is constructing such concepts on her own. This brings us to the critical point: can learning in the community of minds shed light on the acquisition of conceptual knowledge and the differentiation of the developing meaning-memory knowledge system?

Learning in the Community of Minds

Two general questions arise in relation to constructing domain-specific conceptual knowledge, a special interest for children in the later preschool years, and one of considerable concern to educators. One question is, what are the processes of learning and development involved? The other, what is the nature of the knowledge that accrues? The two questions are naturally related.

Many psychologists have constrained notions of teaching and learning tied to their conceptions of the educational process. In the psychological literature, "learning" continues to be held in contrast to "inborn" without further distinction (Pinker, 2002, and many others). One distinguished developmental psychologist stated in a recent article on education that there are two kinds of learning. One (obviously favored) is engaged in through the child's natural exploration and investigation of causal relations in the world. The other involves the practice of things already learned, that is, acquiring skills, such as reading, a type of learning that is seen as dull and difficult. Despite its long history (central to education critiques of the 1960s), this dichotomy is surely a narrow view, and one that is bound to cripple the investigation of how children acquire conceptual knowledge. It ignores the fact that such knowledge is attained through cultural learning, which by definition is collaborative (Rogoff, 2003; Tomasello, Kruger, and Ratner, 1993).

Another view endorses cultural learning of conceptual knowledge: "Human knowledge is socially situated and culturally constructed, that is, children acquire it from interacting with their elders and peers and by participating in their culture" (Astuti, Solomon, and Carey, 2004, p. 153). Yet the focus is "on *what the child brings* to the process of learning within this structured and scaffolded field of relations" (p. 155). Without considering contributions to what the child brings from the long social and cultural journey from birth to age four, five, or six, this focus can yield little that is definitive. We are, of course, interested in what kinds of organizing properties the brain and the cognitive system are capable of and how children apply these in the face of meaningful experiential data. All of those working on problems related to this area make explicit and implicit assumptions that vary as to their emphasis on innate complex content or elementary process. The evidence from the real lives of children about what and how they learn deserves to be accounted for. The least one should expect from a developmental investigation is a reasoned hypothesis (based on available research) about what children of four or five years have learned of cultural concepts and how they have learned, with what cultural aids and tools.

Collaborative Construction

The idea of collaborative construction was sketched in Nelson (1985) around the topic of acquiring taxonomic category knowledge. This model schematizes the successive "rounds" of mother and child contributions occurring over extended periods of time; there is no intensive teaching or quick learning (no fast mapping). The process begins when one of the two (usually the parent) puts a bit of knowledge on the (figurative) table and the other (the child) picks it up, examines it, and determines whether it is meaningful and worth holding on to, thus entering into a meaning-making process with knowledge already in hand. Yes or no, partial or complete, the process continues on another encounter with the same bit of knowledge. At this point, the child has more to offer in terms of memory of the prior encounter and considers the bit of knowledge more carefully, perhaps taking it in and sorting it into a place in memory. On the next turn, the child may take out the bit of knowledge and match it with something new that the parent has said or something new or old in the environment. The parent takes up what the child offers and provides it with more context, which the child may or may not accept. And so on. The sequence is slow and uneven and extends over a significant period of time. An important addition to this model is the reflexive period that follows some of the collaborative interactions. At these times the child may use the interactive meanings derived as resources in her own construction of a complex conceptual structure. Then at the next encounter the child can be seen to "bring" something not previously there.

The outcome of this kind of exchange is hypothesized to be the building up of organized concepts that do not copy those of the parent or of the culture at large, but that are constructed anew by the child and added to in different ways than those from which the material was drawn, such as from other encounters in different contexts. Different relations from other areas of conceptual knowledge are also formed. Figure 8.1 illustrates the interactive process (Nelson, 1985). This figure includes a symbolization of the conceptual structures that exist in cultural forms (e.g., in books), as well as the putative mental representation of the adult interactor (a partial instantiation of the cultural model). The third row shows possible representations in speech to the child. The last row shows the connected bits of the child's relevant concept components prior to interactions with the adult, and the fourth row indicates the child's partial construction in response to the adult's representations. This schematization is designed to illustrate how the child "makes sense" of discourse interactions around topics of interest and incorporates them into developing models of her own that

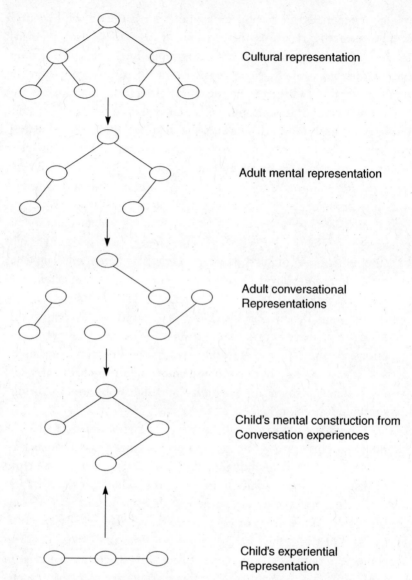

Figure 8.1 Levels of representations of knowledge structures, as received by the child: categorical relations from cultural representations, as in texts; partial representations in adults' concepts; implicit and explicit representations in conversations; and the resulting constructions created by the child, using experiential knowledge in conjunction with conversational experience. Based on diagram in Nelson (1985, 1996).

are never exact copies of either the adult's representations or the cultural models from which they are drawn. In this process, unlike in the scaffolding model derived from Vygotsky's work, the acquisition of new structures is a by-product of interactions, not a prop for teaching. Guiding the child's organization of meaning are the paradigmatic and syntagmatic structures that also characterize the structure of language (Nelson, 1982; see Chapter 6).

Both experiential categories and conventional taxonomies are collaboratively constructed with adults through verbal exchanges. In the case of slot-filler categories, the child's direct experience with different items that belong in different scripts or event contexts is amplified and commented on during the experience, as well as prior to and out of context of the experience. Parents, teachers, and others also talk with young children about the less directly experienced conceptual knowledge that children display, for example, about animals. Such discussions often begin in infancy, as children look at picture books and name animals while parents provide a variety of facts about them, including their classifications (e.g., "a penguin is a funny kind of bird," Adams and Bullock, 1986, p. 187). To study this process, Adams and Bullock used a specially constructed picture book with typical and atypical items from six generic categories (dog, cat, horse, bird, bear, deer) arranged in sets that showed either all items of the same kind together, or all kinds together, or a set with a single "intruder" of a different kind. Children of three ages, fourteen, twenty-six, and thirty-eight months, participated with their mothers. (These children were up to two years younger than those studied in a similar context by Gelman.)

An important finding from the Adams and Bullock study was that the parents used language that emphasized generic families (e.g., dog, animal), providing information about the relation of atypical items to the generic category, and also providing functional information (e.g., "lives at the North Pole," "they swim and catch fish"). Wrote the authors: "Children are told that bats are mammals, penguins are birds, and Newfoundlands are dogs. In addition they are *taught* features that can help them avoid assimilating these exemplars to more or equally compelling categories (bats to *bird* . . .) or features that provide evidence of family membership (e.g., Newfoundlands bark, just like other dogs)" (Adams and Bullock, 1986, p. 161). They also found that mothers tended to provide explanations drawing on experiences from the child's life, particularly with younger children. For example, "That's a penguin. Do you remember when we saw him at the zoo? And how funny he walked?" (p. 188). But even with children at three years of age, parents were already also emphasizing more semantic—that is, symbolic—information.

This study provides a rich lode of material for understanding the nature of collaborative construction of categorical and other conceptual knowledge in early childhood through everyday interactions with parents. It helps to counter the implication from the essentialists' work that children are not taught what they need to know about the immutability of kinds and must therefore invent it for themselves. The children who participate in studies of concepts and categories at age four or later can be expected to have already garnered much *cultural knowledge* from stories, factual books, and expeditions to museums and zoos, as well as through conversations with parents and others on many occasions about many different topics. It is therefore no surprise that older preschoolers have ideas about animals, plants, diseases, and so on that reflect their (imperfect) organization of knowledge purveyed from these sources. What is surprising is that developmental psychologists typically describe this knowledge as though it arose spontaneously within the heads of children who were independently observing the world around them.

In no way do I mean to denigrate the curiosity of young children and the intensity of their interest in the natural world, nor their capacity for absorbing and reconstructing knowledge that is offered to them about things that interest them. (Nor do I intend to denigrate the research of developmental scholars in this area.) Children in fact show great interest in learning the correct classifications of things, such as dinosaurs, and they appear to be very aware that conceptual knowledge resides to a very large extent in the older children and adults in their social-cultural world. As such, cultural knowledge is collaboratively reconstructed in each generation; it is not spontaneously regenerated any more than it is innately provided.

This claim may seem at odds with the study of children's concepts of biology, for example, which are alleged to undergo conceptual change in mid-childhood (Carey, 1985). The assumption is that, in early childhood, children garner odd facts from multiple verbal sources and aggregate them over time, resulting in somewhat fragmentary and error-prone complexes of knowledge. When subject to test, these may produce strange theories as well as conventional ones, but in either case the theory is constructed by the researcher around the child's productions; it is not articulated as such by the child. More longitudinal studies, both short-term and long-term, would sort out how stable and reliable children's organizations are over time and identify the delayed effects on their knowledge structures, similar to that of the consolidation of memory effects reported in Chapter 7.

Community of Mind and Cultural Consciousness

Donald (2001) claims that our unique human individuality is a developmental product of immersion in what he refers to as "mindsharing" (what I have called meaning sharing). Donald puts it this way:

> Our brains coevolved with culture and are specifically adapted for living in culture—that is, for assimilating the algorithms and knowledge networks of culture . . . [O]ur brain design "assumes" the existence of a cultural storage mechanism that can ensure its full development . . . Cultural mindsharing is our unique trait, linked as it is to our conscious capacity. [Language is a by-product] of our brain's evolving symbiosis with mindsharing cultures. Language emerges only at the group level and is a cultural product, distributed across many minds. (2001, p. 11)

The process of mind sharing confers on each individual a unique awareness of place in a larger universe of existence, thus illuminating not only its shared situatedness, but also the strange loneliness of its uniqueness. My claim in this chapter, and the ultimate claim of this book, is that the build up to this existential situation takes place during the preschool years as the child enters into mind sharing, or meaning sharing, and faces the dilemma of maintaining individuality in the face of the multiple sources of experience descending on and invading what had been the ultimate privacy of the mind. The solution is a new form of individuality that draws knowledge but not identity from the invasion and achieves a new, more wary awareness of the totality of culture.

Of course this development does not all happen between four and six years of age; a lot of it waits for the agonies of adolescence, or later. But the beginnings are established as the child gains purchase on unique personal experiences in distinction from those of others, while at the same time extracting meaning from their representations. This new level of cultural consciousness also reveals the irony that Donald (2001, p. 12) notes in the quotation heading this chapter, namely that our species is characterized by a different kind of individualism that "came at the price of giving up the isolationism, or cognitive solipsism, of all other species and entering into a collectivity of mind." But this level of collective or cultural consciousness was not achieved all at once. It is a product of the socialization and enculturation processes that take place interpersonally during the postinfancy years, when language (speech or sign) gradually becomes the dominant mode of both interpersonal communication and intrapersonal cogitation.

৯ 9

The Study of Developing Young Minds

> Symbolizing minds . . . are hybrid products of a brain-culture
> symbiosis. Without cultural programming, they could never
> become symbolizing organs.
>
> ~ *Merlin Donald, 2000*

$\mathcal{I}$N THIS BOOK I HAVE aimed to provide a sense of the coherence of development over the first five years of a child's life. Taking an experiential perspective on the process has revealed how individual children, through specific encounters in social interactions, consolidate the sense of self and move into full participation in their particular cultural world. Each child finds a different path through this developmental maze; no modal child stands for the whole group. Yet at a higher level of generality, the *processes* of development, and the systems in play in these years, set constraints and contexts for the organized life patterns that emerge, however variable they appear on close examination.

In this final chapter I want to highlight the continuities that merge one period of development into the next, as well as the new levels of consciousness and meaning that emerge over time. After summarizing some of the most salient changes, I next examine these developments in terms of the child's expanding consciousness, which maintains continuity through change. The chapter concludes with a discussion of some of the major issues in theory and method that this experiential approach to development brings to the table.

Developmental Change and Continuity

From infancy to school entry at age six, a child changes radically in many dimensions. Such dramatic transformations of body and mind

Table 9.1 Summary of developmental changes in systems from infancy to preschool years

	Social	Communication	Mind	Self	Consciousness
Infancy	I-you	Affective	Private, no representations	I	Awareness → Social →
Toddlerhood	Familiars	Gesture/word	External representations → internal representations	Me	Cognitive →
Early childhood	Groups	Language/symbols	Representation and integration of other sources	My meaning/other meaning	Reflective →
Preschool	Communities	Representational language, external/internal	Differentiated mine/other sources	Self in time: past, future imagined	Narrative → Cultural →

might seem to imply discontinuous stages of development, as Piaget's theory suggested. In contrast, an information processing framework, as well as developmental theories built on modularity and its cousin, domain specificity, emphasize the continuity of mental structures and functions and downplay major change. The developmental systems framework differs from all of these and serves as a platform for understanding change within continuity, according to the following principles:

- There are coherent connections among the parts of the systems.

- There is continuity of development over time.

- Self-organization is continuous and dynamic, involving constant adjustment to new conditions, whether internal or external. Movement in the system is toward continuous organization, not equilibrium.

- The mind undergoes an expansion in complexity and in sources of meaning through experiential transactions.

- Consciousness expands as organization at any level is achieved, revealing new perspectives and new meanings in old memory.

- Individuality of personal characteristics, experiences, and social and cultural conditions implies nonuniformity in developmental sequences and organization.

While each of these points could be expanded into a full theoretical discussion, they are intended as a guide to the principles underlying the discussion of specific developments that take place in this critical period of a child's life. With these principles in mind, a brief overview of the developments will serve to draw out their implications.

Some of the most notable changes of the first five years of life in the domains of social relatedness, communication, mind, self, and consciousness are set out in Table 9.1. The periods of development (infancy, toddlerhood, early childhood, preschool) are deliberately not age specific; individuality of development implies that some changes may take place during different periods for some children. The developments shown in Table 9.1 are clearly not all of those documented in the previous chapters. However, they represent some of the interdependencies of the system as a whole, while still maintaining distinctions

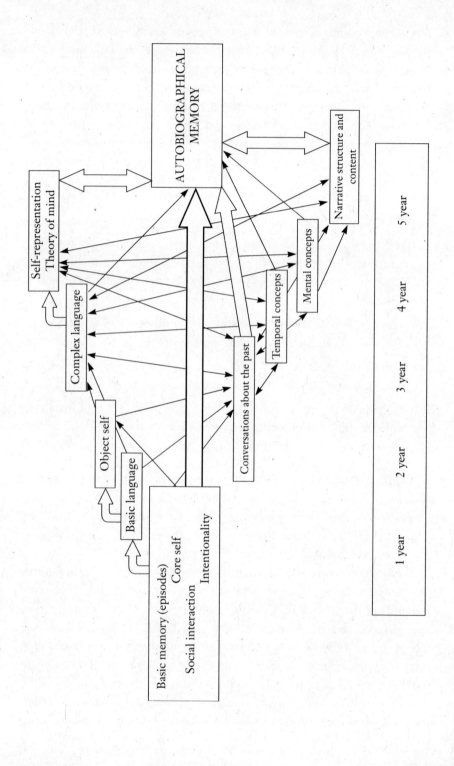

among developments within certain areas. For example, social development appears to expand in a similar way to that of consciousness, from dyadic relations to those that take in wider numbers of familiar people, groups (as in preschools), and eventually different cultural communities. But for a particular child the experience may be much wider than the dyad from the beginning (because the child is in infant day care, for example, or lives with an extended family); no specific constraint is implied. As emphasized in Chapters 4 and 5, communicative functions vary widely during the toddler years, with some children using complex language and others hardly using words at all. Under these different conditions, the system as a whole may be expected to organize meanings in different ways while maintaining balance within the social and embodied complex. Or the child may experience distress in being unable to express what she is learning, thus disrupting the overall self-organization.

The point is that developmental sequences that are common across children may vary in the timing of their appearance and their effects on the system as a whole. There is no one overall sequence of development across even highly interdependent factors. This implies that there will be large variances in our measures, and that the effect of one given factor on another may be obscured by interactions with others as a result of the timing of their appearance within the system. To disentangle some of these influences, we must pay close attention to individual children's experience over time, and also identify patterns of interactions in large numbers of children studied over time. Meanwhile, we can understand developmental sequences in a general way in the context of systems thinking, which can also direct us to particular relations in time and their effects.

This point is illustrated in Figure 9.1 delineating the numerous influences on the construction of autobiographical memory, which emerges at the end of the preschool period in most (but not all) chil-

Figure 9.1. Contributing sources leading to the emergence of autobiographical memory in the late preschool years. The developmental sequence is indicated in terms of the typical "onset age" of each source. Arrows indicate interactions among sources over time, with individual developments shown above the central arrow and social contributions below. Based on Nelson and Fivush (2004), fig. 1. Reproduced with permission from the American Psychological Association.

dren. Influences from "internal" developments are situated in the top of the figure, and those depending on specific contributions from others appear in the lower part. As is evident from the two-headed arrows, there are bidirectional influences not only on memory but among the contributing factors as well. (Most of these influences were discussed in Chapter 7.) These interactions illustrate perhaps better than anything else how interdependent developments are during this period of childhood. Variation in their combinatory patterns is to be expected: for example, some additional experience with narrative storybook reading may lead one child to a more complete understanding of persons and time (and theory of mind) than another, and thus to a point of readiness for the development of autobiographical memory; nonetheless, without specific memory-talk experiences that development might lag. There are many ways to look at the developmental sequence roughly laid out in Table 9.1 and more specifically in Figure 9.1. I find it especially revealing to think of this sequence in terms of the expansion of consciousness.

Expansion of Consciousness

The expansion of consciousness is essentially an expansion of the potential for meaningful experience of different kinds, or on different levels. The levels set out here reflect biological (neurological, bodily) constraints, limitations on experience, learning and accumulated memory, and "meaning sharing" potentials in the different periods of development. Such constraints and limitations on the child's experience necessarily place limits on our interpretations of the child's *Umwelt*, or experience of the world. Consciousness is assumed to expand in relation to opportunities afforded by each prior level of conscious experience. These opportunities appear through the interaction of external and internal factors, especially through the "outside" opportunities provided by social interactions, language use in conversations, and so on, in conjunction with the experiential constraints and memory characteristics of the current consciousness state. Social transactions are critical to the move from one broad level of consciousness to the next and to the consequences that the move has for perceiving new relationships. These are complexes that the child does not control, and opening up to expanded views of the inhabited world at each level takes place very gradually. I hypothesize that as each level is exploited, established meanings of memory may conflict with new experiences that come into awareness, thus motivating the move to the next level of consciousness. These moves may take place slowly or rapidly; they are not tied to specific ages, and individual patterns of reorganization are expected.

It may also be that consciousness is not uniform across types of experience. For example, an adult whose consciousness when enjoying haute cuisine is precise and highly developed may be at a barely reflective level when watching a hockey game. This kind of domain-specific consciousness mirrors the simultaneous functioning of the different levels of the hybrid mind (Donald, 1991, 2001). It also is similar to Karmiloff-Smith's (1992) theory of representational change in domain-specific mode. Following are summary sketches of the characteristics of each level of consciousness.

Basic Awareness

At birth the baby "awakes" to a reality previously unseen. Being awake at this point is being aware of limited aspects of the inhabited world. Many researchers have tried to discern which aspects the newborn is aware of and how those immediate sensations broaden over a few months into familiar sights, smells, tastes, and sounds. It seems most probable that the newborn infant does not inhabit a world of persons and things, as such, but of complexes of familiar faces and comforting bodies, as well as spaces and sights and sounds that take on greater definition over months of exploring the boundaries of self and nonself in both social and nonsocial forms. The infant's systems of sensation, perception, and implicit memory are all at work, attending to patterns of sounds and sights, deriving memory of familiar patterns "unconsciously," and building basic perceptual structures, including, as we now know, statistical regularities in the sounds of language (Saffran, 2003) and presumably in other sensory patterns. These patterns will serve as background "knowledge" for the meaning work that lies ahead.

The meaning that determines memory in this phase of development is that related to the predispositions of the neural structures that, for example, expect and look for "mother," for shapes and objects, for language patterns, and so on. Of course as the infant moves on to the relative sophistication of this phase and develops more and more schemas of her surroundings, she also tunes in more to the verbal and physical interactions of those around her. At some point these perceptions lead into the next significant phase, the expansion of awareness into consciousness.

Social Consciousness

The impact of social consciousness was discussed in some detail in the consideration of the self-other relation of intersubjectivity that comes into play at about nine months (the reigning age for this phase of development is six to eighteen months; see Chapter 3). It is a phase during which the infant pays close attention to his or her social partner for affective, cognitive, and basic security reasons. People and things come together in activities and routines. People are well differentiated, sometimes too much so, as when the baby experiences fear of strangers. Attention to activities and attention to others leads the child into a new experiential space involving comprehension of communicative efforts and language use. Among the most significant developments is attention to the meaning of language and to sharing the meaning of another through words. The child at this point is one member of a dyad or triad—child, parent, object (Hobson, 1993; Werner and Kaplan, 1963). The effects of embodiment change and the potential for self-directed mobility are equally strong, as Campos and others have demonstrated (Campos et al., 2000). The social emphasis of this period, differentiating one person from another, also has the effect of differentiating the child as a person. Comprehending this existential state leads the toddler into the next phase.

Cognitive Consciousness

In this phase the child recognizes herself as a person-object (Chapter 4). She also actively and intentionally externalizes meanings, acting out schemas in play and using words to effect action and to comment on her own action. She sees that others see her, and she sees as well that they see things from a different viewpoint than hers. She organizes toys into their places and asserts her own wants and actions. The child of this age is independently mobile and is receptive to social relations with a variety of different people, with or without the use of language.

Awareness of the self as an object of others' attention provokes feelings of self-consciousness. Acquisition of words to use in sharing meanings brings the child into a new social space, and in the process imposes different meanings on the words she has chosen to use. Interaction around words challenges her own private meanings, a first step toward the linguistic cognition that begins during the following phase. Consciousness of self and other, externalization of memory, and the use of words together facilitate the move to the next level, reflective consciousness.

Reflective Consciousness

This phase of development (usually beginning at about three years but sometimes earlier) becomes possible when activities and discourse are shared between people, when matters are put into a public space. The effect of the externalization of meaning intensifies when children become participants in conversation or in interactive activities in which roles are not routine but must be shared, as in play and games. Learning in language-constituted collaborative constructions becomes possible and even common. The child can take what is offered in a situation into his meaning-memory system and later rerepresent it and reflect on it, manipulate it mentally and come back to it, or come back to the person who introduced it and check out its shared meaning or add to it in new ways. Children frequently express new ideas that they have come to through such reflections (see Chukovsky, 1971, for revealing and charming examples). These possibilities gradually make it possible to expand the span of consciousness in discourse and in narrative so that, over time, a child can take in a whole story (see Chapter 6). This possibility makes the next move inevitable.

Narrative Consciousness

Narrative consciousness makes explicit the differentiation of self in different times and self and other in mind (Chapter 7). Logical sequences of causation unfold in narrative as other times and other places come into view. The world of people expands exponentially from those who are family to all those whose stories can be told in fact or fiction. Personal memory begins to expand from the episodic past to the unknown future. Reflecting on personal memory brings into consciousness the differentiation of others' memory and "my" memory, semantic and episodic. The different perspectives of social and temporal "minds" are manifested in narratives, which lay out many of the secrets of social life, including motivations, successes, failures, deception, and generosity. Imagination is aroused by these different life stories. These perspectives open the secrets of "theory of mind" and lead to the final phase considered here.

Cultural Consciousness

Reflective and narrative consciousness open the windows to cultural consciousness. This is the process I call "entering the community of minds," which expands the child's previously restricted view to encompass an infinite variety of people in the world, of possible experiences and fantasies undreamt of in the child's past, and of domains of knowledge to be explored. The five- or six-year-old who stands on the brink of this phase of consciousness cannot know about these riches but can begin to experiment with them.

Consciousness as Development

Like many developmental proposals, this one appears to involve discrete steps, as though up a ladder, in that each step provides a new position from which to view a broader horizon and to glimpse the next position. A better metaphor, though, would be a climb up a rocky slope, where each resting place offers a chance to view the immediate ground and the surround ahead. The path ahead—when it can be glimpsed—is attractive and enticing for most children, who proceed on to the next place. The higher slopes would not exist without the ground below, and all possibilities inherent in the prior phases of consciousness are present in each succeeding phase.

One may experience basic awareness, for example, in awakening in an unfamiliar place, as one attempts to establish the ground on which to proceed coherently as oneself. The affective feelings of social and cognitive consciousness may come into play whenever one feels at a loss in some new endeavor or new group, before reflective consciousness reestablishes confidence. Narrative consciousness is essential to functioning in social relations as an adult as well as in childhood, and it arises often with or without an accompanying cultural consciousness. Once achieved, all or some levels of consciousness may be accessible at any given time.

How does the expansion of consciousness help us to understand developmental processes? It makes explicit how the child's view of the world outside her private inhabited space expands with experience. Correspondingly, it sets limits on the child's earlier position in the world. It transforms Piaget's egocentrism into an egoist perspective on intersubjective activities, where intersubjectivity does not involve taking both perspectives at once. Rather, the perspective of the self may be temporarily set aside to share that of another, or to enter into a story world, for example, leaving the "real" world behind. This position maintains a phenomenological view of the world, even as the world itself expands in response to the child's consciousness potentials.

Revisiting Major Themes

Experience and Private Minds

Experience is basic in this account because nothing psychological happens without it. I have outlined a multifaceted view of experience, emphasizing its dependence on conditions of the individual (memory, embodiment, inheritance) and the external world (ecological, social, and cultural). Experience acts as an interface between the internal and the external components of an integrated system, where embodiment and inheritance play a major role in what *can* be experienced in a particular setting, and meaning in memory largely influences what *will* be experienced within that constraint. That experience is different for each individual in the same situation follows from the nature of these constraints, as does the related implication that the meaning of the experience is different.

That the infant and young child's mind is a *private space*, and that past and present experiences are thus private as well—private even from the child himself—is not a new or unique claim. Many would agree with it, perhaps with reservations, but I give it particular importance for two reasons: it emphasizes the uniqueness of the modern human mentality in both ontogeny and phylogeny, and it emphasizes the subjectivity of the experiential process. The uniqueness of the human mind stems not from its privacy but from its escape from privacy over the course of the early years, and its acquisition of socially shared symbolic systems. The initial private state and its subsequent openness constitute important conditions for making or remaking a theory of cognitive development, although this is not generally acknowledged. The implication is that it is not just experience that changes but the mind itself, ultimately distinguishing two semidistinct kinds, the private (personal) part and the shared (social and cultural) part.[1]

Meaning

I am more than ever convinced that meaning is the crux of the matter, albeit still the most neglected topic in the study of cognition. It constitutes the answer to the question of why: Why minds (or brains)? Why develop? As noted in Chapter 2, when psychology set out to be an objective science, it left meaning behind, substituting "information" for meaning and thus defining cognitive content in terms of objectively neutral abstractions. However, meaning applies across the biological spectrum, as well as across development. An organism that mindlessly gobbles up information will choke on it; one that seeks out meaning to assuage its mental hunger will be satisfied.

Meaning is relevant to the claim frequently made by strong nativists that there must be structural beginning points—principles, concepts, core knowledge, modules—if the infant is to begin the process of learning from the environment. In the most general sense, I agree. But the process that I envision (together with systems theorists generally) involves not simply a well-wired brain but a brain-body-environment interdependency. Moreover, what is provided by the brain are not "rich" conceptual structures, as so often claimed, but biologically based interests and skeletal processes that are flexible enough to locate and organize the meaningful components for that point in the individual's development, within widely varying environmental encounters.

The development of the means for *meaning sharing* is radical and transformative in cognitive development, as it was in the evolution of the species. By the end of the preschool period (before literacy) the child has become a participant in the community of minds, has joined in the practices of the culture, and has established an identity with its members. By virtue of this membership, a whole universe of meaning—of other people's knowledge, beliefs, and feelings, past and present—opens up for examination and sharing.

Memory

The idea that personal meaning is essentially memory—that indeed, to a large degree, memory is the conservation, organization, and transformation of meaning—is one of the main outcomes of this view of development and cognition. This idea should not be surprising at this point in history. Among the advances that Endel Tulving made in the study of memory decades ago, before he identified episodic and semantic memory, concerned the subjective organization of random lists of words (thus without an objective basis for meaningful organization). Experimental subjects nonetheless found meaningful connections between words and maintained those connections over subsequent recall trials. Different people imposed different organizations on the lists; the basis for the connections was subjective and private, and often unrecognized by the subject.[2] During the same time period (the 1960s), cognitive theory focused single-mindedly on memory and information processing models proliferated, filled with boxes, arrows, decision points, and so on. Today, in contrast, cognition appears to consist of analogies, metaphors, networks, theories, and the like, with memory pushed into the boring background. But these are really all ways of working with meaningful memory representations, in both personal and shared memory. The conclusion is clear: cognition is memory, and *meaning is what memory is about.*[3]

During the preschool period, the "private mind" of direct experience gives way to the realization that the knowledge that emanates from others' minds is distinctive in ways that are important to self-identity, requiring a differentiation of memory. Then what is "mine" must come to be especially marked in memory, and episodic memory emerges as a distinct type. As postulated in Chapter 7, this is but one distinction to be made among types of memory, and how such divisions are to be parceled out (in the mind, brain, or in theory) is a matter for future and ongoing developmental and cognitive work. Social memory is also and particularly meaningful. Shared memory is found in libraries, museums, on the Internet, in universities and other institutions, and in symbolic markers (such as monuments). When such artifacts lose meaning, they are abandoned and left as relics for later generations (perhaps archaeologists) to puzzle over, sifting through the information to find the hidden meanings.

Memory in this conception is a general function of the mind. This has implications for domain specificity in contrast to general processes in learning and cognitive development (Hirschfeld and Gelman, 1994). One way of understanding the claims of domain-specific processes is to think of memory as operating on meaning in domains *after* the specific process has identified and classified the content. This sequence appears to imply that all domains are somehow prespecified as to content. There is also the drawback of keeping the domain knowledge separate from other sectors. The alternative possibility is that the meaning system sifts and identifies the domain of the encountered content on the basis of prior memory work. This alternative gives rise to the possibility of sharing knowledge across domains in metaphors, analogies, and higher-level constructions. This view reflects the position that cognitive processes are an integral part of memory itself.

This suggested relation of the active role of memory in identifying and organizing domain-specific knowledge is relevant to the recent discussion of the role of language in enabling different domains to "talk to each other" across initial boundaries (Carruthers, 2002; Spelke 2003). The idea that specific domains might exist and act independently in the minds of infants and young children (and presumably in other animals without language) entails a divided mind that is the exact opposite of the initially undifferentiated meaning-memory system posited in this book. Many important functions of cognitive development (and adult cognition) are served by language, but there is no good evidence that "talking across domains" is one of these functions (Nelson, 2002).

Social and Cultural

I have emphasized throughout this work the intensive and extensive degree to which human infants depend on the care of others, primarily parents. This is an intensification of the same dependency exhibited among other primates and among mammals in general. In the human case, parents and other adults also are the source of guidance and participatory routines, and the carriers of culture.

But what is culture? This question has various answers, including an emphasis on symbolic forms, tools and artifacts, and institutions. An answer from sociobiology, originally put forth by Dawkins (1976), that has taken on new force in recent years is that culture exists as "memes." Memes are conceived to be bits of "stuff" that live in our brains or minds and that have the power to replicate themselves (like genes), in order to pass from one individual to another. This conception (that bits of independent mental entities design and drive our cultural lives) is antithetical to the idea widely accepted in sociology, anthropology, and psychology that cultures are broad, loosely cohering social entities that integrate and provide identity to groups of people through common beliefs, language, myths, and institutions (political, economic, educational, religious).[4] From a psychological standpoint, whether considered as a whole or as a complex mix of parts and processes, culture is a far broader concept than a collection of random memes regenerating themselves in our "helpless" minds. When considered as the surround of the child's developing life, culture must be seen in terms of practices, symbols, artifacts, media, and technology, as well as the people who use these instruments.

Language carries culture within it, a fact that is strongly contended when it is framed in terms of the Whorfian hypothesis (Whorf, 1956). As usually interpreted, the Whorfian hypothesis holds that the particular language spoken by a group affects the group's thought; the broader interpretation is that it affects thought by imparting cultural conceptions. The chief objection to this idea comes from those who see language as a single universal structure that is imposed on a set of underlying basic concepts; in this view, language is designed to *express* thought, not to *form* it.

However, as argued in Chapter 7, accumulating evidence and argument support the Whorfian claim when it is suitably interpreted as thinking for speaking (Slobin, 2003). Slobin has recently restated the position to include the reverse process of speaking for thinking, recognizing that much of human thinking takes place in language—through inner speech, in Vygotsky's terms—and would not be possible without it. But in Slobin's position on the Whorf hypothesis, what is most relevant to present concerns is the point that, in order to express an observation about the world in language, one must first note the specific details required by the specific spoken language. That is to say, language is critical to the composition of experience itself.

In the same way, language is essential to the child entering into the larger community—the community that speaks the same language and that has knowledge resources to share, as well as ideas and attitudes to contemplate, and stories, myths, and songs to stir the heart. To speak the language is to join the crowd (which is a slightly different take on Wittgenstein's "to learn a language is to enter a way of life").

Individuality

Invoking Barbara McClintock again, and the need to have a "feeling for the organism" (Keller, 1983), I return to the question of individual differences. I strongly believe that we must understand the nature of individual differences if we are to understand development, and that gender differences and cultural variations in child-rearing practices and children's characteristics can be seen in the same light as individual differences. All reflect different ways in which individual systems organize the varying contributions (or constraints) to development over time. As emphasized especially in Chapter 3, social care by adults is as crucial to infants as are the physical conditions of warmth and food. The nature of that care has long-lasting effects on the individual child, as reflected in attachment measures (Weinfield, Sroufe, and Egeland, 2000).

The nature-nurture debate is of little help in understanding these matters. There is now a strong movement toward the position that the inborn characteristics of the individual outweigh any influence of parent care (Harris, 1998), and that individual children "choose" their own environments, including their own social influences, on the basis of innate temperament or personality biases (Scarr, 1992). This generous attitude toward mothers and fathers exempts them from responsibility for children gone astray. It is true that if all environments were exactly the same and similarly bleak, there would still be differences among children, all presumably attributable to biological factors, but children are never raised in identical circumstances, whether severely deprived or expansively rich.[5] We can gratefully recognize the individual resilience of some children who emerge in good health from situations of severe deprivation and isolation without denying that all children benefit from warm and loving parenting and rich opportunities for varied social and nonsocial experience.[6] The experiential model is steadfastly interactive as well as transactive. We can avoid indiscriminate blaming of parents for unwanted outcomes by recognizing the emergence of strong individuality in children, whatever their biological givens and social conditions may be, while still affirming the extraordinarily important role of the social interactions within which they develop.

Theories and Methods

Developmental psychologists have been enormously successful in the past fifty years in undertaking research that has pushed ahead our understanding of what infants and children can see, how they are thinking and remembering in specific circumstances, and learning and gaining knowledge, as well as our understanding of the sequence of language acquisition from words to sentences. However, there are enormous gaps in this record of progress, as I have argued throughout the previous chapters. In the field of cognitive developmental research, it appears that many if not most researchers today find domains of knowledge—space, objects, social beings, numbers, language, and some others—together with types of representation and metarepresentation, such as categories, concepts, relations, and theories, to be meaningful areas of research. The most meaningful ages for study seem to be the first four postnatal months, nine to twelve months, eighteen months, and three to five years, with research at each age focused on a few of the central problems in the areas mentioned. The focus on these ages and problems supports a discontinuous view of development, however; separate abilities appear full-blown at distinct ages, as measured by standard tasks, and little connection is noted with prior, future, or coordinate developments. Further, the task results often report different levels of competence in an area than the levels observed in children's natural environments, and the discrepancy is unresolved.

Only a developmental perspective can explain the course of change in human lives. The complexity involved requires that explanations be based on the principles of developmental systems, systems that are undergoing continuous, dynamic change of many kinds, initiated from many different sources. A major challenge, then, is to understand how the systems maintain coherence across change, and continuity of the whole over time, in the face of strong individual differences and as each interactive system is confronted with problems and responds to challenges.

Interpretation

Current theories in the line of dynamic systems and sociocultural and ecological frameworks offer rich sources for the reinterpretation of well-established findings and facts of development. "Experiential developmental psychology" (or pragmatic psychology) is a framework for interpretation: a framework that can guide both observation and experimentation in the pursuit of particular problems; one that may shed new light on the behavior of children at all ages, and that can lead to new insights about the structure and function of brains, bodies, minds, and social transactions. Clark (1997) discusses the problems of explaining complex dynamic systems, suggesting that such explanations, instead of identifying underlying mechanisms, usually turn out to be merely descriptive. Attempting to explain development in such terms is even more daunting, but I think the challenge of interpreting development in terms of systems—locating connections between components, tracking parts over time—is worth undertaking, without at present attempting a formal theory. Laying out "small theories" within the larger framework may be more feasible.

A focus on interpretation underlines two important facts. First, all of our research results at present are open to different interpretations from different theoretical perspectives. But these differences are often hidden in journal reviews, grant reviews, and publication decisions, rather than acknowledged openly. It is rare for those in the field to publicly expose the contrasting views behind ongoing research programs. More openness to theoretical discussion and critique can help advance our thinking across the board. Science is, after all, a social endeavor, and when differences of interpretation are kept hidden or private, the science suffers. Second, what our minds do is interpret states of the world, including the states of mind of other people (Bogdan, 2003). Interpretation is thus an excellent goal for the study of psychological developmental processes.

Methods and Goals

An experiential developmental psychology should have some implications for future research and research methods. In each of the substantive chapters (Chapters 3 through 8) I have highlighted some areas of research that illustrate and may motivate additional work. The examples come from a variety of areas and programs, and they illustrate characteristics of research programs that may yield productive results:

- They begin with questions that derive from phenomena observed in natural environments. That is, they are grounded in the reality of children's everyday worlds.
- They situate questions within developmental accounts of related behaviors. Although they may begin with an isolated observed phenomenon, its explanation is sought in developmental processes.
- They organize empirical enquiry to document the natural history of the phenomenon, including whether it occurs in other species.
- They carry out ecologically valid experiments in the natural environment to test hypotheses and generate theories.
- They design laboratory experiments to follow up on observations and findings in natural settings, using experimental technologies and controls to achieve higher power.
- They construct theories of the developmental processes involved, to guide further research.

These practices put the emphasis on the child's making sense of experience in the world. This perspective contrasts with the traditional view that the child is engaged in making sense of the world, the goal of genetic epistemology. This traditional view implies that there is an objective body of knowledge to be acquired or expressed and that is known to the adult researcher, who is equipped with a preestablished theory that specifies the categories and mechanisms that could be detected and classified. In contrast, in the experiential view, the infant's perspective on the world is held to be subjective, phenomenological, and pragmatic, not objective and epistemological. What the child learns—what knowledge accrues—through experience depends on the current state of the constraints outlined in Chapter 1: embodiment, ecological context, social interactions, cultural knowledge and symbolic usage, and past experience in terms of conceptual organization and specific memory. These determine what meaning will be found and reorganized in memory to guide further pursuit of the child's interests. The effect of these constraints may be reduced through experimental design, but they cannot be ruled out. For example, previous experience is always variable among children and often unknown to the researcher. What a child learns from an encounter cannot be prespecified or predetermined. Further, behavior in the "real world" may be supported by some of these constraints, so that the same problem, confronted in the laboratory, may be approached differently by the child, and apparently in a less effective or less advanced way. Or the child's response may appear to be more effective in the laboratory setting, as fewer of the real-world constraints interfere. Both outcomes may be misleading.

Many research programs derived from natural observation and from the experimental laboratory exemplify these effects. Judy Dunn's (1988) research on young siblings in family environments brought out many examples of very young children engaging in deception and other behaviors that indicated "knowledge" of theory of mind, findings not achieved in the laboratory until four years of age or older.[7] My own explorations with colleagues of a theory of mind task revealed better performance by children under conditions of greater support in the laboratory, as well as confusions expressed by the children based on their prior "real life" experience (Nelson et al., 2003; Table 8.1). Smith and Thelen's experimental studies of the A not B error, drawing on systems analysis, showed that some variations in conditions, such as body position in space, eliminated the "error" for children who displayed it under standard conditions (Smith, Thelen, Titzer, and McLin, 1999). Such examples, described in previous chapters, indicate that being alert to the relation of the laboratory to real-world conditions and experiences can aid in both designing experiments that probe more deeply and interpreting results from standard designs that seem to contradict natural observations.

The ideal practices listed above do not constitute a methodology. There is no call for a standard method, qualitative versus quantitative, ethology or ethnography versus laboratory, or for a sequence of procedures. Moreover, different stages of knowledge in a field of inquiry may proceed from different points in a program of research. For example, research on language development proceeded from studies of language use in natural home environments in the 1960s and 1970s to laboratory experiments as well as sophisticated analyses of videotaped speech (e.g.,

Bloom, 1993). It is difficult to maintain the conditions of social use in controlled experiments with toddlers; as a result, there are discrepancies between the findings from different settings. Experimental researchers report, for example, that children's attention to "social cues" is a late attainment, whereas it is an important component of beginning language in naturally grounded work. As discussed in Chapter 5, these differences reflect both empirical constraints and theoretical assumptions.

Research in the areas of infant perception and cognition has long been limited by the techniques available, specifically the habituation-dishabituation paradigm (Chapter 3). Testing the theoretical assumptions of innate knowledge against learning in everyday life requires appropriate longitudinal studies that have been slow to emerge (Newcombe, Sluzenskie, and Huttenlocher, 2005).[8] Some ongoing studies of infant cognition, including Adolph's (2000) studies of perceptual and motor skills and Campos's studies of locomotor and cognitive skills (Campos et al., 2000), are outstanding examples of how phenomena observed in situ can be studied effectively in both natural settings and in the laboratory (Chapter 3).

Studies of children's memory have also gone through some of the sequence suggested. Prior to the 1970s there were almost no studies of memory in children younger than school age. Children's reliance on scripts for familiar events in daycare settings was first observed in contrast with their memory for specific events (Nelson, 1986). This work led in two major directions, to controlled laboratory studies (Bauer, 1996, 2006), and to investigating natural conditions for remembering, including a single child's memory talk (Nelson, 1989) and the analysis of parent and child past talk in several longitudinal studies (Fivush, 1994; Nelson and Fivush, 2004; Chapter 7).

Experimental research is clearly one of the most powerful ways of verifying one's intuitions about the factors that influence behavior, or of ruling out one's false hypotheses. There is no call here for doing away with experiments in experiential developmental psychology, but it is important to attend to the meaning of the experiment for the child, as well as its meaning for the adult experimenter (Nelson, Henseler, and Plesa, 2000). Children attempt to relate a present experience to past experiences, rather than confining themselves to the restricted context that the experimenter has devised. Given that meaning always uses past experience to direct present experience, this is not at all unexpected. And it is indeed relevant to our theories of development in these examples and in the general case.

The general case has to do with how the organism—the child—works together as a whole. For the child growing toward school age, much is being learned from others both directly and indirectly. Directly means here that someone else is imparting "information" or acting as a model and providing guidance in an activity in which the child is participating. Indirectly means that the child is absorbing aspects of behavior, much as she did in infancy, in terms of meaningful patterns that become part of what she expects in similar situations and contexts in the future. It is a safe guess that most of the research that takes place in developmental psychology laboratories is designed to test *what* the child has learned from past experience. What is much less often asked is how the child has acquired this knowledge. In an experiential approach to cognitive development, this question is central to understanding development as a process.

The Architecture of Development

What makes development work? According to Piaget, it is the pull toward equilibrium that draws the mind to resolve contradictions.[9] Heinz Werner proposed an all-encompassing principle, the orthogenetic law, by which global forms or conceptions became first differentiated and then reintegrated into more complex creations. Vygotsky claimed that all higher mental processes are experienced first on the interpersonal plane and then later on the intrapersonal plane, a claim that absolutely requires the participation of a partner with a higher-order mind to guide development. No doubt there is truth in each of these conceptions, different as they appear to be, but in none of them is there much sense of what it is that is organizing and being organized.

In the proposal I put forth in Chapter 1, meaning sets the goals of the self-organizing system. The central cognitive component of the system is memory, which is organized in terms of meaning, derived from experience, and continuously recomposed by operations of the system. The basic unit of experience is the event, extracted from the experiential transactions guided by the search for meaning. This formula is in place in the mind even prior to birth and serves the child throughout infancy, as critical aspects of neural development proceed, strengthening and expanding memory in the process. Thereafter, two major transitions take place that change the nature of human cognition and communication.

Externalization

The first of these transitions involves the capacity for explicitation and externalization. This capacity is at the heart of what Donald (1991) identified as mimesis. It enables the individual to represent in internal and external form aspects of what is conserved in the meaning memory. Prior to this development, all memory is what memory theorists refer to as implicit memory, which guides action and perception but is not consciously accessible and cannot be voluntarily called up out of the context of its relevance and use. The first move toward the higher level is the *voluntary recall* that Donald attributed to mimesis, a move that essentially involves representing for the self in thought—a first level of representation. (Again, I reserve the term *representation* for intentional representation; perception and memory are just that, not representations.)[10]

Earlier I speculated that the capacity to represent in thought emerged *after* the capacity to represent externally. For example, intentional recall from memory is primarily evident in the infant and toddler in terms of delayed imitation (or other external representations of knowing), where what has been in memory as a meaningful visual or action pattern is acted out at a later point with materials available for the purpose. The action externalizes and thus represents a previously viewed visual pattern. We do not know that the one-year-old child has a conscious representation in mind that she is attempting to replicate with the props. It may be that acting on the props brings the prior scene to mind. Playing out a scene (e.g., stirring in a bowl or putting a doll to sleep, or, in one of Piaget's examples, lying down and "pretending" to sleep) is a similar kind of externalization. In fact, in Piaget's example the child seemed to recognize that the action was a representation of something only after it was completed, when the child looked up with a smile of satisfaction. The child of this age uses action to represent memory or to represent a familiar activity. To the adult, this activity appears to use an (internal) representation to guide the external evidence of memory or the symbolic pretense; but the reverse seems at least equally likely, based on the behaviors we observe. The internal memory may not be reconstituted as an internal representation before being externally expressed; instead the external form may be the basis for a newly composed internal representation, which then becomes part of the memory.

Either way, the significance of externalization is twofold. It invites the participation of a social partner and initiates social exchanges that can then lead to new content for the child to contemplate, and it enables the child to view the action anew, to reexperience it and subject it to transformations and repetitions (practice).

Some parts of the memory system remain forever inaccessible to recall and representation. It may be that a first bifurcation of the system takes place during the transition from infancy to childhood, allowing some parts to be represented in a different form while others—for example, pattern detectors—remain inaccessible to conscious thought and manipulation.[11] It may also be that the ability to visualize or enact (or later, verbalize) a representation is what determines the possibility of intentional recall.

Language and Thought

The second major transition takes place when symbolic representation becomes possible. When a speech form becomes associated with a meaning derived from the context of use, its production by the child in that context may signal an internal representation of form and content leading toward symbolic representation (see Chapters 4 and 5). As I have argued, learning to speak the language and use it in representations is the most radical cognitive transition of the preschool years. It takes the child beyond the early, intimate social world into the larger world of common culture, into time and space, beyond immediate experiential possibilities.

A major question to be addressed, is how language fits into the structure of the cognitive system. It is odd that this question is so rarely asked in developmental psychology. Several answers are on offer. The standard linguistic position is that language is a separate supramodule (with submodules) that feeds into the cognitive system. An alternative position is that language is basically a system of social communication, acquired through social interaction and use. Vygotsky (1962) proposed that early thought was separate from language, while mature (higher-order) thinking was carried out in inner speech (a more elliptical "self-speech" system). Most developmentalists appear to accept the proposition that language expresses concepts (or ideas and feelings) that exist independently of the language in which they are expressed (P. Bloom, 2000). In mainstream cognitive psychology, verbal thought is not an issue, perhaps because most investigators use verbal materials to examine cognitive processes and have generally not worried much about whether cognition is all verbal, and if so, how that came about in development or in evolution. As discussed in Chapter 6, none of these positions is quite right, in my view. The developmental questions are or ought to be: How and why does a specific language get *into* thought? And what does it do there?

In Donald's conception of the hybrid mind, a level of language representation supplements the earlier implicit and explicit levels of memory, and in turn supports the move to graphic symbolic representations at a still more powerful functional level. In this solution, language representations are not fused with other levels, nor do they override them; instead they provide a separate level of representation and thought. In my reading it is not the *structure* of language that constitutes this level but symbol use itself, which becomes evident in our internal monologues. From this perspective, meaning pervades this level, attaching itself to words and higher-level structures, in effect fusing symbol and meaning, as Vygotsky proposed. But meaning is also maintained at each of the other levels, in interconnections between them as well as in multiple interconnections (integrations) at the same level. Meanings may differ at each level in terms of connections, degree of vagueness or articulateness, metaphoric possibilities, and so on (Lakoff, 1987). Which level reigns at any time depends on the function being served and its usefulness to the current activity.

Tomasello (2003) made a similar point in commenting on the debate over the Whorfian hypothesis, arguing that it is a mistake to privilege something called "nonlinguistic cognition" as the real thing that may or may not be affected by language. Rather, he suggests that we admit that thinking takes many forms, one of which is linguistic cognition; another, is Slobin's (2003) thinking for speaking. As Tomasello rightly notes, the unique property of this *intersubjective system of thought* is its capacity for taking different perspectives on the world and conceptualizing in ways that would not be possible without it.

Memory Partitions

There is at least one further bifurcation or differentiation in memory that may or may not be related to the language capacity. This is the differentiation between episodic and semantic memory. As I have argued, at the beginning of postnatal life and for the next year or two, the child's mental life takes place on a strictly private level, as she is unable to share with other minds or to make her own thoughts explicit in the way she will be able to later, first through nonverbal externalization and more completely with language. This statement implies that at this early developmental point, representations as such are not accessible to the child's thought processes; thinking is confined to ongoing events. Because of this restriction, there is no functional reason for differentiating her own mind from those of others. This must be clear: it is not that the child is confused as to whether her mind is her own, it is that she has no conception of mind as such. Memory at this point can be best thought of as personal knowledge, having been gleaned solely through personal experience, but it is not manifest *as* memory or mind, it is simply background to ongoing activity. Memory then is *neither* episodic nor semantic but simply memory.

By two years of age the contents of memory may be represented for particular purposes and externalized in different ways if an occasion appears to warrant such a process. Experience with exchanging views and knowledge with others, parents, peers, and other persons, then reveals different representations that indicate different knowledge systems— that is, different minds. This becomes the motivation for distinguishing "my memory/mind" from "other memories/minds" and for distinguishing sources of knowledge in terms of episodic memory (I experienced it) and semantic memory (it came from other sources).[12] This differentiation, although arising through verbal representations and their revelations, is orthogonal to the different levels of basic memory (implicit), mimetic representations (external/internal), and inner speech.

Collaborative Construction

A lot of learning takes place without language. I have called this kind of learning "experience." It is a natural result of encountering new salient and relevant things in the world and referring them to the meaning memory. Piaget's theory concentrated on learning through active exploration. In contrast, Vygotsky was most concerned with the kind of learning that occurs when a novice is working with an expert in some knowledge domain, and the expert provides guidance in how to achieve an acknowledged goal. (Ideally both persons are focused on the same goal.) This conception of scaffolded learning is the essence of cultural learning (Rogoff, 2003; Tomasello, 1999; Vygotsky, 1978).

Individual exploration and discovery are exciting but they can go only so far, even in science; all science is socially constructed, built on prior scientific findings as well as on the continuing collaborations and competitions within a field. In fact, most human learning is social, taking place between people, usually in the effort to pass on cultural knowledge and practices. Even when the learner is self-taught through reading, the source of knowledge is social and cultural. Of course our educational disputes are about how best to construct the teaching-learning process to achieve learning by all students in school. Vygotsky's proposal of scaffolding was in fact a proposal for how to address this problem.

Collaborative construction is a kind of generalization of Vygotsky's conception and an extension of Tomasello's ideas on cultural learning, a proposal that all cultural learning takes place through the process of collaboration (Tomasello, Kruger, and Ratner, 1993). It is not confined to the parent-child dyad, or to teachers and children, but may be observed between peers, among groups of adults, and in individuals alone reading a newspaper or book or working with colleagues. The idea is simple: there exist bodies of cultural knowledge, written or passed on orally. Some members of the culture have acquired some fraction of some body of this knowledge, and through discourse (teaching, tutoring, casual conversation, argument, written work) they externalize it for the benefit of others. The value of this external form depends on the skill of the member in making it accessible to others. The receivers or attenders to the discourse (in some cases, the students) receive some part of it—typically not the whole that the imparter believes that she has made available—and that part that is *meaningful* to each individual is then taken into the meaning memory for further construction. In the process, again typically, some parts (often critical) are lost, and when the knowledge is called on again for use in a new context, it is reconstructed from the memory and put forth in its new (now altered) shape.

This description makes the process seem weak indeed, and it is, as university lecturers realize only too well when reading students' exams. But, again, the model reduced to a single trial of teaching-learning is deceptive. When practiced in everyday life between people, such as parent and child, who are interested in the process of teaching and learning, a slow accretion of a reconstructed whole builds up seemingly without effort, as is evident when a child acquires an encyclopedic knowledge of dinosaurs, for example. The larger the structure that is built up in memory (and structures grow with use and practice), the easier it is to find meaningful slots for new related knowledge to fit into it.

The important aspect to collaborative construction is this: it goes on all the time. Collaborative construction is not an instruction for how to achieve teaching or learning (as was Vygotsky's model of scaffolding, which it incorporates) but a description of how human learning takes place. Indeed, the construct of the "meme," discussed previously, is a distorted version of this human learning model. Someone casually mentions a fact (a meme) during a conversation, and a listener "picks it up" and passes it on to the next person, who makes it part of his or her own construction of the "facts of the matter."

Like learning and memory in infancy, learning takes place by virtue of meaning, but in older children and adults meaning often comes through discourse. Organized teaching and learning, as in school, often seems difficult because educators attempt to impart large organized domains of knowledge for which there is no prior basis in the student's meaning memory. The meaning structure must be constructed, and that is the difficult part. For children from a different cultural background, learning may seem difficult for the same reason: they have no prior meaning structure to help them integrate what the teacher is attempting to provide.

There is a danger that collaborative construction may confuse the still undifferentiated memory of the young child prior to its becoming bifurcated into mine/not-mine sources (Chapter 7). Children must become aware of the distinctions of different minds, different thoughts, different sources of knowledge, different times, and different experiences. The conversations that take place during the early childhood years hold the potential to make these distinctions salient and at the same time to threaten the merging of materials from different sources. Reorganization of meaning and memory then becomes necessary. There is no reason to believe that this is its last restructuring; it is only the last to be detailed here.

❧ Finally I come back to Donald's (2001) proposition that symbolizing minds "are hybrid products of a brain-culture symbiosis." This proposition is hard to fathom from the position that symbols are independent products of individual minds. And it is not easy to see the truth of this statement when maintaining that language is only an expression of "underlying" basic concepts and thought. The symbiosis can be understood only in terms of deep changes in mind as culture—a specific culture, carried in a specific language—becomes part of the functioning of the mind itself. Previously I referred to this as the "mediated mind" (Nelson, 1996; Lucariello, Hudson, Fivush, and Bauer, 2004). Although I strongly believe in Donald's symbiosis, I also believe that the mind is not passive in the face of culture seemingly driven to take it over (nor of an ambitious meme demanding entry). Meaning belongs first to persons, and personal meaning filters cultural offerings. Thus the symbiosis grows in developmental time, at least partially through the openness accorded to culture by the child's own mind.

Notes

1. Modern Metaphors of the Developing Child

1. Barbara McClintock, Nobel Prize–winning biologist, quoted in Keller (1983).

2. Or "demons," to use the term introduced in cognitive science models of mind.

3. Based on Wellman (1990), Gopnik (1993a, 1993b), Gopnik and Wellman (1994).

4. I prefer the terms *know, knowledge,* and *known* to *belief, information,* or *learning;* the phenomenological sense of what is known from experience is one of certainty, not of tentativeness, even though it may be easily changed on another encounter.

5. A hug and a push are communicative, as are smiles and frowns.

6. Opponents of connectionist models identify them in these terms, but their vigorous response is that this is an oversimplification (see Elman et al., 1996). These theorists assert that the same neural network models can explain major changes in organization. Smith, an advocate of systems theory, asserts that simple associations can explain much of early development, for example in language learning (Smith, 1999).

2. Perspectives on Meaning

1. Regrettably, I have neither the space nor the expertise to enlarge on these strands of pragmatism and phenomenology and can only point to their significance in the history of the concepts. Heft (2001) provides a good introductory overview of pragmatism.

2. An exception is Bickhard (2002, p. 127): "It is only a pragmatic perspective that can account for the emergence of persons as social beings with a genuine social

ontology, not just processors with a batch of social knowledge to be processed and used."

3. It is important not to confuse this position with a disbelief in the existence of a real "objective" world; it is, rather, the expression of the belief that individuals inevitably view that reality from a distinctive perspective. See Harding (1991) on "strong objectivity."

4. Wilhelm Wundt, professor of inductive philosophy at the University of Leipzig from 1875 to 1917, is known as the father of experimental psychology.

5. The "new science of evo devo" (Carroll, 2005) reveals the role of regulatory genes in the development of embryonic organs and structure, unveiling a major source of evolutionary change. Exciting as these discoveries are (see also Jablonka and Lamb, 2005) they do not appear now to change the psychological landscape of development.

6. It is interesting that the era of EEA is placed (without much rationale) at 1 to 2 million years BP. This point in evolution is well past the point (6 million years BP) at which humans and chimpanzees last shared a common ancestor. Thus this presumed era of human genetic establishment ignores the prior history of genes we share with chimpanzees (approximately 99 percent), as well as any variation in adaptive demands or related gene changes over the past 100,000 years of *Homo sapiens*.

7. Alison Gopnik (quoted in Science Times, *New York Times*, January 4, 2005) goes further in believing that "babies and young children are actually more conscious, more vividly aware of their external world and internal life, than adults are." As explained in Chapter 3, I disagree with this view.

8. However, one should be cautioned that the use of brain imaging is still in its infancy and that many claims are made without sufficient support of replicated studies.

3. Being an Infant, Becoming a Child

1. See Tomasello (1999) for a discussion of the cultural ratchet effect.

2. To retain the advantages of upright posture and a large brain, the human physiological system adapted by curtailing the period of fetal development in utero to enable birthing through a narrow pelvic structure. Even so, for human mothers, giving birth is notably more difficult than it is for other primates, or other mammals, who typically give birth alone and unaided. In contrast, humans almost always give birth with the aid of others, such as midwives and doctors. The difficulty of natural birth for humans is indexed by the high death rate among both mothers and infants in premodern societies (see Hrdy, 1999, for details).

3. See Trevarthen (1980) for a more empathic interpretation.

4. "Mothering" is always to be understood in terms of behavioral practices, no matter who is actually engaged in them: father, nanny, grandmother, or other.

5. Sadly, Esther Thelen passed away in December 2004. She is greatly missed by the developmental community.

6. The term *modular* here is not the same as *modularity*, used to refer to structural modules of the brain dedicated to particular kinds of input analysis. In the dynamic systems construction, modular refers to separate components of the system

that may develop independently before becoming consolidated into a coordinated system of action.

7. Note that this is a phenomenological interpretation of the infant's response; however, it assumes phenomenological awareness of the cognitive level of an emotional response.

8. Basic-level categories are discussed in more detail in Chapters 5 and 6 in connection with word learning.

9. This could be tested by bringing the infant back for a second round of the experiment a week later, to determine if the habituation/dishabituation is completed more rapidly the second time, with a new control category set on the second occasion for comparison.

10. Previous theorists of infant development (Mahler, Pine, and Bergman, 1975) similarly claimed that locomotion brings about the "psychological birth" of the infant, breaking the mother-infant symbiosis and establishing autonomy and willfulness in the infant, as well as "glee," the infant's expression of delight in discovering the world's novelty and in new goals. In turn, infant locomotion was held to provide new challenges for parents and the family system.

11. See Rochat (2001) for an excellent summary and nonpartisan discussion of this and other infant research.

12. Perhaps what is most notable about these research achievements is the amount of public attention that has been given to the findings of "innate theories of core knowledge," demonstrated by theorists showing that infants can perform as they in fact do perform.

4. Toddling toward Childhood

1. The results of this paradigm do not rule out the possibility that the infant's idea of intention may be simply a sense of "trying" based on behavioral cues. It is not necessary to invoke a causal concept of intentionality.

2. The alleged long-run effects of such use remain controversial. However, analogous to the early use of walkers to establish independent locomotion (Chapter 3), the teaching of baby signs at six to twelve months may serve current functions of communication that facilitate the onset of word learning, as advocates claim, with repercussions for other social and self developments. This is not an endorsement of efforts to speed up development of language and cognition in the early years, but it does reflect the current state of the research.

3. When writing this chapter I had hanging in my study a print of the wonderful sixteenth-century painting by Brueghel of villagers of all ages engaged in games in the center of a town square; it kept this aspect of life before me, reminding me that toddlers are but at the beginning of the enjoyment of play, which may be as "real" a part of life for adults and children today as in the past.

4. I am not questioning the research that tracks sequences of play engagement, rather the interpretation of what such sequences imply about symbolic development.

5. DeLoache (2004) considers this to be a dissociation of action, planning, and control mechanisms.

6. By two years of age most children have learned and are using hundreds of

words and are constructing simple sentences. But individual differences in the timing of these accomplishments are huge; language plays different roles for different children during the second year. Unfortunately, the complexity of these processes of language learning require much more space than can be given them in this chapter or even in this book.

7. I recognize that this is a culture-centric view from middle-class America, and that even there, nannies, fathers, other relatives, and daycare workers may play the "mother role." However, the research, including my own, is strongly biased to middle-class mother-centered homes.

8. These analyses will be referred to several times in the succeeding chapters.

9. What is left that requires explanation is not the existence of representational thought but why a much older infant of six months may not "remember" that a toy has gone under a cover and try to retrieve it (Chapter 3).

10. These claims obviously do not constitute a fully developed theory but only the beginnings of some assumptions about the kind of cognitive and memory system that must be in place. Because different developmental theorists have different models in mind, I believe it is necessary for each to state what those assumptions are. This is my attempt.

11. The view of representational development presented here has much in common with Karmiloff-Smith's representational redescription proposal (1992), although the terminology and the details are different. It is also similar to the knowledge-level proposal of Campbell and Bickhard (1986), as well as to my own conception of levels, first outlined in 1986. Karmiloff-Smith proposed the redescription of one layer of representation in terms of the next higher layer. Here, however, the basic levels are not conceived of as representations but as organizations, and the "move" to higher levels comes about through external and internal constructive attempts to bring mental contents into consciousness and thus make them accessible to further manipulation and reflective thought. This way of putting the matter aids one in understanding what Bartlett (1932) meant by "turning around on one's own schema."

5. Experiential Semantics of First Words

1. Apologies to E. Hutchins for the heading "Early Word Learning in the Wild," with its mimetic play on the title of his 1996 book *Cognition in the Wild.*

2. The majority of the observations of children during this period are based on children who are learning English or other European languages in middle-class homes. This is an unfortunate limitation of our current knowledge about experience in infancy and early childhood. I have tried to insert words such as "typically" to indicate that the trends seen in these studies are not necessarily shared by all or seen across social classes, cultures, and language communities. Readers should bear in mind these cautions.

3. This observation is not contradicted by any of the large-scale surveys using the MCDI checklist filled out by mothers; see also L. Bloom, Tinker, and Margulis (1993).

4. It is odd to see claims, such as Bloom's, that children do not make errors in the use of words. Of course children tend to be more correct than not in the experimental paradigms of forced choice, and one can usually make sense of their word

choices, but in comparison to the criteria of adult usage, their word use is frequently far from conventional, especially in the early months (see Clark, 1983, 1993).

5. Indeed, in the 1970s my colleagues and I carried out precisely these kinds of demonstrations in exploring the implications of the functional core hypothesis (Nelson and Kessen, 1976).

6. This was not the conclusion Quine, a behaviorist philosopher, came to, however.

7. The noun bias here may be inflated for a number of reasons, among them the composition of the checklist that mothers filled out that revealed a similar bias (68 percent nouns); another, the probable bias of mothers toward identifying nouns in their children's speech, and the absence of idiosyncratic words and phrases in the checklist itself.

8. Of course novel names for specific places, products, and Web sites, for example, not to mention dogs and people, are assigned all the time by specific individuals, but these are different matters.

9. Clark (1993) emphasizes that children become aware of the need to use conventional words for their meanings. The point here is the reverse: children must hone their meanings to the words that they learn.

6. Entering the Symbolic World

1. Rochat actually attributes the opening of the symbolic gateway to the mother-child social exchanges of infancy, but clearly the more advanced possibilities listed await later developments.

2. See Bates and Goodman (1999) for the argument that grammar emerges from lexical learning, and Tomasello (2003) for the general argument that grammar is constructed from use.

3. In the opinion of many others, however, the quickness and easiness of grammar learning is overemphasized. While three years of language immersion is sufficient for most adults to achieve near-native competence in a new language, most four-year-olds have still to master many subtleties of their grammar.

4. Or as P. Bloom (2000) states, "They don't make mapping errors."

5. This statement implies an agnostic position on the question of whether children come to language with a concept of mind, as well as with concepts of *know* and *think*. I take the position that there are other possible construals of the interpretations of people's beliefs and behaviors than those encoded in our current versions of theory of mind. I therefore await convincing evidence that children believe in the existence of "a mind" prior to meeting the concept in language.

6. This is a theoretically neutral characterization of language structure that derives from the descriptive categories of Saussure (1915).

7. See Nelson (1996) for a summary of the evidence up to 1995. Supporting this constructive view, a recent computer simulation of the learning and organization of a food category indicated the predictive value of eating for forming the category of food (Salon and Nelson, 2000).

8. See also Mandler and McDonough (1998) for evidence of event organization of categories in one-year-olds.

9. See Nelson (2003a) for extended discussion. This analysis has much in

common with more traditional semantic analyses, such as Lyons's (1977) conception of sense in contrast to denotation and Saussure's (1915) conception of the syntagmatic and paradigmatic systems of language structure (Nelson, 1985).

10. See the discussion of similar puzzles in Chapter 4.

11. Recently, as noted in Chapter 4, DeLoache (2003) reported a study using small replicas of larger objects (chair, car), in which eighteen-month-old children attempted to use the replicas as they would the larger object (they tried sitting on the chair, for example). Her results confirm that children do not necessarily consider toys as representations or symbols but as versions of the things in themselves. What reinterpretation of symbolic play this finding demands awaits further study.

12. As reported orally by DeLoache in 2000.

13. Although there is research in the literature on adult memory and representation that is relevant to these processes (see, on text comprehension, Britton and Graesser, 1996; Kintsch, 1998), there has been little on children's processes.

14. See Dunn (1988) for documentation of family socialization experiences.

15. Later studies have suggested that such modality dominance is flexible under different conditions, including familiarity.

16. To my knowledge, Applebee's studies have not been replicated since the advent of the near-universal children's videos that present familiar dramas in a visual as well as auditory medium.

7. Finding Oneself in Time

1. This view is well represented in P. Bloom's (2000) book on learning the meaning of words (see Chapter 5 of this volume). It also forms the basis of "core knowledge" views of cognition that underlie much of the research on cognition in infancy (Chapter 3).

2. Vygotsky's ideas were outlined in opposition to Piaget's (1926) position that language represents thought but does not affect thought.

3. For Vygotsky of course, working in the "new world of socialism," this was definitely a good thing. In terms of American individualist ideologies, it is likely to be seen as a drawback to individual expression and creativity.

4. Those who use imagery in thinking, more than or rather than language, may be thought of as essentially constructing graphs and pictures for the self-observer.

5. Oddly, few developmentalists noted or attempted to investigate this phenomenon prior to the 1970s. Most accepted the common wisdom that the memory of young children was faulty or absent.

6. As always, with the caveat that the children referred to are those who have been observed in research or reported on in other ways: mainly middle-class European American children.

7. The introduction of digital clocks and watches has hastened young children's interest in clock time, also aided by the marking of hours of television shows.

8. This research and its interpretation has been challenged by other studies, but the finding remains robust at this point.

9. From Engel (1986); used with the author's permission.

10. See also Simcock and Hayne (2002) on how children's memory of an event is dependent on the availability of relevant language at the time of the experience.

11. It is possible that her father had presented a more complete version of the coming expedition earlier in the pre-bed conversation. However, it is unlikely that it included all of Emily's speculations. For example, the beach expedition required tens of miles of travel rather than "a couple of blocks."

12. I distinguish "episode memory" in this context from "episodic memory" to make it clear that although the child may give evidence of remembering a specific event, the memory is still not reliably marked as of "my own self."

13. Ratner, Foley, and Gimpert's (2000) study of children's memory of self and other's actions in a project indicates that such confusion is also possible, but in this case, unlike in many everyday routines and studies of action memory, the actions of both participants were the same (pasting stickers); only the objects differed.

8. Entering a Community of Minds

1. Among the populations typically measured in North American psychological laboratories

2. Although (contrary to initial claims) there are significant cultural variations in its achievement, as many have now reported (Lillard, 1998; Lucariello, 2004; Naito, 2004).

3. See Rubin (1995) for an extensive examination of the characteristics of memory in oral cultures.

4. See Nelson (1978) for a report on studies of this bias.

5. Of course it could be that essentialism is innate but that children choose the wrong quality as the essence of kind in the case of racial distinctions, namely physical appearance.

6. Ingold (2004) provides a vigorous objection to the method used by Astuti, Solomon, and Carey and the conclusions to which they respond.

7. Of course the idea of natural kinds may also be questioned in application to children's categories; in the folk language, is this equivalent to animacy?

8. Researchers typically scaffold children's answers very carefully for their experiments, to reduce variance and to be clear as to what is intended as an answer. But this very scaffolding may obscure information relevant to what they are working on, as we found in extending interviews in a ToM task (Nelson et al., 2003). See excerpts in Table 8.1.

9. The Study of Developing Young Minds

1. I definitely do not mean to imply that the young personal or private mind is free from social-cultural influences. Indeed, the child is embedded in a social-cultural "field" from birth. But what she makes of it—how its experiences are conserved and organized—is largely hidden from the view of other minds.

2. In one of my first published research reports, I showed that five- and seven-year-old children also imposed subjective organization in memorizing random lists of words (Nelson, 1969).

3. Maybe this point is obvious; however, in this form it is startlingly new to me, and I am very sure that my fellow developmental psychologists are not persuaded of it. Neuropsychologists, for example Damasio and Donald, apparently accept it implicitly, as do many memory theorists, such as Neisser.

4. See Kuper (1999) for an extensive discussion.

5. See Bronfenbrenner and Ceci (1994).

6. See Rutter (1987, 2006), Curtiss (1977). Rutter (2006) covers recent findings on long-term effects of institutionalization in Romanian children adopted as infants or toddlers by English families.

7. My research group benefited from similar examples from observations of our own children that guided our further research.

8. Piaget's studies of his three children (e.g., Piaget, 1952) should not be simply discarded but taken as a model and informed by modern methods.

9. See Deacon (2005) for an insightful explication.

10. This restriction makes it easier to move back and forth from the brain to mind, as there is no justification for finding representations in the brain.

11. Note in this connection the significance of externalization in learning to read. Reading aloud appears to be a universal preliminary to learning to read silently, internally. This practice seems to imply that the relation of the written symbols to their representation in oral form must be established before they can be transformed into an internal representation for memory. This is different from the child's comprehending words before he or she can produce them; as discussed in Chapters 5 and 6, words comprehended tend to be different from those produced, and the processes involved are different as well.

12. Semantic memory may include general knowledge derived from personal experience but not identified specifically as "mine." This is a difficulty of adapting these terms to the developmental processes being described.

References

Adams, A. K., and Bullock, D. (1986). Apprenticeship in word use: Social convergence processes in learning categorically related nouns. In S. A. I. Kuczaj and M. D. Barrett (Eds.), *The development of word meaning* (pp. 155–197). New York: Springer-Verlag.

Adolph, K. E. (2000). Specificity of learning: Why infants fall over a veritable cliff. *Psychological Science, 11,* 290–295.

Anglin, J. (1977). *Word, object and conceptual development.* New York: Norton.

Applebee, A. N. (1978). *The child's concept of story.* Chicago: University of Chicago Press.

Arbib, M. A. (2002). The mirror system, imitation, and evolution of language. In C. Nehaniv and K. Dautenhahn (Eds.), *Imitation in animals and artifacts.* Cambridge, MA: MIT Press.

Arbib, M. A. (2005). From monkey-like action recognition to human language: An evolutionary framework for neurolinguistics. *Behavioral and Brain Sciences, 28,* 105–168.

Ariel, S. (1992). Semiotic analysis of children's play: A method for investigating social development. *Merrill-Palmer Quarterly, 38,* 119–138.

Astington, J. W., and Baird, J. (Eds.). (2005). *Why language matters to theory of mind.* New York: Oxford University Press.

Astington, J. W., Harris, P. L., and Olson, D. (Eds.). (1988). *Developing theories of mind.* Cambridge: Cambridge University Press.

Astuti, R., Solomon, G. E. A., and Carey, S. (2004). Constraints on conceptual development. *Monographs of the Society for Research in Child Development, 69*(3, Serial No. 277).

Baillargeon, R. (1999). Young infants' expectations about hidden objects: A reply to three challenges; Response to Smith and the commentators. *Developmental Science, 2,* 115–132; 157–162.

277

Baillargeon, R. (2004). Infants' physical world. *Current Directions in Psychological Science, 13*, 89–94.

Baldwin, D. (1991). Infants' contributions to the achievement of joint reference. *Child Development, 62*, 875–890.

Baldwin, D. A. (1993). Infants' ability to consult the speaker for clues to word references. *Journal of Child Language, 20*, 395–418.

Baldwin, J. M. (1902). *Development and evolution.* New York: Macmillan.

Barkow, J. H., Cosmides, L., and Tooby, J. (1992). *The adapted mind: Evolutionary psychology and the generation of culture.* New York: Oxford University Press.

Baron-Cohen, S. (2000). Theory of mind and autism: A fifteen-year review. In S. Baron-Cohen, H. Tager-Flusberg, and D. J. Cohen (Eds.), *Understanding other minds: Perspectives from developmental cognitive neuroscience* (pp. 3–20). Oxford: Oxford University Press.

Barrett, M. D. (1986). Early semantic representations and early word-usage. In I. S. A. Kuczaj and M. D. Barrett (Eds.), *The development of word meaning: Progress in cognitive development research* (pp. 39–68). New York: Springer-Verlag.

Barsalou, L. W. (1999). Perceptual symbol systems. *Behavioral and Brain Sciences, 22*, 577–609.

Barsalou, L. W. (1989). Intraconcept similarity and its implications for interconcept similarity. In S. Vosniadou and A. Ortony (Eds.), *Similarity and analogical reasoning* (pp. 76–121). Cambridge: Cambridge University Press.

Bartlett, F. C. (1932). *Remembering: A study in experimental and social psychology.* Cambridge: Cambridge University Press.

Bartsch, K., and Wellman, H. M. (1995). *Children talk about the mind.* New York: Oxford University Press.

Bates, E., Bretherton, I., Shore, C., and Snyder, L. (1984). Early language inventory. Part 1: Vocabulary checklist. Unpublished document, University of California at San Diego.

Bates, E., Bretherton, I., and Snyder, L. (1988). *From first words to grammar: Individual differences and dissociable mechanisms.* New York: Cambridge University Press.

Bauer, P. J. (1996). Recalling past events: From infancy to early childhood. *Annals of Child Development, 11*, 25–71.

Bauer, P. J. (2006). *Remembering the times of our lives: Memory in infancy and beyond.* Mahwah, NJ: Erlbaum.

Bauer, P. J., Hertsgaard, L. A., and Dow, G. A. (1994). After 8 months have passed: Long-term recall of events by 1-to 2-year-old children. *Memory, 2*, 353–382.

Bauer, P. J., and Mandler, J. M. (1990). Remembering what happened next: Very young children's recall of event sequences. In R. Fivush and J. A. Hudson (Eds.), *Knowing and remembering in young children.* New York: Cambridge University Press.

Bauer, P. J., Wenner, J. A., Dropik, P. L., and Wewerka, S. S. (2000). Parameters of remembering and forgetting in the transition from infancy to early childhood. *Monographs of the Society for Research in Child Development, 65*(4, Serial no. 263).

Bauer, P. J., and Wewerka, S. S. (1997). Saying is revealing: Verbal expression of event memory in the transition from infancy to early childhood. In P. W. van den Broek, P. J. Bauer, and T. Bourg (Eds.), *Developmental spans in event comprehension and representation* (pp. 139–168). Mahwah, NJ: Erlbaum.

Bauer, P. J., Wiebe, S. A., Carver, L. J., Waters, J. M., and Nelson, C. A. (2003). Developments in long-term explicit memory late in the first year of life: Behavioral and electrophysiological indices. *Psychological Science, 14,* 629–635.

Benedict, H. (1979). Early lexical development: Comprehension and production. *Journal of Child Language, 6,* 183–200.

Benson, J. B. (1994). The origins of future-orientation in the everyday lives of 9- to 36-month-old infants. In M. M. Haith, J. B. Benson, R. J. Roberts, and B. Pennington (Eds.), *The development of future-oriented processes* (pp. 375–408). Chicago: University of Chicago Press.

Bickerton, D. (1990). *Language and species.* Chicago: University of Chicago Press.

Bickhard, M. H. (1987). The social nature of the functional nature of language. In M. Hickmann (Ed.), *Social and functional approaches to language and thought.* New York: Academic Press.

Bickhard, M. H. (2002). The biological emergence of representation. In T. Brown and L. Smith (Eds.), *Reductionism and the development of knowledge* (pp. 105–132). Mahwah, NJ: Erlbaum.

Bickhard, M. H. (2004). The social ontology of persons. In J. I. M. Carpendale and U. Muller (Eds.), *Social interaction and the development of knowledge* (pp. 111–132). Mahwah, NJ: Erlbaum.

Bickhard, M. H. (In press). How does the environment affect the person? In L. T. Winegar and J. Valsiner (Eds.), *Children's development within social contexts: Metatheoretical, theoretical and methodological issues.* Hillsdale, NJ: Lawrence Erlbaum.

Bijou, S. W., and Baer, D. M. (1965). *Child development: Vol. 2. Universal stage of infancy.* New York: Appleton-Century-Crofts.

Birch, S. A. J., and Bloom, P. (2003). Children are cursed: An asymmetric bias in mental-state attribution. *Psychological Science, 14,* 283–286.

Bloom, L. (1973). *One word at a time.* The Hague: Mouton.

Bloom, L. (1991). *Language development from two to three.* New York: Cambridge University Press.

Bloom, L. (1993). *The transitions from infancy to language: Acquiring the power of expression.* New York: Cambridge University Press.

Bloom, L. (2000). The intentionality model of word learning: How to learn a word, any word. In R. M. Golinkoff, K. Hirsh-Pasek, L. Bloom, L. B. Smith, A. L. Woodward, N. Akhtar, M. Tomasello, and G. Hollich (Eds.), *Becoming a word learner: A debate on lexical acquisition* (pp. 19–50). New York: Oxford University Press.

Bloom, L., and Lahey, M. (1978). *Language development and language disorders.* New York: Wiley.

Bloom, L., Lahey, M., Hood, L., Lifter, K., and Fiess, K. (1980). Complex sentences: Acquisition of syntactic connectives and the semantic relations they encode. *Journal of Child Language, 7,* 235–261.

Bloom, L., Tinker, E., and Margulis, C. (1993). The words children learn: Evidence against a noun bias in children's vocabularies. *Cognitive Development, 8,* 431–450.

Bloom, P. (1996). Intention, history, and artifact concepts. *Cognition, 60,* 1–29.

Bloom, P. (2000). *How children learn the meaning of words.* Cambridge, MA: MIT Press.

Blum-Kulka, S., and Snow, C. (1992). Developing autonomy for tellers, tales, and telling in family narrative events. *Journal of Narrative and Life History, 2,* 187–218.

Blum-Kulka, S., and Snow, C. E. (Eds.). (2002). *Talking to adults: The contribution of multiparty discourse to language acquisition.* Mahwah, NJ: Erlbaum.

Bogdan, R. J. (2003). *Interpreting minds.* Cambridge, MA: MIT Press.

Booth, J. R., and Hall, W. S. (1995). Development of the understanding of the polysemous meanings of the mental state verb know. *Cognitive Development, 10,* 529–550.

Boroditsky, L. (2001). Does language shape thought? Mandarin and English speakers' conceptions of time. *Cognitive Psychology, 43,* 1–22.

Bowerman, M. (1982). Reorganization processes in lexical and syntactic development. In E. Wanner and L. Gleitman (Eds.), *Language acquisition: The state of the art* (pp. 319–346). New York: Cambridge University Press.

Bowerman, M., and Choi, S. (2000). Shaping meanings for language: universal and language-specific in the acquisition of spatial semantic categories. In M. Bowerman and S. Levinson (Eds.), *Language acquisition and conceptual development* (pp. 475–511). New York: Cambridge University Press.

Bowlby, J. (1982). *Attachment and loss: Vol. 1. Attachment* (2nd rev. ed.). New York: Basic Books.

Brainerd, C. J., and Reyna, V. F. (1990). Gist is the grist: Fuzzy-trace theory and the new intuitionism. *Developmental Review, 10,* 3–47.

Braten, S. (1998). Infant learning by altercentric participation: The reverse of ego-centric observation in autism. In S. Braten (Ed.), *Intersubjective communication and emotion in early ontogeny* (pp. 105–127). New York: Cambridge University Press.

Bretherton, I., and Beeghly, M. (1982). Talking about internal states: The acquisition of an explicit theory of mind. *Developmental Psychology, 18,* 906–921.

Britton, B. K., and Graesser, A. C. (Eds.). (1996). *Models of understanding text.* Mahwah, NJ: Erlbaum.

Bronfenbrenner, U., and Ceci, S. J. (1994). Nature-nurture reconceptualized: A bioecological model. *Psychological Review, 101,* 568–586.

Bronfenbrenner, U., and Morris, P. A. (1998). The ecology of developmental process. In R. M. Lerner (Ed.), *Handbook of child psychology: Vol. 1. Theoretical models of human development* (5th Ed., pp. 993–1028). New York: Wiley and Sons.

Brown, R. (1958). *Words and things.* New York: The Free Press of Glencoe.

Brown, R. (1973). *A first language: The early stages.* Cambridge, MA: Harvard University Press.

Bruner, J. S. (1983). *Child's talk: Learning to use language.* New York: Norton.

Bruner, J. S. (1990). *Acts of meaning.* Cambridge, MA: Harvard University Press.

Bruner, J. S. (1994). The "remembered" self. In U. Neisser and R. Fivush (Eds.), *The remembering self: Construction and accuracy in the self-narrative* (pp. 41–54). New York: Cambridge University Press.

Bruner, J. S., Olver, R. R., and Greenfield, P. M. (1966). *Studies in cognitive growth.* New York: Wiley.

Byrne, R., and Whiten, A. (Eds.). (1988). *Machiavellian intelligence.* Oxford: Oxford University Press.

Callanan, M. (1992). Preschoolers' questions and parents' explanations: Causal thinking in everyday activity. *Cognitive Development, 7*, 213–233.

Campbell, R. L., and Bickhard, M. H. (1986). *Knowing levels and developmental stages.* Basel: Karger.

Campos, J. J., Anderson, D. I., Barbu-Roth, M. A., Hubbard, E. M., Hertenstein, M. J., and Witherington, D. (2000). Travel broadens the mind. *Infancy, 1*, 149–220.

Carey, S. (1985). *Conceptual change in childhood.* Cambridge, MA: MIT Press.

Carni, E., and French, L. A. (1984). The acquisition of before and after reconsidered: What develops? *Journal of Experimental Child Psychology, 37*, 394–403.

Carpendale, J. I. M., and Lewis, C. (2004). Constructing an understanding of mind: The development of children's social understanding and social interaction. *Behavioral and Brain Sciences, 27*, 79–151.

Carpenter, M., Nagell, K., and Tomasello, M. (1998). Social cognition, joint attention, and communicative competence from 9 to 15 months of age. *Monographs of the Society for Research in Child Development, 63* (4, Serial No. 255).

Carroll, S. B. (2005). *Endless forms most beautiful: The new science of evo devo.* New York: W. W. Norton.

Carruthers, P. (2002). The cognitive functions of language. *Behavioral and Brain Sciences, 25*, 657–726.

Carver, L. J., and Bauer, P. J. (2001). The dawning of a past: The emergence of long-term explicit memory in infancy. *Journal of Experimental Psychology, 130*, 726–745.

Caselli, M. C., Bates, E., Casadio, P., Fenson, J., Fenson, L., and Sanderl, L. (1995). A cross-linguistic study of early lexical development. *Cognitive Development, 10*, 159–199.

Ceci, S. J., and Bruck, M. (1993). Suggestibility of the child witness: A historical review and synthesis. *Psychological Bulletin, 113*, 403–439.

Chandler, M. (1988). Doubt and developing theories of mind. In J. W. Astington, P. L. Harris, and D. R. Olson (Eds.), *Developing theories of mind* (pp. 387–413). New York: Cambridge University Press.

Chomsky, N. (1965). *Aspects of a theory of syntax.* Cambridge, MA: MIT Press.

Chukovsky, K. (1971). *From two to five* (M. Morton, Trans., Rev. ed.). Berkeley, CA: University of California Press.

Clark, A. (1997). *Being there: Putting brain, body, and world together again.* Cambridge, MA: MIT Press.

Clark, E. V. (1973). What's in a word? On the child's acquisition of semantics in his first language. In T. E. Moore (Ed.), *Cognitive development and the acquisition of language.* New York: Academic Press.

Clark, E. V. (1983). Meanings and concepts. In J. Flavell and E. Markman (Eds.), *Cognitive development* (Vol. 3, 4th ed.). New York: Wiley.

Clark, E. V. (1993). *The lexicon in acquisition.* New York: Cambridge University Press.

Cole, M. (1996). *Cultural psychology: A once and future discipline.* Cambridge, MA: Harvard University Press.

Conway, M. A., and Rubin, D. C. (1993). The structure of autobiographical memory. In A. F. Collins, S. E. Gathercole, M. A. Conway, and P. E. Morris (Eds.), *Theories of memory* (pp. 103–139). Hillsdale, NJ: Erlbaum.

Curtiss, S. (1977). *Genie: A psycholinguistic study of a modern-day "wild child."* New York: Academic.

Damasio, A. (1999). *The feeling of what happens: Body and emotion in the making of consciousness.* New York: Harcourt.

Damon, W. (Ed.). (1998). *Handbook of child psychology* (5th ed.). New York: Wiley.

Dawkins, R. (1976). *The selfish gene.* New York: Oxford University Press.

Deacon, T. W. (1997). *The symbolic species: Coevolution of language and the brain.* New York: Norton.

Deacon, T. W. (2003). Multilevel selection in a complex adaptive system: The problem of language origins. In B. H. Weber and D. J. Depew (Eds.), *Evolution and learning: The Baldwin effect reconsidered* (pp. 81–106). Cambridge, MA: MIT Press.

Deacon, T. W. (2005). Beyond Piaget's phenocopy: The baby in the Lamarckian bath. In S. T. Parker, J. Langer, and C. Milbrath (Eds.), *Biology and knowledge revisited: From neurogenesis to psychogenesis* (pp. 87–122). Mahwah, NJ: Erlbaum.

DeCasper, A. J., Lecanuet, J.-P., Busnel, M.-C., Granier-Deferre, C., and Maugeais, R. (1994). Fetal reactions to recurrent maternal speech. *Infant Behavior and Development, 17,* 159–164.

DeLoache, J. S. (1990). Young children's understanding of models. In R. F. J. Hudson (Ed.), *Knowing and remembering in young children.* New York: Cambridge University Press.

DeLoache, J. (1991). Symbolic functioning in very young children. *Child Development, 62,* 736–752.

DeLoache, J. S. (2003). Research reported in keynote lecture at the Cognitive Development Society biennial meeting in Park City, Utah, October 2003.

DeLoache, J. S. (2004). Scale errors by very young children: A dissociation between action, planning and control. *Behavioral and Brain Sciences, 27,* 32–33.

Dennett, D. (1994). Language and intelligence. In J. Khalfa (Ed.), *What is intelligence?* (pp. 161–178). Cambridge: Cambridge University Press.

Depew, D. J., and Weber, B. H. (1997). *Darwinism evolving: Systems dynamics and the genealogy of natural selection.* Cambridge, MA: MIT Press.

Dewey, J. (1981). *The philosophy of John Dewey* (J. J. McDermott, Ed.). Chicago: University of Chicago Press.

Dickinson, D. K., and Tabors, P. O. (Eds.). (2001). *Beginning literacy with language.* Baltimore: Paul H. Brookes Publishing.

Dickstein, M. (Ed.). (1998). *The revival of pragmatism: New essays on social thought, law, and culture.* Durham, NC: Duke University Press.

Donald, M. (1991). *Origins of the modern mind.* Cambridge, MA: Harvard University Press.

Donald, M. (2000). The central role of culture in cognitive evolution: A reflection on the myth of the "isolated mind." In L. P. Nucci, G. B. Saxe, and E. Turiel (Eds.), *Culture, thought, and development* (pp. 19–38). Mahwah, NJ: Erlbaum.

Donald, M. (2001). *A mind so rare: The evolution of human consciousness.* New York: Norton.

Dreyfus, H. L. (1991). *Being-in-the-world: A commentary on Heidegger's* Being and Time, *Division 1.* Cambridge, MA: MIT Press.

Dunn, J. (1988). *The beginnings of social understanding.* Cambridge, MA: Harvard University Press.

Edelman, G. M., and Tononi, G. (2000). *A universe of consciousness: How matter becomes imagination.* New York: Basic Books.

Einstein, G., and Flanagan, O. (2003). Sexual identities and narratives of self. In G. Fireman and T. E. McVay (Eds.), *Narrative and consciousness: Literature, psychology, and the brain.* New York: Oxford University Press.

Elman, J. L., Bates, E. A., Johnson, M. H., Karmiloff-Smith, A., Parisi, D., and Plunkett, K. (1996). *Rethinking innateness: A connectionist perspective on development.* Cambridge, MA: MIT Press.

Engel, S. (1986). *Learning to reminisce: A developmental study of how young children talk about the past.* Unpublished doctoral dissertation, City University of New York Graduate Center, New York.

Fagan, J. F. I. (1984). Infant memory: History, current trends, relations to cognitive psychology. In M. Moscovitch (Ed.), *Infant memory: Its relation to normal and pathological memory in humans and other animals* (pp. 1–28). New York: Plenum.

Fenson, L., Dale, P. S., Reznick, J. S., Bates, E., Thal, D. J., and Pethick, S. J. (1994). Variability in early communicative development. *Monographs of the Society for Research in Child Development, 59*(5).

Fernald, A. (1992). Human maternal vocalizations to infants as biologically relevant signals: An evolutionary perspective. In J. H. C. Barkow, L. Cosmides, and J. Tooby (Eds.), *The adapted mind: Evolutionary psychology and the generation of culture* (pp. 391–428). New York: Oxford University Press.

Fernald, A. (2005). *Young children's inferential use of verb information in learning new objects.* Paper presented at the Symposium on Inferential Processes in Word Learning, biennial meeting of the Society for Research in Child Development, April 9.

Fischer, K. W., and Bidell, T. (1991). Constraining nativist inferences about cognitive capacities. In S. Carey and R. Gelman (Eds.), *The epigenesis of mind: Essays on biology and cognition* (pp. 199–236). Hillsdale, NJ: Erlbaum.

Fischer, K. W., and Rose, S. P. (1993). Development of coordination of components in brain and behavior: A framework for theory and research. In G. Dawson and K. W. Fischer (Eds.), *Human behavior and the developing brain.* New York: Guilford Press.

Fivush, R. (1994). Constructing narrative, emotion, and self in parent-child conversations about the past. In U. Neisser and R. Fivush (Eds.), *The remembering self: Construction and accuracy in the self-narrative* (pp. 136–157). New York: Cambridge University Press.

Fivush, R., and Hamond, N. R. (1990). Autobiographical memory across the preschool years: Toward reconceptualizing childhood amnesia. In R. Fivush and J. A. Hudson (Eds.), *Knowing and remembering in young children* (pp. 223–248). New York: Cambridge University Press.

Fivush, R., and Nelson, K. (2004). Culture and language in the emergence of autobiographical memory. *Psychological Science, 15,* 573–577.

Fivush, R., and Nelson, K. (2006). Parent-child conversations locate the self in the past. *British Journal of Developmental Psychology, 24,* 235–251.

Fivush, R., and Reese, E. (1991). *Parental styles for talking about the past.* Paper presented at the International Conference on Memory, Lancaster, England, July.

Flanagan, O. (1992). *Consciousness reconsidered.* Cambridge, MA: MIT Press.

Fodor, J. A. (1975). *The language of thought.* New York: Crowell.

Fodor, J. A. (1981). *Representations.* Cambridge, MA: MIT Press.

Fodor, J. A. (1983). *Modularity of mind.* Cambridge, MA: MIT Press.

Fogel, A. (2001). A relational perspective on the development of self and emotion. In H. A. Bosma and E. S. Kunnen (Eds.), *Identity and emotions: Development through self-organization.* New York: Cambridge University Press.

Fontaine, R. G. (2002). *Preschoolers' understanding of story books: The influence of story genre, affect, and language.* Unpublished doctoral dissertation, City University of New York Graduate School, New York.

Frege, G. (1892). On sense and reference. In P. Geach and M. Black (Eds.), *Translations from the philosophical writings of Gottlob Frege.* Oxford: Blackwell, 1960.

French, L. A., and Nelson, K. (1985). *Young children's understanding of relational terms: Some ifs, ors and buts.* New York: Springer-Verlag.

Furrow, D., Moore, C., Davidge, J., and Chiasson, L. (1992). Mental terms in mothers' and children's speech: Similarities and relationships. *Journal of Child Language, 19,* 617–632.

Gelman, S. A. (2003). *The essential child.* New York: Oxford University Press.

Gelman, S. A., and Markman, E. M. (1986). Categories and induction in young children. *Cognition, 23,* 183–209.

Gentner, D. (1982). Why nouns are learned before verbs: Linguistic relativity versus natural partitioning. In S. A. I. Kuczaj (Ed.), *Language development: Vol. 2. Language, thought, and culture* (pp. 301–334). Hillsdale, NJ: Lawrence Erlbaum.

Gentner, D. (2003). Why we're so smart. In D. Gentner and S. Goldin-Meadow (Eds.), *Language in mind: Advances in the study of language and thought* (pp. 195–236). Cambridge, MA: MIT Press.

Gergely, G., and Watson, J. S. (1999). Early socio-emotional development: Contingency perception and the social-biofeedback model. In P. Rochat (Ed.), *Early social cognition: Understanding others in the first months of life* (pp. 101–136). Mahwah, NJ: Erlbaum.

Gerhardt, J. (1989). Monologue as a speech genre. In K. Nelson (Ed.), *Narratives from the crib* (pp. 171–230). Cambridge, MA: Harvard University Press.

Gershkoff-Stowe, L., and Thelen, E. (2004). U-shaped changes in behavior: A dynamic systems perspective. *Journal of Cognition and Development, 5,* 11–36.

Gesell, A. L., and Amatruda, C. S. (1945). *The embryology of behavior: The beginnings of the human mind.* New York: Harper.

Gibson, E. J., and Walk, R. (1960). The "visual cliff." *Scientific American, 202,* 64–71.

Gibson, J. J. (1979). *The ecological approach to visual perception.* Boston: Houghton Mifflin.

Glenberg, A. M. (1997). What memory is for. *Behavioral and Brain Sciences, 20,* 1–55.

Goldin-Meadow, S. (1997). When gestures and words speak differently. *Current Directions in Psychological Science, 6,* 138–143.

Goldman, S. (2003). *Unshared lives: Fictional and personal narrative productions in high-functioning autistic children.* Unpublished doctoral dissertation, City University of New York, New York.

Golinkoff, R. M., Hirsh-Pasek, K., Bloom, L., Smith, L. B., Woodward, A. L., Akhtar, N., et al. (2000). *Becoming a word learner: A debate on lexical acquisition.* New York: Oxford University Press.

Golinkoff, R. M., Hirsh-Pasek, K., and Hollich, G. (1999). Emergent cues for early word learning. In B. MacWhinney (Ed.), *The emergence of language* (pp. 305–330). Mahwah, NJ: Erlbaum.

Goodman, G. S., Rudy, L., Bottoms, B. L., and Aman, C. (1990). Children's concerns and memory: Issues of ecological validity in the study of children's eyewitness testimony. In R. Fivush and J. A. Hudson (Eds.), *Knowing and remembering in young children* (pp. 249–284). New York: Cambridge University Press.

Goodwin, S. W., and Acredolo, L. P. (2000). *Baby minds.* New York: Bantam Books.

Goody, E. N. (1997). Social intelligence and language: Another Rubicon. In A. Whiten and R. W. Byrne (Eds.), *Machiavellian intelligence II: Extensions and evaluations.* (pp. 365–377). Cambridge: Cambridge University Press.

Gopnik, A. (1993a). How we know our minds: The illusion of first-person knowledge of intentionality. *Behavioral and Brain Sciences, 16,* 1–14.

Gopnik, A. (1993b). Theories and illusions. *Behavioral and Brain Sciences, 16,* 90–100.

Gopnik, A., and Choi, S. (1990). Language and cognition. *First Language, 10,* 199–216.

Gopnik, A., Glymour, C., Sobel, D. M., Schulz, L. E., Kushnir, T., and Danks, D. (2004). A theory of causal learning in children: Causal maps and Bayes nets. *Psychological Review, 111,* 3–32.

Gopnik, A., and Meltzoff, A. (1996). *Words, thoughts and theories.* Cambridge, MA: MIT Press.

Gopnik, A., Meltzoff, A., and Kuhl, P. K. (1999). *The scientist in the crib: Minds, brains, and how children learn.* New York: Morrow.

Gopnik, A., and Wellman, H. (1994). The theory theory. In L. A. Hirschfeld and S. A. Gelman (Eds.), *Mapping the mind* (pp. 257–293). New York: Cambridge University Press.

Gottlieb, G. (1997). *Synthesizing nature-nurture.* Mahwah, NJ: Erlbaum.

Gould, S. J. (1977). *Ontogeny and phylogeny.* Cambridge, MA: Harvard University Press.

Greenfield, P. M., and Smith, J. (1976). *The structure of communication in early language development.* New York: Academic Press.

Greenough, W. T., Black, J. E., and Wallace, C. S. (1987). Experience and brain development. *Child Development, 58,* 539–559.

Haden, C. A., Ornstein, P. A., and Didow, S. M. (2001). Mother-child conversational interchanges as events unfold: Linkages to subsequent remembering. *Child Development, 72,* 1016–1031.

Haith, M. M., and Benson, J. B. (1998). Infant cognition. In D. Kuhn and R. S. Siegler (Eds.), *Cognition, perception, and language* (pp. 199–254). *Handbook of Child Psychology* (5th ed., Vol. 2). New York: Wiley.

Hall, G. S. (1904). *Adolescence: Its psychology and its relation to physiology, anthropology, sociology, sex, crime, religion, and education.* New York: Appleton.

Hampson, J. (1989). *Elements of style: Maternal and child contributions to the expressive and referential styles of language acquisition.* Unpublished doctoral dissertation, City University of New York Graduate Center, New York.

Hampson, J., and Nelson, K. (1993). The relation of maternal language to variation in rate and style of language acquisition. *Journal of Child Language, 20,* 313–342.

Harding, S. (1991). *Whose science? Whose knowledge? Thinking from women's lives.* Ithaca, NY: Cornell University Press.

Harris, J. R. (1998). *The nurture assumption.* New York: Free Press.

Harris, P. L. (2005). Conversation, pretense and theory of mind. In J. Astington and J. Baird (Eds.), *Why language matters to theory of mind* (pp. 70–83). New York: Oxford University Press.

Harris, P. L., and Kavanaugh, R. D. (1993). Young children's understanding of pretense. *Monographs of the Society for Research in Child Development, 58*(1, Serial No. 231).

Hart, B., and Risley, T. R. (1995). *Meaningful differences in the everyday experiences of young children.* Baltimore: Paul B. Brookes Publishing.

Heath, S. B. (1983). *Ways with words.* Cambridge: Cambridge University Press.

Heft, H. (2001). *Ecological psychology in context: James Gibson, Roger Barker, and the legacy of William James's radical empiricism.* Mahwah, NJ: Erlbaum.

Hendriks-Jansen, H. (1996). *Catching ourselves in the act: Situated activity, interactive emergence, evolution, and human thought.* Cambridge, MA: MIT Press.

Hewes, G. (1976). The current status of the gestural theory of language origin. In S. R. Harnad, H. D. Steklis, and J. Lancaster (Eds.), *Origins and evolution of language and speech* (vol. 280, pp. 482–504). New York: Annals of the New York Academy of Sciences.

Hirschfeld, L. A. (1995). Do children have a theory of race? *Cognition, 54,* 209–252.

Hirschfeld, L. A., and Gelman, S. A. (Eds.). (1994). *Mapping the mind: Domain specificity in cognition and culture.* New York: Cambridge University Press.

Hirsh-Pasek, K., Golinkoff, R. M., and Hollich, G. (2000). An emergentist coalition model for word learning: Mapping words to objects is a product of the interaction of multiple cues. In R. M. Golinkoff, et al. (Ed.), *Becoming a word learner: A debate on lexical acquisition* (pp. 136–164). New York: Oxford University Press.

Hobson, R. P. (1993). *Autism and the development of mind.* Hillsdale, NJ: Lawrence Erlbaum Assoc.

Hoff, E., and Naigles, L. (2002). How children use input to acquire a lexicon. *Child Development, 73,* 418–433.

Hollich, G. J., Hirsh-Pasek, K., and Golinkoff, R. M. (2000). Breaking the language barrier: An emergentist coalition model for the origins of word learning. *Monographs of the Society for Research in Child Development, 65*(3).

Homer, B., and Nelson, K. (2005). Seeing objects as symbols and symbols as objects: Language and the development of dual representation. In B. Homer and C. Tamis-LeMonda (Eds.), *The development of social cognition and communication.* Mahwah, NJ: Erlbaum.

Homer, B., and Tamis-LeMonda, C. (Eds.). (2005). *The development of social cognition and communication.* Mahwah, NJ: Lawrence Erlbaum.

Hrdy, S. B. (1999). Mother Nature: A history of mothers, infants, and natural selection. New York: Pantheon Books.

Hudson, J. A. (1986). Memories are made of this: General event knowledge and the development of autobiographic memory. In K. Nelson (Ed.), *Event knowledge: Structure and function in development* (pp. 97–118). Hillsdale, NJ: Lawrence Erlbaum.

Hudson, J. A. (1990). The emergence of autobiographic memory in mother-child conversation. In R. Fivush and J. A. Hudson (Eds.), *Knowing and remembering in young children* (pp. 166–196). New York: Cambridge University Press.

Hudson, J. A. (2004). The development of future thinking: Constructing future events in mother-child conversation. In J. M. Lucariello, J. A. Hudson, R. Fivush, and P. J. Bauer (Eds.), *The development of the mediated mind: Sociocultural context and cognitive development* (pp. 127–150). Mahwah, NJ: Erlbaum.

Hutchins, E. (1996). *Cognition in the wild.* Cambridge, MA: MIT Press.

Huttenlocher, J., Haight, W., Bryk, A., Seltzer, M., and Lyons, T. (1991). Early vocabulary growth: Relation to language input and gender. *Developmental Psychology, 27,* 236–248.

Huttenlocher, J., and Higgins, E. T. (1978). Issues in the study of symbolic development. In W. A. Collins (Ed.), *Minnesota Symposium on Child Psychology* (Vol. 11, pp. 98–140). Hillsdale, NJ: Erlbaum.

Ingold, T. (2004). Conceptual development in Madagascar: A critical comment. *Monographs of the Society for Research in Child Development, 69*(3), 136–144.

Inhelder, B., and Piaget, J. (1958). *The growth of logical thinking from childhood to adolescence.* New York: Basic Books.

Jablonka, E., and Lamb, M. J. (2005). Evolution in four dimensions: Genetic, epigenetic, behavioral, and symbolic variation in the history of life. Cambridge, MA: MIT Press.

Jackendoff, R. (2002). *Foundations of language: Brain, meaning, grammar, evolution.* New York: Oxford University Press.

Jacques, S., and Zelazo, P. D. (2005). Language and the development of cognitive flexibility: Implications for theory of mind. In J. W. Astington and J. A. Baird (Eds.), *Why language matters for theory of mind* (pp. 165–185). New York: Oxford University Press.

James, W. (1890). *The principles of psychology.* New York: Dover Publications, 1950.

Johnson, C. N., and Maratsos, M. P. (1977). Early comprehension of mental verbs: Think and know. *Child Development, 48,* 1743–1747.

Johnson, M. H. (Ed.). (1993). *Brain development and cognition.* Oxford: Blackwell.

Johnson, M. H. (1998). The neural basis of cognitive development. In D. Kuhn and R. S. Siegler (Eds.), *Handbook of child psychology: Vol. 2. Cognition, perception, and language* (5th Ed., pp. 1–50). New York: John Wiley and Sons.

Johnson, M. K., and Raye, C. L. (2000). Cognitive and brain mechanisms of false memories and beliefs. In D. L. Schacter and E. Scarry (Eds.), *Memory, brain and belief* (pp. 35–86). Cambridge, MA: Harvard University Press.

Johnson-Laird, P. N. (1987). The mental representation of the meaning of words. *Cognition, 23,* 189–211.

Jusczyk, P. W. (2000). *The discovery of spoken language.* Cambridge, MA: MIT Press.

Kagan, J. (1991). The theoretical utility of constructs for self. *Developmental Review, 11,* 244–250.

Karmiloff-Smith, A. (1992). *Beyond modularity.* Cambridge, MA: MIT Press.

Keil, F. C. (1987). Conceptual development and category structure. In U. Neisser (Ed.), *Concepts and conceptual development: Ecological and intellectual factors in categorization* (pp. 175–200). New York: Cambridge University Press.

Keller, E. F. (1983). *A feeling for the organism: The life and work of Barbara McClintock.* New York: W. H. Freeman.

Kemler Nelson, D. G. (1999). Attention to functional properties in toddlers' naming and problem-solving. *Cognitive Development, 14,* 77–100.

Kemler Nelson, D. G., Egan, L. C., and Holt, M. B. (2004). When children ask, "What is it?" What do they want to know about artifacts? *Psychological Science, 15,* 384–390.

Kessler Shaw, L. (1999). *The development of the meanings of "think" and "know" through conversation.* Unpublished doctoral dissertation, City University of New York Graduate Center, New York.

Kintsch, W. (1998). *Comprehension.* New York: Cambridge University Press.

Klein, R. G., and Edgar, B. (2002). *The dawn of human culture.* New York: Wiley.

Kloppenberg, J. T. (1998). Pragmatism: An old name for some new ways of thinking? In M. Dickstein (Ed.), *The revival of pragmatism: New essays on social thought, law, and culture* (pp. 83–127). Durham, NC: Duke University Press.

Krauss, R. (1952). *A hole is to dig: A first book of first definitions.* New York: Harper and Brothers.

Kuczaj, S. A., and Barrett, M. D. (Eds.). (1986). *The development of word meaning: Progress in cognitive developmental research.* New York: Springer-Verlag.

Kuhn, T. S. (1970). *The structure of scientific revolutions* (2nd ed.). Chicago: University of Chicago Press.

Kuper, A. (1999). *Culture: The anthropologists' account.* Cambridge, MA: Harvard University Press.

Labov, W. (1973). The boundaries of words and their meanings. In C. J. N. Bailey and R. W. Shuy (Eds.), *New ways of analyzing variation in English.* Washington, DC: Georgetown University Press.

Lakoff, G. (1987). *Women, fire, and dangerous things.* Chicago: University of Chicago Press.

Laland, K. N., and Brown, G. R. (2002). *Sense and nonsense: Evolutionary perspectives on human behavior.* New York: Oxford University Press.

Landau, B., Smith, L. B., and Jones, S. S. (1988). The importance of shape in early lexical learning. *Cognitive Development, 3,* 299–331.

LeDoux, J., Debiec, J., and Moss, H. (Eds.). (2002). *The self: From soul to brain.* New York: New York Academy of Sciences.

Lehrman, D. S. (1970). Semantic and conceptual issues in the nature-nurture problem. In L. Aronson (Ed.), *Development and evolution of behavior* (pp. 17–52). San Francisco: W. H. Freeman.

Lerner, R. M., and Kauffman, M. B. (1985). The concept of development in contextualism. *Developmental Review, 5,* 309–333.

Leslie, A. M. (1987). Pretense and representation: The origins of "theory of mind." *Psychological Review, 94,* 412–426.

Levinson, S. C. (2001). Covariation between spatial language and cognition, and its implications for language learning. In M. Bowerman and S. Levinson (Eds.), *Language acquisition and conceptual development* (pp. 566–588). New York: Cambridge University Press.

Levy, E., and Nelson, K. (1994). Words in discourse: A dialectical approach to the acquisition of meaning and use. *Journal of Child Language, 21.*

Lewis, M. (1997). The self in self-conscious emotions. In J. G. Snodgrass and R. L. Thompson (Eds.), *The self across psychology* (pp. 119–142). New York: New York Academy of Sciences.

Lewis, M., and Brooks-Gunn, J. (1979). *Social cognition and the acquisition of self.* New York: Plenum.

Lieven, E. V. M., Pine, J. M., and Dresner Barnes, H. (1992). Individual differences in early vocabulary development: Redefining the referential-expressive distinction. *Journal of Child Language, 19,* 287–310.

Lillard, A. S. (1993). Pretend play skills and the child's theory of mind. *Child Development, 64,* 348–371.

Lillard, A. S. (1998). Ethnopsychologies: Cultural variation in theory of mind. *Psychological Bulletin, 123,* 3–30.

Loftus, E. F. (1979). *Eyewitness testimony.* Cambridge, MA: Harvard University Press.

Loftus, E. F. (2004). Memories for things unseen. *Current Directions in Psychological Science, 13,* 145–147.

Lucariello, J. (2004). New insights into the functions, development and origins of theory of mind: The functional multilinear socialization (FSM) model. In J. Lucariello (Ed.), *The development of the mediated mind* (pp. 33–58). Mahwah, NJ: Erlbaum.

Lucariello, J., Hudson, J. A., Fivush, R., and Bauer, P. (Eds.). (2004). *The development of the mediated mind: Sociocultural context and cognitive development.* Mahwah, NJ: Erlbaum.

Lucariello, J., Kyratzis, A., and Engel, S. (1986). Event representations, context, and language. In K. Nelson (Ed.), *Event knowledge: Structure and function in development* (pp. 137–160). Hillsdale, NJ: Lawrence Erlbaum.

Lucariello, J., Kyratzis, A., and Nelson, K. (1992). Taxonomic knowledge: What kind and when. *Child Development, 63,* 978–998.

Lucariello, J., and Nelson, K. (1985). Slot-filler categories as memory organizers for young children. *Developmental Psychology, 21,* 272–282.

Lucariello, J., and Nelson, K. (1987). Remembering and planning talk between mothers and children. *Discourse Processes, 10,* 219–235.

Lucy, J. A. (1992). *Language diversity and thought: A reformulation of the linguistic relativity hypothesis.* New York: Cambridge University Press.

Luo, Y., and Baillargeon, R. (2005). Can a self-propelled box have a goal? Psychological reasoning in 5-month-old infants. *Psychological Science, 16,* 601–608.

Lyons, J. (1977). *Semantics* (Vol. 2). Cambridge: Cambridge University Press.

Mahler, M. S., Pine, F., and Bergman, A. (1975). *The psychological birth of the human infant: Symbiosis and individuation.* New York: Basic Books.

Mandler, J. M. (2004). *The foundations of mind: Origins of conceptual thought.* New York: Oxford University Press.

Mandler, J. M., and McDonough, L. (1998). Studies in inductive inference in infancy. *Cognitive Psychology, 37,* 60–96.

Markman, E. M. (1981). Two different principles of conceptual organization. In M. Lamb and A. Brown (Eds.), *Advances in developmental psychology* (Vol. 1). Hillsdale, NJ: Lawrence Erlbaum Assoc.

Markman, E. M. (1987). How children constrain the possible meanings of words. In U. Neisser (Ed.), *Concepts and conceptual development: Ecological and intellectual factors in categorization* (pp. 255–287). New York: Cambridge University Press.

Markman, E. M., and Hutchinson, J. E. (1984). Children's sensitivity to constraints on word meaning: Taxonomic vs. thematic relations. *Cognitive Psychology, 16,* 1–27.

McClamrock, R. (1995). *Existential cognition: Computational minds in the world.* Chicago: University of Chicago Press.

McDonough, L. (2002). Early concepts and early language acquisition: What does similarity have to do with either? In N. Stein, P. Bauer, and M. Rabinowitz (Eds.), *Representation, memory, and development* (pp. 115–144). Mahwah, NJ: Erlbaum.

McDonough, L., and Mandler, J. M. (1998). Inductive generalizations in 9- and 11-month-olds. *Developmental Science, 1,* 227–232.

McNeill, D. (1992). *Hand and mind: What gestures reveal about thought.* Chicago: University of Chicago Press.

Mead, G. H. (1934). *Mind, self, and society.* Chicago: University of Chicago.

Medin, D., and Ortony, A. (1989). Comments on Part I: Psychological essentialism. In S. Vosniadou and A. Ortony (Eds.), *Similarity and analogical reasoning* (pp. 179–195). Cambridge: Cambridge University Press.

Mehler, J., and Dupoux, E. (1994). *What infants know.* Cambridge, MA: Blackwell.

Meltzoff, A. N. (1995). *Infantile amnesia? New data from infancy.* Symposium paper presented at the biennial meeting of the Society for Research in Child Development, Indianapolis, April.

Meltzoff, A. N., and Gopnik, A. (1993). The role of imitation in understanding persons and developing theories of mind. In S. Baron-Cohen, H. Tager-Flusberg, and D. Cohen (Eds.), *Understanding other minds: Perspectives from autism* (pp. 335–366). New York: Oxford University Press.

Meltzoff, A. N., and Moore, M. K. (1985). Cognitive foundations and social function of imitation and intermodal representation in infancy. In J. Mehler and R. Fox (Eds.), *Neonate cognition: Beyond the blooming buzzing confusion* (pp. 139–156). Hillsdale, NJ: Erlbaum.

Meltzoff, A. N., and Moore, M. K. (1999). A new foundation for cognitive development in infancy: The birth of the representational infant. In E. K. Scholnick, K. Nelson, S. A. Gelman, and P. H. Miller (Eds.), *Conceptual development: Piaget's legacy* (pp. 53–78). Mahwah, NJ: Erlbaum.

Menand, L. (2001). *The metaphysical club: A story of ideas in America.* New York: Farrar, Straus and Giroux.

Merleau-Ponty, M. (1964). *The primacy of perception and other essays on phenomenological psychology, the philosophy of art, history and politics.* Evanston, IL: Northwestern University Press.

Merriman, W., and Tomasello, M. (Eds.). (1995). *Beyond names for things.* Hillsdale, NJ: Erlbaum.

Miller, G. A., and Johnson-Laird, P. N. (1976). *Language and perception.* Cambridge, MA: Harvard University Press.

Miller, P. J., Hoogstra, L., Mintz, J., Fung, H., and Williams, K. (1993). Troubles in the garden and how they get resolved: A young child's transformation of his favorite story. In C. A. Nelson (Ed.), *Memory and affect in development* (Vol. 26, pp. 87–114). Hillsdale, NJ: Lawrence Erlbaum Assoc.

Miller, P. J., Potts, R., Fung, H., Hoogstra, L., and Mintz, J. (1990). Narrative practices and the social construction of self in childhood. *American Ethnologist, 17*, 292–311.

Mithin, S. (1996). *The prehistory of the mind.* New York: Thames and Hudson.

Montgomery, D. E. (1997). Wittgenstein's private language argument and children's understanding of the mind. *Developmental Review, 17*, 291–320.

Montgomery, D. E. (2002). Mental verbs and semantic development. *Journal of Cognition and Development, 3*, 357–384.

Moore, C. (1999). Intentional relations and triadic relations. In P. D. Zelazo, J. W. Astington, and D. R. Olson (Eds.), *Developing theories of intention* (pp. 43–62). Mahwah, NJ: Erlbaum.

Moore, C., Bryant, D., and Furrow, D. (1989). Mental terms and the development of certainty. *Child Development, 60*, 167–171.

Moore, C., and Corkum, V. (1994). Social understanding at the end of the first year of life. *Developmental Review, 14*, 349–372.

Naito, M. (2004). Is theory of mind a universal and unitary concept? *International Society for Behavioral Development Newsletter, 28*, 9–11.

Namy, L., and Waxman, S. R. (1998). Words and gestures: Infants' interpretations of different forms of symbolic reference. *Child Development, 69*, 295–308.

Napolitano, A. C., and Sloutsky, V. M. (2004). Is a picture worth a thousand words? The flexible nature of modality dominance in young children. *Child Development, 75*, 1850–1870.

Neisser, U. (1997). The roots of self-knowledge: Perceiving self, it, and thou. In J. G. Snodgrass and R. L. Thompson (Eds.), *The self across psychology: Self-recognition, self-awareness, and the self concept* (pp. 19–33). New York: New York Academy of Sciences.

Nelson, K. (1969). The organization of free recall by young children. *Journal of Experimental Child Psychology, 8*, 284–295.

Nelson, K. (1973). Structure and strategy in learning to talk. *Monographs of the Society for Research in Child Development, 38*(1–2, Serial No. 149).

Nelson, K. (1974). Concept, word, and sentence: Interrelations in acquisition and development. *Psychological Review, 81*, 267–285.

Nelson, K. (1978). Semantic development and the development of semantic memory. In K. E. Nelson (Ed.), *Children's language* (Vol. 1). New York: Gardner.

Nelson, K. (1982). The syntagmatics and paradigmatics of conceptual development. In S. Kuczaj (Ed.), *Language development: Vol. 2. Language, thought, and culture* (pp. 335–364). Hillsdale, NJ: Erlbaum.

Nelson, K. (1985). *Making sense: The acquisition of shared meaning.* New York: Academic Press.

Nelson, K. (1986). *Event knowledge: Structure and function in development.* Hillsdale, NJ: Lawrence Erlbaum.

Nelson, K. (1989a). Monologue as representation of real-life experience. In K. Nelson (Ed.), *Narratives from the crib* (pp. 27–72). Cambridge, MA: Harvard University Press.

Nelson, K. (1989b). Monologue as the linguistic construction of self in time. In K. Nelson (Ed.), *Narratives from the crib* (pp. 284–308). Cambridge, MA: Harvard University Press.

Nelson, K. (Ed.). (1989c). *Narratives from the crib.* Cambridge, MA: Harvard University Press.

Nelson, K. (1991). Remembering and telling: A developmental story. *Journal of Narrative and Life History, 1,* 109–127.

Nelson, K. (1993). The psychological and social origins of autobiographical memory. *Psychological Science, 4,* 1–8.

Nelson, K. (1995a). The dual category problem in lexical acquisition. In W. Merriman and M. Tomasello (Eds.), *Beyond Names for Things* (pp. 223–250). Hillsdale, NJ: Erlbaum.

Nelson, K. (1995b). From "spontaneous" to "scientific" concepts. In L. Martin, K. Nelson, and E. Tobach (Eds.), *Sociocultural psychology: Theory and practice of doing and knowing.* New York: Cambridge University Press.

Nelson, K. (1996). *Language in cognitive development: The emergence of the mediated mind.* New York: Cambridge University Press.

Nelson, K. (1997). Finding oneself in time. In J. G. Snodgrass and R. Thompson (Eds.), *The self across psychology. Annals of the New York Academy of Sciences.* New York: New York Academy of Sciences.

Nelson, K. (2001). Language and the self: From the "experiencing I" to the "continuing me". In C. Moore and K. Lemmon (Eds.), *The self in time: Developmental issues* (pp. 15–34). Mahwah, NJ: Erlbaum.

Nelson, K. (2002). Developing dual-representation processes. *Brain and Behavioral Sciences, 25,* 693–694.

Nelson, K. (2003a). Making sense in a world of symbols. In A. Toomela (Ed.), *Cultural guidance in the development of the human mind* (pp. 139–162). Westport, CT: Greenwood.

Nelson, K. (2003b). Narrative and self, myth and memory. In R. Fivush and C. Haden (Eds.), *Autobiographical memory and the construction of a narrative self: Developmental and cultural perspectives* (pp. 3–28). Mahwah, NJ: Erlbaum.

Nelson, K. (2004). Construction of the cultural self in early narratives. In C. Daiute and C. Lightfoot (Eds.), *Narrative analysis: Studying the development of individuals in society* (pp. 87–110). London: Sage Publications.

Nelson, K. (2005a). Cognitive functions of language in early childhood. In B. Homer and C. Tamis-LeMonda (Eds.), *The development of social cognition and communication* (pp. 7–28). Mahwah, NJ: Erlbaum.

Nelson, K. (2005b). Emerging levels of consciousness in early human development. In H. S. Terrace and J. Metcalfe (Eds.), *The missing link in cognition: Origins of self-reflective consciousness* (pp. 116–141). New York: Oxford University Press.

Nelson, K. (2005c). Evolution and development of human memory systems. In B. Ellis and D. Bjorklund (Eds.), *Origins of the social mind: Evolutionary psychology and child development* (pp. 319–345). New York: Guilford Publications.

Nelson, K. (2005d). Language pathways to the community of minds. In J. W. Astington and J. Baird (Eds.), *Why language matters to theory of mind.* New York: Oxford University Press.

Nelson, K., and Fivush, R. (2004). The emergence of autobiographical memory: A social cultural developmental theory. *Psychological Review, 111,* 486–511.

Nelson, K., Hampson, J., and Kessler Shaw, L. (1993). Nouns in early lexicons: Evidence, explanations, and implications. *Journal of Child Language, 20,* 61–84.

Nelson, K., Henseler, S., and Plesa, D. (2000). Entering a community of minds: A feminist perspective on theory of mind development. In P. Miller and E. S. Scholnick (Eds.), *Toward a feminist developmental psychology* (pp. 61–84). New York: Routledge.

Nelson, K., and Kessen, W. (1976). *Report to the Carnegie Foundation on infant categories.* Unpublished report, Yale University.

Nelson, K., and Kessler Shaw, L. (2002). Developing a socially shared symbolic system. In E. Amsel and J. Byrnes (Eds.), *Language, literacy and cognitive development* (pp. 27–58). Mahwah, NJ: Erlbaum.

Nelson, K., Plesa, D., Goldman, S., Henseler, S., Presler, N., and Walkenfeld, F. F. (2003). Entering a community of minds: An experiential approach to theory of minds. *Human Development, 46,* 24–46.

Nelson, K., Plesa, D., and Henseler, S. (1998). Children's theory of mind: An experiential interpretation. *Human Development, 41,* 7–29.

Nelson, K., and Ross, G. (1980). The generalities and specifics of long-term memory in infants and young children. In M. Perlmutter (Ed.), *Children's memory: New directions for child development* (Vol. 10, pp. 87–101). San Francisco: Jossey-Bass.

Newcombe, N. S., Sluzenski, J., and Huttenlocher, J. (2005). Preexisting knowledge versus on-line learning: What do young infants really know about spatial location? *Psychological Science, 16,* 222–227.

Nguyen, S. P., and Murphy, G. L. (2003). An apple is more than just a fruit: Cross-classification in children's concepts. *Child Development, 74*(6), 1783–1806.

Noble, W., and Davidson, I. (1996). *Human evolution, language and mind.* New York: Cambridge University Press.

Ochs, E., and Schieffelin, B. (1984). Language acquisition and socialization: Three developmental stories. In R. Schweder and R. LeVine (Eds.), *Culture theory: Essays on mind, self and emotion* (pp. 276–320). Cambridge: Cambridge University Press.

Ogden, C. K., and Richards, I. A. (1949). *The meaning of meaning,* 10th ed. London: Routledge and Kegan Paul. (Originally published 1923.)

Ong, W. J. (1982). *Orality and literacy: The technologizing of the word.* New York: Routledge.

Oyama, S. (1985). *The ontogeny of information: Developmental systems and evolution.* New York: Cambridge University Press.

Oyama, S. (2000). *Evolution's eye: A systems view of the biology-culture divide.* Durham, NC: Duke University Press.

Oyama, S. (2001). Terms in tension: What do you do when all the good words are taken? In S. Oyama, P. E. Griffiths, and R. D. Gray (Eds.), *Cycles of contingency: Developmental systems and evolution* (pp. 177–194). Cambridge, MA: MIT Press.

Oyama, S., Griffiths, P. E., and Gray, R. D. (Eds.). (2001). *Cycles of contingency: Developmental systems and evolution.* Cambridge, MA: MIT Press.

Peirce, C. S. (1897). Logic as semiotic: The theory of signs. In J. Buchler (Ed.), *The philosophical writings of Peirce* (pp. 98–110). New York: Dover Books, 1955.

Perner, J. (1991). *Understanding the representational mind.* Cambridge, MA: MIT Press.

Perner, J. (2001). Episodic memory: Essential distinctions and developmental implications. In C. Moore and K. Lemmon (Eds.), *The self in time: Developmental perspectives* (pp. 181–202). Mahwah, NJ: Erlbaum.

Piaget, J. (1926). *The language and thought of the child.* New York: Harcourt, Brace.

Piaget, J. (1929). *The child's conception of the world* (J. A. Tomlinson, Trans.). New York: Harcourt Brace and World.

Piaget, J. (1952). *The origins of intelligence in children.* New York: Norton Library.

Piaget, J. (1962). *Play, dreams, and imitation in childhood.* New York: Norton.

Pillemer, D. B. (1998). *Momentous events, vivid memories.* Cambridge, MA: Harvard University Press.

Pinker, S. (1984). *Language learnability and language development.* Cambridge, MA: Harvard University Press.

Pinker, S. (1994). *The language instinct: How the mind creates language.* New York: William Morrow.

Pinker, S. (1997). *How the mind works.* New York: Norton.

Pinker, S. (2002). *The blank slate.* New York: Penguin Putnam.

Poti, P. (1989). Early sensorimotor development in macaques. In F. Antinucci (Ed.), *Cognitive structure and development in nonhuman primates* (pp. 39–54). Hillsdale, NJ: Erlbaum.

Povinelli, D. J., and Eddy, T. J. (1996). What young chimpanzees know about seeing. *Monographs of the Society for Research in Child Development, 61*(3).

Povinelli, D. J., Landau, K. R., and Perilloux, H. K. (1996). Self-recognition in young children using delayed versus live feedback: Evidence of a developmental asynchrony. *Child Development, 67,* 1540–1554.

Povinelli, D. J., and Simon, B. B. (1998). Young children's understanding of briefly versus extremely delayed visual images of the self: Emergence of the autobiographical stance. *Developmental Psychology, 34,* 118–194.

Power, T. G. (2000). *Play and exploration in children and animals.* Mahwah, NJ: Erlbaum.

Premack, D. (1988). "Does the chimpanzee have a theory of mind?" revisited. In R. Byrne and A. Whiten (Eds.), *Machiavellian intelligence* (pp. 160–179). Oxford: Oxford University Press.

Premack, D., and Woodruff, G. (1978). Does the chimpanzee have a theory of mind? *Behavioral and Brain Sciences, 1,* 515–526.

Presler, N. (2000). *Pre-writing memories: From anticipatory discourse to children's personal narratives.* Unpublished doctoral dissertation, City University of New York Graduate School, New York.

Prinz, J. J. (2002). *Furnishing the mind: Concepts and their perceptual basis.* Cambridge, MA: MIT Press.

Quine, W. V. O. (1960). *Word and object.* Cambridge, MA: MIT Press.

Ratner, H. H., Foley, M. A., and Gimpert, N. (2000). Person perspectives on children's memory and learning: What do source-monitoring failures reveal? In K. P. Roberts and M. Blades (Eds.), *Children's source monitoring* (pp. 85–114). Mahwah, NJ: Erlbaum.

Reed, E. S. (1996). *Encountering the world: Toward an ecological psychology.* New York: Oxford University Press.

Reese, E. (2002a). A model of the origins of autobiographical memory. In J. W. Fagen and H. Hayne (Eds.), *Progress in infancy research* (Vol. 2, pp. 215–260). Mahwah, NJ: Erlbaum.

Reese, E. (2002b). Social factors in the development of autobiographical memory: The state of the art. *Social Development, 11,* 124–142.

Reese, E., Haden, C. A., and Fivush, R. (1993). Mother-child conversations about the past: Relationships of style and memory over time. *Cognitive Development, 8,* 403–430.

Rescorla, L. A. (1980). Overextension in early language development. *Journal of Child Language, 7,* 321–335.

Ricciuti, H. N. (1965). Object grouping and selective ordering behaviors in infants 12- to 24-months old. *Merrill-Palmer Quarterly, 11,* 129–148.

Roberts, K. P., and Blades, M. (Eds.). (2000). *Children's source monitoring.* Mahwah, NJ: Erlbaum Assoc.

Rochat, P. (2001). *The infant's world.* Cambridge, MA: Harvard University Press.

Rogoff, B. (1990). *Apprenticeship in thinking: Cognitive development in social context.* New York: Oxford University Press.

Rogoff, B. (2003). *The cultural nature of human development.* New York: Oxford University Press.

Rogoff, B., and Mistry, J. (1990). The social and functional context of children's remembering. In R. Fivush and J. Hudson (Eds.), *Knowing and remembering in young children* (pp. 197–223). New York: Cambridge University Press.

Rosch, E., Mervis, C., Gray, W., Johnson, D., and Boyes-Braem, P. (1976). Basic objects in natural categories. *Cognitive Psychology, 8,* 382–439.

Rovee-Collier, C., and Hayne, H. (1987). Reactivation of infant memory: Implications for cognitive development. In H. W. Reese (Ed.), *Advances in child development and behavior* (Vol. 20, pp. 185–283). New York: Academic Press.

Rubin, D. C. (1995). *Memory in oral traditions.* New York: Oxford University Press.

Russell, J. (1992). The theory theory: So good they named it twice? *Cognitive Development, 7,* 485–519.

Rutter, M. (1987). Resilience in the face of adversity: Protective factors and resistance to psychiatric disorder. *British Journal of Psychiatry, 147,* 598–611.

Rutter, M. (2006). The psychological effects of early institutional rearing. In P. J. Marshall and N. A. Fox (Eds.), *The development of social engagement: Neurobiological perspectives* (pp. 355–391). New York: Oxford University Press.

Saffran, J. R. (2003). Statistical language learning: Mechanisms and constraints. *Current Directions in Psychological Science, 12,* 110–114.

Salon, J., and Nelson, K. (1999). A connectionist model of the acquisition of a slot-filler category of food. Unpublished manuscript, City University of New York Graduate Center.

Saussure, F. de (1915). *Course in general linguistics.* New York: The Philosophical Library, 1959.

Sawyer, R. K. (1997). *Pretend play as improvisation.* Mahwah, NJ: Erlbaum Assoc.

Scarr, S. (1992). Developmental theories for the 1990s: Development and individual differences. *Child Development, 63,* 1–19.

Schacter, D. L., Wagner, A. D., and Buckner, R. L. (2000). Memory systems of

1999. In E. Tulving and F. M. I. Craik (Eds.), *The Oxford handbook of memory* (pp. 627–643). New York: Oxford University Press.

Schank, R. C. (1982). *Dynamic memory: A theory of reminding and learning in computers and people*. New York: Cambridge University Press.

Schneider, W., and Weinert, F. E. (1995). Memory development during early and middle childhood: Findings from the Munich longitudinal study (LOGIC). In F. E. Weinert and W. Schneider (Eds.), *Memory performance and competencies: Issues in growth and development* (pp. 263–282). Mahwah, NJ: Erlbaum.

Schneirla, T. C. (1957). The concept of development in comparative psychology. In D. B. Harris (Ed.), *The concept of development* (pp. 78–108). Minneapolis: University of Minnesota Press.

Scribner, S. (1985). Vygotsky's use of history. In J. Wertsch (Ed.), *Culture, communication and cognition: Vygotskian perspectives* (pp. 119–145). New York: Cambridge University Press.

Seidman, S., Nelson, K., and Gruendel, J. (1986). Make believe scripts: The transformation of ERs in fantasy. In K. Nelson (Ed.), *Event knowledge: Structure and function in development* (pp. 161–187). Hillsdale, NJ: Erlbaum.

Siegal, M., and Peterson, C. C. (1994). Children's theory of mind and the conversational territory of cognitive development. In C. Lewis and P. Mitchell (Eds.), *Children's early understanding of mind: Origins and development* (pp. 427–456). Hillsdale, NJ: Erlbaum.

Skinner, B. F. (1957). *Verbal behavior.* New York: Appleton-Century-Crofts.

Slobin, D. I. (1987). Thinking for speaking. In J. Askew, N. Beery, L. Michaelis, and H. Filip (Eds.), *Proceedings of the Thirteenth Annual Meeting of the Berkeley Linguistics Society* (pp. 435–445). Berkeley: University of California.

Slobin, D. I. (2001). Form-function relations: How do children find out what they are? In M. Bowerman and S. C. Levinson (Eds.), *Language acquisition and conceptual development* (pp. 406–449). New York: Cambridge University Press.

Sloutsky, V. M., and Napolitano, A. C. (2003). Is a picture worth a thousand words? Preference for auditory modality in young children. *Child Development, 74,* 822–833.

Smith, L. B. (1999). Children's noun learning: How general learning processes make specialized learning mechanisms. In B. MacWhinney (Ed.), *The emergence of language* (pp. 277–304). Mahwah, NJ: Erlbaum.

Smith, L. (2003). Learning to recognize objects. *Psychological Science, 14,* 244–250.

Smith, L. B., and Thelen, E. (2003). Development as a dynamic system. *Trends in Cognitive Science, 7,* 343–348.

Smith, L., Thelen, E., Titzer, R., and McLin, D. (1999). Knowing in the context of acting: The task dynamics of the A not B error. *Psychological Review, 106,* 235–260.

Snow, C. (1986). The social basis of language development. In P. Fletcher and M. Garman (Eds.), *Language acquisition* (2nd ed.). Cambridge: Cambridge University Press.

Snow, C. (1999). Social perspectives on the emergence of language. In B. MacWhinney (Ed.), *The emergence of language* (pp. 257–276). Mahwah, NJ: Erlbaum.

Spelke, E. (1988). The origins of physical knowledge. In L. Weiskrantz (Ed.), *Thought without language.* New York: Oxford University Press.

Spelke, E. S. (2003). What makes us smart? Core knowledge and natural language. In D. Gentner and S. Goldin-Meadow (Eds.), *Language in mind: Advances in the study of language and thought* (pp. 277–312). Cambridge, MA: MIT Press.

Spelke, E. S., and Newport, E. L. (1998). Nativism, empiricism, and the development of knowledge. In *Handbook of Child Psychology*, R. M. Lerner (Ed.), *Theoretical models of human development* (5th ed., Vol. 1, pp. 275–340). New York: Wiley.

Spitz, R. (1945). Hospitalism: An inquiry into the genesis of psychiatric conditions in early childhood. *Psychoanalytic Study of the Child, 1,* 53–74.

Stern, D. N. (1985). *The interpersonal world of the infant: A view from psychoanalysis and developmental psychology.* New York: Basic Books.

Stetsenko, A. (2003). Alexander Luria and the cultural-historical activity theory: Pieces for the history of an outstanding collaborative project in psychology. *Mind, Culture, and Activity: An International Journal, 10,* 93–97.

Stetsenko, A. (2004). Scientific legacy: Tool and sign in the development of the child. In R. W. Rieber and D. K. Robinson (Eds.), *The essential Vygotsky* (pp. 501–512). New York: Kluwer Academic/Plenum.

Sugarman, S. (1983). *Children's early thought.* New York: Cambridge University Press.

Sutton-Smith, B. (1997). *The ambiguity of play.* Cambridge, MA: Harvard University Press.

Tardif, T. (1996). Nouns are not always learned before verbs: Evidence from Mandarin speakers' early vocabularies. *Developmental Psychology, 32,* 492–504.

Tardif, T. (2006). But are they really verbs? Mandarin words for action. In K. Hirsh-Pasek and R. M. Golinkoff (Eds.), *Action meets word: How children learn verbs.* New York: Oxford University Press.

Taylor, M. (1999). *Imaginary companions and the children who create them.* New York: Oxford University Press.

Terrace, H. S., and Metcalfe, J. (Eds.). (2005). *The missing link in cognition: Origins of self-reflective consciousness.* New York: Oxford University Press.

Tessler, M. (1986). *Mother-child talk in a museum: The socialization of a memory.* Unpublished manuscript, City University of New York Graduate Center, New York.

Tessler, M., and Nelson, K. (1994). Making memories: The influence of joint encoding on later recall. *Consciousness and Cognition, 3,* 307–326.

Thelen, E., and Smith, L. B. (1994). *A dynamic systems approach to the development of cognition and action.* Cambridge, MA: MIT Press.

Thelen, E., and Ulrich, B. D. (1991). Hidden skills: A dynamical systems analysis of treadmill stepping during the first year. *Monographs of the Society for Research in Child Development, 56* (serial no. 223).

Tomasello, M. (1992). *First verbs: A case study of early grammatical development.* New York: Cambridge University Press.

Tomasello, M. (1999). *The cultural origins of human cognition.* Cambridge, MA: Harvard University Press.

Tomasello, M. (2003). *Constructing a language: A usage-based theory of language acquisition.* Cambridge, MA: Harvard University Press.

Tomasello, M., and Call, J. (1997). *Primate cognition.* New York: Oxford University Press.

Tomasello, M., Kruger, A. C., and Ratner, H. H. (1993). Cultural learning. *Behavioral and Brain Sciences*, 495–552.

Tomasello, M., Striano, T., and Rochat, P. (1999). Do young children use objects as symbols? *British Journal of Developmental Psychology*, *17*, 563–584.

Trevarthen, C. (1980). The foundations of intersubjectivity: Development of interpersonal and cooperative understanding in infants. In D. R. Olson (Ed.), *The social foundations of language and thought* (pp. 316–342). New York: W. W. Norton.

Tronick, E. Z., Als, H., Adamson, L. B., Wise, S., and Brazelton, T. B. (1978). The infant's response to entrapment between contradictory messages in face-to-face interaction. *Journal American Academy of Child Psychiatry*, *17*, 1–13.

Tulving, E. (1993). What is episodic memory? *Current Directions in Psychological Science*, *2*(3), 67–70.

Tulving, E., and Lepage, M. (2000). Where in the brain is the awareness of one's past? In D. L. Schachter and E. Scarry (Eds.), *Memory, brain, and belief* (pp. 208–228). Cambridge, MA: Harvard University Press.

Turati, C. (2004). Why faces are not special to newborns: An alternative account of the face preference. *Current Directions in Psychological Science*, *13*, 5–8.

Valsiner, J. (1987). *Culture and the development of children's action.* New York: Wiley.

Valsiner, J. (1998). The development of the concept of development: Historical and epistemological perspectives. In R. M. Lerner (Ed.), *Handbook of child psychology: Vol. 1. Theoretical models of human development* (5th Ed., pp. 189–232). New York: Wiley.

van Geert, P. (1998). A dynamic systems model of basic developmental mechanisms: Piaget, Vygotsky, and beyond. *Psychological Review*, *105*, 634–677.

Varela, F. J., Thompson, E., and Rosch, E. (1991). *The embodied mind.* Cambridge, MA: MIT Press.

Vygotsky, L. (1962). *Thought and language* (E. Hanfmann and G. Vakar, Trans.). Cambridge, MA: MIT Press.

Vygotsky, L. (1978). *Mind in society: The development of higher psychological processes.* Cambridge, MA: Harvard University Press.

Vygotsky, L. (1986). *Thought and language* (translation revised and edited by A. Kozulin). Cambridge, MA: MIT Press.

Vygotsky, L. (2004). The function of signs in the development of higher mental processes. In R. W. Rieber and D. K. Robinson (Eds.), *The essential Vygotsky* (pp. 539–550). New York: Kluwer Academic/Plenum.

Wang, Q. (2001). Cultural effects on adults' earliest childhood recollection and self-description: Implications for the relation between memory and the self. *Journal of Personality and Social Psychology*, *81*, 220–233.

Watson, J. (1913). Psychology as the behaviorist views it. *Psychological Review*, *20*, 158–177.

Weinfield, N. S., Sroufe, L. A., and Egeland, B. (2000). Attachment from infancy to early adulthood in a high-risk sample: Continuity, discontinuity, and their correlates. *Child Development*, *71*, 695–702.

Weist, R. M. (1986). Tense and aspect: Temporal systems in child language. In P.

Fletcher and M. Garman (Eds.), *Language acquisition* (2nd ed.). Cambridge: Cambridge University Press.

Wellman, H. M. (1990). *The child's theory of mind.* Cambridge, MA: MIT Press.

Wellman, H. M., Cross, D., and Bartsch, K. (1986). Infant search and object permanence: A meta-analysis of the A-not-B error. *Monographs of the Society for Research in Child Development, 54* (No. 214).

Wellman, H. M., Cross, D., and Watson, J. (2001). Meta-analysis of theory-of-mind development: The truth about false belief. *Child Development, 72,* 655–684.

Wellman, H. M., and Gelman, S. A. (1992). Cognitive development: Foundational theories of core domains. *Annual Review of Psychology, 43,* 337–375.

Werner, H., and Kaplan, B. (1963). *Symbol formation.* New York: Wiley.

Wertsch, J. V. (Ed.). (1985a). *Culture, communication and cognition: Vygotskian perspectives.* New York: Cambridge University Press.

Wertsch, J. V. (1985b). *Vygotsky and the social formation of mind.* Cambridge, MA: Harvard University Press.

Wertsch, J. V. (1991). *Voices in the mind.* Cambridge, MA: Harvard University Press.

Wetzler, S. E., and Sweeney, J. A. (1986). Childhood amnesia: An empirical demonstration. In D. C. Rubin (Ed.), *Autobiographical memory* (pp. 191–201). New York: Cambridge University Press.

Wheeler, M. A. (2000). Episodic memory and autonoetic awareness. In E. Tulving and F. I. M. Craik (Eds.), *Oxford handbook of memory* (pp. 597–625). New York: Oxford University Press.

White, S. H. (1965). Evidence for a hierarchical arrangement of learning processes. In L. P. Lipsitt and C. C. Spiker (Eds.), *Advances in child development and behavior* (Vol. 2, pp. 187–220). New York: Academic Press.

White, S. H., and Pillemer, D. B. (1979). Childhood amnesia and the development of a socially accessible memory system. In J. F. Kihlstrom and F. J. Evans (Eds.), *Functional disorders of memory* (pp. 29–74). Hillsdale, NJ: Lawrence Erlbaum Assoc.

Whorf, B. L. (1956). *Language, thought and reality: Selected writings of Benjamin Lee Whorf.* Cambridge, MA: MIT Press.

Wilson, E. O. (1975). *Sociobiology: The new synthesis.* Cambridge, MA: Harvard University Press.

Wittgenstein, L. (1953). *Philosophical investigations.* New York: Macmillan.

Wolf, D., and Gardner, H. (1979). Style and sequence in symbolic play. In M. Franklin and N. Smith (Eds.), *Early symbolization.* Hillsdale, NJ: Lawrence Erlbaum Assoc.

Wolf, S. A., and Heath, S. B. (1992). *The braid of literature: Children's worlds of reading.* Cambridge, MA: Harvard University Press.

Acknowledgments

During the years of working through the ideas laid out in this book (1999 to 2005), I benefited from discussions and feedback at workshops, lectures, and conferences that I want to acknowledge. Thanks, first, to Stephen von Tetzchner for giving me the opportunity to introduce the experiential perspective and the idea of the "community of minds" in a workshop at the University of Oslo in October 2000. Thanks also to Professor Harald Welzer and Professor Hans J. Markowitz and their group at the Kulturwissenschaftliches Insitut in Essen, Germany, for inviting me to participate (in October 2002) in their early discussions of the biological and social contributions to autobiographical memory over the life span (reflected in Chapter 7; see also Nelson and Fivush, 2004). I thank Yasuji Kojima of the Japan Society of Developmental Psychology for the invitation to present a weeklong workshop in Tokyo (in August 2003), where I further developed many of the arguments in this book, aided by questions from participants in the workshop; my thanks to the group and its leaders for their interest and generous hospitality.

Many thanks to Manuel de la Mata and his colleagues at the University of Seville for the opportunity to spend ten days there in March 2004 lecturing on major parts of what are now Chapters 4 to 8 of this book. Thanks to Oscar Vilarroya for the invitation to participate in the extraordinary "Social Brain Dialogue" at the Universal Forum of Cultures, Barcelona 2004; as well as for his book *The Dissolution of Mind*, a magical lens that provided me with an inside-out view of my own theory. Thanks also to Evelyn Fox Keller for including me in her 2004 workshop on dynamic systems in developmental psychology at the University of Minnesota. Many others whom I met at conferences and workshops added to my understanding gained through the written word. I note especially Endel Tulving, whose work has influenced mine in different ways since my graduate student days, and Merlin Donald, whose theories and scholarly work have played such an important part in the direction of my thinking and writing over the past fifteen years.

I would also like to acknowledge the following individuals for helpful discussions of issues and ideas: longtime colleague and coauthor Robyn Fivush, on autobiographical memory; Patricia Bauer, on the course of infant and toddler memory; Janet Astington, on language and theory of mind (thanks also for reading and commenting on Chapter 1); Twyla Tardif, on lexical acquisition; Mike Tomasello and colleagues at the Max Planck Institute in Leipzig, Judy DeLoache, and Terry Deacon, on symbols and representation.

I am indebted to Joe Glick, coleader of the New Models seminar at CUNY, for his provocative insights, and to the several groups of students (and occasional faculty) who have participated, for their critical seminar discussions. The group of doctoral students who worked closely with me during this work in process contributed through their own work to its eventual content as well as to ongoing research and publications. They include Zena Eisenberg, Robin Goldstein Fontaine, Sylvie Goldman, Sarah Henseler, Daniela Plesa, Nechama Presler, Lea Kessler Shaw, and Faye Walkenfeld. Bruce Homer, briefly a post-doc and now a colleague at New York University, has worked with me on the issues of symbols and representation that loom large in several chapters here. The contributions of all are happily acknowledged.

The discussion of symbols in Chapters 4 and 5 is based in part on Nelson (2003a), and part of Chapter 6 is based on Nelson (2005a), which is in a volume that grew out of a conference held at New York University in October 2001 (Homer and Tamis-LaMonda, 2005). The discussion of community of minds and theory of mind is based in part on Nelson et al. (2003) and on a chapter of an edited volume from a conference held in Toronto in April 2002 (Astington and Baird, 2005). The idea of developing levels of consciousness was introduced in Nelson (2003a) and Nelson (2005b); the latter is part of an edited volume from a conference held at Columbia University in April 2003 (Terrace and Metcalfe, 2005). Parts of this work on memory development and theory of mind were supported by a grant from the National Science Foundation.

Several people read and commented on versions of the book. Laraine McDonough's careful reading and critical commentary on the penultimate version of the manuscript was extremely helpful. Daniela Plesa's close and insightful reading and commentary was as always inspirational. Thanks also to Philippe Rochat and to an anonymous reviewer for their appreciative readings of the manuscript.

In addition, three family members outside the field volunteered to read the manuscript for comprehension and readability in whole or in part: my daughter Laura Nelson (an anthropologist), my sister-in-law Joan Nelson (a political scientist), and my husband, Richard Nelson (an economist). Their contributions and support are gratefully acknowledged. As always, Richard provided invaluable intellectual and moral support throughout the book's long generative process.

I am dedicating this book to my granddaughter, Noa Nelson Perlmutter, who could not yet critique the manuscript but who, from birth to age two and a half, served faithfully to inspire and illustrate much of what I have written here.

Finally I thank Elizabeth Knoll, senior editor of behavioral sciences at Harvard University Press, whose confidence in and support for this project preceded my own initial vision of its form, and Julie Ericksen Hagen for her sensitive and insightful editing of the manuscript.

Index

Abstraction, 144, 151, 152, 153–164, 168, 181
Acredolo, L. P., 97
Action, 18, 31, 32, 33, 52, 96, 108, 121, 224, 246, 247
Action systems, 65–66
Activity context, 155, 161
Activity theory, 53
Adolph, Karen, 67–68, 84, 259
Adultomorphism, 7, 45
Adults, 71, 98, 142–143, 144, 147, 162, 208
A-not-B task, 72–73, 81, 258
Applebee, A. N., 174–175, 176, 274
Association, 163, 165
Associationism, 22, 23
Astuti, R., 229, 230, 232
Attachment, 51, 63, 64, 66, 80, 83, 182
Attention: and awareness, 15; and experience, 8; and gesture use, 76–77; in infant development, 65–66, 76–81; and infant locomotor activity, 80–81; joint, 76–78, 80–81; and language, 102, 140, 149, 150, 167, 168; shared, 16–17, 78, 82, 92, 102, 121, 217; in social sphere, 246; and story narratives, 172, 173; tracking of, 78, 81, 85. *See also* Gaze following
Autism, 196, 215
Autobiographical memory, 184–193, 196, 200–201, 205, 242, 243–244

Autonoesis, 186, 187, 203, 204
Awareness, 15, 25, 85, 245–246, 248

Baillargeon, Renee, 71
Baldwin, Dare, 123, 129
Baldwin, James Mark, 52
Barker, Roger, 35
Barsalou, L. A., 37
Bartlett, F. C., 204, 272
Bates, Elizabeth, 119, 273
Bauer, Patricia J., 76, 94, 259
Behavior genetics, 43–44, 45
Behaviorism, 2, 35
Being and becoming, 21, 57, 59, 65–66, 87
Beliefs, 157, 209, 210, 212, 213, 214, 219
Bickhard, M. H., 37, 52, 269, 272
Biocultural developmental theory, 40–41, 53–56
Biology, 4, 7, 9, 10, 12, 15, 31, 60, 236–237, 244, 250. *See also* Body
Bloom, Lois, 103, 119, 125, 143, 154, 190, 272
Bloom, Paul, 73, 129–130, 144, 147, 153, 226, 263, 272, 273, 274
Body: and A-not-B task, 72; change in, 9, 20–21, 65; in cognitive psychology, 35–36; and constraints on experience, 18, 20–21, 34; growth of, 24, 66; infant posture of, 61–62, 64, 65, 68–69, 72, 82, 258; and meaning, 10, 250. *See also* Biology

Bogdan, R. J., 12, 216–218, 219
Bowerman, Melissa, 119, 134, 182
Bowlby, John, 62, 77
Brain, 3–4, 10, 47, 48–50, 60, 61, 90, 135, 163, 180, 250; brain-culture symbiosis, 267. *See also* Neural systems
Bronfenbrenner, U., 37, 276
Brown, Roger, 125, 128–129, 142
Bruner, Jerome, 9, 29–30, 105, 129, 224–225

Campos, Joseph, 79, 80, 81, 82, 84, 246, 259
Carey, Susan, 4, 227, 228
Carpendale, J. I. M., 77, 218
Carpenter, M., 76, 77
Categories: basic *vs.* global, 74, 101, 134; of child *vs.* adult, 138; in collaborative construction, 236; construction of, 11, 73–74, 111, 112, 114, 161; construction theory of, 138; covert, 181; and culture, 161; development of, 73; everyday, experiential basis for, 160, 161; extension of, 103; and functional core concepts, 124; global, 222; and indexes, 145; infant, 73–74, 83, 112; as innately specified, 133–134; and language acquisition, 126, 128, 130, 133–134; and overextension of words, 123, 124; and representation, 89, 110; slot-filler, 160; and sorting, 101; structure of, 227; superficial *vs.* deeper qualities in, 225–226; taxonomic, 232
Causality, 225, 226, 231, 247
Causal terms, 154–157, 161, 162
Change, 5, 6–7, 8–9, 11, 20, 45, 62, 65–67, 69, 79–82, 85, 239–244; models for, 21–26
Child-directed speech (CDS), 118–119
Chimpanzees, 44, 47, 61. *See also* Primates
Chomsky, Noam, 3–4, 83, 127, 129, 135
Clark, Andy, 30, 36, 256
Clark, Eve V., 123, 154, 157, 273
Cognition: change in architecture of, 5; and community of minds, 212; computational, 7, 11, 45, 46; and contextualism, 37; and culture, 66, 88; demands of symbolic representation in, 50; and domain-specificity, 6; embodied, 36; evolution of, 37, 48–50; and hybrid mind, 49, 112; in infancy, 58, 70–73; and language, 104–105, 130, 168, 180, 183, 262; as layered, 112, 113; and memory, 49, 88, 184, 185, 251; mimetic, 88; and mimetic representations, 91; as modular, 5–6, 67;

and narratives, 176; and nativism, 45–47; naturalistic, 47–48; and nonverbal thinking, 181; representation as functional mode of, 111; and scientific thought, 51–52; sense making in, 14; situated, 37; and socio-cultural sphere, 66; and speech, 70; and story narratives, 172; study of, 259; subjectivity of, 111; and symbols, 56, 144; syntagmatic and paradigmatic dimensions of, 160–161; and theory of mind, 215, 221; in theory theories, 215-216
Cognitive psychology, 3, 35–36, 52, 263
Cognitive science, 11, 29–31, 52, 56, 84, 89, 109
Cole, Michael, 53
Collaborative construction, 232–237, 247, 264–267
Communication: changes in, 240; and developmental systems, 240, 241; and infant locomotion, 80, 81–82; by infants, 69–70, 85; intention in, 121; interpretation of, 117, 121; and mimetic representations, 91; of mother with infant, 75; and relational expressions, 93; and social attentiveness, 83; types of, 135. *See also* Conversation; Language
Community, 136, 138, 219, 221, 254. *See also* Social sphere
Community of minds, 13–14, 27–28, 117, 209–238, 248, 250–251. *See also* Culture(s); Social sphere
Concept(s): aggregative, 223–224; of causal relations, 226–227; of child *vs.* adult, 74, 138, 222; collaborative construction of, 232–237; and community of minds, 212; construction of, 103, collaborative, 232-237; construction theory of, 138; content of, 227-229; core, 6, 46; and cultural consciousness, 221–238; development of, 73, 74, 111, 227, 228; and essences, 227–231; of everyday function *vs.* similarity, 223; and experience, 160, 221, 222, 257; functional core, 103–104, 123–124; of functions of things, 226, 227; and human goals and actions, 32; infant formation of, 73–74, 83, 112; as innately specified, 83, 133–134, 135, 232; and language, 130, 139, 147, 151, 222, 263; logical, 182; matching of, 142–143; and meaning, 11, 139; natural-kind, 228, 229; organization of, 225–231; and participatory interactions, 224; personal, 221–222;

and pictures, 222; and representation, 110; in semiotic triangle, 136, 137; sorting, 222–223; sources of, 222; in speech, 224; spontaneous *vs.* conventional, 222; structuring of, 222–223; syntagmatic and paradigmatic dimensions of, 160–161; and temporal and causal terms, 154; and theory theory, 227; tuning of, 136, 138, 147, 153; universal, 30; and words, 74, 121, 123, 135, 136, 147, 148, 153, 222

Consciousness: changes in, 240; cognitive, 114-115, 178, 246-247, 248; cultural, 15, 220, 221-238, 248, 249; as development, 248–249; and developmental systems, 240, 241; expansion of, 9, 241, 243, 244–249; and imaginary play, 170–171; in infancy, 84–85; and language, 178, 183; levels of, 15, 24–26, 178; narrative, 212, 218, 247–248; orders of, 34; reflective, 247; social, 25, 114, 243, 244, 246, 248, 249; of time and self, 184

Context, 37, 142–143, 161–162, 165, 167, 235

Continuity: and change, 7; in cognitive science, 11; developmental, 45, 46; in developmental systems theory, 255–256; in evolution, 18; of expanding consciousness, 239–244; and experience, 8–9; in language development, 140; of memory, 205; in nativism, 45, 46; of self, 27, 189, 205, 215; in self-other relationship, 77; theories about, 22; in theory theory, 7

Conversation: and abstract terms, 153; and autobiographical memory, 192, 205, 244; and collaborative construction, 233, 234, 235; development of, 193, 194; expansion of consciousness through, 244; and infant-mother relationship, 75; and language acquisition, 166; and memory, 200, 204; and oral culture, 223; and reflective consciousness, 247; and self in time, 193–205; and time, 188, 189. *See also* Communication; Language; Speech

Culture(s): change in, 66; and cognition, 66, 88; and collaborative construction, 234, 236; and community of minds, 209, 212; constraints of, 20, 257; and contextualism, 37; and conventional categories, 161; coordination with, 7; defined, 252–253; development in, 42, 53–56; evolution of, 48–50; and experience, 13–14, 33; of

family, 66; hybrid, 24; and imitation, 95; infant in, 59–60; and interaction patterns, 105; and interpretation, 12; and language, 129, 140–141, 144, 152, 161, 183, 253–254, 262; and learning, 105, 232, 265; and meaning, 10, 30, 111, 250–251; and memory, 192–193, 201; and nativism, 46; oral, 183; and play, 171; in pragmatism, 38; ratchet effect of, 55; scaffolding by, 105, 265; and self history, 188; and sense of time, 189; shaping by, 46; and symbols, 151; and theory of mind, 217, 218, 219; and theory theories, 7; tuning to, 147, 149; variability in, 64; and Vygotsky, 2, 52, 53, 54–55

Damasio, A., 36, 85, 114, 275
Darwin, Charles, 38
Darwinism, 31, 33
Deacon, Terrence, 50–51, 144, 145, 146, 151, 159, 163, 164, 276
DeLoache, Judy, 99, 164, 165, 271, 274
Development: architecture of, 260–267; as discontinuous, 255; evolutionary, 48, 49; and experiential child, 11–12; as movement to new levels, 23–26; nature *vs.* nurture debate in, 254–255; sequence of, 50, 243, 244; stages of, 21; theory and method concerning, 255–260; in theory theories, 215–216; variability in, 108, 115, 239, 241, 243–244

Developmental systems theory (DST), 22, 38–48, 59, 81, 240, 241, 243–244, 255–256

Dewey, John, 7, 31, 32, 33, 34, 35, 36, 52, 106

Domain-specificity, 4, 6, 23, 59, 63, 81, 227, 231, 241, 245, 252

Donald, Merlin, 23, 24, 48–50, 51, 59, 88, 92, 95, 150, 151, 181, 183, 209, 237, 238, 245, 261, 263, 266, 275

Dunn, Judith, 258, 274

Dynamic systems theory, 39, 42, 44, 46, 67, 72–73, 84

Ecological setting, 19, 20, 21, 108, 161, 249, 256, 257

Ecological theory, 35, 37, 84

Embodiment, 18–19, 36, 46, 60–62, 87, 246, 257

Emergence, 15, 25, 27, 38, 40, 41, 49, 51, 88, 92, 95, 105, 110, 112, 114, 239, 243, 251, 254-255, 261

Emotion, 66, 81, 157, 158
Environment, 62, 250, 257, 258
Episodic memory. *See* Memory
Essence/essentialism, 6, 10, 73, 227–231, 236
Event(s), 14, 89, 90, 91, 111, 124, 159, 160, 235, 260
Evo devo, 270n5
Evolution, 18, 31, 33, 36–37, 38–48, 49, 50, 63–64, 76, 187, 270n6
Evolutionary psychology, 36, 43-44
Experience: abstraction from, 161–163; and action, 18, 32; and change, 8–9, 64–65; and collaborative construction, 234, 235; and community of minds, 212; and concepts, 160, 221, 222, 257; constraints on, 17–21, 257; in culture, 33; definition of, 8–9, 14; and development, 1, 23, 82, 244; direct, 206–207; discovery through, 59; as double-sided, 93; event as unit of, 14, 111, 260; and expansion of consciousness, 244; externalization of, 93, 138; and future events, 197; history of, 64, 104; and knowledge, 38, 224, 227; and language, 9, 103, 146, 151, 152, 161–163, 199–200, 253; learning as, 264–265; and locomotion, 81, 82; making sense of, 257; and meaning, 8, 9–10, 15, 16, 17, 110–111, 116, 161–163, 244, 257; and memory, 192, 257; and narrative, 172, 177; nature of, 15–17; personal *vs.* reported, 201, 202, 203, 204; perspective on, 37–38, 257–258; as private, 9, 65, 75, 78, 249–250; as process, 14–21; repeated, 89; and representation, 74, 113; of self *vs.* others, 220, 250; shared, 86, 93, 138, 172, 188, 189; and theory of mind, 215, 218, 220; and theory theories, 6; and thought, 32, 224; use of past, 9, 19, 20, 110, 115, 166, 189, 192, 195, 214, 259–260
Experiential child, 1, 7, 8–14
Externalization, 92, 93, 95, 100, 102, 103, 104–105, 106, 114, 138, 225, 246, 247, 261–262

Fischer, Kurt, 39, 42
Fivush, Robyn, 89, 105, 185, 195, 259
Frege, Gottlob, 133, 145

Gaze following, 76, 78, 79, 81. *See also* Attention
Gelman, Susan, 227–228, 230, 231
General process theory, 22, 24

Genetic determinism, 43, 44, 45
Genetic epistemology, 52
Gesture(s), 76, 80, 81–82, 85, 89, 91, 93, 96–97, 100, 101, 111, 145
Gibson, E., 68, 83
Gibson, J. J., 35, 37
Golinkoff, Roberta, 128, 130
Goody, E. N., 117, 141
Gopnik, Alison, 2, 5, 75, 101, 216, 227, 269, 270n7
Gottlieb, G., 39, 42
Gould, S. G., 48
Grammar, 132, 133, 150, 152–153, 154, 161, 164, 167, 182, 189–191
Greenfield, P. M., 119

Habituation-dishabituation paradigm, 73–74
Hall, G. Stanley, 2, 48
Hampson, J., 122, 132, 166
Harding, S., 12
Harris, P. L., 4, 98, 170, 177
Heath, S. B., 172, 176
Heft, H., 32, 35, 37, 269
Heidegger, Martin, 33, 34, 106
Heider, Fritz, 35
Hendriks-Jansen, Horst, 37, 41, 56, 66
Hirsh-Pasek, K., 128, 130
Hobson, R. P., 69, 76, 77
Hrdy, Sarah Blaffer, 51, 63–64, 83
Husserl, E., 33
Hutchins, E., 30, 272
Huttenlocher, Janelllen, 98–99, 259
Hybrid mind, 23, 24, 49, 50, 112, 181, 245, 263, 266
Hypernymic terms, 159–161

Iconicity, 164–165
Icons, 144, 145, 173–174
Image schema, 74, 111
Imagination, 115, 171, 205, 206, 210, 215, 220, 248
Imitation, 75–76, 85, 88, 89, 90, 93–95, 100, 101, 186, 261. *See also* Mimesis
Indexes, 144, 145, 146, 163, 165
Individual(s), characteristics of, 254-255; children, 239; differences, 87, 119, 125, 132, 243–244, 249; pathways, 14; individuality, 241
Induction, 124, 126, 130, 227, 228
Infancy/infant: attachment in, 51; and attention, 65, 66, 78, 79, 80–81; body of, 61–62, 64, 65, 66, 68–69, 72, 82, 258; and

categories, 73–74, 83, 112; and change, 62, 69, 79–82, 85; and cognition, 58, 70–73; and communication, 69–70, 75, 80, 81–82, 85; competent, 3–8, 45, 46; and concepts, 73–74, 83, 112; and culture, 59–60; dependency in, 18, 20, 59, 62, 65, 69, 252; development in, 58–86, 240; early, 6, 26, 51, 58, 70, 71; existence in, 59–67; gesture use by, 96; and imitation, 93–94; and locomotion, 60, 67–68, 72–73, 79–82, 87, 109, 121–122, 188, 271n10; and memory, 76, 85–86, 89–90, 246; newborn, 3, 40, 45, 60, 61, 65, 66, 67, 70, 75, 85, 245; private mind of, 264; and representation, 58, 70–73, 264; in social sphere, 51, 62–64, 65, 69–70, 75–79, 80; and time, 190; vision in, 63

Inference. *See* Interpretation

Information, 9, 15, 22, 111, 250

Information processing, 3, 7, 110, 241, 251

Innateness, 42; and cultural learning, 232, 236; and essentialism, 229, 230; of knowledge, 5, 7, 51, 259; and language acquisition, 4, 83, 127, 130, 133; and maternal care, 63; and nativism, 45, 46; in nature *vs.* nurture debate, 254; and phylogeny, 47; in theory theories, 23

Intention(s), communicative, 93, 96, 121; and community of minds, 212; and imaginary play, 170–171; and imitation of action goals, 95; and language, 102, 123, 129, 168; in narrative of parent-child conversations, 195; and reference, 118; and representation, 88, 90, 91, 110, 111, 112; in sign language *vs.* gestures, 96; and story narratives, 172; and theory of mind 216; tracking of, 85; and word learning, 144

Intentionality, 76, 81, 82, 144; and signs, 145; and ToM, 216

Interpretation: of communications, 117, 121; and community of minds, 210; from experience, 17; and experiential child, 12; of goals of others, 216, 217; and language, 141, 161–162, 167, 168; from observation, 12; of perception, 111; and representation, 71; shared, 142; and temporal and causal terms, 155; and theory of mind, 216, 217, 219; of words, 104, 122–123

Intersubjectivity, 17, 65, 69, 77, 78, 82, 105, 246, 249, 263. *See also* Self; Social sphere

Jackendoff, Ray, 135, 136

James, William, 31, 32, 35, 36, 52

Johnson, Marcia, 203

Joint attention. *See* Attention

Joint interaction, 104–105

Karmiloff-Smith, A., 91, 245, 272n11

Kessler Shaw, L., 132, 157, 158, 166

Knowledge: and action, 31–32, 33, 52; background, 104; and cognitive architecture, 5; and collaborative construction, 232, 233; and community of minds, 212; domains of, 6, 255; and everyday events, 90; from experience, 38, 224, 227; explicit, 216; externalization of, 95, 100, 106, 225; gathering of, 15; and identity, 237; and imitation, 93–95; infant representation of, 70–73; internalization of, 54; and language, 152, 168; metarepresentational, 32; and modularity, 22–23; of others, 220; as perspectival, 12; pragmatic, 12, 31, 47, 59; procedural, 32; reflection on, 104; shared, 210, 252; and temporal and causal terms, 154; and theory of mind, 220; without representation, 36

Lakoff, George, 74, 263

Landscape of Consciousness, 195

Language: and abstraction, 152, 163, 168, 181; and action, 246; age of development in, 70, 87, 119, 139, 140, 150, 151, 152, 153, 154, 155, 156, 157, 158, 169–171, 172, 175, 177, 178; and basic awareness, 245; of child *vs.* adult, 138; Chomsky on, 3–4; and cognition, 5, 6, 104–105, 130, 168, 180, 182, 262; and collaborative construction, 235; and community of minds, 210, 212, 213; and comprehension, 119–120, 121, 167, 168, 169; and concepts, 73, 147, 151, 222, 263; and consciousness levels, 25; construction theory of, 138; as core capacity, 46; and culture, 129, 140–141, 144, 152, 161, 183, 253–254, 262; and domains, 6, 122, 252; early responsiveness to, 70, 102–104; emergence of, 77, 88; evolution of, 48–50; expansion of consciousness through, 244; and experience, 9, 103, 146, 151, 152, 161–163, 199–200, 253; expressive and receptive, 166–169; and gesture, 96; and imitation, 95; and intentionality, 76; learning of, 117–148, 247; and

Language (*continued*)
locomotion, 109, 121–122; and meaning, 10, 11, 17, 92, 93, 103, 128, 133, 135, 139, 142, 143, 147, 149, 151–152, 153, 159, 161–162, 168, 169, 246, 262, 263; and memory, 166, 167, 168, 173, 174, 182, 183, 263, 264; and modules, 6, 83; and mother, 69–70, 104–105, 128–129, 138, 140; and personal style, 101, 105, 117, 119, 120, 122, 195; and principles, 128, 130; and private mind, 117, 139, 141–142, 147, 181–182; production of, 119–120, 121–122; and reference, 77, 149, 150, 151; and representation, 45–46, 92, 109, 150, 151–165, 167, 180, 181, 182, 188, 200, 207, 212, 213, 215, 218, 262, 263; and self-other distinctions, 207–208; and shared attention, 121; and social consciousness, 246; social pragmatic theory of learning, 117, 118, 140, 143, 144; and social sphere, 34–35, 83, 125, 128, 129, 130, 131, 140–141, 144, 181, 262–263; and story narratives, 172; study of, 258–259; and symbols, 56, 104, 144–147, 163–164, 200, 262; and syntagmatic and paradigmatic dimensions, 160; and theory of mind, 215, 217, 218; and thought, 147, 179–184, 224, 262; and time, 189–191; variability in, 120, 121–122, 132, 243. *See also* Communication; Conversation; Speech; Word(s)
Language acquisition device (LAD), 3, 127, 129
Language acquisition support system (LASS), 129
Learning: and advancement to new levels, 24; in community of minds, 231–232; by computational mind, 52; in cultural and social spheres, 265; experience as, 264–265; and imitation, 85; and inborn concepts, 232; and infant-mother relationship, 69; in language, 247; and meaning, 11, 265, 266; and pragmatic contexts, 161; scaffolding in, 224–225, 265; and temporal and causal terms, 155
Lehrman, D. S., 41
Levy, Elena, 156, 163
Lewis, Charles, 77, 218
Lewis, Michael, 106
Lillard, A. S., 169–171
Lyons, J., 274

MacArthur Communicative Development Inventory (MCDI), 119
Making sense, 14, 15, 17, 85, 233, 257
Mandler, Jean M., 73–74, 84, 110, 112, 273
Mapping: and collaborative construction, 233; fast, 128, 130–131, 155, 233; and language, 125, 127–128, 130–131, 133, 134, 138, 142, 143, 144, 146, 147; and object concepts, 73; and shared meanings, 142; and temporal and causal terms, 155
Markman, Ellen M., 127–128
McClintock, Barbara, 1, 7–8, 14, 254
McDonough, Laraine, 74, 273
Mead, G. H., 35
Meaning: and aggregative thinking, 224; and biology, 9, 10, 15; and body, 10, 250; collaborative, 233, 235; conceptual theory of, 136–137; and consciousness expansion, 244, 245; construction of, 143, 144, 233, 235; and context, 157, 158; conventional, 118, 120, 122–125, 135, 136, 143; and culture, 30, 111, 250–251; definition of, 9; development in terms of, 1, 9–10, 23; and experience, 8, 9–10, 15, 16, 17, 110–111, 116, 161–163, 244, 257; externalization of, 92, 246, 247; and language, 10, 11, 17, 93, 103, 128, 133, 135, 139, 142, 143, 147, 151–152, 153, 159, 161–162, 168, 169, 246, 262, 263; and learning, 265, 266; and locomotion, 82; and memory, 11, 15, 17, 110–111, 113, 157, 185, 245, 251, 260; and narratives, 173, 176, 196; and objective self, 105; private, 10, 135, 139, 247; as process, 14–21; and public discourse, 141; and representation, 71, 92, 101, 109–114, 152–153; and self-organization, 23, 260; and semiotic triangle, 136, 137; shared, 10, 16, 92, 93, 104, 111, 117, 135, 136, 138–147, 148, 193, 209, 237, 244, 246, 247, 250–251; and social sphere, 29, 30, 32, 34–35; sources of, 10, 142; as subjective, 10, 11; unconscious, 96; universal, 134–135; from use, 138, 156–157. *See also* Making sense
Meaning system: adult tuning to, 104; and development, 24; and domain-specificity, 252; and language, 135, 147, 149, 151, 153, 162; and memory, 113, 151; and objectivity, 105; for persons *vs.* artifacts, 95; private *vs.* enculturated, 147; and source confusion, 206; and theory of mind, 215; tuning of, 149; and word use, 103, 104

Meltzoff, Andrew, 2, 5, 75, 93–94, 95, 101
Memory: autobiographical, 184–193, 196, 200–201, 205, 242, 243–244; in basic awareness, 245; as basic mental construct, 111–112; and cognition, 49, 88, 184, 185, 251; in collaborative construction, 233; and conversations, 200, 204; development of, 89, 90, 91, 94, 185, 186, 202, 244, 245, 251, 264; and domain-specificity, 252; dynamic, 116, 139; early, 185–186; episode, 202; episodic, 14, 177, 184, 186–187, 188, 192, 193, 200, 202, 204–205, 206, 214, 220, 247–248, 251, 264; and event, 48–49, 111; and experience, 192, 257; explicit, 32, 90–91, 204, 261; and externalization, 247, 261–262; factual, 186; functional, 200–201; and hybrid mind, 112; and imitation, 76, 94; implicit, 32, 90–91, 110, 185–186, 245, 261; infant, 85–86, 89–90, 264; as information processing, 110; internal, 95; and language, 166, 167, 168, 173, 174, 182, 183, 263, 264; and meaning, 10, 11, 15, 17, 110–111, 113, 151, 157, 185, 245, 251, 260; and mother's style, 196–197; and narrative, 173, 174, 177, 244, 247–248; and neural systems, 61, 261; perceptual, 110; personalization of, 192; and play, 171; procedural, 110, 184; and reality monitoring, 205, 206; and representation, 89, 91, 109–110, 113; research on, 259; and self, 177, 186, 187, 188, 191–193, 202, 204–205, 220, 248; semantic, 184, 187, 192, 206, 220, 248, 251, 264; shared, 251–252; short term, 186; social, 251–252; sources of, 201–206, 207, 214, 215, 216; and suggestibility, 201–203; and theory of mind, 215, 219–220; and time, 188; voluntary recall of, 90, 261; of mine *vs.* others', 186, 205, 206, 220, 251, 266
Mental event representation (MER), 91
Mental state terms, 157–159, 161
Merleau-Ponty, M., 33, 34
Metarepresentation, 32, 215, 216, 217, 255
Miller, Peggy, 174, 176, 201
Mimesis: and cognition, 88; emergence of, 112; in evolution, 49; and externalization, 114; and hybrid mind, 112; and language, 165, 168; and meaning sharing, 93; and memory, 261; and play, 170; prevalence of, 50; and representation, 90–92, 101, 109, 110, 164. *See also* Imitation

Mind: in behaviorism, 35; changes in, 240; as closed, 30–31; in cognitive psychology, 35–36; computational, 30–31, 46, 52; and developmental systems, 240, 241; differences among, 219; hybrid, 23, 24, 49, 50, 112, 181, 245, 263, 266; and interactions, 41; layers in, 112; mediated, 266; as private, 249–250; of self *vs.* other, 177; sharing of, 92–93, 209, 237; solipsistic, 46
Mirror test, 106–107, 108, 191
Modularity, 22–23, 24, 116, 215, 241, 270n6
Monologues, bedtime, 107, 108, 115, 156, 166, 168, 176, 197-200
Moore, Chris, 77, 93–94, 157
Mother: care by, 254–255; and collaborative construction, 233; communication with, 75; and concepts, 231; elaborative, 195; gaze of, 76, 78, 79; and infant, 62, 63, 65, 69; and intersubjectivity, 77; and language, 69–70, 104–105, 128–129, 138, 140; leaving by, 78; style of, 105, 122, 195, 196–197. *See also* Parent
Mother-child-object, triangle, 77; mother-child-object-word, quadrangle, 140
Motor ability. *See* Infancy/infant

Naming game, 125–126, 128–129
Narrative, 25, 49, 88, 108, 150, 151, 154, 169–177, 184, 195–197, 212, 244, 247–248
Narrative consciousness. *See* Consciousness
Nativism, 23, 42, 45–47, 68, 74, 84, 153, 250
Neisser, U., 85, 275
Nelson, Katherine, 9, 13, 48, 50, 54, 88, 89, 90, 91, 101, 103, 105, 107, 108, 111, 115, 117, 120, 121, 122, 123, 132, 134, 154, 155, 156, 159, 160, 161, 162, 165, 166, 168, 171, 173, 176, 187, 188, 189, 190, 194, 196, 197, 199, 201, 205, 210, 212, 215, 217, 222, 232, 233, 235, 252, 259, 266, 267
Neural systems, 5, 6, 7, 10, 18, 20–21, 22–23, 24, 61, 261. *See also* Brain
Newborns. *See* Infancy/infant
Newport, E., 45, 46, 68, 84
Noun, 131–133

Object categories and concepts, 70-74, 114, 134, 153
Object(s): boundaries of, 83; and concept construction, 103; independence of, 72;

Object(s) *(continued)*
infant attention to, 66; and intended
reference problem, 118; knowledge, 70-
73; and language acquisition, 131, 140;
and mapping, 127–128; and mind *vs.*
event, 15; permanent, 115; preverbal
conceptual understanding of, 125;
representation of, 164; and self, 77, 85,
100; and semiotic triangle, 136, 137
Object words, 70, 120, 121, 152, 162–163
Ong, Walter, 183, 223
Oral language/culture, 13, 88, 175, 183,
223–225
Oyama, Susan, 38, 39, 40, 42

Paradigmatic organization, 159, 160, 161,
184, 235
Paradigmatic style, 196–197
Parent: attention of, 78; and collaborative
construction, 233; conversation with, 188,
189, 193–205; and language use, 117, 122;
and nature *vs.* nurture debate, 254–255;
and word learning, 118–119. *See also*
Mother
Peirce, C. S., 31, 32–33, 144, 163
Perception: in basic awareness, 245; as basic
mental construct, 111–112; changing, 65;
and concepts as innately specified, 134;
and constraints on experience, 18; early
theories of, 3; of essence or core, 73; as
evolved tool, 37; and functional core
concepts, 124; by infants, 60–61, 62, 63,
67–69, 80, 81; interpretation of, 111; and
language acquisition, 125; and nativism,
45; and object concepts, 73–74; of objects,
83; of patterns, 10; primacy of, 34; and
representation, 91, 109–110, 111; of
similarity, 73; and speech, 70; study of,
259; and words, 123, 157, 158
Perspective(s): and change, 64–65; of child,
57; and cognitive self, 107; and
community of minds, 209; and expansion
of consciousness, 249; and experience,
37–38, 257–258; infant, 61–62, 63, 75,
84–85; from intersubjectivity, 263; and
knowledge, 12; and language, 103; and
meaning, 30; and narrative, 172; and new
words, 161; of other, 246; outsider, 208;
real world independent of, 30; in self-
other contrasts, 193–194; shared, 16, 179
Phenomenology, 12, 33–35, 257
Phylogeny, 41, 44, 47, 51, 88, 249; and
ontogeny, 48-51

Piaget, J., 58, 74, 84, 88, 154; Piagetian
theory, 2, 3, 23, 51-52, 55, 70-71, 72, 95,
103, 110, 112, 115-116, 146, 202-203,
227, 241, 260, 274, 276
Pictures, 164, 173–174
Pinker, Steven, 43, 132, 232
Play, 93, 97–102, 169–172, 246
Povinelli, D. J., 191
Pragmatic sense, 1, 5, 8, 12, 47, 48, 59, 140,
218, 227, 257
Pragmatism, 31–38, 52, 54, 56; Pragmatic
psychology, 34, 256
Pretending, 169–172, 175
Primates, 44, 47, 49, 50, 51, 55, 60, 61, 63,
83, 97, 217, 226, 252
Private mind: and autobiographical
memory, 205; and community of minds,
209, 210; and concept making, 221–222;
emergence from, 92, 114, 250; and
experience, 249–250; and functional core
concepts, 124; of infant, 65, 75, 78, 264;
and language, 117, 139, 141–142, 147,
181–182; and meaning, 10, 135, 139, 247;
and mind, 249–250; and play, 101; and
self history, 188; and story narratives, 172;
and theory of mind, 215; and views of
others, 219–220; and word meanings, 135
Psychologists' fallacy, 7, 32

Quine, W. V. O., 126–127, 129, 142, 145

Ratner, H. H., 232, 275
Reality, 38, 98–99, 100, 101, 175, 205, 206–
207, 220
Recapitulation hypothesis, 50
Reconstruction: and concept formation,
229; and culture, 221; and meaning, 113;
and memory, 92, 183, 199, 204; of
narratives, 176, 177; of observed event,
93, 94; of representations, 153; of shared
experience, 27; and theory of mind, 217,
218; in thinking process, 183
Reese, Elaine, 195
Reference: and icons, 145; indeterminacy of,
126; intended, 118; and language, 127,
130, 131, 132, 133, 149, 150, 151, 163,
165; and sense, 133; shared, 149
Reflection, 25, 32, 33–34, 95, 104, 106, 115,
194, 207, 248
Reflective consciousness, 178, 247
Representation: in cognition, 111–113; and
community of minds, 212, 213;
construction of, 109, 113; development

of, 71–72, 112; dual, 99; and experience, 74, 113; and externalization, 92, 261–262; of future, 197; and hybrid mind, 112; and imitation, 95; in infancy, 58, 74, 264; and intention, 88, 90, 91, 111, 112; knowing without, 36; and language, 45–46, 92, 109, 150, 151–165, 167, 180, 181, 182, 188, 200, 207, 212, 213, 215, 218, 262, 263; and meaning, 71, 92, 101, 109–114, 152–153; and memory, 89, 91, 109–110, 113; and mimesis, 90–92, 101, 109, 110, 164; and object knowledge, 70–73; and perception, 91; and play, 100; of representations, 217; and self, 89, 205, 261; as shareable, 104; and story narratives, 173, 176; and symbols, 98, 113, 146–147; as term, 110, 113; and theory of mind, 215, 218, 220; and thought, 190, 225; of unknown events, 181
Rescorla, Leslie, 119, 134
Robotics, 30, 36
Rochat, Philippe, 98, 150, 271, 273
Rogoff, Barbara, 53, 54, 232, 265
Rovee-Collier, Caroline, 89
Rubin, David, 275

Saussure, F. de, 136, 274
Scaffolding: and autobiographical memory, 193; and collaborative construction, 235; by culture, 105; and dynamic systems theory, 84; and infant cognition, 59; and language acquisition, 129; in learning, 224–225, 265; and problem-solving, 54; and sense of time, 189; and toddler, 104; in Vygotsky, 2
Schemas, 11, 14, 74, 89, 90, 91, 111, 112, 197, 245–246
Schneirla, T. C., 41
Scientist, child as, 1–2, 3
Scripts, 11, 89, 90, 98, 101, 111, 112, 139, 154, 160, 171, 186, 190, 197, 235
Self: and attention of other, 247; autobiographical, 114; boundary of, 85; changes in, 240; cognitive, 105, 106, 107–108; in community of minds, 213; and consciousness levels, 25; continuity of, 27, 189, 205, 215; conversation about, 193–205; and developmental systems, 240, 241; emergence of, 105–115; and experience, 8, 188, 189; and externalization, 104–105; independent, 107; of infant, 61; and language use, 178; meaning as related to, 110; and memory,

177, 186, 187, 188, 191–193, 202, 204–205, 220, 248; mirror, 106–107; and narrative, 175, 176, 177, 247; natural and social origins of, 35; new consciousness of, 188; objective, 105–106, 114, 246–247; and objects, 85, 100; and other, 25, 85, 106, 184, 191–193, 204, 205, 207–208, 213, 219–220, 229, 246, 247; and representation, 89, 205, 261; social consciousness of, 246; subjective, 187; symbolization of, 115; and time, 115, 184–189, 191, 192, 193–205, 215
Self-consciousness, 106, 114, 247
Self-mobility, 78, 80, 188, 246
Self-organization, 23, 24, 39–40, 41, 73, 82, 108–109, 241, 260
Semiotic function, 71, 115
Semiotic triangle, 136, 137
Sensorimotor period, 2, 58, 110, 112, 115
Simulation theory, 215
Skinner, B. F., 2, 22
Slobin, D. I., 182, 253, 263
Smith, Linda, 39, 42, 46, 67, 72, 73, 84, 258
Social referencing, 79
Social sphere: attention in, 246; and autobiographical memory, 192–193, 205; awareness of, 88; care in, 254–255; changes in, 21, 66, 240; and cognitive development, 6, 66; and community of minds, 209, 212; and concept formation, 229; and concept tuning, 136, 138; and consciousness expansion, 243, 244; and consciousness levels, 25; constraints of, 19–20, 34, 257; and contextualism, 37; coordination with, 7; and core capacities, 46; and development, 42, 58, 69, 76, 240, 241; differentiation in, 246; and experiential child, 13–14; and externalization, 104–105, 262; infants in, 51, 62–64, 65, 69–70, 75–79, 80; influence of, 252–254; and intersubjectivity, 77; and language, 34–35, 83, 125, 128, 129, 130, 131, 140–141, 144, 181, 262–263; learning in, 265; and meaning, 29, 30, 32, 34–35; and mimetic representations, 91; and nativism, 46; Piaget's neglect of, 52–53; and private mind, 250; and reflective consciousness, 178; and representation, 89; and self, 106, 108, 188, 204; and self-organization, 41; shared meaning in, 10; and symbols, 145, 146, 151; and theory of mind, 215, 217,

Social sphere *(continued)*
218, 219, 221; and variability in
development, 108
Sociobiology, 36–37, 42–43, 253
Source monitoring, 203, 214, 216
Speech, 70, 118–119, 122, 182, 183, 224,
253, 263. *See also* Conversation; Language
Spelke, E. S., 4, 45, 46, 68, 71, 84, 252
Stern, Dan, 77
Subjectivity, 9, 10, 11, 111, 187, 249–250,
257
Suggestibility, 192, 201–203
Superordinate terms, 159–161
Symbol(s), 149–178; age at use of, 99, 100;
and cognition, 50, 56, 144; and
communication, 135; and community of
minds, 13; and evolution, 49; and hybrid
mind, 263; and icons and indexes, 144;
and intention, 145; and language, 56, 104,
144–147, 163–164, 200, 262; and neural
adaptations, 50; and play, 98–102, 169–
171; and private mind, 250; for self, 115;
and social sphere, 145, 146, 151; in theory
of mind, 218; and tuning, 53; and words,
146
Syntagmatic relations, 159, 160, 161, 235

Temporal terms, 154–157, 161, 162, 163
Thelen, Esther, 39, 42, 46, 67, 72, 73, 84,
258, 270
Theorist, child as, 1–2, 3–5, 45, 48
Theory of mind (ToM), 5–8, 77, 196, 211,
213–221, 248, 258; defined, 4–5, 213
Theory theory, 7, 22, 23, 215–216, 227
Thought: and language, 147, 179–184, 224,
262; nonrepresentational, 113; nonverbal,
181; in parent-child conversations, 195;
representational, 74, 115; scientific, 51–
52; and speech, 182, 183, 253, 263;
theoretic, 49
Time: awareness of, 188–191; and
consciousness levels, 25, 188;
conversation about with parents, 193–
205; and conversational discourse, 166;
and culture, 189; developing sense of,
190, 200; differentiation of, 220; and
experience, 15; expressions of, 181, 182;
and infant, 65; and memory, 188; and
narrative, 177, 179, 247–248; and self,
115, 184–189, 191, 192, 193–205, 215;
and story narratives, 172, 175; and theory
of mind, 220
Toddlers: concept sorting by, 222–223, 228;

and developmental systems, 240; gesture
use by, 96–97; imitation by, 93–95;
interpretation of word reference by, 122–
123; and language acquisition, 102–104,
132, 139; and memory, 89–90; and
mimetic representation, 90–92; play by,
97–102, 170; and self, 105–115; and time,
190
Tomasello, M., 17, 51, 55, 56, 59, 76, 77, 95,
98, 100, 117, 122, 129, 138, 143, 144,
165, 192, 217, 226, 232, 263, 265, 270,
273
Toys, 98–99, 101
Trevarthan, C., 77, 270
Tulving, Endel, 186, 187, 204, 251
Tuning: of concepts, 147, 153; to cultural
community, 147, 149; in infant-mother
relationship, 69; and language, 140, 196;
to meaning system, 104; of perception,
64; by symbolic resources, 53; and word
meanings, 136, 138

Valsiner, J., 53
Van Geert, P., 39
Verbs, 133, 189
Vision, 6, 45, 60–61, 62, 63, 65, 68–69. *See
also* Perception
Visual cliff, 68–69, 83
Vocalization, 50, 91
Vygotsky, Lev, 56, 100, 129, 147, 189, 193;
and collaborative construction, 235;
concepts in, 223; and cultural-historical
child, 2; and cultures, 52, 53, 54–55;
development in, 260; and human telos,
51; and imaginary play, 170–171; inner
speech in, 253; and language, 103, 180,
181–182, 262–263, 274; scaffolding in,
224, 265, 266; spontaneous *vs.* scientific
concepts in, 222; and thinking in *vs.*
outside of language, 183

Weist, R. M., 190
Wellman, Henry, 216, 269
Werner, Heinz, 2, 260
Wertsch, James, 53
Whorf, B. L., 138, 181, 183, 253, 263
Wilson, E. O., 42–43
Wittgenstein, Ludwig, 34, 138, 139, 141,
142, 157, 159
Word(s): and abstraction, 161–163; and
aggregative thinking, 224; for artifacts,
153; for beliefs, 157; comprehension of,
119–120, 121, 157, 167; and concepts, 74,

121, 123, 135, 136, 147, 148, 153, 222; and context, 142, 157, 158, 161; and conventions, 122–125, 135, 136; definition of, 135; and directives, 102; and discourse, 142, 159; for emotion, 157; and experience, 161–163; and icons, 165; and infant speech, 70; and intention, 93; kinds of, 131–133; as labels, 180; learning of, 117–118, 122, 140, 161–163; meaning of, 34–35, 103, 122–125, 133, 134–135, 136, 138–147, 152–153, 157, 158, 159, 224; and memory, 157; as mutually interpretable, 104; new, 128, 161–163; nonobject, 131, 133, 134; number of learned, 119–120; and objective self, 114; object/referential *vs.* social/expressive aspects of, 122; over- and underextension of, 103, 123–124, 134, 139, 148; for perception, 157, 158; production of, 93, 103, 119–120, 121–122, 157, 167; and public discourse, 141; reference of, 127–128, 133, 163; relevance of, 143; and representation, 89; responsiveness to, 102–104; and semiotic triangle, 136; shared, 138–147; and symbols, 146, 165; use of, 87, 123, 144, 157, 161–162, 163. *See also* Language

Wundt, Wilhelm, 270

Zone of proximal development, 225